THE

DE ARTE POETICA

OF MARCO GIROLAMO VIDA

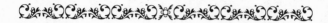

THE

DE ARTE POETICA

OF MARCO GIROLAMO VIDA

Translated with commentary,
& with the text of c. 1517 edited,
by Ralph G. Williams

COLUMBIA UNIVERSITY PRESS

New York

1976

The Andrew W. Mellon Foundation,
through a special grant, has assisted the Press
in publishing this volume.

Library of Congress Cataloging in Publication Data
Vida, Marco Girolamo, Bp. of Alba, d. 1566.
 The De arte poetica of Marco Girolamo Vida.
 Bibliography: p.
 1. Poetry—Early works to 1800. I. Title.
PN1040.V4813 1976   871'.04   75-44367
         ISBN 0-231-03959-X

Columbia University Press
New York   Guildford, Surrey

To

WILLIAM & MARGARET

who served in their generation

*Questo . . . darà lume a coloro che sono
in tenebre e in oscuritade, per lo usato
sole che a loro non luce.*

DANTE, Convivio 1.13

CONTENTS

ACKNOWLEDGMENTS

This work has been with me for nearly nine years now, quite long enough to fulfill Horace's injunction, "nonumque prematur in annum." Over those years I have added substantially to the bulk of the work, the appendix being the most considerable of the additions, and I have tried to give the work an appropriate finish. I hope that it may be of use in its present form; were I to begin again, I should do some things otherwise, particularly in the matter of the Introduction. But it seems to me good to send it forth now rather than to write another book on the same subject. I have found Vida's remark that after time one may return to one's work and scarcely recognize oneself there to be in good measure true: for several years now my interests have been primarily elsewhere, and the return to this text has been rather like the experience of seeing an old photograph of oneself.

The complexity of the task has often made it seem one whose center—not to misappropriate a phrase—is everywhere, and whose circumference nowhere. I have been aided over the years, however, by extraordinarily generous and learned teachers and colleagues. I hope that F. L. Huntley, H. V. S. Odgen, Warner G. Rice, and Gerald F. Else will recognize in the work some results of their good counsel at the outset of the project. For the past six years Mario A. Di Cesare has been a never-failing source of advice, information, correction, and astounding good cheer. James Hutton has recently read the entire manuscript and made many valuable suggestions; those acquainted with him will know how generously and courteously he shares his enormous learning. Robert H. Super has been good enough to answer queries and to make encouraging suggestions. Russell A. Fraser was instrumental in the publishing of the work. I owe a special debt to the anonymous reader for the Columbia University Press, who was finely helpful, particularly in making useful suggestions for revisions. And in the preparation for press of an unusually difficult text, William Bernhardt has been a model of patience and precision.

Among all those whom I might further mention—and they are many—I feel a special debt to Marian Warder Bain; her tutoring in Latin literature and composition for three years was splendidly enabling. And one day sixteen years ago she read aloud a few Latin hexameters, expressing wistfully the hope that one day we could catch their beauty. In doing so she opened to me a world of loveliness I might otherwise have missed.

To my brother Barrie best thanks; to my wife Mary Jane that silence which expresses what is beyond thanks. The dedication is to remembered joy.

R. G. W.

Ann Arbor, December 1975

INTRODUCTION

THE TRANSLATION AND COMMENTARY

Saepe etenim occurrunt haud dictu mollia, ubi haeret
Cura diu. . . .

DE ARTE POETICA I. 441–42

The need for a fresh translation of Marco Vida's *De arte poetica*—and of numerous other Renaissance critical documents as well—is obvious. The only English version of the *De arte poetica* with any currency is that of Christopher Pitt, whose 1725 rendering into heroic couplets is included in A. S. Cook's *The Art of Poetry* (1892; repr. 1926). While Pitt's poem has many felicitous passages, it qualifies more as a loose verse paraphrase of Vida than as a translation. Too frequently his version suggests either more, less, or something quite other than what Vida wrote. Its style and tone, indeed, are less Vida's than Pitt's, for the latter's eighteenth-century diction and unrelentingly lofty style reflect poorly the charm, grace, and occasional wit of his original.

The text which I used in translating is that of the *editio princeps* published at Rome in 1527; the edition reproduced here photographically is that published by the Volpi brothers in Padua in 1731. I have noted in the appropriate places the few misprints the latter text contains. Otherwise, excepting for a few matters of orthography (e.g., "quum" [1731] for "cum" [1527]), and for punctuation, the two texts are identical. The Padua edition recommended itself for use here by its high degree of accuracy, its historical interest, and its superior format.

In an appendix to this work I present, for the first time, the text of the much longer version of the poem which Vida completed c. 1517, and in an introductory essay (pp. 199–211) discuss its rather checkered history. I have also examined a version of the poem published at Paris in July of 1527, which is much closer in length and in its readings to the Rome edition; presumably (see p. 199) it is an unauthorized edition, based on a manuscript of the text which had not yet received Vida's final revisions. For most of Vida's other works I have relied on the Volpi (or "Cominiana") edition referred to above. I have found a number of other editions useful in a variety of ways, though all, I fear, are basically weak. L'Abbé Batteux's translation, in his *Les quatres poëtiques* (Paris, 1771), is often by his own admission closer to paraphrase than to translation (see pp. 4–5); this procedure relieves him of a number of obligations to the text which were better paid, for his version becomes not only stylistically but conceptually untrustworthy. The German translation by Joseph Aigner, in his *Die Christliche-Lateinische Muse* (Munich, 1825), is uneven but it is on the whole rather closer ot its text than is either Pitt's or Batteux's version. Among commentaries, those by Thomas Tristram in the Oxford edition of 1723 and by Richard Russel in the London edition of 1732 are solid, if scant and a little prone to wander after irrelevant analogues. A. S. Cook's notes are regrettably capricious and inaccurate. But to each of these I am indebted, and to each grateful.

My purpose in this translation is to present a prose version which is at once literal and literate. I have followed the sense and syntax of the poem faithfully, while attempting to convey at the same time a notion of the tone and style of the original. It is hoped that this translation will be useful to those who need only an occasional helping hand in reading Vida's poem as well as to those who have no Latin. For these reasons, while attempting to avoid making bad English out of good Latin, I have kept strictly to my text. If the translation seems at times to strain prose rhythms, the effect usually represents a considered attempt to convey some idea of the pace of the original. In diction, too, I have tried to keep as close as possible to the level of the language of the poem itself, neither being too technical and prosaic nor too elegant and artificial.

The commentary presented here is not exhaustive, particularly and by design in the matter of individual words or phrases which Vida takes from Vergil, for to have included a notice of every possible reference to the latter's works would have burdened the commentary unconscionably and unnecessarily. I do intend the commentary, however, as an adequate presentation of Vida's sources and of such analytic and interpretative comment as will enable the reader to make an informed appraisal of Vida's purposes and achievement in his best-known and most influential work.

Always, "between the conception and the creation falls the shadow . . ."; and working, as he must, in that shadow, one may with anticipation repeat the lines of an anonymous thirteenth-century author:

> Mes ains . . .
> Proi tous ceulx qui liront cest livre
> Que, se je mespreng a escrire
> Ou a dire que je ne doie,
> Corrigent moi.

VIDA'S LIFE AND WORKS

"Loud o'er the rest Cremona's trump doth sound . . ."
MILTON, "The Passion"

The precise date of Vida's birth is unknown. One can disregard the guesses put forward by most of the editors and biographers of the seventeenth and eighteenth centuries: Russel, for instance, following Arisius, placed the date at 1470; [1] Batteux placed it at 1507. [2] The best estimate, argued by Marcheselli, and supported by Tiraboschi (1782), places birth between 1480 and 1485. [3] His birthplace was

[1] Richard Russel, *Marci Hieronymi Vidae . . . Poemata quae extant omnia* (London, 1732), p. 1: "Marcus Hieronymus Vida Cremonae natus est Anno 1470."

[2] L'Abbé Batteux, *Les quatres poëtiques* (Paris, 1771), p. 1: "Marc-Jérome Vida naquit à Crémone, Ville d'Italie, l'an de Jésus-Christ 1507. En 1532 il fût fait évêque d'Albe."

[3] In the *De reipublicae dignitate* Book 1, in an autobiographical passage, Vida suggests that the reason Leo X might have chosen to commission him to write the *Christiad* was "quia fortasse legisset meae adolescentiae lusus, versus, inquam, illos quos olim adolescens de re ludicra, sed non parum difficili atque involuta (Scacchia vulgo vocant) conscripseram, nec non duos quoque libros de Bombyce." From Vida's letter of 1519 to Isabella d'Este, we learn that the *Bombyx* was composed about 1512. If Vida had been born in 1470, he would have been forty-two in 1512 (scarcely an *"adolescens"*). The date 1507 is preposterous; Vida wrote an elegy and two epigraphs in memory of Serafino d'Aquila who died in 1500; he had entered the priesthood certainly by 1510.

Cremona, some thirty or thirty-five miles west of Mantua, where Vergil was born.[4] His parents, Guglielmo and Leona (Oscasale) Vida, of "honorable lineage" but relatively modest circumstances, christened their son Marco Antonio, a name he kept until his entrance into orders sometime in the early years of the cinquecento. Marco Antonio had brothers and at least two, perhaps three, sisters, but we know almost nothing of them; one brother, Giorgio, was a captain in the Venetian military, and two sisters, Lucia and Helena, are named, but of the rest we have no record.[5] Vida refers to his brothers and sisters in the will he wrote in 1564, but only to order that masses be said for them at their tombs.[6]

Despite their restricted means, Vida's parents gave him a superb education;[7] his early teacher at Cremona was Niccolò Lucari, the

Supposing that the rule that one not be ordained until he was twenty-four was observed in this case, one may reasonably suppose that Vida was born somewhere between 1480 and 1485. See Girolamo Tiraboschi (*Storia della letteratura italiana* [Milan, 1824], tome 7, pt. 4, pp. 2106 f.) and Vincenzo Cicchitelli (*Sulle opere poetiche di Marco Girolamo Vida* [Naples, 1904], pp. 2–3, n. 1) for further details.

The best modern biographies of Vida are those of Mario Di Cesare (*Vida's Christiad and Vergilian Epic* [New York, 1964], pp. 1–39), Hazel S. Alberson ("Marcus Hieronymus Vida," unpublished Ph.D. dissertation, University of Wisconsin, 1935]), and Vincenzo Cicchitelli (as above). Di Cesare's account is the most useful, and I have relied almost exclusively, even on occasion to matters of phrasing, on the account which he has painstakingly provided; but as he himself notes, "a full biography of Vida remains a desideratum" (p. 296).

[4] Although Vergil's actual birthplace was Andès, just outside of Mantua, the latter is traditionally given as the place of his birth. Donatus quotes the epitaph on Vergil's tomb at Naples, a couplet which Donatus rather naïvely believed was written by Vergil himself:

Mantua me genuit, Calabri rapuere, tenet nunc
Parthenope: cecini pascua, rura, duces.

[5] See Francesco Novati, "Sedici lettere inedite di M. G. Vida, Vescovo d'Alba," *Archivio storico lombardo*, XXVI (1899), 51–60, cited in Cicchitelli, p. 3, and Di Cesare, p. 296, n. 3.

[6] "Volens, iubens, et mandans, quod Haeres eius infrascriptus perpetue teneatur et pariter successores teneantur successive celebrari facere missam unam in ecclesia parochiali Sancti Baxiani, agri et dioecesis cremonensis, pro anima ipsius Rev. Midomini Testatoris et parentum suorum, fratrum quoque et sororum, ubi etiam illi sepulti sunt." See Novati, p. 135.

[7] See Vida's poem "Gelelmi Vidae et Leonae Oscasalae Parentum Manib.," especially lines 60–66:

Vos claras me scilicet artes
Re licet angusta, potius voluistis adire

humanistic disciple of Vittorino da Feltre, the great pedagogue of the early quattrocento. Subsequently he studied at Mantua, where Vittorino had instituted his famous school in 1423 [8] and where, during the time of Vida's presence, Pietro Marcheselli and Francesco Viglio taught the *studia humanitatis*. Here, too, Vida came to admire at closer range the brilliant and gracious Isabella d'Este, to whom he would later dedicate his *Bombyx*.[9] Vincenzo Cicchitelli supposes, moreover, and doubtless rightly so, that Vida's stay at Mantua had a profound influence on him: "Beneath that golden sky, where Battista Spagnuoli—the man whom they called Vergil resurrected—and Battista Fiera composed in elegant Latin, he not only studied carefully Latin and Greek letters but dedicated all his love to the poets of ancient Rome."[10] Vida himself states that he had given himself over to humane studies from the time he was a boy.[11]

> Quam genere indignis studiis incumbere nostro
> Atque ideo doctas docilem misistis ad urbes
> Quamvis in nostris lusisset lubrica rebus
> Iampridem fortuna, et opes vertisset avitas
> Et res fluxa alias potius revocaret ad artes.

[8] See Stefano Davari, *Notizie storiche intorno allo studio pubblico ed ai maestri del secolo XV e XVI, che tennero scuola in Mantova* (Mantua, 1876), cited in Cicchitelli, p. 6.

[9] Vida not only inscribed the poem to her, and praised her lavishly in a letter which accompanied the copy he sent her ("quella che fra tutte le gran Signore di virtu, bontà, et altri beni di corpo è la prima"), but he invoked her at the beginning of the poem (ll. 7–10)

> Tuque ades, et nostro succurre Isabella labori
> Nympha, Padi in ripa magnis e regibus orta,
> Quae gentem pulchra auxisti pulcherrima prole
> Gonsagam; exiguis ades huc non aspera coeptis.

As Di Cesare remarks (p. 299, n. 21), this praise is not that of a man in need of patronage. Vida was well provided for by papal largess at the time of the letter to Isabella. Vida genuinely admired her excellent qualities, among which was a patriotism they both shared ("Quae vastas fessae Italiae miserata ruinas" [*Bombyx* 2.3]).

[10] Cicchitelli, p. 8: ". . . e sotto quell' aureo cielo, ove cantavano in elegante latino Battista Spagnuoli che chiamavano il Virgilio redivivo e Battista Fiera, ei non solo studiò con cura le lettere latine e greche, ma dedicò anche tutto il suo amore ai poeti dell' antica Roma."

[11] *De reipublicae dignitate* 1: "Ego inquam . . . negare non possum posuisse multum temporis et quasi aetatem trivisse in illis studiis, quibus a puero me totum dedissem. . . ." Giuseppe Toffanin, *L'umanesimo al concilio di Trento. In appendice: M. Gerolamo Vida, Elogio dello stato (De rei publicae dignitate)* (Bologna, 1955), p. 111.

Early in the first decade of the cinquecento [12] Vida returned home to Cremona and immersed himself first in philosophy and then theology.[13] Sometime later, though the exact date is uncertain, he took orders in the Lateran Canons of St. Peter, and shortly thereafter went to Rome to further his studies.[14] To mark his ordination he changed his name from Marco Antonio to (Marco) Girolamo.

Notices of Vida's literary activity in the years following are reasonably frequent, but of his actual movements we know little enough. Vida rose steadily to prominence, and by 1513 was in a position to solicit Leonardo della Rovere, the brother of Pope Julius II, for assistance in publishing a revised version of his epic *Juliad*, a substantial part of which Vida had completed earlier, by 1511.[15]

It was under Leo X (Giovanni de' Medici), the great humanist pope, however, that Vida attained that public eminence which he never afterward lost. Vida was already acquainted with prominent literary and ecclesiastical figures, men of the stature of Bembo, Castiglione, and Sadoleto, and had written, sometime about 1511–13, two poems, the *Ludus scacchiae* and the *Bombyx*, which were to bring him to the attention of Leo. There is no need to elaborate here on the nature of the pontificate of Leo. Under him Rome became the focus of the humanistic culture of Europe, with papal funds being used lavishly and often discerningly for the support of artists and men of letters. Some of the attitude of this cultured and generous son of *Il Magnifico* toward the office of St. Peter is expressed in the

[12] Cicchitelli, p. 9, suggests the year 1505 for Vida's return to Cremona, and 1510 for his removal to Rome. Both seem a little late, since by early 1511 Vida was quite far along in an epic *Juliad* on the warlike feats of Julius II.

[13] See *De reipublicae dignitate* 1: "Quum enim iam adolevissem, relictis studiis illarum artium quas qui tenent eruditi vocantur, me totum philosophis, tum theologis tradideram erudiendum" (Toffanin, p. 111). Lancetti states that Vida also studied in Padua and Bologna, citing the line "Atque ideo doctas docilem misistis ad urbes" as proof (*Della vita e degli scritti di Gerolamo Vida* [Milan, 1840], p. 9). Di Cesare takes him to task for this conjecture (pp. 296–97, n. 5). Perhaps Lancetti had the "philosophis" (Padua?) and "theologis" (Bologna?) of the above passage in mind as well as the line cited; it seems likely in any case that he is simply following Tiraboschi, *Storia*, pp. 2107–8.

[14] See *De reipublicae dignitate* 1: "gravissimisque illis studiis Romam adductus, operam strenue navabam" (Toffanin, p. 111).

[15] Tommaso Vairani, *Monumenta cremonensium Romae exstantia* (Rome, 1778), pp. 36–60, cited in Di Cesare, p. 297, n. 8. See, too, Cicchitelli, pp. 39–40.

exclamation he purportedly made after his election: "Godiamoci il papato chè Iddio ce n'ha dato" ("Let's enjoy the papacy, since God has given it to us"). And when Leo received and read a copy of the *Ludus* he was not the man to miss its poetic excellences, or boggle at the sheer fun of it. Tartessio tells Leo's reaction:

When Leo the tenth, the Pontifex Maximus, a man of unsurpassed authority and judgment, had read carefully a poem sent to him by Lascaris in which its author, Marco Girolamo, describes a farcical battle, he was much taken with the man's talent and with both the facility and stately excellence of his style, and affirmed solemnly that this was the one for whom he had fervently prayed for so long, whose sublime and elegant style would be adequate for a poem extolling the wondrous and excelling deeds of Christ, a theme which many had attempted, but developed with too little splendor. Leo's encouragement met with success, and Vida undertook to treat the subject in verse, and began his work.[16]

The extent of Vida's growing reputation during this period, based not only on the *Ludus* and *Bombyx* but on the *Tredecim pugilum certamen,* the *De arte poetica,* and the as-yet-uncompleted *Christiad* as well, is signaled by Giraldus' enthusiastic comment in his *De poetis nostrorum temporum:*

As you are undoubtedly aware, I am a long-standing admirer of Marco Girolamo Vida of Cremona, one of that brotherhood whom we call "canons" from their "rule" of life. He, to my mind, is the only one in this age whom we see to have attained that rank which a poet can achieve without the

---

[16] Marco Paulo Tartessio's comments in his "In M. Hieronymi Vidae poeticam praefatio" are included in the "Cominiana" edition of Vida's works (*Poemata omnia,* published by Josephus Cominus, 2 vols. [Padua, 1731], Vol. II, p. xii). Note the characteristic Renaissance touch of calling the pope the "Pontifex Maximus," the designation of the "chief priest" in Roman paganism. The reference was of course designed to call up the grandeur of Rome:

"Leo X Pont. Max. summa auctoritate, summo iudicio, quum ad se a Lascare . . . allatum M. Hieronymi carmen quo ludicrum proelium describitur, accurate lectitasset, hominis ingenio et scribendi tum facultate, tum dignitate allectus, persancte affirmavit hunc illum esse quem summis votis diu expetivisset, cuius sublimi, et eleganti stylo Christ res gestae mirae, et insignes a nonnullis jam tentatae, sed parum luculenter expressae, carmine celebrari possent; easque ut versibus attingeret, atque inchoaret, hortatu suo perfecit."

Vida himself mentions that Leo commissioned him to write the *Christiad* because he was impressed with the *Ludus* and *Bombyx;* see the quotation from *De reipublicae dignitate* in note 3.

Greeks, with Vergil as one's principal guide. Indeed he is said by his detractors to be more of a thief than an adaptor. Certainly no one else's work is so thoroughly imbued with Maro; he hammers on this anvil night and day, devotedly following his one model. He has a vast and poetical spirit: his special virtue, it seems to me at least, is his extraordinary and wonderful facility in arranging and ornamenting his poetic materials. No one will conclude—at least with any justice—that I am mistaken in this if he reads either his "Game of Chess" which the author calls "Ludus scacchiae," or the two books on the silkworms, or the battle between the thirteen Italian soldiers and an equal number of Gauls (a poem which he recently sent to Baldassare Castiglione of Mantua, a man of eminence both at home and abroad, a zealous student of all polite arts, and a most courteous poet), or his *Poetics* and *Christiad*, which he has not published to date, since he has not yet put them in their final form. But enough about Vida at this point, for fear I should seem to make the man larger than life in my praises.[17]

And Ariosto, in completing his monumental epic, *Orlando furioso*, placed Vida among those worthies whom he envisioned on the shore to welcome the safe arrival in harbor of his poetical bark:

> See . . . there is Vida of Cremona,
> An ever-flowing channel of lofty eloquence.[18]

Having accepted Leo's commission, Vida set to work on the *Christiad* in the middle years of the pontiff's reign. Mario Di Cesare

[17] Lilius Gregorius Giraldus, *De poetis nostrorum temporum,* ed. Karl Wotke (Berlin, 1894), pp. 29–30: "Admirari ego soleo, id quod vos minime fugit, Marcum Hieronymum Vidam Cremonensem, unum ex sodalibus, quos a vitae regula canonicos appellamus. Quem unum hac tempestate meo iudicio eo pervenisse videmus, quo sine Graecis duce cum primis Vergilio pervenire poeta potest, adeo ut a malevolis surripere nedum sumere dicatur. In nullo certe Maro magis deprehenditur; hanc ille incudem die nocteque tundit, uni insistit. Vastus illi animus atque poeticus, praecipua eius, ut mihi quidem videtur, virtus excellens ac mira quaedam in poeticis materiis disponendis inlustrandisque felicitas. Qua in re me decipi iure quidem nemo iudicarit, qui vel eius latrunculorum ludum, quem scacchorum ille appellat, legerit, vel bombycum duos libellos et tredecim Italorum pugilum cum totidem Gallis certamen, quod nuper ille Balthasari Castalioni Mantuano, viro domi forisque egregio omniumque bonarum artium studioso et poetae percomi, misit, nec non et poeticarum et Christiados, quae in opertum nondum ille rettulit nec quibus manus adhuc extrema accessit. Sed iam de Vida satis, ne nos illum magis quam se ipse laudare videamur." Giraldus was writing probably between 1515 and 1520.

[18] *Orlando furioso*, 46.13.1, 5, 6:

> Ecco . . . il Vida Cremonese
> D'alta facondia inessicabil vena.

The first edition of the *Orlando* was published in Ferrara in 1516.

suggests that the pope's expectations were great: that Leo hoped to be the spiritual Augustus at whose request the Christian Vergil was to write the great Christian epic.[19] Leo is even said to have echoed thus, *mutatis mutandis,* Propertius' comment on the long-awaited *Aeneid:*

> Cedite Romani scriptores, cedite Graii
> Nescio quid maius nascitur Aeneide.
>
> (Give way you Roman authors, give way you Greeks,
> A work greater than the Aeneid is being born.)

Vida was comfortably settled at St. Sylvester in Frascati in the Tusculan hills southeast of Rome, where, during the years that followed, years which saw Italy the battleground and prize in the Franco-Spanish struggles, and the terrible sack of Rome in 1527, he worked diligently on his magnum opus. Leo did not live to see the work completed, but Vida's commission was reaffirmed by Clement VII, Giulio de' Medici, Leo's cousin, who endowed Vida liberally both with money and with benefices.[20] Vida gave intermittent readings of his work as it progressed, including, in 1530, one before the Pope and Emperor at Bologna. By 1532 the work was complete, although the first edition was not published until 1535, at Cremona.

If the comment which Vida makes in the *De reipublicae dignitate* (mid-1540s) is to be believed, the task of composing the *Christiad* was not always either light or pleasing; the tone of his remarks is almost bitter.

. . . poets compose whatever they sing or write of their own free will, and with a certain unfettered delight of the spirit, but I wrote my works, such as they are [sc. the *Christiad*] on command, not to say compulsion; they might almost be more correctly called Leo X's poems than mine. Finally, when that poetic heat had died in me, without which Democritus says that no one can be a great poet, I returned to myself, although later than I could have wished, and resumed my former studies.[21]

[19] Di Cesare, p. 26, remarks that Leo may even have hoped, like Augustus, that the epic would legitimatize the rule and ways of Rome—this time, however, to the German heretics.

[20] See Novati, "Sedici lettere . . . ," pp. 26–30, cited in Di Cesare, p. 301, n. 34.

[21] *De reipublicae dignitate* 1 (Toffanin, p. 112): ". . . poetae quae canunt scribuntve ea suapte sponte atque animi libera quadam oblectatione faciunt; ego vero ista, qualiacumque, iussus, ne dicam coactus, scripsi: rectiusque fere Leonis X poemata quam

The *Christiad* was an international success, however. With predict-
able humanistic smugness, Lotichius wrote: "Maro is Caesar's bard:
but Vida preferred to be/ The poet of Jehovah and of his Christ," [22]
apparently assuming that if Jehovah is greater than Caesar, then the
Christian Vergil's poem must inevitably be greater than Vergil's
own. The remark is illustrative of the fervent desire the humanists
had for a Christian poem to equal the *Aeneid*. And the fame of the
Christiad grew with the years. Bartholomew Botta wrote to Vida in
1540 asking his permission to write a commentary on the *Christiad*
and soliciting his cooperation in preparing a biographical sketch.
Vida's reply glances at the fame of his epic; the poet says he is grati-
fied with Botta's quick acceptance of the work for pedagogical purposes:

It is very gratifying to me that, among those who mold the minds of youth
to humanity and excellence through the liberal arts, you were the first to
recite in public and to interpret in the schools my poem which I published in
recent years concerning Christ, at once God and man.[23]

Other passages in Vida's letter to Botta may help to explain the
poet's actions and attitudes in the years after the composition of the

---

mea dici possunt. Tandem, restincto in me calore illo, sine quo negabat Democritus,
quemquam poetam magnum esse posse, serius quam voluissem, ad me ipsum redii
meque retuli ad pristina studia."

One of Vida's more original remarks in the *De arte poetica* (1.50–53) is to much the
same point: ". . . [take care that] whatever you project, prepare for, and, finally, undertake suits your taste and has aroused spontaneous pleasure in your mind. Do not
write on command, unless you are forced to it by the authority which great monarchs
wield. . . ."

> quodcumque paratus
> Aggrederis, tibi sit placitum, atque arriserit ultro
> Ante animo. nec iussa canas, nisi forte coactus
> Magnorum imperio regum. . . .

[22]   Caesaris est vates Maro: Vida sed esse Jehovae
>   Et Christi vates maluit esse sui.

Quoted in Di Cesare, p. 27.

[23] Cominiana ed., II, 129: "Quod vero apud istos quibus adolescentulorum mentes
bonis artibus finguntur ad humanitatem et virtutem, poematis meis, quod de J.
Christi, Dei simul et hominis, rebus, proximis annis edidi, publice enarrandi, atque in
scholis interpretandi, autor fueris, mihi gratissimum fuit. . . ."

Botta published his commentary in 1569.

Christiad. Vida had little of the pretentious pride of many of the humanists; he insists that in writing the *Christiad* he had no interest in gaining glory:

> I, indeed, did not undertake so arduous and so perilous a work through hope of immortality or glory: I did not forget that I was writing the deeds of one whose spirit was unwavering in his willingness to be lowly and downcast and wholly without glory for the salvation of humankind, although he was nonetheless God and the son of God, king of all kings, and not only Lord, but also the author and creator of all things.

And he would not give Botta materials for a vita, though he was willing to give his blessings to a commentary:

> You add also that, on account of the difficulty of some things, particularly those which have to do with religion, you wish a commentary; and that if none are yet published, you will enter into this territory yourself, and begin a treatment of the whole poem for the benefit of the public. I not only wish, indeed I fervently desire that your project will turn out well and happily for you. . . . But I ask, Botta, that you not expect us [to send you] any commentaries on our life and accomplishments—if any are worth mentioning—from which you can gain information to compose the customary "Life of the Author" in the beginning of your work.[24]

One could wish that Vida had been a little less reticent.

In 1533 Vida accepted the bishopric of Alba, a city southeast of Turin. The benefice was not a great one, though even so it was sufficient to occasion the usual carping. Viglius Zuichemus claimed that "because of his *Christiad,* inscribed to the Pope, Vida was given an episcopacy." But even he admitted the extent of Vida's fame: "His

---

[24] Cominiana ed., II, 129–30: "Ego certe opus tam arduum, atque adeo periculosum, non spe immortalitatis, aut gloriae, adortus sum: non oblitus, me scribere res illius, qui pro humani generis salute, humilis, et abjectus, ac plane inglorius animi certo judicio esse voluit: cum nihilominus esset et Deus, et Dei Filius, regum omnium rex, ac rerum non tantum Dominus, verum etiam autor, et fabricator.

"Addis etiam, te, propter rerum difficultatem, earum praesertim, quae spectant ad religionem, in huiusmodi poema desiderare commentaria; teque, si nondum ulla edita sunt, hanc provinciam aggressurum, totumque ipsum poema, publicae utilitatis gratia, tractandum suscepturum: quod tibi bene ac feliciter non modo volo, sed etiam cupio. . . .

"Te tamen, Botta, rogo, ne a nobis vitae nostrae, aut rerum nostrarum, si quae sunt, commentarios exspectes ullos, quibus edoctus, possis in operis initio Autoris vitam de more contexere."

poems and those of a certain Fracastoro gain the highest praise among the Italians." [25]

At any rate, Vida went north within two years of his consecration and remained in this post until his death. Much of the time he resided at Cremona, but he was an active and effective bishop, constantly working for the benefit of his poor and troubled diocese. After his elevation to the bishopric he wrote almost no poetry excepting the "Divine Hymns." The tone of his comments in the *De reipublicae dignitate* seems to indicate that he felt himself burned out, and, at any rate, he was convinced that his duties now lay elsewhere.

His diocese was almost constantly disturbed by the Franco-Spanish wars, and sovereignty over unhappy Alba frequently shifted from one power to the other. Vida's efforts to spare his flock were unstinting, and much of whatever mercy they were shown was due to his personal intercession. [26]

From time to time the documents allow us further glimpses of Vida's activity during these years. Of great personal purity of life himself, and unswerving in his devotion to his religion, Vida was an energetic persecutor of heretics and critic of the Lutheran heresy. In a letter which he wrote in 1540 to Pope Paul III, he calls Luther a "most loathsome monstrosity" ("portentum teterrimum") and labels the Lutheran movement "madness" ("amentia") and a "plague" ("pestis"). [27] In a letter to Guillaume Du Bellay, [28] the French viceroy, Vida admonishes him to show absolutely no mistaken mercy to a man from Alba who was under the charge of having preached heresy: "You could not offer a better sacrifice to immortal God." [29] Concerning his stringent recommendation, he says only, "A love for the common good and righteous sorrow took hold of me and impelled me on" ("Momordit me atque impulsit reipublicae charitas et

[25] "Vida . . . ob Christeida Pontifici dicata episcopatu donatus est. Huius ac Fracastorii cuiusdam carmina primam laudem apud Italos obtinent." Quoted in Di Cesare, p. 27.

[26] For the details, which need not be recounted here, see Di Cesare, p. 29.

[27] Quoted in Di Cesare, p. 31. The text of the whole letter may be found in Novati, "Sedici lettere . . . ," pp. 270–73.

[28] Guillaume Du Bellay was the uncle of the French poet and critic Joachim Du Bellay.

[29] Quoted in Di Cesare, p. 31.

iustus dolor"). And he was personally responsible for the deaths of at least two other heretics.[30]

But Vida was not blind to the scandals within the church. In a poem to Clement VII which stops just short of despair, Vida reflects on the disasters of the campaign which resulted in the sack of Rome in 1527. After describing the carnage, "the terrible devastations of the cities, the deaths of so many men, the endless disasters" (ll. 22–24), he suggests that God may yet return and dwell in and with them. Only they must first cleanse themselves of sin:

> But first each man must purge his mind
> Of hidden ills: dissipating habits
> Must be suppressed; nor may we pursue further
> The road down which we have started.
>
> ("Clementi VII Pont. Max." 53–56) [31]

He attended the sessions of the Council of Trent, but was predictably discouraged and disgusted by the maneuverings of the delegates, and by their arid debates. In an interesting letter cited in Di Cesare, Vida aims a blast at the dereliction of the clergy, suggesting that if they had tended to their charges the church would not have found itself in such great difficulties.[32]

Vida's loyalty to his people, as well as his unbending will, remained with him throughout his life. In 1552, when Vida heard that Alba was about to be attacked, this time by the forces of his old friends, the Gonzagas, he put his friendship aside and addressed a burning letter to Fernando Gonzaga, bitterly protesting the planned assault. Vida only infrequently wrote in Italian, but, as Di Cesare remarks, the power of his feeling emerges through the tumbling clauses of the vernacular:

As Bishop of Alba, I protest in God's name, if you carry out this adventure . . . , you will not have honor. . . . If the season of the year were not so hostile to it and I could hope that the harshness of the weather would per-

---

[30] See Di Cesare, pp. 303–4, n. 45.
[31]   Sed ante mens est cuique latentibus
          Purganda morbis: sunt quoque luridi
               Mores retractandi; nec ultra
                    Progrediendum iter institutum.
[32] Di Cesare, pp. 31–32. For the text of the letter see Novati, "Sedici lettere . . . ," pp. 21–25.

mit me in my already feeble and fast-declining age sufficient command of myself to endure the journey, nothing would stop me from going to the walls of Alba . . . not, indeed, to preserve those few rags and remnants assigned as my living, which I would willingly give up along with all my bishopric for the safety of any the least of those citizens, all of them my beloved children, and conjoined with me in love founded in the heart and blood of Jesus Christ, but to die with them, if that were the case, so that my spirit could go with those tortured and tormented souls before the tribunal of God to seek from divine justice vengeance for their innocent blood against whoever had shed it by hand, by counsel, or by commands; for it is not fitting that the shepherd outlive his flock when it is wholly slaughtered by wild beasts.[33]

Vida's letter was successful, in part at least; though the attack was made, little or no blood was spilled, there was no looting, and the citizens were spared the worst horrors of war.

Vida died on September 27, 1566. He was buried in the Cathedral Church to the left of the high altar, his epitaph a simple "Here lies M. Hieronymus Vida of Cremona, bishop of Alba" ("His situs est M. Hieronymus Vida Cremon. Albae Episcopus"). When the cathedral was remodeled in 1870, his remains were placed in a new tomb at the entrance to the sanctuary. His final epitaph reads:

M. HIERON. VIDAE

CREMONENSIS

AB ANNO MDXXXIII AD MDLXVI ALB. EPISC.

[33] Cominiana, ed., II, 131–32: "Come Vescovo d'Alba le protesto in nome di Dio, se va alla suddetta impresa. . . . , non avrà onore. . . . Se la stagion dell' anno non fosse tanto contraria, e potessi sperare, che l' asprezza del tempo permettesse all' età mia già fiacca e precipitata, di potermi reggere, e durare in cammino, non mi terrebbe alcun rispetto, che io non venissi alle mura d' Alba con l' esercito Cesareo, non già per conservare quelli pochi stracci e reliquie assegnate al viver mio, quali volontieri con tutto 'l Viscovato lascerei per la salute di qualsivoglia minimo di quelli cittadini, tutti miei filguoli cari, e congiunto meco in amore, fondato in le viscere e sangue di Gesu Cristo; ma per morire insieme con essi, venendo 'l caso, perchè lo spirito mio potesse ire in compagnia di quelle anime tribolate, e maltratte avanti il tribunal di Dio, e chiedere vendetta alla divina giustizia con mano, consiglio e con commissioni: non convenendo al pastore sopravivere al gregge suo tutto dalle fiere ucciso."

The phrase "per la salute di qualsivoglia minimo di quelli cittadini, tutti miei filguoli cari" is particularly effective, recalling as it does Christ's "Inasmuch as you have done it unto one of the least of my brothers, you have done it unto me" ("quamdiu fecistis uni ex his fratribus meis minimis, mihi fecistis," Vulgate, Matt. 25:40).

Fernando replied in a brief and respectful letter in which he protests his innocence of such intentions as Vida suggests. See the text of the whole letter in Cominiana ed., II, 132.

CHRISTIANO CARMINE VIRGILIO FAMAM

AEMULATI

RELIQUIAE OLIM AD LAEVAM ARAE MAX.

DEPOSITAE

NE TANTO VIRO DEBITUS HONOS

PLANE DEFICERET

INSTAURATO TEMPLO

HOC MONUMENTO CONDITAE SUNT

ANNO MDCCCLXX

(Here lies M. Hieronymus Vida, from the year 1533 to 1566 Bishop of Alba, who with his song of Christ rivaled the fame of Vergil. His remains were formerly laid at the left side of the high altar, but when this temple was rebuilt in 1870, they were placed in this monument so that the honor due so great a man should not be wholly lacking.)

ON THE *DE ARTE POETICA*

Tempora mutantur et nos mutamur in illis.

Vida's contemporaries lavished high praise on his *De arte poetica;* the poem went through numerous editions in his lifetime and was widely used as a text in the schools.[34] Almost forty years after the work was completed, Julius Caesar Scaliger compared Vida's ordering of his materials with Aristotle's and Horace's and pronounced Vida "accuratius"—"more just"; in a later passage in which he analyzes the *De arte poetica* in erratic detail, he makes the even more sweeping statement: "Praeterea tanto maiore laude quam Horatius dignus Vida est: quanto artificiosius de arte agit hic quam ille" ("Moreover, Vida is as much more worthy of praise than Horace, as his treatment of the art of poetry is more artful than his").[35] A

[34] Professor Di Cesare has recently published a complete bibliography of works by and on Vida: *Bibliotheca Vidiana, Biblioteca Bibliographica Italica* (Florence, 1974). In the section on the *De arte poetica* (pp. 167–98), I count nineteen printings of the poem through 1566.

[35] *Poetices libri septem* (Lyons, 1561), pp. iv–v, 310; the first passage occurs in Scaliger's dedicatory letter to Sylvius his son, the second in his general analysis of Vida's work.

hundred years later, Boileau seems to have paid Vida the compliment of imitation, though he was not gracious enough to avow the debt. Pope, however, made good for Boileau's *gaucherie* by hailing Vida as

> Immortal *Vida!* on whose honour'd Brow
> The Poet's *Bays* and Critick's *Ivy* grow:
> Cremona now shall ever boast thy Name
> As next in Place to *Mantua,* next in Fame! [36]

Numerous passages in the *Essay on Criticism* testify further to Pope's close and admiring knowledge of the *De arte poetica*. Particularly noteworthy is his brief and witty imitation of Vida's passage on imitative harmony:

> 'Tis not enough no Harshness gives Offence,
> The *Sound* must seem an *Eccho* to the *Sense.*
> *Soft* is the Strain when *Zephyr* gently blows,
> And the *smooth Stream* in *smoother Numbers* flows;
> But when loud Surges lash the sounding Shore,
> The *hoarse, rough Verse* shou'd like the *Torrent* roar.
> When *Ajax* strives, some Rocks' vast Weight to throw,
> The Line too *labours,* and the Words move *slow;*
> Not so, when swift *Camilla* scours the Plain,
> Flies o'er th'unbending Corn, and skims along the Main.[37]

Vida's fame was clearly widespread during the first three quarters of the eighteenth century. Thomas Tristram published an excellent edition of his poems in 1723, and Samuel Johnson suggests that it was owing to the popularity of this edition that Christopher Pitt produced his well-known translation of the *De arte poetica* in 1725.[38] Doubtless the translation enhanced Vida's reputation, but the result has been that English readers ever since have seen Vida through Pitt's spectacles. It was consequently almost inevitable that Vida should thereafter be considered both in style and in doctrine a precursor of Boileau and Pope.

Vida's popularity did not survive the general overthrow which the reputations of "neoclassical" authors suffered at the hands of the

---

[36] See Boileau, *L'Art poétique,* ll. 165–70, and Pope, *An Essay on Criticism,* ll. 705–8; cf. pp. 183–85, below.

[37] *Essay on Criticism,* ll. 364–73; see Vida *De arte poetica* 3.373–454.

[38] See Samuel Johnson, *Lives of the Poets* (New York), Everyman Library series, II, 279.

poets and critics of the Romantic movement. It is not so much that he is damned: he is ignored. Those who wished to emphasize the primacy of unfettered individual imagination and expression had more proximate devils to exorcise.

Notices of Vida do indeed occur in the nineteenth century. One might cite Jules Lefèvre-Deumier's essay in his *Etudes biographiques et littéraires* (Paris, 1854), a trifling and splenetic production. Cook republished Pitt's translation with notes of his own in 1892, coupling Vida with Horace and Boileau; [39] Cook's attitude toward these texts is summed up in his introduction:

> But these treatises are more than historic documents, testifying to a state of things which has passed away. In that aspect they are indispensable, as disclosing the principles which, with varying authority in different countries, have held sway from Tasso to Leopardi, from Malherbe to Victor Hugo, and happily for us—if we except sporadic phenomena, like Ben Jonson in the early seventeenth century—from Pope only to Burns.[40]

In 1899 J. E. Spingarn published his immensely influential *History of Literary Criticism in the Renaissance*. His notices of Vida are mostly brief and generally negative in tone; the language of revolt against neoclassicism is still pervasive: "The mechanical conception of poetic expression, in which imagination, sensibility, and passion are subjected to the elaborate and intricate precepts of art, is everywhere found in Vida's poem." [41] Spingarn's references to Vida are divided between statements which summarize the poem and evaluative analysis. The latter, as the above citation illustrates, is often not particularly penetrating; at times his analysis even suggests that he has not understood the text at all.[42]

[39] See "The Translation and Commentary," pp. xi–xii.
[40] A. S. Cook, *The Art of Poetry* (Boston, 1892), p. xvii.
[41] J. E. Spingarn, *A History of Literary Criticism in the Renaissance* (New York, 1899), p. 127.
[42] In Book 2, where his comments largely concern invention and disposition, Vida remarks that one's material need not be unique to oneself but that one may use the same materials as the ancient poets (2.541 ff.); Spingarn glosses, unjustifiably:
"The highest originality becomes for Vida merely the ingenious translation of passages from the classic poets:—

Haud minor est adeo virtus, si te audit Apollo,
Inventa Argivum in patriam convertere vocem,
Quam si tute aliquid intactum inveneris ante."

In the early twentieth century, George Saintsbury saw Vida's influence as even more pernicious than did Cook; of Vida he says that

he seems by a sort of intuition to have anticipated, at the beginning of the sixteenth century, almost the whole critical orthodoxy of the sixteenth, seventeenth, and eighteenth. . . . Had it not been for the astonishing accuracy with which . . . Vida actually anticipated the dominant critical taste of something like three hundred years, and the creative taste of about half that period, not many more lines than we have given pages might have been devoted to him.

In concluding his discussion he sums up:

Such are the principles that we find in Vida, and such their inevitable result. Only let us once more repeat not merely that he may well, in the admirable words of Lord Foppington, "be proud to belong to so prevailing a party" as the Neo-Classicists of the following three centuries, but that he actually led and almost made that party himself.[43]

If Cook thinks that he has detected too pedestrian and confining an influence in Vida, Saintsbury seems to feel he has caught the devil behind the deviltry and proceeds to the exorcism which had been neglected earlier.

A more temperate account of the *De arte poetica* is given by Vincenzo Cicchitelli in his *Sulle opere poetiche di Marco Girolamo Vida* (Naples, 1904). His discussion of the *De arte poetica* (pp. 85–173) provides generally competent summary and some source analysis but is superficial in evaluating the poem's general orientation and achievement.

The most widely circulated criticism of the *De arte poetica* within recent years is that of Bernard Weinberg in his monumental *A History of Literary Criticism in the Italian Renaissance,* and the most extensive that of Mario Di Cesare in *Vida's Christiad and Vergilian Epic.*[44] Superb as Weinberg's study is as a whole, his brief essay on Vida is weakened from the first by his methodology, with the result that he misses much of the significance of Vida's poem; indeed, he does not

[43] George Saintsbury, *A History of Criticism and Literary Taste in Europe* (Edinburgh and London, 1902), II, 30, 33–34. For an extended discussion of Saintsbury's point see pp. xlii–li.
[44] Bernard Weinberg, *A History of Literary Criticism in the Italian Renaissance* (Chicago, 1961), II, 715–19, and Di Cesare, pp. 13–23, 40–86.

really examine the work within its own terms or context, but rather as it relates to the (largely subsequent) theorizings of the cinquecento: "Marco Girolamo Vida's *De arte poetica,* the first of the 'arts' to concern us, exists in a pre-Platonic and pre-Aristotelian world, one in which there is as yet no trace of the fructifying ideas of those two traditions." That Vida's poem was written just before the introduction of Aristotle's *Poetics* into the mainstream of Renaissance literary criticism is undoubtedly true; that the *De arte poetica* shows no signs of Platonism—or Neo-Platonism—is not quite so clear.[45] Weinberg, one may note, is largely interested in a diachronic analysis of the discussion in the cinquecento of particular concepts, and hence his prime interest in Vida is not in the over-all orientation of the poem but in what it says on imitation, for example, or on the nature of the poet's audience. His methodology serves him excellently when he is discussing cinquecento commentaries or polemics on Aristotle and Horace, but ill here, for Vida is not writing a polemic, and Weinberg poses questions to which Vida really never intended to address himself systematically.

Di Cesare's comments on the *De arte poetica* are well informed and vigorous; he has read his text with great care and is free of prejudices, whether aesthetic or methodological, that might hinder him from making a just analysis of it. Apt and incisive as many of his comments are, however, he does not seem to know quite what to make of the poem as a whole. He refers to the "simultaneous richness and poverty of this treatise on poetry"; the richness, he feels, derives from such technically impressive passages as those he quotes liberally and justly in the continuation of his analysis. Summing up what he feels Vida's achievements to be, he speaks quite warmly:

---

[45] The description of the poet's possession by the divine furor at 2.430 ff. is strongly reminiscent of the Neo-Platonic ecstasy, as is the tone and temper of the hymn to Vergil which ends the poem (see 3.554 ff. and note 55); the Neo-Platonists of the mid- and late quattrocento referred principally of course to the *Ion* and *Phaedrus* for their notion of the poetic *mania.* Note that in the Cremona text at 1.622 ff. Vida seems to be making a clear reference to Plato's *Republic* 10.

Curiously, Weinberg preserves the idea that Vida's model is Horace's *Ars poetica,* ignoring the basic differences between the two works both in matters of structure and in matters of orientation. Vida's poem is in many respects patterned rather after Vergil's *Georgics;* see below, p. lxi.

On the whole, Vida makes his points competently and clearly. His verse is appropriate, frequently elegant; at times, he manifests a striking virtuosity. The tone of the work is warm, sensible, moderate; for all the magisterial quality, Vida's manner is consistently genial. Frequently he speaks with tongue in cheek and even parodies his master. The treatment of hyperbole, metonymy, apostrophe, and irony is jovial.[46]

One is a little unprepared, then, for the general impeachment of the work which Di Cesare pronounces at the beginning of the chapter entitled "Vida's *Ars poetica* and Vergilian Humanism," which deals in a suggestive and usefully discursive way with quattrocento Vergilian humanism:

Julius Caesar Scaliger credits Vida's *Ars poetica* with organization and thoroughness superior to Horace's. But the praise is faint; indeed, Vida's major weakness is his lack of thoroughness. The *Ars poetica* discusses fully neither poetry nor the poet, does not define epic or treat it comprehensively, subordinates such matters as characterization to the passion for decorum, and ignores many problems in Vergilian epic. It is a very commonplace piece of work, drawn from common sources.[47]

And elsewhere he refers to the "dull aestheticism" of the *De arte poetica*. Apparently Di Cesare means to praise warmly the virtuosity and personal geniality which Vida exhibits in making "competently and clearly" what Di Cesare himself feels are trite points, though for reasons which will become clear below, such an evaluation of the poem, while not wholly unfair, is unsatisfying. Di Cesare himself suggests a more valid understanding of the poem when he refers to Bembo's statement that the *De arte poetica* was "a pleasing poem which had nothing to do with theory." [48] Unfortunately he does not follow up this suggestion as he might, but concludes the matter by calling the *De arte poetica* "Vida's notes on his experience with the *Scacchia* and *Bombyx*" and by criticizing Saintsbury for "suggesting that Vida and his contemporaries really believed the rhetorical excesses they glorified." [49]

---

[46] Di Cesare, p. 21.   [47] Di Cesare, p. 40.   [48] Di Cesare, p. 22.

[49] Di Cesare, p. 23. This last comment is a little difficult to accept, but taken in connection with the next paragraph, it obviously asserts that Vida's emphasis on rhetoric was something conventional in which he himself did not really believe, and that humanists generally pursued the mastery of rhetoric as a sort of cultural ritual. Such a thesis seems not only exceedingly inappropriate in Vida's case but rather unlikely as a

Even the best of Vida's critics, then, seems unclear as to the nature and significance of the *De arte poetica*. The most hostile commentators seem scarcely to have read him, and certainly have not done so carefully. Those who praise the poem do so hesitatingly and, excepting in the matter of Vida's verbal and prosodic brilliance, uneasily. Most unfortunate is the almost unanimous agreement among modern critics that Vida is writing an essay on poetic theory which essentially presents and is nothing but critical *crambe repetita*.

The next few pages represent an attempt to sketch out a more satisfactory appraisal of the structure and orientation of the *De arte poetica* as a means of providing the reader with a suitable vantage point from which to begin his own examination of the work. The analysis is not presented with the fond hope that Vida's work may be seen to deserve a place among the greatest of critical documents. Clearly (to me at any rate) the poem is not of that rank, either intrinsically or— though less obviously—historically. My goal is a rather more modest one: to suggest that Vida's poem is other and better than it has latterly been said to be.

To begin with a notice of how Vida structures his material: the poem as a whole is disposed into three books. Since, as is clear from the invocation and proposition to the poem, Vida's purpose includes doing for the humanist poet what Quintilian had done for the orator—that is, describe the early education required for his nurture and the specific knowledge and skills necessary for success in his profession—he takes up his topics in an order suggested by the needs of a gradually maturing student. After placing his reader *in medias res* [50] with a few general comments (ll. 27–29) on the antiquity and diverse nature of the poetic genres, the special excellence of epic, and the preparations one can make for writing his poem, Vida shifts gracefully to consider the early education which must precede instruction in the complex rules for writing an epic. Embedded in this discussion is an evaluative history of poetry to Vida's time (ll. 134–215), which is presented as a guide for the youth's reading; as

---

generality; cf. Hanna H. Gray, "Renaissance Humanism: The Pursuit of Eloquence," in *Renaissance Essays*, ed. Paul O. Kristeller and Philip P. Wiener (New York, 1968), pp. 199–216.

[50] See at 2.60 ff. Vida's explication of this device and its usefulness.

we shall see below, it is also of considerable significance for an understanding of Vida's intentions in the work as a whole. Book 1 is
rounded out with a long passage which rises out of an observation
that quiet in the countryside and freedom from care are necessary
for successful composition (ll. 486–96) and then proclaims (497–563)
the happiness and holiness of the life of the poet. The closing lines
of the book comprise a "history" which states the ancient and divine
origins of poetry and an ecstatic hymn to the as-yet-unnamed god of
poetry ("whoever you are, a god surely . . .").

After a reinvocation of the Muses in the opening lines of Book 2,
Vida takes up in detail the task he had begun in the most general
way at the beginning of Book 1 but had deferred in order to deal
with the primary education of the poet-to-be; he is now ready to
"set down the first rules for the composition of the work." Book 2
is devoted to "invention" and "disposition," in poetic-rhetorical
theory traditionally the first and second of the three great concerns
of the poet, the third—to be discussed in Vida's Book 3—being "elocution." After the invocation and proposition, then, almost the whole
book—with the significant exceptions of a medial and final passage—
is given over to quite specific suggestions, well illustrated from
Vergil and Homer, as to how to "invent" and "dispose" one's material effectively, starting with instructions especially applicable to the
beginnings of a poem, then proceeding to considerations relevant to
the poem as a complete structure, and so to points which might be
applicable almost anywhere in the poem (e.g., digressions, *sententiae,*
bravura passages, or indelicate matters). The source of one's "inventions," clearly a pivotal consideration in poetic theory, is dealt with in
a medial passage for which Vida's cryptic remark at Book 2.13–14
has prepared. This medial section follows naturally from preceding
lines which declare and illustrate the poet's ability so to invent and
dispose his poetic materials as to re-create in language the effect of
reality, and describes vividly the poetic furor and how one ought to
handle the gifts it brings. Coupled with this statement on the su-
prarational origin of some of the poet's subject matter is one immediately following which balances it by emphasizing the role the poet's
intellect plays in finding his material. The final passage of Book 2, a
series of brilliant and impassioned lines, rises with the utmost ease

out of the preceding material. This final passage is closely tied by theme, imagery, and tone to the literary history in Book 1, to the hymn which closes that book, and to the brilliant paean of praise to Vergil which closes the poem.

The final book of the *De arte poetica* takes up the third major poetic concern, "elocution"—the investiture in fitting and brilliant language of the material one is presenting. Much of the comment here is devoted to instructions on and illustrations of the various figures which one uses to avoid obscurity and provide variety—that variety which, Vida remarks, is a prime characteristic of the poets' exemplar, Nature. The first group of figures presented consists largely of tropes and "figures of thought" (metaphor, synecdoche, irony, and simile, for example), the second, "figures of words" (archaisms, periphrasis, compounds, tmesis, syncope, and so on). For reasons which will be made clear below, this whole book confronts in its most obvious form the problem of literary imitation. A long and celebrated section (ll. 373–454) illustrates the techniques of borrowing from the ancients and the effects one may achieve by emulating their excellence. The poet's final task is obviously revision, and Vida therefore ends his instructions with suggestions on this topic (ll. 455–526). After a brief section which states Vida's hopes for his own work, and a modesty *topos,* the whole poem is brought to a magnificent close in a section containing an encomium to Vergil. These last lines recall the themes, images, and tone of the brilliant passages at the ends of Books 1 and 2 and constitute a conceptual and stylistic coda to the work as a whole.[51]

What emerges clearly from even a brief examination of the structure of the *De arte poetica* is the fact that Vida has formed his poem with elaborate care. The poem is anything but rambling and loosely strung together; its deceptive ease of development and smooth style should not obscure for us that meticulous workmanship which we should expect from one who insists that disposition is the area in which "poets chiefly hope to gain glory" (2.16).

We turn now from this brief comment on structure to focus more sharply on matters of content: although Vida is not developing a

[51] This point is developed in considerable detail, below, pp. xxxvii–xli.

"theory" in the sense in which Aristotle and Scaliger do, his poem clearly does have a critical orientation. It will be useful to state here the chief theoretical distinctions which Vida employs, using the old categories "poeta," "poiesis," and "poema" as rubrics. The "poet" as Vida describes him is the special recipient of the divine "furor." He cannot successfully will the god's presence, but like the Christian mystic he can woo him and prepare for his coming by reading the words which the god has before inspired in his servants. When in the grip of this furor, the poet composes with marvelous power, but, of course, through no ability of his own (2.395–444). This view of the poet's inspiration resembles closely, if it is not identical with, the Renaissance Neo-Platonist conception of the poetic *mania,* which itself rests ultimately on a (mis)interpretation of the *Ion* and the *Phaedrus.* Vida introduces the concept with some frequency: earlier—at 2.13–14—he had mentioned that "those whom the god regards with favor will often discover quickly materials answering to their wishes," and the passages at the end of Books 1 and 3 presuppose and express a theory of inspiration. But a work such as Vida's is intended, at least in part, as instruction in how to educate oneself and others in the "art" of poetry. Hence his insistence that the poet have wide experience of the world and complete knowledge of the "invention," techniques of "disposition," and "elocution" of the great poets of antiquity. Vida makes no definitive statement on the relationship between the poet's own quite learnable activity in the matter of invention, and the uncontrollable, in fact capricious, gusts of inspiration imparted by "the gods." He does take care, however, to warn his pupil that painstaking art must review and "revise everything that blind frenzy cast[s] up in [his] mind" (2.454). It is significant, too, that immediately after discussing inspiration, Vida chooses to emphasize further the rational components of the act of composition:

You are surely aware, too, that art functions only by imitating nature, and conforms to it closely. For the poets have set Nature before them as their sole mistress, and in whatever their undertaking they always follow her footsteps. Thus, using words as their medium, they create likenesses. . . . (2.455 ff.)

Clearly, while Vida asserts the importance of the furor which
derives from the gods, and the innate aptitude which comes as a gift
from nature (1.312–13), he stresses at least equally those acquired
abilities which depend on one's own efforts. If pressed to reconcile
his two emphases, Vida would perhaps have referred to Horace's
formulation:

> natura fieret laudabile carmen an arte
> quaesitum est: ego nec studium sine divite vena
> nec rude quid prosit video ingenium.
> (*Ars poetica* 408–10)

Besides, says Vida, it is not through excellence in invention (the area
in which we presumably owe our chief debt to the "god" and to natural ability), but through outstanding "disposition," a task "wholly a
question of art," that poets "chiefly hope to gain glory" (2.15, 16).[52]
Vida therefore directs his best pedagogical efforts toward giving his
students a loving and close understanding of the supreme works of
poetry in order that they may achieve a complete mastery of the material and—even more—of the formal techniques and language
which are the poet's rightful heritage and tools.

As is clear from the preceding remarks, the second category,
"composition" ("poiesis"), as Vida understands it, involves inspiration, or the "furor," to be sure, but insofar as poetry is an art, pre-
supposes intelligent, expert, and unremitting human effort as well.
This labor is expended upon the three tasks mentioned above which
theoretically follow upon one another, "invention," "disposition,"
and "elocution." Vida's instructions on these topics in Books 2 and 3
center on an exegesis of the practice of the best ancient authors,
whose works, he is unshakably convinced, are the only defensible
paradigm for the "poiesis" of the modern student.

Finally, the "poem" which the student produces will take its place
as a work of art within a carefully patterned tradition. It will have a
form and meaning referable to and intelligible in terms of the poetic heritage preceding it, and will be praised in all subsequent ages
(see 2.542–62; 3.516–24, 538–41, 554–92). The audience the poem

[52] See Commentary, pp. 148–49, for a fuller exposition of this point.

may expect will obviously be a learned and judicious one, for the
warnings in Books 2 and 3 are based on what the readers will find
admirable and what odious. The poem, if well made, is the undying
"offspring" of the poet (3.251–54, 509–15), his best hope for a secular immortality through fame.

If one considers the sources of Vida's individual precepts, the first
fact that must strike him is that Vida's debt to ancient poets, critics,
and rhetoricians in matters of diction and specific precepts is in-
calculable; most critics would say that it is complete, excepting in the
matter of what they see as his servility to his predecessors: this characteristic they attribute to his humanist education. Vida himself joyfully acknowledges his profound debt to the ancients, and to Vergil
in particular: "Whatever worth and art and invention are ours in this
work come from you; my pupils whom I have taught and led over
the steeps of your holy mountain owe these most excellent gifts to
you alone; for I tread in your sure footsteps; I follow you alone, O
glory of Italy, O supreme splendor of the poets!" (3.580–85). The
authors to whom Vida is chiefly indebted are Quintilian (for most of
his precepts on education and for general rhetorical theory), Cicero
(for specific remarks on rhetorical devices), Horace (for numerous
phrases, and "rules" on decorum), Plutarch (for instructions on the
proper education of children), Homer (whom Vida uses—frequently
disapprovingly—as a mine of illustrations), Plato—through whatever
paths Platonism, or Neo-Platonism, was mediated to him (for general notions on the divine furor), and Vergil (in whom Vida as a
poet virtually lived and moved and had his being). Indeed, there is
scarcely a phrase or precept in the whole of the *De arte poetica* which
cannot be referred to an ancient source.[53]

But for understanding and evaluating the content of Vida's poem,
it is equally important to mark the extraordinary way in which the
work is conceived and executed as to note the theoretical orientation
of the work or the sources of its individual precepts. As we saw, the
title, *De arte poetica*, has misled numerous modern critics into looking
for the same sort of emphasis on theoretical distinctions and exhaus-

---

[53] It would be pointless to reproduce here what is illustrated massively in the Commentary; for the annotation of Vergilian phrases in the long passage on imitative harmony (3.373–454), for example, see Commentary, pp. 183–93.

tive elaboration of the materials of a discipline (or concept within that discipline) that we find in Aristotle or Longinus or the cinquecento "Aristotelians" Scaliger and Castelvetro. When the critics have discovered that Vida does not proceed in the manner they expect, they have concluded that he simply filched some material from Cicero, Vergil, and Quintilian, and compacted—more or less loosely—a poem.

What one must note, however, is the particular combination of materials which Vida chooses, and the apparent purpose for which he chooses them. To proceed serially through the work with this focus in view: The proposition to the first book announces the nature of the poem as a whole: Vida is as concerned with his pupil as he is with the "discipline"; his aim is to write a general work which, itself a work of art, will guide a youth well into worthwhile poetic activity. The inclusion of detailed instructions on the education of the young man in preparation for his life as a poet—and this in itself is a departure in verse "arts of poetry"—implies, as indeed turns out to be the case, that Vida intends not polemic or technical instructions only but, as was suggested above (see p. xxxi), the presentation of a cultural paradigm parallel to that of Quintilian.[54] Just as for Quintilian the best type of citizen is he who is prepared to participate most fully in the civic and cultural life about him, that is, the orator, so for Vida the best and most exalted life open to youth is that of the humanist poet, one who can exercise all his powers in fulfilling Rome's function of teaching the nations, since her ability to rule the world has gone:

[54] Vida does indeed, in the 1520 letter to the *patres* of Cremona (see pp. 212–13), say of his poem that it deals with its subject "as fully as may be." The massive revisions Vida made in his poem between 1520 and the publication of the final version in 1527 might encourage one to reply that the poem's emphasis is different in the two versions, and in some measure this is true. But while the 1520 version is indeed "fuller" than the 1527, in neither version is the poem primarily "technical" and "theoretical," at least as later cinquecento writers would have understood those terms. The revisions Vida made—involving the excision of many references to contemporaries and a mass of illustrative detail—serve primarily to throw into higher relief in the 1527 poem his emphasis on the general cultural paradigm he is presenting. The "fullness" of his poem is, in both versions, that of general presentation and significant illustration, rather than of detailed definition and argumentation. Note, for example, his dismissal of basic prosody as a matter to be dealt with by a classroom teacher (1.415 ff.).

Native gods of Rome, and you, Apollo, protector of Troy, whence our race lifted itself to the stars of the sky, let this glory, at least, never be taken from the Latins: let Italy always excel in the arts and the pursuits of learning, and Rome, loveliest of all things, always teach the nations. For fortune in arms has departed entirely, so great is the discord which has grown among Italy's princes. We draw violent swords, and war upon one another. . . .

2.558–65

The particular goal of the humanist poet was the production of a great Christian epic. Nowhere is that expectation made more obvious and compelling than in the brief sketch of the "cycle . . . [and] fortunes of the poets of the past" which Vida presents at 1.129–215. Vida describes literary history in terms of three great movements: the first began at a peak of achievement with Homer; thereafter everything Greek declined; the Latins subsequently labored upward from the crude and undistinguished literature with which their cultural life had begun, until Vergil carried literary art to unprecedented and unsurpassable heights; after Vergil, says Vida, "one could see everything hastening in tumult without a pause from bad to worse" (l. 178). Finally Europe brought forth the Medici who initiated the ascent to yet a third peak.[55] The implication of the pattern is obvious; Vida's generation was to produce an epic comparable to Homer's and Vergil's which would be the capstone of its (renewed) culture. The way to educate a youth in preparation for that task forms the substance of the first book. The leader on the journey is a poet-priest;[56] the cultural paradigm into which he is initiating the youth is a quasi-religious one with an *ascesis,* a *doctrina,* and a rhetoric of its own.

Vida's praise of the Medici patronage as the cause of the Muses' return to Italy not only is a graceful compliment but states as well his profound belief that what started and defines Italy's cultural resurgence is the renewed contact with ancient literature which the Medici encouraged and, through the collection of manuscripts, made possible. It is inevitable, then, that when Vida begins in Books

[55] This reading of cultural history is typically humanist, and is not new with Vida, of course; for analogues, particularly of Vida's view of Roman, medieval, and Renaissance cultural history, see W. K. Ferguson, *The Renaissance in Historical Thought* (Boston, 1948), pp. 7–28.
[56] See 1.561 ff.

2 and 3 to present specific precepts on invention, disposition, and elocution, he should turn for guidance and illustration to those ancient exemplars which he feels are his true cultural inheritance, an inheritance only recently recovered from the "sheer neglect" it suffered under a "savage race." Vida clearly feels that Latin literature renewed—and one must always bear in mind the *Romanitas* which the humanists claimed for themselves and their works—could do no better than to follow the course taken by the ancients, and Vergil in particular. For just as Vergil accepted a great deal, particularly in terms of "invention," from the Greeks (i.e., Homer), but then through his miraculous art improved everything he took, so, Vida feels, his cultural descendants can do no better than to accept what the ancients have provided for them and direct their own artistic efforts toward attaining in modern times an excellence as nearly equivalent as possible to Vergil's in the past. Hence Vida's loving, patient, and incisive analysis of the practice of Homer and, above all, Vergil in order to provide the aspiring humanist poet with a reliable guide to excellence. The lengthy passage which closes the second book picks up and explores further the cultural *Romanitas* of the literary history in Book 1 and the comparisons between Homer and Vergil throughout Book 2.[57] The cultural supremacy of ancient Rome had been accompanied by a political supremacy, and Vida shared the typical humanist longing for a full reinstatement of Roman preeminence. Pope Leo X, Giovanni de' Medici, had shown some promise of reviving Rome's political importance, but his plans were cut short by his early death.[58] No doubt the dream that Leo might have recov-

---

[57] For a fuller discussion of this passage and the imagery which Vida uses, see Commentary, pp. 168–72.

[58] The exceedingly significant part of this passage which relates to Leo's death is nearly identical with the corresponding passage in the early (1517) version; Leo's name has simply been substituted for Giuliano's. The substitution is explicable in one context in terms of Leo's and Clement's patronage of Vida, for aside from Vida's personal gratitude to Leo, Clement himself might be expected to react more strongly to a lament on Leo, who occupied the papal chair and hence was a preeminently illustrious member of the family, than to one on Giuliano. More significant for the poem, however, is the fact that Leo was perhaps the last strong pope who (in Vida's eyes at least) might have asserted the authority of Rome in political affairs as well as religious, and hence stood as a wholly satisfactory focus for possibilities Vida thought to be now lost.

ered the power of ancient Rome is, from our vantage point, an almost ludicrously impractical one, but Vida did indeed hope for such
a resurgence. He sees clearly that disunity has been the cause of
Italy's woes, and passionately denounces the laying open of the
"homeland" to "foreign tyrants" (i.e., Francis I and Charles V). But
he realizes too that with Leo's death all hope for a renewed Roman
imperium is finally gone. He prays for what is left—that the humanist
cultural *magisterium,* at least, might not be taken away. The *Romanitas*
of Vida's political and cultural allegiance is made clear again and
again in the *De arte poetica;* Aeneas is "ours" ("nostro Aeneae,"
1.126); the ancient Latin poets are "ours" (1.131, 149; 2.190, 541); it
is the "youth of Italy" whom he is teaching (2.8); Italy is our homeland ("patria," 2.566), Latin is the student's native tongue (3.279–87,
esp. l. 284), and it is our homeland ("patriam," 2.566) which has
been laid open to foreign tyrants by those who are fighting what
Vida sees as a civil war ("Ipsi nos inter saevos distringimus enses,"
2.565). That Leo, the one who could draw all the eyes of Europe to
Rome as the center of political power, has died is grievous to Vida.
But the cultural *magisterium* might yet remain, and it is to educate
youth who will support and extend this *magisterium* that Vida is writing.

The hymn to Vergil which closes Book 3 completes the pattern of
meaning which Vida has been developing through the whole poem.
Vergil is the Latins' glory (3.555); he is their "prince" (l. 565). Where
he has led the way, Italy's poets have followed (l. 567). All Latin eyes
are turned, not on Leo (2.581–82), the symbol of political power,[59]
but on Vergil (ll. 570–71), their cultural *princeps.* In his literary history and throughout the poem Vida proclaimed Vergil the supreme
poet, and by implication the everlasting support and inspiration for
that continuing Roman cultural *magisterium* for which he prays at the
end of Book 2. The identification of Vergil with this hope is made
explicit in the hymn which closes the poem; indeed, the language of
invocation to which Vida rises clearly connects the praise of Vergil
with the paean to the unknown god of poetry at the end of Book 1.
The figure of the god of poetry and that of Vergil coalesce, and

[59] See Commentary, pp. 171–72, for a full discussion of the imagery in the passage
which supports this identification.

Vida's prayer askes in Christian Neo-Platonic fashion that this god unite his people to himself, and inspire them—that they may, presumably, produce those literary works which would constitute the most worthy act of *pietas* in their power.

In this context, then, it seems a little ungracious to tax Vida with "lack of thoroughness" for neither defining fully the epic nor presenting the wealth of technical distinctions which Scaliger, for example, later does so energetically. One had almost as well tax Vergil for not being exhaustive in his treatment of agriculture in the *Georgics*. The analogy is a better one than might appear to be the case at first glance, for the *Georgics* is the poem which, in many respects, Vida has used as his closest model. Both, in spite of their apparently didactic intent, are really more celebrations of their topics than exhaustive technical discussions; both have persistent political and cultural themes elaborated in a complex way throughout their length; both concentrate the development of their poems' conceptual focus in lengthy passages at the end of each book; and both intersperse the highly selective but carefully ordered details they discuss with epic similes and anecdotes. Di Cesare speaks well, if cryptically, when he states that "the *Ars poetica* . . . emphasizes the value of the classics, especially Vergil, in forming poets to preserve Italy's cultural supremacy," and that the *De arte poetica* is "an essay on poetry as Vida conceives Vergil might have written that essay." [60] To Vida's intent to create of his teaching a work of art, we shall return below.

That characteristic for which Vida is most often cited is the unswerving devotion to the ancients, and to Vergil in particular, to which I have already made reference. Admittedly, the student poet is urged to imitate Nature (2.455 ff.), but one soon becomes aware that, in Vida's eyes, the best way to follow Nature is to accept the guidance of those who saw her most clearly, that is, the poets of antiquity. The extent to which he insists on their authority and example, most obviously in the matter of diction, is evident not only in his precepts but in his practice as well. Vida's language and style are single-mindedly Vergilian, so much so that, as we saw, Giraldus,

---

[60] Di Cesare, p. 15; for further comment on this point see below, pp. li–lii.

writing in Vida's own day, makes reference to some who called Vida "more of a thief than an adapter." Doubtless these are the same critics whom Vida scorns for considering themselves wise ("in [their] self-conceit") because they have discovered his "thefts" (3.259). Clearly, however, many of Vida's contemporaries did not consider his theory or practice either servile or bizarre: he was celebrated as the best poet of the age and his *De arte poetica* was hailed as the best guide to the art ever written. I have discussed above the carefully developed conceptual focus which Vida provides for his poem, and the complex structure which sustains it; his is the first poetic presentation of the cultural paradigm of literary humanism, and his the remarkably successful adaptation of the *Georgics'* tone and structure to another topic. It is appropriate now to examine more fully his concept of literary imitation. There can be no doubt that Vida means precisely what he says; indeed, as I shall emphasize below, the *De arte poetica* is intended as a poetic realization of its own precepts.

At Book 3.170–293 Vida discusses the ways in which one may most profitably imitate the language and style of the ancients, just as in Book 2 he gives instructions as to how one may profit by their excellence in invention and disposition. Of particular interest are two related points: his quiet insistence on the use of Latin, and his assertion that one must look to the ancients—particularly Vergil—as the absolute arbiters of style. It is this section in particular that most earns for Vida the stern rebukes of nineteenth- and twentieth-century critics. The topic is important enough to justify quotation of the passage *in extenso:*

> Consider now the choice to be made in vocabulary and the principle governing that choice. Not all words are suitable for verse, nor should you consider all which are as of equal rank, for they are also differentiated by the measures to which they are suited; indeed, words differ as widely one from another as do poems, although here and there you will find a number of words which are common to all types of verse. . . . Discard the base mass of words which are devoid of all splendor and are mere unseemly ciphers, lest your vocabulary be undistinguished. That you may reach this goal, follow the path of the old poets: it will lead you aright. . . . Then if one author should far surpass all the others, I should direct you to learn excellence and the principles of expression from him. . . .
>
> I should scarcely discourage you, however, from exploring at the same

time the productions of the rest of the poets . . . collecting noteworthy phrases from their works. . . . Nor would I personally hesitate to survey frequently and attentively the verses of a rude poet, searching as I read to see if some phrases might not occur here and there which would be suitable if rendered in my own verse and which I with better auspices might turn to my own purposes so soon as I had quite polished away the rust of ages with which they were encrusted. . . .

As these observations indicate, it is from the ancient poets that we ought always to learn how to express ourselves. . . . Note how, that we may fit to our own use the spoils and noble trappings of the ancients, we appropriate in one instance their brilliant inventions, in another the order they employ, in others yet the spirit of their words, and even the words themselves—for one need not be ashamed of having sometimes spoken with another's tongue.

But when you are attempting thefts from the polished poets, proceed with particular caution; remember to conceal what you have stolen by altering the forms of the words and to escape detection by switching word order. Give everything a new countenance and a wholly new form. Once this task is complete (and it will not occupy you long), you yourself will scarcely recognize the altered words of the ancient poet.

Certain authors frequently commit their theft quite in the open and, intrepid as they are, wish their action to be noted by all; when caught, they glory in the very theft: in some cases, they have made no change in the order of the words, but with impunity have stripped them of their former significance and given them a wholly different meaning; in others, aflame with a desire to compete with the ancients, they delight in vanquishing them by snatching from their hand even material which has long been their peculiar possession, but which is, however, ill-fashioned, and improving it. . . .

Therefore, my pupils, let each of you follow my example; commit your thefts fearlessly and draw your booty from every quarter. For he is a hapless poet (though there are many to be found) who trusts rashly in his own powers and skill and, as though he stood in no need of another's aid, brashly refuses to follow the trustworthy steps of the ancients, abstaining, alas, too much from taking booty, having decided to spare "others' property"—a vain scrupulosity this, an effort not sanctioned by Phoebus. Their rejoicing on that account is pitiably short-lived, however, and often they survive their own monuments; unpraised, they have wept ere their final day for their dead offspring, and, yet living, have seen the funeral of their own fame. How they might wish that they had avoided vain labor, and learned other arts from their parents!

Often I enjoy playing with phrases from the ancients and while using precisely the same words expressing another meaning. Nor shall anyone (no matter how wise in his self-conceit) prove my thefts guilty ones, for soon my borrowings will be obvious to all, and our sons' sons and their descendants will aprove them. Heaven forbid that I should wish to conceal my thefts or hide my spoils because I feared the punishment of disrepute!

You may not entrust yourself to the ancients entirely, however, since they will not supply you with everything you need. For, if you inquire well into [even] a few matters, [you will find that] there will remain things as yet unheard by any man which you must attempt [to express] through your own efforts. For this reason, we also are under no sanction forbidding us to fashion certain new locutions and publish freely words never spoken before. That these may elicit a measure of recognition, however, let them declare their origin, be able to show the family to which they are cognate, and rely [for acceptance] on their descent from a well-known lineage.

If the poverty of your native language is a sufficiently serious hindrance, it is quite legitimate for you to import a formless mass [of linguistic ore] from the prosperous lands where the Greeks dwell, and by shaping it on the Latin anvil, compel it to renounce the characteristics of its [verbal] forebears. It was thus that anciently the riches of the Ausonian tongue grew. Thus, too, Latium flourished, whither contact transferred an overwhelming variety of usages from Argos as the Italians took up their inheritance from prostrate Athens. Note how many Greek expressions there are which have been lifted from their Mycenaean milieu and now shine brightly, mingled with our own, with no apparent distinction made between the two sorts of vocabulary; both citizen and foreigner pass everywhere through Latian lands with like marks of honor. Our language ceased to be poor a long time since; only rarely will the plenty and splendor of your native land fail you. Cicero himself will provide all that you require from his own riches, and other artists born in those years of felicity (and do not rely on the poets alone) will fully suffice for your needs.

Moreover, I have often seen among the songs of the ancient bards verses which, though barbarous in style, are a splendid hoard: Gaul has sent its Belgian "war-wains" across the Alps into Latium, and long Macedonian "pikes" too have come. And shall I fear lest I find myself without a copious stock of words, and the poverty of a confined language limit me? [61]

---

[61] Saintsbury is particularly intemperate in his censure of Vida, fixing on this passage as exquisitely worthy of damnation; indeed, he excerpts a considerable part of it for inclusion (out of context) in his *Loci Critici* (New York, 1903), pp. 85–86 (Scaliger, it might be mentioned, rates only a two-line citation). In his *History of Criticism*, II, 34, 35, he dismisses Vida contemptuously: "Had it not been for the astonishing accuracy with which, as has been said, Vida anticipated the dominant critical taste of something like three hundred years, and the creative taste of about half that period, not many more lines than we have given pages might have been devoted to him. . . . His doctrines themselves are, whether we look at them in gross or in detail, some of the poorest and most beggarly things to be found in the whole range of criticism. . . . Vida's idea of poetry is simply and literally shoddy."

It is not my intent in the following remarks to present a defense of Vida's position: I wish chiefly to "place" it historically and conceptually. Vida's contention that Latin is the instrument of culture, the poet's "native tongue," was at any rate fairly common in his own day. While from the mid-quattrocento on strong voices (such as Alberti's, Lorenzo Il Magnifico's, Landino's, Castiglione's, and Bembo's) had been heard in defense of the use of the vernacular tongue for literary endeavour (indeed, Bembo's *Prose della volgar lingua* was published in 1525 while Vida was still revising his poem), many humanist writers, Vida among them, clung to the exclusive use of Latin. Mario Marti, indeed, suggests in the introduction to his edition of Bembo's *Prose* that the issue was, by Bembo's time, largely a dead one:

In fact, the rights of the vernacular were no longer trampled upon save by the tardy and anachronistic defenders of Ciceronian Latinity, by the likes of the Strozzi, Amaseo, Bonamico, and by all those whom an ill-understood aristocracy of culture led to a blind and fanatic, even if excited exaltation of the classical languages. Often in the dialogues of the early cinquecento dedicated to language and to rhetoric, one chapter at least is reserved for the polemic concerning the ideal and practical priority of Latin or of the vernacular. Even in the *Prose* of Bembo, part of the first book is dedicated to this argument. But it is a polemic with no biting, no urgent necessity: a simple homage to a traditional aspect of the whole question.[62]

But if, he cites later, the *Stanze* of Poliziano and the *Arcadia* of Sannazaro had, among other works, helped to decide the issue, one must remember that Poliziano wrote some of his loveliest and most influential work in Greek and Latin (cf. the *Sylvae*) and that Sannazaro's would-be-great epic *De partu virginis* (1526) is not only in Latin but is notoriously laden with classical phrases and conven-

---

[62] Pietro Bembo, *Prose della volgar lingua*, ed. Mario Marti (Padua, 1967), p. ix. In verità, i diritti del volgare non erano ormai calpestati più che dai tardi e anacronistici difensori della latinità ciceroniana, dagli Strozzi, dagli Amaseo, dai Bonamico e da tutti coloro che una malintesa aristocrazia di cultura conduceva alla cieca e fanatica, anche se commossa, esaltazione delle lingue classiche. Spesso nei dialoghi del primo Cinquecento, dedicati alla lingua e alla retorica, un capitolo almeno è riservato alla polemica intorno alla priorità ideale e pratica del latino o del volgare. Anche nelle *Prose* bembesche, parte del I libro è dedicata a quest'argomento. Ma è una polemica senza più alcun mordente e senza urgente necessità; un semplice omaggio ad un aspetto tradizionale dell'intera questione.

tions. Vida was not alone, then, in his practice in his own day, and stood in a long tradition which insisted on the use of Latin as the instrument of a polished culture. Giancarlo Mazzacurati's description of the humanist position is eloquent:

> Latin represented for the humanists, still more than a language, a symbol at once both ethical and political: a symbol of the universal and of the exemplary, a channel of communication with the past, and with a present not municipal but national and European. Against its death as a spoken language they counterpoised an eternal life in writings and in the usage of the learned: to write in Latin signified for them as well to set counter to the natural corruption of things, of states, of tongues, an act of faith in intelligence and wisdom, an aspiration to transcend and deny the contingent in order to attain universality in time and space.[63]

More controversial than his preference for Latin, however, though again his position is not idiosyncratic, is Vida's insistence on the virtually absolute preeminence of the ancients, and particularly Vergil and Cicero, in matters of style. Certainly his advice on literary imitation differs substantially, to give historically significant examples, from the position of his predecessors Quintilian, Petrarch, and Poliziano, and from his contemporary Erasmus. The crucial issue is the matter of fidelity to the diction, idiom, and style of the authoritative models. It may be useful to cite here Quintilian's and Erasmus' remarks so that the reader may compare them to Vida's own. Quintilian's *Institutio oratoria* 10.1.2 is largely concerned with imitation, and presents a summary discussion of the authors Quintilian considers most worthy of imitation. In ending his discussion of individual authors, Quintilian comments:

> It is from these and other authors worthy of our study that we must draw our stock of words, the variety of our figures and our methods of composi-

---

[63] Giancarlo Mazzacurati, *Pietro Bembo e la questione del "volgare"* (Naples, 1964), p. 16. Il latino rappresentava per gli umanisti, più ancora che una lingua, un simbolo etico e politico insieme: un simbolo di universalità, di esemplarità, un tramite di colloquio col passato e con un presente non municipale, ma nazionale ed europeo. Alla sua morte come lingua parlata essi contrapponevano una vita eterna nelle scritture e nell'uso dei dotti: scrivere in latino significava per loro anche opporre alle naturale corruzione delle cose, degli stati, delle lingue, un atto di fede nell'intelligenza e nella sapienza, una aspirazione a superare e negare il contingente per attingere l'universalità, nel tempo e nello spazio. Mazzacurati's whole discussion is a useful presentation of the history of the *questione* from Dante's time to Bembo's.

tion, while we must form our minds on the model of every excellence. For there can be no doubt that in art no small portion of our task lies in imitation, since, although invention came first and is of special importance, it is expedient to imitate whatever has been imitated with success. And it is a universal rule of life that we should wish to copy what we approve in others. (10.2.1; H. E. Butler, trans.)

But further on he enters a caveat:

But the very fact that in every subject the procedure to be followed is so much more easy for us that it was for those who had no model to guide them, is a positive advantage with caution and judgement.

The first point, then, that we must realize is that imitation alone is not sufficient, if only for the reason that a sluggish nature is only too ready to rest content with the inventions of others. . . . It is a positive disgrace to be content to owe all our achievements to imitation alone. . . . For the man whose aim is to prove himself better than another, even if he does not surpass him, may hope to equal him. But he can never hope to equal him if he thinks it his duty merely to tread in his footsteps. . . . For the models which we select for imitation have a genuine and natural force, whereas all imitation is artificial and moulded to a purpose which was not that of the original orator. . . . Consequently, there are many who, after excerpting certain words from published speeches or borrowing certain particular rhythms, think that they have produced a perfect copy of the works which they have read, despite the fact that words become obsolete or current with the lapse of years, the one sure standard being contemporary usage. (10.2.4, 7, 10, 11, 13; H. E. Butler, trans.)

In his devastatingly satiric *Ciceronianus*, Erasmus, through the interlocutors Bulephorus and Nosoponus, glances at the excessive admiration and slavish imitation of both Cicero and Vergil; his own position, which emerges quite clearly, is similar to Quintilian's:

Bu.—I acknowledge that there are certain general principles that can be applied to any theme; such as purity, clearness, elegance of expression, order, and such things, but this does not satisfy those apes of Cicero. They demand the absolute reproduction of words—the very thing, which, granting that it could be done somehow or other, in certain allied subjects, would be impossible in wholly different subjects. You will acknowledge, I think, that Vergil holds first place among Latin poets just as Cicero among Latin orators.

No.—Yes.

Bu.—Well, if you are preparing to write lyric verse, will you place before you Horace or Vergil?

No.—Horace is the greatest in his class.

Bu.—What if satire?

No.—Horace, with much more reason.

Bu.—What if you are contemplating comedy?

No.—I will go to Terence for a model.

Bu.—To be sure, on account of the great difference of theme.

No.—But the language of Cicero has some peculiar, indefinable adaptability.

Bu.—Exactly the same I could say, "indefinable." Immoderate love for Cicero deceives many, because to adapt the language of Cicero to an entirely different theme is to come out unlike him. . . . That is not necessarily best which is most like Cicero: for, as I was going to say, no animal in all its members approaches nearer to the figure of man than the ape, and so like is it that if nature had added a voice it could seem a man; again nothing is more unlike man than a peacock or a swan—and yet, I think, you would prefer to be a swan or a peacock rather than an ape. . . . They play the fool who distort themselves to copy Cicero exactly; for it would not be possible, if it were desirable; and it would not be desirable, if it were possible. But he can be expressed exactly in this way: if we strive in our imitation to express not his exact virtues, but as great ones, or it may be greater. Thus it can happen that he is most a Ciceronian who is most unlike Cicero, that is, who speaks best and most pointedly, though in a different way; and this is not surprising for the environment is now entirely different. (Izora Scott, trans., *The Imitation of Cicero*, pp. 76–78)

Vida's attitude clearly contrasts with that of his source for so many critical assertions, Quintilian, and with that of the great northern Latinist. But again Vida's position is in no way surprising historically: the debate over the question of proper models was very warm indeed as Vida was writing and revising his poem, and he was anything but alone in his assertions. One need only cite here the names of Bembo, Cortesi, and Longolius, all of whom insisted on a more or less strict fidelity to the practice of Cicero in prose, to remind oneself of the prestige of the party to which Vida's remarks join him. One may easily fit Vida into the pattern of literary battles in his own day, then.[64] It remains, however, a less simple matter to appreciate the

---

[64] For a discussion of Ciceronianism and the question of literary "models," see Remigio Sabbadini, *Storia del ciceronianismo e di altre questioni letteraria nell' eta della rinascenza* (Turin, 1885); J. E. Sandys, *Harvard Lectures on the Revival of Learning* (Cambridge, Mass., 1905), pp. 145–73; Izora Scott, *The Imitation of Cicero* (New York, 1910); Giorgio Santangelo, *Pietro Bembo e il principio d'imitazione* (Florence, 1950); and Giancarlo Mazzacurati, *Misure del classicismo rinascimentale* (Naples, 1967).

conceptual basis of such a position. Mazzacurati's remarks, cited above, are suggestive. I will add only a few further observations on the central interests of humanism and the difficulty in appreciating them which our changed presumptions create.[65]

Central to all forms of humanism is the question of the existence and nature of normative values in human affairs. A twentieth-century modern, accustomed to think of reality as the sum of all the diverse and diversifying phenomena of the universe, and of standards and consistency as imposed only temporarily and provisionally upon an intractable mass of phenomena, is likely to find the search for eternally valid norms in philosophy, in moral conduct, in politics, and in aesthetics absurd in the root sense of the word; such an attempt is simply inappropriate in terms of the metrics currently employed in analyzing and evaluating our universe. While many of the fulminations of "Romantic" critics against humanists like Vida were based on radically altered notions of aesthetic norms and of what— or who—produces and validates them, twentieth-century perplexities are more likely to be based on a fundamental distrust of the very idea of norms, particularly if it is claimed that they are immutable for all time.

The Renaissance Christian humanist, however, had long been used to the idea that history was structured, and that at a specific point in time a definitive declaration of God's will and nature had been given. That revelation was considered determinative, and it was only by recourse to the records of the revelation that one could validate his theology or ethics or philosophy; in brief, at any point on which the revelation impinged, one was bound to accept its authority. The church exercised a continuing *magisterium,* of course, but both tradition and the biblical record encouraged an allegiance to standards revealed at a particular historical moment. As readers of Dante and Petrarch are aware, moreover, the conviction that Augustan Rome as the secular milieu of the definitive revelation was di-

[65] The word "humanist" is used both to denote one's profession (as was the case in its earliest usage) and to characterize his thought-complex. It is in the latter, and looser, sense that I use the term here. For a history of the term "humanism," see Charles Trinkaus, art. "Humanism," in *The Encyclopedia of World Art,* Vol. VII, cols. 702 ff., and A. Campana, "The Origin of the Word 'Humanist,' " *Journal of the Warburg and Cortauld Institute,* IX (1942), 60–73.

vinely ordained, displayed a normative excellence in political structure, and represented the high point of world culture was immensely appealing and widespread. When Petrarch and men like Ciriaco
d'Ancona went about "to awaken the dead," it was with the certainty
that they were returning to the best cultural, linguistic, and aesthetic
tradition the world had ever known—in short, to that *Romanitas*
which was their proper and rightful inheritance. By Vida's adulthood
some century and more later the battle over whether or not a Christian should be interested in recovering this secular heritage was
largely concluded, and won for the humanists; with some important
exceptions the texts which we now possess had been recovered, and
the study of the linguistic medium of that culture, Latin, had been
refined by generations of scholars—scholars who laterly would find
Petrarch's own style shot through with "barbarisms."

When access to a "recovered" culture considered to be normative
comes solely through and is increasingly marked by a proficiency in
the recovered language of that culture, and more particularly by an
ability to wield the language as it was spoken and written at a specific
point in its history, then stylistic excellence is certain to be considered of the first importance. Indeed, one's intellectual and social
standing within the "recovered" culture is likely to be determined on
that basis to a degree which might seem to us perplexing. And when
all contemporary stylistic criteria and the testimony of antiquity itself
point to one author in poetry and another in prose as supreme, their
works will almost inescapably become the standard of literary merit.
For when one commits himself to the final excellence of a "recovered" language, one cannot easily hope to excel its own best exemplars. Though one might hope to use material not available to the
ancient author and still do excellently, and might hope to do as well
as he in the disposition of his material, one clearly might not hope to
surpass him in language. In such a case, one may only pore over and
cull out the stylistic excellences of the antique authors and make
them his own as much as possible. Given these postulates, the process of achieving excellence is of necessity a process of "recovery."

Vida's highly schematic literary history, which we discussed earlier, pp. xxxvii–xl (see also Book 1.129 and note 23), shows his understanding of the pattern of world culture. The paradigm points in-

evitably to the production of a third great epic characteristic of its age. In language, it must be Latin, and hence in style Vergilian, if it would hope to compare with the ancient performance; in subject it must of course be heroic (though, one may note, the "hero" might be a Christian one, even perhaps Christ himself). In planning the "disposition" of what one has "invented," Vida felt that the poet must look to the practices of antiquity, since Vergil in particular showed an unerring decorum in the arrangement of his material.

It was not, then, that by some odd "intuition" Vida "anticipated, at the beginning of the sixteenth century, almost the whole critical orthodoxy of the sixteenth, seventeenth, and eighteenth [centuries]," an orthodoxy which Saintsbury seems to identify with what he calls elsewhere an eccentric "Gospel of Plunder," but that Vida's theory of literature is part of a larger and coherent theological, political, cultural, and aesthetic paradigm. One may, indeed, reject that pattern because he finds it inadequate aesthetically, historically, or culturally, but it is worthy of interest and understanding.

This, in bold but I think essentially just outline, is the structure which Vida has given his poem, the conceptual focus which that structure expresses and sustains, and the thought-complex within which we must understand his verse essay. It is true enough that Vida's poem is one of the final statements of an aesthetic paradigm which in its main outlines had been known for a century and a half, and whose individual components were much older yet. Almost every line of the *De arte poetica* has the patina of the years upon it. It was "timely" only in that it took (generally classicizing) positions on questions which were of current interest. Nonetheless, it is an impressively wrought synthesis, powerful in its presentation of cultural humanism, striking in its disposition of material and in its variation of tone, and consummately graceful in execution.

It is important to insist, finally, on what has received episodic mention above, and will be amply illustrated in the commentary and appendix (see esp. pp. 183–93 and 201–10): Vida's unremitting effort to produce a poem which should delight as well as teach. That he intended the latter is clear from his letter to the *patres* of Cremona (see pp. 212–13), and from the poem itself; it is indeed this aspect of his work which has aroused most controversy and which the preceding pages attempt to assess. But no one could (or should) read the poem without appreciating the extent to which it is itself intended as a work of art. Dryden observed that Vergil's *Georgics* was "the best poem of the best poet"; clearly the *Georgics'* excellence as a treatise on husbandry was not the critical criterion, great as that excellence might be. What Dryden remarked was the almost incredible finish of the *Georgics,* the delicacy of vocabulary, the grace of style, the polished rhythms. And so, to the very considerable extent of his abilities, with Vida. The *De arte poetica* intends to teach and delight not only through its matter (audaciously enough, the practice and nature of poetry itself), but through the disposition and elocution of that matter. The poem, in short, is to have its effect not only through what it says but through what it is. Just as Vida supposes that Vergil was attempting through his poetic practice in a patriotic epic to be giving "instructions on the poetic art itself," "transforming and improving what [he] received from others" (p. 213), so Vida feels that by the same process, and writing on the art of poetry itself, he may produce a poem worthy if not "innovative" in doctrine, and instructive and pleasing in its art. It is that achievement of Vergil's which Vida perhaps most admired, and which with rather striking success he emulated.

THE TEXT OF

1527

AND THE TRANSLATION

NOTE

The meter which Vida uses here is the dactylic (hexameter),
the basic measure in Latin prosody; his style is consciously and
overwhelmingly Vergilian. For a detailed stylistic examination of
Vida's passage illustrating the effects of imitative harmony,
see the commentary, below, pp. 183–93,
on DE ARTE POETICA 3. 355–454.

Ex æneo nomismate, apud Vulpios.

M. HIERONYMI VIDÆ
CREMONENSIS
ALBÆ EPISCOPI
POETICORUM
AD FRANCISCUM FRANCISCI REGIS F.
FRANCIÆ DELPHINUM
LIBER PRIMUS.

 IT fas veſtra mihi vulgare arcana per orbem,
Pierides , penituſque ſacros recludere fontes ,
Dum vatem egregium teneris educere ab annis,
Heroum qui facta canat , laudeſve deorum,
Mente agito, veſtrique in vertice ſiſtere montis. 5

Ecquis erit juvenum, ſegni qui plebe relicta
Sub pedibus, pulchræ laudis ſuccenſus amore,
Auſit inacceſſæ mecum ſe credere rupi,
Lætæ ubi Pierides, cithara dum pulcher Apollo
Perſonat, indulgent choreis, & carmina dicunt?   10
Primus ades, FRANCISCE. ſacras ne deſpice Muſas,
Regia progenies, cui regum debita ſceptra
Gallorum, quum firma annis acceſſerit ætas.
Hæc tibi parva ferunt jam nunc ſolatia dulces,
Dum procul a patria raptum, amplexuque tuorum,   15

THE FIRST BOOK

OF

❦ THE POETICS[1] ❦

OF

M. HIERONYMUS VIDA
OF CREMONA
BISHOP OF ALBA

[*Dedicated*]

To Francis, Son of King Francis of France
& Dauphin of France

SANCTION MY SPREADING YOUR SECRETS ABROAD THROUGH THE
world, Pierians, and revealing to their depths your sacred springs,
as I consider how to foster from his boyhood years and place on
your mountain's peak a surpassing poet, fitted to sing the heroes'
deeds or the praises of the gods.[2]

What youth will he be who will spurn the sluggish crowds
beneath his feet, and enflamed by a love of fair glory will dare to
commit himself with me to the inaccessible heights where, as
handsome Apollo sounds his lyre, the joyous Muses abandon
themselves to the dance and chant their songs? Be the first to
come forward, Francis. Do not spurn the sacred Muses, prince of
a royal line, heir to whom the scepter of Gaul's monarchs will pass
when manhood has come with the increase of years. Even now in
their gentleness they bring you these slight lines as a solace while,
torn far from your homeland and your family's embrace

Ah dolor! Hifpanis fors impia detinet oris
Henrico cum fratre . patris fic fata tulerunt
Magnanimi, dum Fortuna luctatur iniqua .
Parce tamen, puer o, lacrimis. fata afpera forfan
Mitefcent, aderitque dies lætiffima tandem,   20
Poft trifte exfilium patriis quum redditus oris
Lætitiam ingentem populorum, omnefque per urbes
Accipies plaufus, & lætas undique voces :
Votæque pro reditu perfolvent debita matres.
Interea te Pierides comitentur. in altos   25
Jam te Parnaffi mecum aude attollere lucos.
Jamque adeo in primis ne te non carminis unum
Prætereat genus effe, licet celebranda reperti
Ad facra fint tantum verfus, laudefve deorum
Dicendas, ne relligio fine honore jaceret.   30
Nam traxere etiam paullatim ad cætera Mufas,
Verfibus & variis cecinerunt omnia vates.
Sed nullum e numero carmen præftantius omni,
Quam quo poft divos heroum facta recenfent,
Verfibus unde etiam nomen fecere minores,   35
Munere conceffum Phœbi venerabile donum
Phemonoes, quæ prima dedit (fi vera vetuftas)
Ex adyto haud aliis numeris refponfa per orbem.
Tu vero ipfe humeros explorans confule primum,
Atque tuis prudens genus elige viribus aptum.   40
Nam licet hic divos, ac dîs genitos heroas
In primis doceam canere, & res dicere geftas,
Hæc tamen interdum mea te præcepta juvabunt.
Seu fcenam ingrediens populo fpectacula præbes,
Sive elegis juvenum lacrimas, quibus igne medullas   45

Urit

(O sorrow!), a cursed mischance holds you, and Henry your brother
as well, on Spain's shores. For so your noble father's fates have
decreed it shall be while he struggles with an unjust Fortune. Cease
weeping, lad. Bitter fate will perhaps grow gentle; that most joyous
of days will come at last: then, once again on home shores, sad exile
past, you will know the people's measureless joy; they will shout their
tributes of praise as you pass through each city and raise their
jubilant cries on every hand; then mothers will offer the votive gifts
they pledged for your return. In the meantime let the Muses be
your companions; be bold now to climb with me to the groves on
Parnassus' heights.

Let us begin now: first, note that Song is not all of one genre. It is
true that verses were devised in the beginning solely for the
glorification of things sacred or for speaking the gods' praises, so
that religion might not lack some particular mark of distinction; but
little by little poets drew the Muses to other subjects and in differing
meters composed songs on every theme.[3] Of all these genres of
song, none is so excellent (save songs of the gods) as that in which
poets recount heroes' deeds [4]—whence, in fact, posterity derived the
name for the verses.[5] This meter, a sacred gift, was granted by favor
of Apollo to Phemonoe, who first (if the ancient tale is true) and in
precisely this measure [6] sent [the sun-god's] oracles out of his temple
and through the world.

First, taking thought, try what your shoulders will bear, and
choose with prudence a genre suited to your abilities.[7] Although my
first concern here will be with teaching how one may tell the praises
and deeds of the gods and the heroes descended of gods, my
precepts will, however, be of [further] use to you now and then.
Should you enter the theater and present plays to the public,
[for example,] or choose to sing of youths' tears, with which, as with
fire, love scorches the heart,

Urit amor, feu paftorum de more querelas,
Et lites Siculi vatis modularis avena,
Sive aliud quodcumque canis, quo carmine cumque,
Numquam hinc (ne dubita) prorfum inconfultus abibis.
Atque ideo quodcumque audes, quodcumque paratus   50
Aggrederis, tibi fit placitum, atque arriferit ultro
Ante animo. nec juffa canas, nifi forte coactus
Magnorum imperio regum; fiquis tamen ufquam eft
Primores inter noftros qui talia curet.
Omnia fponte fua, quæ nos elegimus ipfi,   55
Proveniunt: duro affequimur vix juffa labore.
Sed neque quum primum tibi mentem inopina cupido,
Atque repens calor attigerit, fubito aggrediendum eft
Magnum opus. adde moram, tecumque impenfius ante
Confule, quicquid id eft, partefque expende per omnes 60
Mente diu verfans, donec nova cura fenefcat.
Ante etiam pelago quam pandas vela patenti,
Incumbafque operi incipiens, tibi digna fupellex
Verborum, rerumque paranda eft: proque videnda
Inftant multa prius, quorum vatum indiget ufus.   65
Illis tempus erit mox quum lætabere partis.
Sponte fua, dum forte etiam nil tale putamus,
In mentem quædam veniunt, quæ forfitan ultro,
Si femel exciderint, numquam revocata redibunt,
Atque eadem ftudio fruftra exfpectabis inani.   70
Nec mihi non placeant qui, fundamenta laborum
Quum jaciunt, veterum explorant opera inclyta vatum
Noctes atque dies, paffimque accommoda cogunt
Auxilia, intentique aciem per cuncta volutant.
Quin etiam prius effigiem formare folutis,   75

To-

should you compose debates after the shepherd's manner, and pipe on your reed the contests the Sicilian poet sang, or, indeed, should you write in some other form, whichever mode you select, and whatever measure it may involve, you shall not (have no doubt) leave this work without profiting from it.[8]

And since one's own abilities are of such importance, take care that whatever you project, prepare for, and, finally, undertake suits your taste and has aroused spontaneous pleasure in your mind. Do not write on command, unless you are forced to it by the authority which great monarchs wield—supposing that among our princes one exists somewhere who would trouble himself on such a matter. All things which we personally choose to attempt flourish of their own will, but we scarcely accomplish with hard toil what we do on command.[9]

You ought not to undertake a great work suddenly, when first some chance whim or sudden poetic fervor strikes you. Delay, and first consider painstakingly the nature of the subject; ponder its every part, and reflect on the matter at length, until the young project matures in your mind. Moreover, before you spread your sails to the open sea and, at the outset, launch into the work,[10] you must prepare a worthy stock of words and matter, for there are many pressing subjects required by the poet's practice which demand your prior attention. The time will soon come when you will rejoice in these riches.[11] Of its own volition—perhaps while your thoughts are quite elsewhere—certain material will occur to you which, once forgotten, will perhaps never return freely, though you should call for it back, so that with vain industry you will wait to no purpose for the same thoughts to recur.[12]

Nor would those displease me who in laying the foundations of their labors pore over the illustrious works of the ancient poets day and night, draft fit auxiliaries from every direction, and eagerly cast their gaze over all their array.[13] It will also be useful to fashion beforehand in prose a likeness,

Totiufque operis fimulacrum fingere verbis
Proderit, atque omnes ex ordine nectere partes,
Et feriem rerum, & certos tibi ponere fines,
Per quos tuta regens veftigia tendere pergas.
Jamque hic tempus erat dare vela vocantibus Euris,   80
Condendique operis primas præfcribere leges.
At prius, ætati teneræ quæ cura colendæ,
Dicendum, quantus puero labor impendendus.
Nulli etenim infignem dabitur geftare coronam,
Pieridum choreas teneris nifi norit ab annis.   85
Poftquam igitur primas fandi puer hauferit artes,
Jam tunc incipiat riguos accedere fontes,
Et Phœbum, & dulces Mufas affuefcat amare.
Ille autem parvum qui primis artibus ante
Imbuit, atque modos docuit, legefque loquendi,   90
Syncerus vocis cuperem, ac puriffimus oris
Contigerit; fandi ne fors puer, atque nefandi
Nefcius, imbiberit male gratæ femina linguæ,
Quæ poft infecto ex animo radicitus ulla
Non valeas meliora docens evellere cura.   95
Iccirco mihi ne quifquam perfuadeat oro,
Ut placeant qui, dum cupiunt fe numine lævo
Tollere humo, & penitus jactant fe ignota docere,
Conventu in medio, feptique impube corona
Infolito penitus fandi de more magiftri   100
Obfcuras gaudent in vulgum fpargere voces
Irrifi, fœdam illuviem, atque immania monftra.
Non minus a recta mentis ratione feruntur
Decepti, quam qui, liquidi quum pocula fontes
Sufficiant, malunt grave olentem haurire paludem.   105

Ne

or image, of the whole work, to connect in order all of the constituent parts, to fix the sequence in which your material is to be presented, and to set for yourself clear limits within which you may direct your footsteps safely and proceed with vigor on your journey.[14]

And now this would be the time to spread the sails to the sounding winds and to set down the first rules for the composition of the work. But first I must speak of the pains to be taken in the education of the youth, the mighty effort which must be expended on the fledgling poet.[15] For truly, no one will ever be permitted to wear the crown of supreme achievement who has not been acquainted with the chorus of Muses from his earliest years. Therefore, after the child has learned the first elements of speech, let him even then approach the full-flowing fountains and learn to love Apollo and the sweet Muses.[16] I should wish, to be sure, that he who instructed the boy in the rudiments of learning and taught him the modes and rules of speaking be of unblemished voice and faultless enunciation, so that the youngster, ignorant of what is and is not proper in the use of language, may not harbor seeds of ill-pleasing speech, which you will never afterwards be able to eradicate wholly from his infected mind whatever effort you spend on giving instruction in better diction.[17] Therefore let no one, I beg you, urge me to suffer gladly men who, hoping to raise themselves from the dirt through the favor of heaven, surround themselves with a circle of immature youths, and, claiming unreservedly to be professors of knowledge which they do not have, knowing nothing of a master's manner of speech, delight, fools as they are, in throwing out to those who know no better a vile flood of obscure terms and barbarous monstrosities. These men are deluded, and no less out of their wits than those who would prefer to swallow foul-smelling swamp water when there are clear fountains from which they might fill their cups.

Ne mihi ne teneræ talis se admoverit auri;
Sed procul o procul ista ferat, natosque Getarum
Imbuat, aut siqua est gens toto obtusior orbe.
Jamque igitur mea cura puer penetralia vatum
Ingrediatur, & Aonia se proluat unda.   110
Jamque sacrum teneris vatem veneretur ab annis,
Quem Musæ, Mincî herbosis aluere sub antris,
Atque olim similem poscat sibi numina versum,
Admirans artem, admirans præclara reperta.
Nec mora. jam favet Ascanio, tactusque dolore   115
Impubes legit æquales, quos impius hausit
Ante diem Mavors, & acerbo funere mersit.
Multa super Lauso, super & Pallante peremto
Multa rogat, lacrimas inter quoque singula fundit
Carmina, crudeli quum raptum morte parenti   120
Ah miseræ legit Euryalum, pulchrosque per artus
Purpureum, leto dum volvitur, ire cruorem.
Necnon interea Grajos accedere vates
Audeat, & linguam teneris assuescat utramque
Auribus, exercens nunc hanc, nunc impiger illam.   125
Nulla mora est. nostro Æneæ jam conferet igneis
Æaciden flagrantem animis, Ithacumque vagantem:
Atque ambos sæpe impellet concurrere vates.
Nunc geminas puer huc aures, huc dirige mentem.
Nam, quia non paucos parte ex utraque poetas   130
Nostrosque, Grajosque tibi se offerre videbis,
Quos hic evites, quibus idem fidere tutus
Evaleas, dicam, ne quis te fallere possit.
Haud multus labor auctores tibi prodere Grajos,
Quos inter potitur sceptris insignis Homerus.   135

                                                    Hunc

Let this type of fool never come near me or my pupil's ear; far, rather,
far away let him deliver his cant, and corrupt the children of the
Getae [18]—or those of some other nation, if the world holds one more
dull.

Let my young pupil enter then, even thus early, into the poets'
secret sanctuary and wash himself in the Aonian waters; let him learn
from his childhood years to revere the sacred poet whom the Muses
nourished beneath Mincio's grassy caves, and entreat the gods that he
may someday attain a like mastery of verse, as he marvels at that art
and wonders at that brilliant invention.[19] Straightway he takes
Ascanius' part, and touched with sorrow reads of youths his own age
whom savage Mars swallowed long ere their day, sinking them deep
in death before they had come to ripeness of years. Many are the
questions about Lausus, and about slain Pallas many, too, the
questions he asks; he weeps from each verse to the next as he reads of
Euryalus, snatched in bitter death from his wretched parent (ah,
sorrow!), and of the purple gore which flowed over his handsome
limbs as he writhed in his final agony.[20]

Meanwhile the pupil should not hesitate to approach the Greek
poets and familiarize his youthful ears to both tongues, diligently
practicing his Greek and Latin in turn.[21] No delay is advisable; let him
compare our Aeneas with Aeacides, who flames in spirit, and with the
wandering Ithacan, making the two bards compete often before him
thus.[22]

And now, give ear and particular attention to what I am about to
say, young student. For since you will see many poets who have
written in either language—both ours and the Greek—come
forward to claim your attention, I shall here tell you whom to avoid,
and whom you may safely trust, lest one should mislead you.[23]
It is no great task to tell of the Greek authors: among them
illustrious Homer rules supreme;

Hunc omnes alii obfervant. hinc pectore numen
Concipiunt vates, blandumque Heliconis amorem.
Felices quos illa ætas, quos protulit illi
Proxima! divino quanto quifque ortus Homero
Vicinus magis, eft tanto præftantior omnis.   140
Degenerant adeo magis, ac magis ufque minores
Obliti veterum præclara inventa parentum.
Jamque fere Inachiæ reftincta eft gloria linguæ
Omnis, & Argolici jufli concedere avitis
Sunt pulfi reges foliis, civefque coacti   145
Diverfa exfilia, atque alienas quærere terras.
Huc illuc inopes errant. habet omnia victor
Barbarus, & verfis nunc luget Græcia fatis.
Noftri autem ut fanctum divas Helicona colentes
Cœperunt primum in Latium transferre, fluebant   150
Verfu incompofito informes, artifque Pelafgæ
Indociles Mufa fundebant carmina agrefti
Silvicolas inter Faunos. tunc omne fonabat
Arbuftum fremitu filvai frondofai.
Nondum acies, nondum arma rudi pater Ennius ore   155
Tentarat, qui mox Grajo de vertice primus
Eft aufus viridem in Latio fperare coronam.
Tum rerum cauffas naturæ arcana latentis
Explorare aufi cecinerunt carmine dulci,
Omnia Pierio fpargentes nectare, vates.   160
Atque ita deinde rudes paullatim fumere verfus
Cœperunt formam infignem, penitufque Latini
Agreftem exuerunt morem, liquidiffima donec
Tempeftas veluti cæli poft nubila, & imbres
Extulit os facrum foboles certiffima Phœbi   165

Vir-

he it is whom all the others revere, and from whom poets
conceive deep in their breast their inspiration and sweet love of
Helicon. They were fortunate men whom that age and the next
brought forth, for the nearer the date of a poet's birth to the time
of the divine Homer, the greater his preeminence over all his
successors. Their descendants declined ever further and further,
ignorant of the brilliant [poetic] invention achieved by their
predecessors of old. And now the glory of Inachus' tongue is
virtually extinguished. The kings of Argolis are forced into
submission and are driven from their ancestral seats; the citizens
are compelled to seek exile here and there in foreign lands, and
wander aimlessly about in poverty. The victorious barbarian
possesses all, and now Greece mourns, her fortunes
in ruin.[24]

Conversely, when our poets first began to convey into Latium
the goddesses who dwell on Helicon, their poetic technique was
crude and their verse unpolished. Unlearned in the Pelasgian art,
they poured out among forest-dwelling fauns songs inspired by a
rustic muse. Then all the wood resounded to the rustling of the
forest leaves. Father Ennius, rude of speech, had not yet sung of
battle lines and arms—Ennius, who afterward became the first
Latin poet to dare hope for the laurel crown from the Greek's
head.[25] Then, venturing to explore the causes of things, the
hidden secrets of nature,[26] the poets sang in sweet verse on all
themes, sprinkling them with the nectar of Pieria. And thus at last
crude verses began little by little to assume excellence of form.
The Latin poets freed themselves of their rustic manner until, like
purest-shining day after clouds and squalls of rain have left the
heavens, that most certain of Phoebus' sons, Vergil, godlike in
voice and spirit, raised up his sacred voice,

Virgilius, qui mox, veterum fqualore, fituque
Deterfo, in melius mira omnia rettulit arte,
Vocem, animumque deo fimilis. date lilia plenis,
Pierides, calathis, tantoque affurgite alumno.
Unus hic ingenio præftanti, gentis Achivæ   170
Divinos vates longe fuperavit, & arte,
Aureus, immortale fonans. ftupet ipfa, pavetque,
Quamvis ingentem miretur Græcia Homerum.
Haud alio Latium tantum fe tempore jactat.
Tunc linguæ Aufoniæ potuit quæ maxima virtus   175
Effe, fuit, cæloque ingens fe gloria vexit
Italiæ. fperare nefas fit vatibus ultra.
Nulla mora, ex illo in pejus ruere omnia vifa,
Degenerare animi, atque retro res lapfa referri.
Hic namque ingenio confifus pofthabet artem :   180
Ille furit ftrepitu, tenditque æquare tubarum
Voce fonos, verfufque tonat fine more per omnes.
Dant alii cantus vacuos, & inania verba
Incaffum, fola capti dulcedine vocis,
Pierides donec Romam, & Tiberina fluenta   185
Deferuere Italis expulfæ protinus oris.
Tanti cauffa mali Latio gens afpera aperto
Sæpius irrumpens. funt juffi vertere morem
Aufonidæ victi, victoris vocibus ufi.
Ceffit amor Mufarum. artes fubiere repente   190
Indignæ, atque opibus cuncti incubuere parandis.
Jampridem tamen Aufonios invifere rurfus
Cœperunt, Medycum revocatæ munere, Mufæ,
Tufcorum Medycum, quos tandem protulit ætas
Europæ in tantis folamen dulce ruinis.   195

Tom. II.   B   Illi

cleansed the filth and neglect left by the ancients, and set everything forth anew, made more excellent by his miraculous art. Give him lilies, O Pierians, from your brimming baskets; rise to acclaim your greatest foster child. This one man had a genius and art excelling all the sons of the Greeks, surpassing by far their godlike poets. All golden he is, a singer of immortal songs. Greece herself, though she admires great Homer, reels and trembles before him. Of no other time can Latium so boast herself, for then the Ausonian tongue achieved its highest excellence, and the mighty fame of Italy was borne to the sky. It would be blasphemous for poets to hope for anything excelling this.[27]

From that time, one could see everything hastening in tumult without a pause from bad to worse. The spirits of men grew degenerate, and all the arts declined from sheer neglect. For here, one man, trusting in his genius, spurns art; there, another is full of the fury of sound, attempts to equal trumpet blasts with his voice, and thunders endlessly through all his verses. Others offer vapid songs and inane words, captivated solely by the sweetness of their own voice. Finally, the Pierians deserted Rome and flowing Tiber, driven away from Italy's shores. The cause of this boundless evil for Latium, open [to attack], was the frequent irruption of a savage race. Italy's conquered sons were ordered to change their customs and use the language of the victor. Love of the Muses died; [28] despicable pursuits straightway took their place, and everyone flung himself into the acquisition of riches.

Some time ago, however, the Muses began again to visit the Italians, recalled by the largess of the Medici, the Medici of Tuscany, whom Europe in her old age brought forth at last as a welcome solace amid such great disasters.

Illi etiam Grajæ miferati incommoda gentis,
Ne Danaûm penitus caderet cum nomine virtus,
In Latium advectos juvenes, juvenumque magiſtros,
Argolicas artes quibus eſſet cura tueri,
Securos Muſas juſſere, atque otia amare.   200
Illi etiam captas late miſere per urbes,
Qui doctas tabulas veterum monimenta virorum
Mercati pretio adveherent, quæ barbarus igni
Tradebat, Danaûm regnis, opibuſque potitus.
Et tentamus adhuc ſceptris imponere noſtris   205
Externum, nec dum civiles condimus enſes.
Hæc ætas omnis, vatum hæc fortuna priorum.
Ergo ipſum ante alios animo venerare Maronem,
Atque unum ſequere, utque potes, veſtigia ſerva;
Qui ſi forte tibi non omnia ſufficit unus,   210
Adde illi natos eodem quoque tempore vates.
Parce dehinc, puer, atque alios ne quære doceri,
Nec te diſcendi capiat tam dira cupido.
Tempus erit, tibi mox quum firma advenerit ætas,
Spectatum ut cunctos impune accedere detur.   215
Interea, moniti, vos hic audite, parentes.
Quærendus rector de millibus, e que legendus,
Sicubi Muſarum ſtudiis inſignis, & arte,
Qui curas dulces, carique parentis amorem
Induat, atque velit blandum perferre laborem.   220
Illa ſuis niti nondum auſit viribus ætas,
Externæ ſed opis, alienæque indiga curæ eſt.
Nam puerum, ni præſentis vis fida regentis
Adſit, & hunc dulcem ſtudiorum infundat amorem,
Illecebræ ſacris avertant mille Camœnis   225

                                                    Dece-

These men took pity on the distresses of the Greeks, and lest, with the name, the excellence of the Danaans should wholly perish, brought youths and young men's tutors into Latium whose task should be to preserve the arts of Greece and to cultivate in safety the Muses and a scholar's leisure. They also sent emissaries far and wide through the captive cities to purchase, at whatever the cost, and bring back those monuments of the ancients, learned books, which the barbarian who had taken possession of the Danaan kingdoms and its riches was consigning to the fire.[29] —And yet we are trying to place a foreign scepter above those of our homeland and have not yet sheathed the sword of civil war! [30]

This is the whole cycle, these the fortunes of the poets of the past. Revere Maro in your mind before all others, then; follow him only, and as far as you are able, keep to his steps. Should it happen that he alone does not suffice for all your needs, then read in addition those poets born also in that same age.[31] Stop at that point, youth, and do not ask to be taught other authors. Avoid the grip of such a pernicious impulse for learning. The approved time will come when, having reached stable maturity, as soon will be the case, you will be allowed to approach the others, and no harm will ensue.

In the meantime parents, be cautioned, and pay close heed: you must seek out and choose your son's tutor from among thousands, if you are ever to find a man remarkable for his learning and skill who will take up these pleasant duties, assume the love a parent bears his child, and be willing to carry through this agreeable task. Youth does not yet dare rely on his own powers; it needs outside support and another's care. For unless a master's steady influence is consistently present and instills this sweet love of studies, a thousand enticing objects may divert the youth from the sacred

Deceptum falsa melioris imagine curæ.
Sic quoque ubi cultis plantas defodit in hortis
Agricola, & teneras telluri credidit almæ,
Fraxineos contos subito erigit, & sua cuique
Robora, ut innixæ ventos, cælique ruinam   230
Contemnant, surgantque leves impune per auras.
Ille autem pueri cui credita cura colendi
Artibus egregiis, in primis optet amari,
Atque odium cari super omnia vitet alumni:
Ne forte & sacras simul oderit ille Camœnas   235
Imprudens, & adhuc tantæ dulcedinis expers,
Deficiantque animi studiorum in limine primo.
Ponite crudeles iras, & flagra, magistri,
Fœda ministeria, atque minis absistite acerbis.
Ne mihi ne quæso puerum quis verbera cogat   240
Dura pati; neque enim lacrimas, aut dulcis alumni
Ferre queunt Musæ gemitus, ægræque recedunt;
Illiusque cadunt animi, nec jam amplius audet
Sponte sua quicquam egregium: ingratumque laborem
Invitus trahit ægre, animoque ad verbera durat.   245
Vidi ego qui semper levia ob commissa vocabat
Ad pœnam pueros, furiis insurgere, & ira
Terribilem, invisos veluti sæviret in hostes.
Hinc semper gemitus, hinc verbera dira sonabant.
Atque equidem memini quum formidatus iniquis   250
Urgeret pœnis, solitoque immanior ille
Terreret turbam invalidam, miserabile visu,
Forte puer prima signans nondum ora juventa
Insignis facie ante alios exegerat omnem
Cum sociis ludens lucem, oblitusque timoris   255

B 2   Post-

Muses and deceive him with the cheating image of better
pursuits. The task is like that of the farmer who has planted his
shoots in well-dug gardens and entrusted the slips to the
nurturing soil; he straightway erects ash-wood stakes as supports
for each one so that, twined on these, the plants may scorn
winds and cloudbursts, and, though tender, grow up in safety in
the midst of the winds.[32]

Further, let the man who is entrusted with the youth's
cultivation in the excelling arts desire as his first care to be loved,
and avoid above all the hatred of his dear charge, lest perhaps the
boy imprudently hate the sacred Muses at the same time, and
while he is yet unaware of the boundless pleasure which is in
store, his zeal for his studies should fail at the very outset.
Tutors, suppress your cruel rages; put down those shameful
ministers, your whips, and abstain from hard threats. Let no
one, I beg you, force my pupil to submit to cruel lashings, for the
Muses cannot endure the tears or groans of the youth they love,
and, sick at heart, they withdraw. The boy's spirits fall, and he no
longer dares attempt anything excellent on his own; he balks,
and carries on poorly a task he hates and becomes hardened in
mind to the floggings.[33]

I personally saw a master who, for niggling misdeeds, invariably
summoned his students to punishment, rose up in gusts of fury,
and, fearful in his wrath, raged as though against a hated enemy.
Hence incessant groans and hence the terrible whips sounded on
and on. And, indeed, I remember that on one occasion when the
dreaded master was pressing hard his unjust punishments, and,
more savage than usual, was meting out protracted terror to the
helpless class—it was a pitiful sight—there happened to be one
youngster, his face still unmarked by youth's first beard, of a
nobler countenance than his classmates, who had spent all the day
in sport with his friends, and, forgetting his fear,

Posthabuit ludo juffos edifcere verfus.
Ecce furens animis multa increpat ille, minifque
Infurgens, fævo pavitantem territat ore
Horrendum, & loris dextram crudelibus armat.
Quo fubito terrore puer miferabilis acri   260
Corripitur morbo. parvo is poft tempore vitam
Crefcentem blanda cæli fub luce reliquit.
Illum populifer Padus, illum Serius imis
Seriadefque diu Nymphæ flevere fub undis.
Tempore jam ex illo vatem quum dura jubentem   265
Phœbigenam Alcides animo indignante peremit
Vocali invifam feriens teftudine frontem,
Debuerat fævos factum monuiffe magiftros.
Vos tamen, o juffi juvenes, parete regentum
Imperiis, ultroque animos fummittite veftros.   270
Siquem igitur clari formandi gloria vatis
Digna manet, verbis puerum compellat amicis
Sæpe rogans, laudifque animum pertentat amore.
Quandoquidem, hunc imis poftquam femel offibus ignem
Implicuit, labor inde levis: fe fe excitat ardens   275
Sponte fua, durofque volens fert ille labores;
Et tacito vivens crefcit fub pectore flamma.
Quid memorem (focium nam mos æqualibus annis
Jungere, cui paribus ftudiis contendat alumnus)
Æmula quum virtus ftimulis agitarit honeftis?   280
Præfertim fi victori fua præmia rector
Pollicitus celeremve canem, pictamve pharetram.
Continuo videas ftudio geftire legendi
Ardentem, ac fera fub nocte urgere laborem,
Dum timet alterius capiti fpectare coronam.   285

                                                          Aft

had preferred to play rather than memorize the verses set. Lo, in the
fury of his soul the master thundered rebuke after rebuke, rose up
with threats, and terrified the trembling boy with his savage scolding,
a veritable monster, his right hand brandishing his cruel lashes. From
the sudden shock the terror brought on, the unhappy child was
gripped with a harsh sickness, and within a little time he left his
growing life under heaven's sweet light. Po, the father of poplars,
wept him; and deep beneath the waves Serio and the Serian nymphs
wept long for him.[34] When Apollo's son Alcides, indignant in spirit,
slew his poet-tutor because of the harsh demands he made, striking
the brow he detested with the singing tortoise shell, his deed ought to
have served as a warning to cruel tutors.[35] Nonetheless, young men,
when your teachers give you orders, obey their commands and freely
submit your minds [to their direction]. For the master who is destined
to the glory due one who trains a brilliant poet will encourage his
pupil with friendly words and will question him often and imbue his
mind with the love of praise. For indeed, when once the tutor has set
this fire deep in his student's bones, the youthful poet thenceforth
finds his work light; in an eager glow he himself fuels the fire in his
frame and willingly shoulders difficult tasks, as deep in his silent
breast the living flame grows.

Since the practice of associating a pupil with a companion his own
age with whom he may compete in studies equally advanced is
common, what need to describe here [what must occur] when the will
to excel, with its noble spurs, impels [the boy's efforts]—particularly if
the tutor has promised as the victor's reward a swift-running dog or a
painted quiver? Immediately you may see the youngster in a perfect
fever to study his literature and, fearful of seeing the laurel crown on
another's head, persevering in his lessons late into the night.

Aſt ubi ſponte ſua ſtudia hæc aſſuerit amare,
Jam non laudis amor, non illum gloria tantum
Sollicitat, ſed mira operum dulcedine captus,
Muſarum nequit avelli complexibus arctis.
Nonne vides, duri natos ubi ſæpe parentes   290
Dulcibus amôrunt ſtudiis, & diſcere avaras
Juſſerunt artes, mentem ſiquando libido
Nota ſubit, ſolitaque animum dulcedine movit,
Ut læti rurſum irriguos accedere fontes
Ardeſcant ſtudiis, & nota reviſere Tempe?   295
Exſultant animis cupidi, pugnantque parentum
Imperiis: nequit ardentes vis ulla morari.
Sic aſſuetus equus jam duris ora lupatis ,
Forte procul notis ſi armenta aſpexit in arvis,
Huc veterum ferri cupit haud oblitus amorum,   300
Atque hic atque illic hæret, freniſque repugnat:
Quove magis ſtimulis inſtas, hoc acrius ille
Perfurit. it tandem multo vix verbere victus
Cœptum iter. ipſa tamen reſpectans crebra morâtur
Paſcua, & hinnitu late loca complet acuto.   305
Ah quoties aliquis ſacros reminiſcitur æger
Fontes incaſſum, & lucos ſuſpirat amatos
Dulcibus ereptus Muſis puer, atria ut alta
Incoleret regum, rebus præfectus agendis!
Tibure quam mallet, gelido aut ſub Tuſculo iniquam   310
Pauperiemque pati, & ventos perferre nivales!
Contra autem, vanum multi effudere laborem,
Quos fruſtra excoluiſſe ſolum male pinguis arenæ
Pœnituit, ventiſque viam tentaſſe negatis.
Quod ne cui ſero contingat forte docenti,   315

Con-

But when once his own inclinations have fixed his love on these
studies, neither a passion for praise nor glory alone is his care;
captive then to the wonderful sweetness of the poets' works, he is
held beyond release in the Muses' encircling embrace.[36] Indeed, you
will surely have observed how, even after parents have withdrawn
their children from those lessons they love—as frequently
occurs—and ordered them to learn the arts of avarice, if ever the old
impulse slips into their thoughts and charms their minds with its
well-known sweetness, the delighted youngsters straightway long to
return in their studies to those full-flowing fountains and visit the
Tempe they knew. In their eagerness their spirits swell up, and they
rebel against their parents' commands; ardent as they are, no force
can stay them.[37] In the same way, if a steed, though already broken
to the painful bit in his mouth, chances to catch a distant glimpse of
his herd in the fields of home, he yearns to be led there,
remembering keenly [former] loves, and he balks, first here, then
there, and fights against the reins. The more you press on the spurs,
the more violently he rages. Finally only just curbed by repeated
blows of the quirt, he resumes the course he began, though still he
pauses to look back on those crowded pastures, and fills the fields far
and wide with his shrill whinny. Ah, how often some youth, sick at
heart, calls back to his mind (in vain!) the sacred fountains, and sighs
for the groves he loves, torn away from the sweet Muses to dwell in
kings' lofty courts as "Prefect of Royal Affairs." How he would
prefer to bear harsh poverty beneath Tibur's banks or Tusculum's [38]
cool hill, and endure winter's blasts!

There are many pupils, however, who have expended their labor
in vain, who regret that they tilled to no avail infertile desert soil,
and pressed on with the journey though the winds were to their
faces. Lest this should come to the tutor's notice too late,

Continuo poterit certis præfcifcere fignis.

Namque puer nullis rectorum hortatibus ipfe

Sponte fua exercetur, amatque, rogatque docentes

Primus, inardefcitque ingenti laudis amore.

Provocat hinc focios pulchra ad certamina primus,   320

Exfultatque animo victor, fuperatus amaris

Mordetur curis, latebrafque, & fola requirit

Infelix loca. ad æquales pudet ire, gravefque

Vultus ferre nequit cari rectoris inultus.

Nec lacrimis penitus caruerunt ora decoris.   325

Hic mihi fe divis, fatifque volentibus affert :

Huic Mufæ indulgent omnes, hunc pofcit Apollo.

At nullam prorfus tibi fpem fruftra excitet ille

Quem non ulla movet prædulcis gloria famæ,

Et præcepta negat duras dimittere in aures   330

Immemor auditi: cui turpis inertia mentem

Dejicit, atque hebetes torpent in corpore fenfus.

Huic curam moneo ne quifquam impendat inanem.

Nec placet ante annos vates puer. omnia jufto

Tempore proveniant. ah ne mihi olentia poma   335

Mitefcant prius, autumnus bicoloribus uvis

Quam redeat, fpumetque cadis vindemia plenis.

Ante diem nam lapfa cadent, ramofque relinquent

Maternos: calcabit humi projecta viator.

Nec ludos puero abnuimus. fubducere mentem   340

Interdum ftudiis liceat. defeffus amœna

Rura petat, fæpe & mores obfervet agreftum,

Et venator agat de vertice Tiburtino

Veloces capreas, aut tendat retia cervis.

Non ille interea penitus patietur inanem   345

Ire

he may determine the matter beforehand without delay by noting
unmistakable signs. For the poet-to-be practices of his own accord
with no urging from his master; he is the first to love and question his
teachers, and burns with a great desire for praise. Hence he is
foremost in urging his classmates on to praiseworthy competitions.
His heart is glad when he is the victor; when bested, he is eaten with
bitter regrets and, feeling miserable, seeks out hiding places and
solitary spots. He is ashamed to meet his fellows, and, until he has
vindicated himself, cannot bear to face the stern looks of the tutor he
loves; his face is streaked with becoming tears. This youth comes to
me recommended by both the gods and the fates. He is the darling of
all the Muses; Apollo asks him for his own. But from the beginning
have no vain hopes of the boy who is quite unmoved by a passion for
glory and sweet fame, who shuts stony ears to instruction and is
forgetful of what he has heard, whose mind is debased by a shameful
laziness, and whose sluggish senses lie listless in his body. Be advised:
expend no effort on him, for it will be useless.

But neither do I approve of a youth's being a poet before his
time. All things should flourish in their proper season. I cannot
wish that the juicy apples should ripen before autumn returns with
her twin-hued grapes and the vintage froths in brimming wine jars.
For apples which drop before they ought will fall and leave the
nourishing branches, and, strewn on the ground, will be trampled
underfoot by a traveler.[39]

Nor would I discourage the lad from games, for from time to time
the mind ought to be drawn away from its studies.[40] When the boy is
weary, let him seek the sweet fields and there oftimes watch the
peasants' customs; let him hunt and drive swift-fleeing mountain
goats from Tivoli's crest or spread out his nets for deer. But the
promising pupil will not let the day pass wholly by in empty diversion;

Ire diem. comitum cœtu fe fubtrahet ultro
Interdum, & fola fecum meditabitur umbra
Agreftem Faunis laudem; Mufafque fub alta
Confulet Albunea vitreas Anienis ad undas.
Nempe etiam alternis requiefcere fœtibus arva   350
Permittunt fponte agricolæ, & ceffare novales.
Interea vires tellus inarata refumit,
Quique fubit, largis refpondet frugibus annus.
Verum non eadem tamen omnibus effe memento
Ingenia. inventus fæpe eft cui carmina curæ,   355
Cui placeant Mufæ, cui fit non læva voluntas,
Nititur ille tamen fruftra, & contendit inani
Delufus ftudio, vetitifque accingitur aufis.
Numina læva obftant, precibufque vocatus Apollo.
Orabit melius cauffas fors ille, animoque   360
Naturam, & cæcos rerum fcrutabitur ortus.
Sæpe tamen cultufque frequens, & cura docentum
Imperat ingeniis, naturaque flectitur arte.
Nec labor ille quidem rectoribus ultimus, acres
Incauto juveni ftimulos avertere amoris,   365
Donec crefcentem doceat maturior ætas
Ferre jugum, atque faces, fævique Cupidinis iras.
Sæpe etenim tectos immitis in offibus ignes
Verfat amor, mollefque eft intus cura medullas,
Nec miferum patitur vatum meminiffe, nec undæ   370
Caftaliæ. tantum fufpirat vulnere cæco.
Ante oculos fimulacra volant noctefque, diefque
Nuntia virginei vultus, quem perditus ardet.
Nec potis eft alio fixam traducere mentem
Saucius. ignari fruftra mifcere parentes   375

Pæo-

he will withdraw from time to time of his own accord from his knot of friends and meditate in the lonely shade on some rustic hymn to the Fauns; [41] high up where Albunea springs, at Anio's sparkling waters, he will talk with the Muses. In like manner farmers deliberately let their fields rest by planting alternate crops and letting the lands lie fallow; for while the earth remains untilled, it regains its strength and then repays its debt the following year with a bountiful harvest.[42] Remember, however, that not all pupils have the same abilities. One often sees a youth who sincerely cares about poetry, who delights in the Muses, and whose willingness is propitious, but who struggles nonetheless in vain, and, deluded, struggles on with fruitless diligence, preparing himself for projects denied him to perform. For unpropitious divinities stand in his way, and Apollo, though [the boy] has invoked him in prayer. Perhaps he will plead cases or ponder nature and the hidden sources of the universe with greater success.[43] Frequently, however, constant labor and tutors' efforts overrule natural disposition, and nature is bent by art.[44]

Certainly not the last of the master's tasks is to protect the foolhardy youngster from the sharp spurs of love until maturer age teaches the growing lad to bear merciless Cupid's yoke, his outbursts of rage, and his fiery brands. For cruel love often pours hidden fire through his frame, pain penetrates to the tender marrow, and love blots from the poor wretch all memory of the poets and of Castalian waters, so greatly does he groan with his hidden wound. Images swim before his eyes night and day—the features of that maiden for whom with utter abandon he burns. The smitten boy cannot turn his mind to other topics, so firmly are his thoughts fixed. His parents, quite ignorant [of what is the matter], vainly mix Paeonian syrups

Pæonios fuccos; medicafque Machaonis artes
Confulere. interea penitus calor ille reliquit
Picrius. torquent alii cor molle calores.
Quum vero jam pubefcens mente altius haufit
Mufarum dulcem, fanctique Heliconis amorem,   380
Et fe fe Phœbo addixit, propriumque facravit,
Haud tantum exploret vatum monimenta, fed idem
Confulat, atque alios auctores difcat, ut acri
Nulla fit ingenio quam non libaverit artem.
Proderit in primis linguam Ciceronis ad unguem   385
Fingere, & eloquii per campos ire patentes.
Ille decus Latii, magnæ lux altera Romæ
Ore effundit opes, fandi certiffimus auctor,
Tantum omnes fuperans præclaræ munere linguæ,
Quantum iit ante alias Romana potentia gentes.   390
Profuit & varios mores hominumque, locorumque
Exploraffe fitus, multas terraque, marique
Aut vidiffe ipfum urbes, aut narrantibus illas
Ex aliis noviffe, & pictum in pariete mundum.
Quid referam qui, ut fæva queant æquare canendo   395
Prœlia, non horrent certamina Martis adire,
Per mediafque acies vadunt, & bella laceffunt?
At quia dura vetant longum nos fata morari
In cunctis, revocatque angufti terminus ævi,
Vos fat erit, pueri, tantum omnes iffe per artes,   400
Quarum fumma fequi faltem faftigia oportet.
Nec refert, rate qui varias legit æquoris oras,
Mercis ut in patriam referat fe dives opimæ,
Si non cuncta oculis luftraverit oppida paffim,
Et circumfufis longum terat otia terris.   405

Sat

and consult Machaon's *Medical Arts*.[45] Meantime the Pierian flame
has completely deserted him; other flames now torment his yielding
heart.[46]

When the pupil is reaching maturity and his mind has drunk deep
of sweet love of the Muses and sacred Helicon, and he has sworn his
allegiance to Apollo as one wholly consecrated to him, let him then
read not only the poets' works but examine and learn other authors as
well, so that there may be no kind of knowledge his eager spirit has
not tasted. It will be useful above all for him to hone his diction to a
fine edge like Cicero's, and to roam over the wide-spreading fields of
rhetoric. For Cicero, that ornament of Latium, great Rome's second
light, surest master of oratory, pours riches from his mouth, and as
far excels all others in the wealth of his magnificent speech as Roman
might surpassed that of all nations besides.[47]

It has been helpful for students to have explored the varied
manners in which men live and the sites of celebrated places, and,
traveling both by land and by sea, to have seen many cities in person
or known them from others' accounts, and have learned of the world
as it is depicted in wall paintings.[48] Need I recall the example of those
who, to enable themselves to describe savage battles with accuracy,
have no fear of entering the war-god's struggles, and, passing
through the midst of the battle lines, urge on the wars? But since the
inexorable fates forbid us to pause long in every new scene, and the
end of life's brief span summons us,[49] it will suffice, students, if you
have simply touched upon all the arts, whose principal points you will
find it useful at least to have examined. It does not matter if the
merchant who brings his ship to port on the various shores of the
ocean that he may return home rich with sumptuous goods has not
peered through every city everywhere with his own eyes and whiled
away long periods of leisure in far-flung lands.

Sat fuerit portus, extremaque litora tantum
Exploraffe : fecus toto vagus exfulet ævo,
Et ferus natos dulces, patriamque revifet.
Nulla dies tamen interea, tibi nulla abeat nox,
Quin aliquid vatum facrorum e fontibus almis   410
Hauferis, ac dulcem labris admoveris amnem.
Sed tibi præfertim princeps tunc hæreat illa
Cura animo, noctem atque diem te te excitet una,
Omnem quam propter libuit perferre laborem.
Non hic te quibus aut pedibus, fpatiifve monebo   415
Tendantur ducti verfus. labor ifte regentum
Poftulat haud multum curæ, qui fæpe morando
Ipfa minutatim metiri carmina fectis
In partes membris, & tempora certa docebunt.
Continuo edico jam tunc animofus alumnus   420
In numerum incipiat fub leges cogere verba.
Jam tunc fummiffa meditetur carmina voce
Sermonum memor antiquis quos vatibus haufit.
Tum votis fibi centum aures, tum lumina centum
Exoptat dubius rerum, metuenfque pericli :   425
Dividit huc illuc animum, cunctamque pererrat
Naturam rerum, verfatque per omnia mentem,
Quis rebus dexter modus, aut quæ mollia fandi
Tempora. vertuntur fpecies in pectore mille.
Nec mora nec requies, dubio fententia furgit   430
Multa animo, variatque. omnes convertitur anceps
In facies, nefcitque etiam notiffima, & hæret
Attonitus. nunc multa animum, nunc confulit aures
Secum mente agitans fi qua olim audita recurfent
Sponte fua, & memorem mentem excitat, atque repoftas 435

Tom. II.   C   The-

It suffices him to have explored simply the harbors and coastlines; otherwise he will wander as an exile all his life and only too late see his homeland and children again.[50] In the meantime, however, let no day or night pass without your drawing something from the full-flowing springs of the sacred poets, bringing their sweet waters to your lips. But above all keep your principal task firmly fixed in your mind; let that one goal for which you chose to endure every labor spur you on night and day.

I shall not give technical instructions here on the various meters and measures into which one arranges the verses he has drawn up [in rough]; this is the masters' task and requires few pains. For the tutors will pause frequently and show their students how to do an exact prosodic analysis of the particular verse lines by breaking down metrical units into the constituent parts and will teach them precision in handling a meter. Just at this point, I direct my pupil—who is already eager at the prospect—to begin working words into metrical patterns according to the rules, and, this done, to practice reading his verses aloud in a low voice, paying close attention to the phrases which he drew from the ancient bards. Then he wishes devoutly that he had a hundred ears and a hundred eyes, suspecting everything, and fearful of pitfalls; he turns his attention to every quarter and scans the whole nature of things, poring over everything to discover which meter might be suitable for expressing his conceptions or which rhythms might be smooth. He turns a thousand expressions over in his breast. [Leaving him] neither pause nor rest, many a notion rises in his mind, and then modifies. He is undecided, and resorts to every expedient; he is ignorant of even what he knows best, and comes to a dazed halt. He makes constant appeals, now to his mind, now to his ears,

Thefauris depromit opes, lætufque laboris
Ipfe fui parto fruitur. multa ecce repente
Fors inopina aperit cunctanti, aliudque putanti.
Jamque hæc jamque illa attentat, texitque, retexitque,
Et variis indefeſſus conatibus inſtat.   440
Sæpe etenim occurrunt haud dictu mollia, ubi hæret
Cura diu, multoque exercita corda labore.
Nunc hos nunc illos aditus veſtigat, & omnia
Attentans fcopulo longum luctatur iniquo,
Dum fe qua oſtendat facilis via. denique multa   445
Aut vi, aut cæli, & fortunæ munere victor
Exfultat, domitoque animis it ad æthera monſtro.
Aſt ubi nulla viam nec vis, nec dextra aperit fors,
Nec prodeſt vires feſſas renovare, nec aptum
Nunc hic, nunc illic captare ad carmina tempus,   450
Invitus cura abiiſtit, triſtifque relinquit
Cœpta infecta, pedem referens; ceu forte viator
Siquis tendat iter campis, cui fe amnis abundans
Ecce viæ in medio objiciat, fpumifque fragofos
Poſt imbrem volvens montis de vertice fluctus,   455
Horrefcit, ripaque moratus obambulat anceps :
Tum demum metuens retro redit æger, iterque
Aut alia tenet, aut, cedant dum flumina, differt.
Sed neque inexpertus rerum jam texere longas
Audeat Iliadas, paullatim aſſuefcat, & ante   460
Incipiat graciles paſtorum inflare cicutas.
Jam poterit culicis numeris fera dicere fata,
Aut quanta ediderit certamine fulmineus mus
Funera in argutas, & amantes humida turmas,
Ordirive dolos, & retia tenuis aranei.   465

Con-

racks his brain to see if something which he heard once will recur to him freely, belabors his memory, and rifles the wealth laid up in its treasuries, and happy in [the results of] his efforts, rejoices in what his mind has brought forth. Indeed, unforeseen good luck itself suggests many things to him suddenly when he is bogged down and his thoughts are elsewhere. He tries one set of devices and then another, weaves [his poem] together and then unravels it, and wearilessly perseveres with the various experiments he attempts. Often there occur to him conceptions difficult to express, at which his efforts, and his mind itself, weary with incessant toils, stick fast. [To achieve his goal], he follows up one approach after another, and trying every expedient, struggles long with the problem which stands in his way like a giant crag, until some natural path suggests itself, and victor by dint of great effort or by gift of heaven and Fortune, he rejoices, and his spirits rise to the sky, his dragon slain. But when neither effort nor an opportune piece of luck clears the way, and it is of no use for him to revive his sagging strength or to seize here and there on a time auspicious for composition, he turns away from his effort unwillingly and sadly leaves unfinished what he has begun, and retreats. So, too, a traveler who chances to make his way through the fields and finds his way blocked by a storm-swollen brook which foams and swirls in crashing torrents down from the mountain's peak trembles in fear, pauses on the bank, and walks up and down, uncertain what to do.[51] Finally he turns back, afraid and sick at heart, and either takes his journey by another path or defers it until the rivers subside.

[A youngster], unskilled in matters [poetic], ought not to venture to compose long *Iliads,* but should gain experience little by little, making his debut by playing on the shepherds' slender pipes. Soon he will be able to tell in verse of the fearsome fates of a gnat, or of how in boundless battle the murderous mouse dealt death to the croaking troops of marsh-loving frogs, or weave a tale of the stratagems and webs of the subtle spider.[52]

Confiliis etiam hic noftris, vobifque, docentes,
Eft monitis opus; ingeniis nam parcere multa
Fas teneris, donec paullatim attollere fe fe
Incipiant animi, videantque in carmine labem
Per fe ipfi, & tacito rubeant ultro ora pudore.   47 0
Nam maculas fi forte omnes per carmina monftret
Quæfitor ferus, abjiciant fpem protinus omnem,
Atque alias animo potius vertantur ad artes.
Noftrum igitur fi forte adeat puer indole limen
Egregia, ut confulta petat parere paratus,   475
Quique velit fe fe arbitrio fupponere noftro,
Excipiam placidus. nec me juvenile pigebit
Ad cælum vultu fimulato extollere carmen
Laudibus, & ftimulos acres fub pectore figam.
Poft tamen ut multa fpe mentem arrexerit ardens,   480
Siquis forte inter veluti de vulnere claudus
Tardus eat verfus, quem non videt infcius ipfe,
Delufufque fonis teneras fallacibus aures,
Haud medicas afferre manus, ægroque mederi
Addubitem, & femper meliora oftendere pergam.   485
Quod fupereft, etiam moneo, creberque monebo,
Ne quifquam nifi curarum, liberque laborum
Inchoet egregium quicquam: verum procul urbis
Attonitæ fugiat ftrepitus, & amœna filentis
Accedat loca ruris, ubi Dryadefque puellæ,   490
Panefque, Faunique, & montivagi Silvani.
Hic læti haud magnis opibus, non divite cultu
Vitam agitant vates. procul eft fceleratus habendi
Hinc amor, infanæ fpes longe, atque impia vota:
Et numquam diræ fubeunt ea limina curæ.   495

                    C 2   Dul-

Even here, tutors, you need our counsels and warnings; for it is proper to exercise much forbearance with tender spirits until, little by little, their minds begin to mature, and themselves seeing the faults in their poems, their faces blush unbidden with silent shame. For should some harsh critic point out all the defects in their compositions, they would immediately cast away all hope and their minds would be wrenched too strongly toward other arts. Therefore, if a youth who shows unusual abilities should come to my door to ask for advice, ready to follow it—the sort [of youngster] willing to submit himself to my direction—I will not hesitate to assume an expression of delight and extol his boyish poem to the skies in my praises, and will fix the sharp spurs deep in his heart. Afterward, however, when, all afire, he has excited his mind with high hopes, should there chance meantime to come along a verse which is sluggish as though lame from a wound, which he, lacking expertise, his inexperienced ears fooled with deceptive sounds, has not observed, I would not hesitate in the least to lay my healing hands on it and cure the invalid, always going on, moreover, to present better techniques.[53]

Finally, and I urge this repeatedly, let no one begin any ambitious project unless he is free from worries and duties. Let him rather flee far from the din of the reeling city and come to the pleasant places of the silent countryside where dwell the Dryad maids,[54] and Pans, and Fauns, and the rural gods who wander the hills. Here poets lead a happy life, without great riches and sumptuous surroundings. Criminal love of gain is remote here, and mad hopes and evil desires; wasting cares never cross their thresholds;

Dulcis, & alma quies, ac paucis nota voluptas!
At nimium trux ille, ferifque e cautibus ortus,
Qui fanctos, genus innocuum, populumque deorum
Aut armis audet vates, aut lædere dictis.
Vidi ego qui ad fummos Mufarum munere honores   500
Evecti, mox ingratos contemnere Mufas,
Nec vates faltem alloquio dignarier ipfos.
Parcite, mortales, facros vexare poetas.
Ultores fperate deos, fub numine quorum
Semper vita fuit vatum defenfa piorum.   505
Illi omnes fibi fortunas pofuere volentes
Sub pedibus; regumque & opes, & fceptra fuperba
Ingenti vincunt animo, ac mortalia rident.
Non illis ufquam fcelerum mens confcia cæcos
Horrefcit cæli crepitus, ignemve corufcum,   510
Quum pater omnipotens præruptas fulmine turres
Ingeminans quatit, ac montes diverberat altos.
Securi terrorum hilares ad fidera mentes
Arrexere, deûmque agitant fine crimine vitam.
Dona deûm Mufæ. vulgus, procul efte, profanum.   515
Has magni natas Jovis olim duxit ab aftris
Callidus in terras infigni fraude Prometheus,
Quum liquidos etiam mortalibus attulit ignes.
Quippe rudes hominum mentes, & pectora dura
Ipfe fagax animo miferatus, ubi aftra per aurea   520
Ire datum, ac fuperûm lætis accumbere menfis,
Miratus fonitum circumvolventis olympi
Ingentem, magnique argutos ætheris orbes,
Quos, fua quemque, cient vario difcrimine Mufæ;
Continuo utilius ratus eft mortalibus addi   525

here are sweet and genial rest and pleasure known only to a few.
That man is too savage and born of rough mountain crags [55] who
dares either with weapons or with words to harm the holy poets, a
group which gives no offense, the gods' peculiar people. I have
seen men who have been raised by the gift of the Muses to the
highest honors soon after spurn the Muses as displeasing and
scarcely deign a word to the poets themselves. Mortals, molest not
the sacred singers: you must look for the gods to be their
avengers, under whose divinity the life of devout bards has always
found refuge. They have all willingly spurned their fortunes
under their feet; they prevail over the riches of kings and proud
scepters through their great spirit, and laugh at mortal concerns.
Their conscience, knowing itself untarnished by crimes, is
untroubled at heaven's invisible thunders or its flashes of fire,
when the all-powerful Father redoubles his fury and shakes
soaring towers with his thunderbolt and flails lofty mountains.
Secure from these terrors, they raise cheerful minds to the stars
and live without reproach the life of the gods. The Muses are the
gift of the gods; uninitiate crowd, keep your distance! [56]

It was cunning Prometheus who once, long ago, committed the
astounding theft, and, when he brought bright fire to mortals,
brought too these daughters of mighty Jove from the stars to the
earth. For, wise himself, he pitied the rude minds and hard hearts
of men. And in the days when [the eternal ones still] allowed him
to pass through the golden stars and recline at the glad tables of
the gods, he marveled at the mighty music of Olympus as it
whirled and the pure-singing spheres of vast heaven, each tended
by a Muse who spun and turned her own to a different pitch.
Immediately he deemed that, fire only excepted,

Poft ignem nil poffe, animumque ad callida movit
Furta vigil. dii mox cæleftia dona volentes
Conceffere, doli licet audentiffimus ipfe
Auctor Caucafeo fævas det vertice pœnas.
Quo terrore nifi multo poft tempore inertes   530
Non aufi dias homines accerfere Mufas.
Sed ventura prius pandebant carmine foli
Cælicolæ, dubiifque dabant oracula rebus.
Ipfe pater divûm Dodonæ carmina primus,
Et Libycis cecinit lucis: mox Phocidis antro   535
Infonuit Themis alma: fuos quoque pulcher Apollo
Refponfis monuit Delphos: nec defuit olim
Antiquis Faunus caneret qui fata Latinis.
Tum Solymûm prifci vates, tum facra Sibyllæ
Nomina divinas cæli in penetralia mentes   540
Arripuere, deumque animis haufere furentes.
Nec mora, quæ primum Fauni, vatefque canebant,
Carmina mortales paffim didicere per urbes,
Poft epulas laudes heroum, & facta canentes.
Quid mirandum homini cælo divinitus æque   545
Conceffum? mortale genus tua numina fentit,
Quifquis es ille, deus cérte, qui pectora vatum
Incolis, afflatafque rapis fuper æthera mentes.
Te fine nil nobis lætum, nec amabile quicquam.
Ipfæ etiam volucres vario tua numina cantu   550
Teftantur, pecudefque feræ, mutæque natantes
Ad tua juffa citæ properant. tua munera faxa
Dura movent, filvafque trahunt hinc inde fequentes.
Te quoque fenferunt olim impia Tartara, & umbræ
Pallentes ftupuere. minas tibi janitor Orci   555

Obli-

nothing more profitable could be given to mortals, and, ever on the watch, he planned his cunning thefts. The gods soon freely resigned these "gifts" from heaven, though he who was so bold and committed the fraud suffered cruel punishments on the heights of Caucasus.[57]

Paralyzed with fear at this, men only much later dared to invite the divine Muses to them. But it was in song alone that the heaven-dwellers prophesied beforehand of events yet to come and gave oracles [to settle] doubtful matters. First the Father of the gods himself chanted verses at Dodona [58] and in the Libyan groves; then kindly Themis intoned [her will] in the cave at Phocis; handsome Apollo, too, instructed his special shrine, Delphi, with his oracles, and Faunus long ago recited to the ancient Latins their destinies. Then the ancient bards of Solyma, and then the Sibyls, whose names are sacred, laid hold of the supernal minds in the inner courts of heaven, and raging [with the divine fury], drank deep of the souls of the gods. Immediately mortals everywhere from city to city learned the poems which the Fauns and the bards had been the first to recite, and after their feasts they sang the heroes' praises and deeds.[59] What has heaven's divine ordination given to man which equally claims our wonder?

The race of mortals feels your majesty, whoever you are, a god surely. You inhabit the hearts of the poets, and draw above the heavens the minds which you have inspired.[60] Without you, nothing is pleasing to us, nothing is amiable; the very birds themselves bear witness to your godhood in diverse song; and the wild beasts and the silent swimmers in the sea hasten to do your will. Your gifts move hard rocks and draw forests now here and now there in their train. Cursed Tartarus, too, once felt your presence long ago, and the pale shades reeled. The keeper of hell gate because of you forgot his threats,

Oblitus, fævas pofuere & Erinnyes iras.
Tu Jovis ambrofiis das nos accumbere menfis,
Tu nos diis æquas fuperis. tu blanda laborum
Sufficis, & duræ præfens folatia vitæ.
Salve, hominum dulcis requies, divûmque voluptas.   560
Ipfe tuæ egregios audax nunc laudis honores
Ingredior, vates idem, fuperûmque facerdos,
Sacraque dona fero teneris comitatus alumnis.

and the Erinyes ceased their wild ragings. You grant us to sit
down at Jove's ambrosial feasts and make us the equals of the
gods above. You are the caressing recompense for our labors, and
the ever-present solace of a toil-weary life. Hail, sweet repose of
men and pleasure of the gods! I boldly take up now the excelling
honors of your praise, who am myself a poet and a priest of the
most high gods, and, as your attendant, bear to your young
novices your sacred gifts.[61]

M. HIERONYMI VIDÆ
C R E M O N E N S I S
A L B Æ   E P I S C O P I
P O E T I C O R U M
AD FRANCISCUM FRANCISCI REGIS F.
F R A N C I Æ   D E L P H I N U M
L I B E R   S E C U N D U S.

ERGITE, Pierides natæ Jovis. en mihi totum
Nunc fas venturis Helicona recludere feclis.
Infpirate animum. templa ipfe in veftra facerdos
Sacra ferens juvenes florentes mollibus annis
Duco audens durum per iter. vos mollia, divæ, 5
Siqua latent, vobis tantum divortia nota,
Præfentes monftrate, novofque oftendite calles,
Quos teneam. Vos en omnis, vos Itala pubes,
Quæ juga fub noftris nunc tendit ad ardua fignis,
Supplicibus pofcit votis, facilefque precatur.   10
Nam mihi nunc reperire apta, atque reperta docendum
Digerere, atque fuo quæque ordine rite locare.
Durus uterque labor. fed quos deus afpicit æquus,
Sæpe fuis fubito invenient accommoda votis.
Altera nempe arti tantum eft obnoxia cura,   15

Unde

THE SECOND BOOK

OF

❧ THE POETICS ❧

OF

M. HIERONYMUS VIDA
OF CREMONA
BISHOP OF ALBA

[Dedicated]

To Francis, Son of King Francis of France

& Dauphin of France

PRESS ON, PIERIANS, DAUGHTERS OF JOVE: HEARKEN, AND GRANT ME now the right to reveal Helicon fully to ages to come. Breathe through my spirit, for, priest and sacrament-bearer, I am boldly guiding youths in the prime of their impressionable years into your sanctuaries, and the path is arduous. You goddesses, if there are easier byways which are hidden and known to you alone, be present and point them out; show me new paths to take.[1] See! To you all the youth of Italy who now, under my banner, approach your mountain fastnesses [2] make appeal in suppliant prayers, and implore from you godspeed. For now I must teach the invention of fit matter, and when once it is discovered, its disposition, the just assignment of each part to its proper position.[3] Both tasks are difficult, but those whom the god regards with favor will often discover quickly materials answering to their wishes. The other concern is, of course, wholly a question of art,

Unde folent laudem in primis optare poetæ.
Veftibulum ante ipfum, primoque in limine femper
Prudentes leviter rerum faftigia fumma
Libant, & parcis attingunt omnia dictis,
Quæ canere ftatuere. fimul cæleftia divûm   20
Auxilia implorant, propriis nil viribus aufi.
Quos ores autem non magni denique refert,
Dum memor aufpiciis cujufquam cuncta deorum
Aggrediare. Jovis neque enim nifi rite vocato
Numine fas quicquam ordiri mortalibus altum.   25
Nec fat opem implorare femel, Mufafque ciere:
Sed quoties, veluti fcopuli, duriffima dictu
Objicient fe fe tibi non fuperanda labore
Mortali, divos toties orare licebit.
Incipiens odium fugito, facilefque legentum   30
Nil tumidus demulce animos, nec grandia jam tum
Convenit, aut nimium cultum oftentantia fari.
Omnia fed nudis prope erit fas promere verbis.
Ne fi magna fones, quum nondum ad prœlia ventum,
Deficias medio irrifus certamine, quum res   35
Poftulat ingentes animos, virefque valentes.
Principiis potius femper majora fequantur.
Protinus illectas fuccende cupidine mentes,
Et ftudium lectorum animis innecte legendi.
Jam vero quum rem propones, nomine numquam   40
Prodere conveniet manifefto. femper opertis
Indiciis, longe & verborum ambage petita
Significant, umbraque obducunt. inde tamen, ceu
Subluftri e nebula, rerum tralucet imago,
Clarius & certis datur omnia cernere fignis.   45

                       Hinc

and it is in this task that poets chiefly hope to gain glory.[4]

At the very entrance, just at the threshold of their works, the [poets] prudently skim lightly over the highlights of their material, touching in a few words on everything which they have decided to make the subject of their song.[5] At the same time they beseech the gods' divine aid, attempting nothing in their own strength. It finally makes no great difference, however, which [gods] you call upon, provided you remember in undertaking anything to use the rites proper to each god; for unless Jove's divinity is invoked in the prescribed manner, mortals may compose nothing lofty.[6] Nor is it sufficient to invoke the Muses and implore their bounty once only. You may call on the gods as often as, like crags at sea, things exceptionally difficult to express and unmanageable by human effort obstruct your course.[7]

Avoid giving offense at the outset; lure on the ready minds of your readers by avoiding bombast. At this point, things grand and ostentatiously overwrought are inappropriate; rather, one ought to express everything in words almost wholly free of ornamentation. If you wax magniloquent before you come to the wars, you will fail ludicrously in the midst of the battle when the material demands high spirits and unabated powers. Rather, let the sequel always be more lofty than the beginnings.[8] From the start kindle with eagerness the minds enticed [to take up your work]; fix in your readers' spirits the desire to read on.[9] Indeed, when you present the argument, it will be appropriate to relate it without reference to a proper name. For the poets always intimate their meaning by covert references and recondite circumlocutions, and cover it with a shadow. As through a light-suffused cloud, however, so here the likeness of things shines through quite clearly, and one may identify everything by its sure characteristics.

Hinc fi dura mihi paffus dicendus Ulyffes,
Non illum vero memorabo nomine, fed qui
Et mores hominum multorum vidit, & urbes
Naufragus everfæ poft fæva incendia Trojæ.
Addam alia, anguftis compleétens omnia diétis.   50
Ergo age quæ vates fervandi cura fatiget
Ordinis intentos operi, quum carmine aperto
Rem tempus narrare, loco ut difpofta decenti
Omnia fint opere in toto, nec meta laborum
Ufquam diffideat ingreffibus ultima primis.   55
Principio invigilant non exfpeétata legenti
Promere, fufpenfofque animos novitate tenere,
Atque per ambages feriem deducere rerum.
Nec, quacumque viam fuadet res gefta, fequuntur.
Plerumque a mediis arrepto tempore fari   60
Incipiunt, ubi faéta vident jam carmine digna.
Inde minutatim geftarum ad limina rerum
Tendentes, prima repetunt ab origine faétum.
Hoc faciunt, operum primo ne in limine leétor
Hæreat ignarufque viæ, incertufque laborum.   65
Namque ubi eum metam jam tum ftatuere fub ipfam,
Lætior ingreditur, fpe mentem arreétus inani,
Dum putat exigui finem prope adeffe laboris.
Sed portus, quos ante oculos habet ufque propinquos
Approperans, jam jamque tenet, fimilifque tenenti eft,   70
Longa procul longo via dividit invia traétu.
Fleétendi retro curfus: via plurima eunti
Reftat adhuc, multumque illi maris æquor arandum.
Haud fapiens quifquam, annales ceu congerat, Ilii
Inchoet excidium veteri paftoris ab ufque   75

Hence, if I am to speak of Ulysses, who endured many hard
trials, I will certainly not mention him by name, but will speak
of him as "the shipwrecked man, who, after Troy was overturned
and cruelly put to the torch, saw the customs and cities of many
men." [10] I would add other details, too, encompassing everything
in a few words.

Now mark the exhausting effort which writers who pay close heed to
their work expend to preserve due sequence, when, having begun their
song, it is time to so narrate the action that every event in the whole work
occupies its proper position and the conclusion of their toils fulfills
precisely what they undertook at the outset. [11] In the early portion of their
poems, authors are at pains to provide surprises for the reader; they hold
his mind in suspense with novelty and conduct the sequence of events
along roundabout paths, refusing [simply] to follow wherever the action
leads. Often they take time prisoner and begin their narrative in the midst
of events, where they see exploits worthy of a poem ready to hand. From
that point, they little by little retrace their steps to the threshold of events
and retell the action from its very outset. [12] Their purpose in so doing is to
prevent the reader's sticking fast at the very threshold of their works
through ignorance of the journey to be traveled and uncertainty as to the
labors involved. For when the poets have placed him immediately at a
point just before his destination, the reader screws up his courage with
vain hopes and sets out more cheerfully, thinking that he is almost at the
end of a brief undertaking. But as he hastens toward ports which even
now lie just before his eyes (now, surely, he is reaching harbor, he is
virtually there . . .), a long trackless journey divides him by a vast space
[of ocean] from the faraway shore. He must reverse his course: the chief
part of our traveler's journey is still to come; he must yet furrow a great
expanse of sea.

One would scarcely be acting wisely if, as though compiling
chronicles, he should begin a "Fall of Troy" [13] right from the decision
of that shepherd of long ago

Judicio, memorans ex ordine fingula, quicquid
Ad Trojam Argolicis ceffatum eft Hectore duro.
Conveniet potius prope finem prœlia tanta
Ordiri, atque graves iras de virgine rapta
Averfi Æacidæ præmittere: tum fera bella   80
Confurgunt, tum pleni amnes Danaûmque, Phrygumque
Xanthufque, Simoifque, & inundant fanguine foffæ.
Haud tamen interea quæ præceffere filendum,
Aulide jurantes Danaos, vectafque per æquor
Mille rates, raptufque Helenes, & conjugis iras,   85
Quæque novem Troja eft annos perpeffa priores.
Atque etiam in patriam fiquis deducere adortus
Errantem Laertiaden poft Pergama capta,
Non illum Idæo folventem e litore claffem
Cum fociis primum memoret, Ciconefque fubactos,   90
Sed jam tum Ogygiam delatum fiftat ad alta
Virginis, amiffis fociis, Atlantidos antra.
Exin poft varios Phæacum in regna labores
Inferat. hic pofitis demum ipfe miferrima menfis
Errorefque fuos narret, cafufque fuorum.   95
Ante tamen fi gefta canunt, ab origine cauffas,
Expediunt quis dehinc ftatus, aut quæ tempora rerum.
Primus at ille labor verfu tenuiffe legentem
Sufpenfum, incertumque diu, qui denique rerum
Eventus maneant, quo tandem durus Achilles   100
Munere placatus regi rurfum induat arma
In Teucros, cujufve dei Laertius heros
Auxilio, Polypheme, tuis evadat ab antris.
Lectores cupidi exfpectant, durantque volentes,
Nec perferre negant fupereft quodcumque laborum,   105
                                                       Inde

and recount in order each separate incident, including the long delay
before Troy which implacable Hector imposed on the Argives. It will
be appropriate rather to recount the mighty battles [around Troy]
toward the end [of the work], and to place first sulking Aeacides'
ruinous wrath at the confiscation of his [captive] maiden. Then savage
battles burst out, then the rivers Xanthus and Simois run full with the
bodies of Danaans and Phrygians, and the ditches overflow with blood.
In the meantime, however, one must not omit wholly the events which
preceded: the Danaans swearing their oaths at Aulis, the thousand
ships borne through the sea, the abduction of Helen, the rages of her
husband, and the sufferings endured by Troy throughout the first
nine years of the war. Again, should one undertake to guide the
wandering son of Laertes back to his native land after the capture of
Troy, he should not begin by telling of his launching the fleet from the
shores of Ida with his friends, nor of the subjugation of the Cicones;
rather he should show him already on Ogygia, his friends lost, standing
before the lofty caves of the daughter of Atlas. He should carry him
thence, after various toils, to the kingdom of the Phaeacians, where,
when at last the feast is ended, he may tell with his own lips the
calamities which beset him, his wanderings, and the misfortunes of his
followers.[14]

Moreover, if the poets sing of actions which took place long ago, they
sketch out from the beginning the causes of the events, and the result of
what occurred, and the times at which the events took place.[15] But the
poet's first task is so to mold his verse as to keep his reader in suspense and
long uncertainty as to what final outcome of the [present] events might be
in store. By what gift will stubborn Achilles be at last reconciled to the king
so that he will once more arm himself against the Teucrians? By the aid of
which god, Polyphemus, will the heroic son of Laertes escape from your
caves?[16] The readers are in eager expectation, and press on willingly and
without balking at completing whatever tasks remain.

Inde licet feffos fomnus gravis avocet artus,
Aut epulis placanda fames, Cererifque libido.
Hoc ftudium, hanc operam fero dimittimus ægri.
Nonne vides ut fæpe aliquis nimis arte fuperbit
Improbus, & captis animis illudere gaudet,   110
Et nunc huc, deinde huc mentes deducit hiantes,
Sufpenditque diu miferos, torquetque legentes?
Ille quidem fi te magnum certamen Atridæ
Et Paridis, multo promiffum carmine nuper,
Exfpectare avidum, fævaque cupidine captum   115
Senferit, ufque moras trahet ultro, & differet arma,
Dum celfa Priamo, patribufque e turre Lacæna
Nomine quemque fuo reges oftendit Achivos.
Ipfa procos etiam ut juffit certare fagittis
Penelope, optatas promittens callida tedas   120
Victori, per quanta moræ difpendia mentes
Sufpenfas trahet ante, viri quam proferet arcum
Thefauris claufum antiquis, penitufque repoftum!
Haud tamen omnino incertum metam ufque fub ipfam
Exactorum operum lectorem in nube relinquunt.   125
Sed rerum eventus nonnullis fæpe canendo
Indiciis porro oftendunt in luce maligna,
Subluftrique aliquid dant cernere noctis in umbra.
Hinc pater Æneam, multique inftantia vates
Fata docent Latio bella, horrida bella manere,   130
Atque alium partum Trojanis rebus Achillem.
Spem tamen incendunt animo, firmantque labantem
Spondentes meliora, & res in fine quietas.
Ipfe quoque agnovit per fe, quum in limine belli
Navibus egreffus turmas invafit agreftes,   135

Languid sleep, or hunger, that craving for Ceres' [gifts] which demands to be satisfied with rich feasts, may call our weary limbs away, but it is [only] with heavy hearts, and then late at night, that we give over our reading of this work.

You will note that often some impudent poet who suffers from an excess of art grows haughty and takes pleasure in toying with the minds he has in his power. He leads eager minds first here and then there and continually baits and tortures his unhappy readers. Indeed, if he should sense that you are caught in the grip of a consuming curiosity and are waiting eagerly for the great battle between Atreus' son and Paris which he had promised earlier with much fanfare, he will prolong delay after delay and put off the fighting while the lady of Lacedemonia, standing on a lofty turret, points out to Priam and the elders of Troy each of the Argive kings by name.[17] Again, when Penelope herself has commanded the suitors to compete in archery, cunningly promising marriage—for that is what they wished—to the winner, through what innumerable delays which she is at pains to provide does she drag our suspense-ridden minds before she produces her husband's bow which had been locked in the ancient treasuries, stored deeply away! [18]

But the poets do not, of course, leave the reader in a cloud, totally uncertain right up to the very conclusion as to how their works will end; rather as they sing they often foreshadow dimly the outcome of events through numerous signs, and grant him some measure of sight in the half-lit darkness. Hence it is that Aeneas' father and many prophets besides tell him the fortunes that will straightway befall Latium, that wars, savage wars, and another Achilles born to [plague] the Trojan cause are to come. Nonetheless they light the flame of hope in his mind and shore up his slipping resolve with promises of better things and, in the end, peace in all his ways.[19] But Aeneas also recognized through his own insight [what the future must hold] when, on the threshold of war, he disembarked from his ships, attacked the peasant hordes,

Atque (omen pugnæ) proſtravit marte Latinos
Occiſo, ante alios qui ſe ſe objecerat, hoſte.
Fata Menœtiades etiam prædixerat olim
Victori moriens majori inſtare ſub hoſte,
Quamvis haud fuerit res credita. tu quoque, Turne,   140
Prævidiſſe tuos poteras heu, perdite, caſus
Longe ante exitium, quum crebro obſcœna volucris
Per clypeum, perque ora volans ſtridentibus alis
Omine turbavit mentem, admonuitque futuri.
Hinc tibi tempus erit, magno quum optaveris emtum   145
Intactum Pallanta, & quum ſpolia aurea baltei
Oderis, atque tibi haud ſtabit victoria parvo.
Nam juvat hæc ipſos inter præſciſſe legentes,
Quamvis ſint & adhuc confuſa, & nubila porro.
Haud aliter longinqua petit qui forte viator   150
Mœnia, ſi poſitas altis in collibus arces
Nunc etiam dubias oculis videt, incipit ultro
Lætior ire viam, placidumque urgere laborem;
Quam quum nuſquam ullæ cernuntur quas adit arces,
Obſcurum ſed iter tendit convallibus imis.   155
Tuque ideo niſi mente prius, niſi pectore toto
Crebra agites quodcumque canis, tecumque premendo
Totum opus ædifices, iterumque, iterumque retractes,
Laudatum alterius fruſtra mirabere carmen.
Nec te fors inopina regat, caſuſque labantem.   160
Omnia conſiliis proviſa, animoque volenti
Certus age, ac ſemper nutu rationis eant res.
Quandoquidem ſæpe incerti huc, illucque vagamur,
Inque alia ex aliis inviti illabimur orſa,
Dum multa ac varians animis ſententia ſurgit.   165

Sæpe

killed the enemy champion who first blocked his way, and (an omen of battle to come) laid the Latins low by his might.[20] And again, long before the event, Menoetius' son as he died foretold to his conqueror that his fate [in turn] was imminent at the hands of a greater adversary, though the prophecy was scarcely believed.[21] And you, too, Turnus (alas, you were doomed), could foresee your misfortunes long before your death when an ill-omened bird, the wind whistling in its wings, flew across your shield and face again and again and troubled your mind with foreboding and warned of the future.[22] Hence the time will come to you when you will wish that you had never touched Pallas, whom you bought so dearly, and you will hate that golden spoil, his belt, since your victory will cost no small price.[23] For it pleases the readers to know these things in advance as the story proceeds, although the events which will precede them may be confused [in their minds] and those which will follow nebulous. The same reaction is characteristic of a traveler who chances to be heading for a distant city. If he catches now even doubtful glimpses of turrets built on lofty hills, he begins to travel more cheerfully and pushes on with a labor he finds more pleasing than when he never glimpses the fortifications toward which he is journeying, but makes his way along a dusky road deep in the valleys.

Therefore, unless you first consider the subject of your song repeatedly and with full attention and, as you mull it over, structure the entire work and then revise it again and again, you will marvel in vain at someone else's much-praised poem. Do not let unconsidered chance and random circumstance rule you because you are indecisive; rather conduct everything with assurance according to a plan predetermined by deliberation and your own wishes, and let the whole work proceed on the basis of rational design. For often we are unsure of ourselves and roam here and there, and without planning to, begin one set of topics and then turn to another as a mass of ideas rises and shifts in our minds.[24]

Sæpe vides, primis ut quidam longius orſis
Digrediuntur, & obliti quaſi cœpta priora
Longe aliis hærent nulla ſermonibus arte,
Et longos peragrant tractus, aliena canentes.
Ac velut in patriam peregrina ſiquis ab ora   170
Ire cupit poſt exſilium, duroſque labores,
Ille tamen recto non qua via tramite ducît,
Carpit iter, ſed nunc vagus hac, nunc errat & illac,
Undique dum ſtudio fontes inviſit inani,
Fonteſque, fluvioſque, & amœnos frigore lucos.   175
Nam quid opus gemmis armatos pingêre currus,
Multa ſuperque rotas, ſuper axes multa morari
Tunc quum bella manus poſcunt, atque arma fremit Mars?
Nec ſiquem indecoremque animi, pugnaſque peroſum
Egregios inter memoras heroas in armis   180
Caſtra ſequi, cupidi exſpectant audire legentes,
Qua facie, quibus ille humeris, qualive capillo
Incedat, captus ne oculo, an pes claudicet alter,
Aut longo vertex ductu conſurgat acutus,
Ordine cuncta, aliud quaſi nil tibi reſtet agendum.   185
Aptior Auſonius Drances, cui frigida bello
Dextra quidem, ſed conſiliis non futilis auctor,
Dives opum, pollens lingua, & popularibus auris.
Multa tamen Grajæ fert indulgentia linguæ,
Quæ noſtros minus addeceant graviora ſequentes.   190
Quid tibi nonnullas artes, ſtudiumque minorum
Indignum referam? ſunt qui, ut ſe plurima noſſe
Oſtentent, pateatque ſuarum opulentia rerum,
Quicquid opum congeſſerunt, ſine more, ſine arte
Irriſi effandunt, & verſibus omnia acervant,   195

Præ-

You often see authors who depart far from the topics they started with:
as though they have forgotten what they began earlier, they dwell at
length and unartfully on something else, and wander through long
passages singing of matters quite irrelevant. It is as though someone
wished to return home from a foreign land after exile and punishing
labors, and chose not to travel by the direct route, but rather wandered
aimlessly here and there, and at every point fruitlessly spent his time in
visiting fountains—fountains and rivers and cool lovely groves. For what
is the use of depicting chariots encrusted with jewels, and pausing
lovingly over their wheels and lengthily over their axles, at a time when
the wars demand close combat and Mars is brandishing his weapons? [25]
If while you are recounting tales of outstanding heroes in arms you
should tell of a camp follower who is shamefully lacking in courage and
has a thorough distaste for battles, your eager readers will not be
anxious to hear of the expression on his face, how his shoulders are set,
how his hair is dressed as he marches along, or whether he has lost an
eye, his left foot is lame, or he has a pointed head atop an elongated
neck.[26] Rather dispose each part of your material as carefully as though
its treatment were your final task. A more suitable subject is the
Ausonian Drances; his hand in war was feeble indeed, but he was no
worthless counselor, he was rich in goods, and powerful in speech and
popular acclaim. There are, however, many things which the laxness of
the Greek tongue allows which would be less fitting for our bards, who
concentrate on graver topics.[27]

Why should I tell you of the numerous tricks and shameful practices
of petty poets? For there are many who in order to show themselves
polymaths and to display the wealth of topics at their command
spew out inappropriately and unartfully whatever riches they have
collected (fools!), and make their verses a congeries of everything—

Præcipue fiquid fummotum, fiquid opertum,
Atque parum vulgi notum auribus, aut radiantis
De cæli arcana ratione, deûmve remota
Natura, aut animæ obfcuro impenetrabilis ortu.
Sæpe etiam accumulant antiqua exempla virorum　　　200
(Carminis ingratum genus) hinc atque inde petita,
Quamvis fæpe illis tempufque, locufque repugnet.
Ne, pueri, ne talem animis inducite morem,
Nec vos decipiat laudis tam dira cupido.
Haud fum animi dubius, magnos memorare poetas　　　205
Interdum Solifque viàs, Lunæque labores,
Aftrorumque ortus: qua vi tumida æquora furgant,
Unde tremor terris, quamvis illi orfa fequantur
Longe alia, aut duri cantantes proelia Martis,
Aut terræ mores varios, cultufque docentes.　　　210
At prius invenere locum, dein tempore capto
Talia fubjiciunt parci, nec fponte videntur
Fari ea. rem credas hoc ipfam pofcere; ita aftum
Diffimulant, aditufque petunt fuper omnia molles.
Cur pater Anchifes natum opportuna rogantem　　　215
Non doceat, rurfus ne animæ femel æthere caffæ
Ad cælum redeant, blandique ad luminis auras?
Igneus an ne ollis vigor, & cæleftis origo
Seminibus, quantum non noxia corpora tardant?
Quandoquidem ut varium fit opus (namque inde voluptas 220
Grata venit) rebus non ufque hærebis in iifdem.
Verum ubi vis animis varius fuccurrere feffis,
Ingraderifque novas facies, rerumque figuras,
Paullatim capto primis delabere cœptis
Tempore, nec pofitis infit violentia rebus.　　　225

Omnia

particularly if that "everything" is something remote or obscure, and [hence] little known to the ears of the masses, or concerns the secret system which rules the shining sky, or the hidden nature of the gods, or the obscure origin of the impenetrable soul. Often, too, they heap up hoary examples of men "who did such-and-so" (a disagreeable sort of poem), drawing their instances from far and wide, even though it is often the wrong time and the wrong place to adduce them. Students, introduce no such habit into your minds; avoid being deceived by so disastrous a desire for praise.[28]

I am quite aware that, whether singing of cruel Mars' combats, or teaching the varying characteristics of soil or techniques of cultivation, the great poets mention from time to time the courses of the sun, the eclipses of the moon, the risings of the stars, the force which makes the swelling seas rise, and the sources of earthquakes, even though they are presently pursuing topics quite alien to these.[29] But they have first devised a natural setting [for these digressions]; then seizing on a suitable opportunity, they introduce such passages sparingly, seeming not to speak of them by their own choice. You would believe that the subject itself required their inclusion, so carefully do they conceal their cunning, for they aim above all at ease of development.[30] When Aeneas is asking questions fit and just, why should his father Anchises not instruct him whether souls once deprived of the bright air return to the sky and the winds [which blow] in the sweet light; whether the seeds of life are of fiery vigor and heavenly descent insofar as our noxious bodies do not hamper them? [31] Indeed, for a poem to be various (surely a source of charm and enjoyment) you must avoid focusing continually on the same subjects. But when you wish to refresh our weary minds by being varied, and you introduce new matter and a new mode of treatment, pick the proper time, slip gradually away from the topics with which you began, and avoid doing violence to the material already presented.

Omnia fponte fua veniant, lateatque vagandi
Dulcis amor, cunctamque potens labor occulat artem.
Sic olim Æneæ, venturi haud infcius ævi,
Res Italûm in clypeo, Romanorumque triumphos
Fecerat ignipotens, pugnataque in ordine bella,   230
Stirpis ab Afcanio quondam genus omne futurum.
Tum fi quis Latio cretus de fanguine vates
Profequitur varias oras, morefque locorum
Medofque, Æthiopafque, & dites arboris Indos,
Immemor ille nimis patriæ, oblitufve fuorum,   235
Si non Italiæ laudes æquaverit aftris,
Cui neque Medorum filvæ, neque Bactra, neque Indi,
Totaque turiferis Panchaïa certet arenis.
Quare etiam, egregii vates, ego carmina veftra
Haud equidem arguerim, qui pectora feffa legentum   240
Interdum, atque aures recreatis carmine dulci.
Non ego poft Celei crates, poft tribula dicta,
Raftraque, plauftraque, & inflexo cum vomere aratra
Addubitem flere exftincti miferabile funus
Romani ducis, aut ruris laudare quietem   245
Poft vites dictas Bacchi, & filveftria dona.
Vidi etiam qui jam perfecto munere longam
Subjecere moram, extremo fub fine vagantes
Exactorum operum, vacua dum carmina Mufa
In longum traherent, cujus dulcedine mira   250
Feffi animi cuperent iterumque iterumque redire.
Me nulla iccirco quiret vis fiftere, quin poft
Naturas & apum dictas, & liquida mella,
Triftis Ariftæi queftus, monitufque parentis
Profequerer dulci fermone, & Protea vinctum.   255

                                              Addam

Let everything arise spontaneously; hide your cherished fondness for digressions and labor strenuously to conceal all your art.[32] Thus once the mighty fire-god, in full knowledge of the ages to come, figured on Aeneas' shield the fate of the Italians, the Romans' triumphs, the wars which one after another they fought, and Ascanius' yet unborn sons, [Aeneas'] whole line of descendants.[33]

Should, then, any poet of Latin blood be describing various countries, the customs of different lands, Medes Ethiopia, and Indians wealthy in trees, he has forgotten too much his homeland and his countrymen if he neglects to raise Italy's praises to the stars; for neither the forests of Media, nor Bactra, nor the Indians, nor all Panchaia with her incense-bearing sands can compete with her.[34] It follows then, bards of great skill, that I would scarcely be the man to criticize your works because you revive your readers' weary minds and ears from time to time with gentle strains. For after I had told of Celeus' harrows, of threshing sledges and of rakes, of wagons, and of plows with their inflexible blade, I, too, would not hesitate to lament the pitiable fall of the dead Roman leader [35] or to praise the peace of the countryside when I had sung of Bacchus' vines and the fruits of the forest.[36]

I have known authors to introduce a long delay at the end of their poem, digressing just when their works were virtually complete, and with their Muse at leisure, to spin out long passages whose wonderful sweetness made weary minds eager to return again and again. Therefore, if I have sung of the nature and habits of bees and of their smooth-flowing honey, no force could prevent me from telling in sweet song of the laments of Aristaeus in his sorrow, of his parent's admonition, and of captive Proteus.

Addam Threicii carmen miferabile vatis,
Qualis populea queritur philomela fub umbra,
Ut Rhodope, ut Pangæa fleant, Rhefi ut domus alta,
Atque Getæ, atque Hebrus, atque Actias Orithyia.
Non aliam ob cauffam, reges qui in prœlia euntes   260
Dinumerant, populofque, moram traxere canentes
Aut Ligurum regi, ob cafum Phaetontis amati
Dum gemit, & mœftum Mufa folatur amorem,
In filvis cano natas in corpore plumas,
Aut rurfum Hippolytum fuperas veniffe fub auras   265
Pœoniis revocatum herbis, & amore Dianæ.
Nec vero interea, quæ cuique infignia, quæ arma,
Prætereunt: pingunt clypeos, atque Hercule pulchro
Pulcher Aventinus fatus olim infigne paternum
Centum angues, cinctamque gerit ferpentibus Hydram. 270
Sæpe etiam loca amœna canunt, & frigida Tempe.
Nunc variis pingunt cum floribus auricomum ver,
Nunc virides liquidis inducunt fontibus umbras,
Crebraque fluviorum in ripis fpatiantur opacis
Aut Veneti Eridani, aut Ætoli Acheloi.   275
Addunt & Panas, Faunos, Dryadafque puellas,
Et centum æquoreas Nereo genitore forores.
Sæpe tamen memorandum inter ludicra memento
Permifcere aliquid, breviter mortalia corda
Quod moveat, tangens humanæ commoda vitæ,   280
Quodque olim jubeant natos meminiffe parentes.
At non exiguis etiam te infiftere rebus
Abnuerim, fi magna voles componere parvis,
Aut apibus Tyrios, aut Troja ex urbe profectos
Formicis, Libycum properant dum linquere litus.   285

Sed

I would tell of the pitiful song the Thracian poet sang like
Philomela sobbing out her lament in the poplar shade, a song so
sad that Rhodope and Pangaea and Rhesus' lofty home and the
Getae and the Hebrus and Athenian Orithyia would weep to hear
it.[37] For the same reason, when listing kings and peoples on the
march into battle, poets insert a pause and tell [for example] of
how in the forest feathers sprang up on the pale, aged body of
the Ligurians' king as he lamented the fall of Phaëthon, who was
dear to him, and eased the ache of his love by his Muse; [38] or of
Hippolytus, who was returned to the upper air by Paeonian herbs
and Diana's love.[39] But the poets do not pass over each warrior's
regalia and weapons. They depict [the heroes'] shields: handsome
Aventinus begotten once by handsome Hercules bears his father's
device—a hundred snakes and Hydra girt with serpents.[40] Often,
too, the poets sing of lovely vistas and cool Tempe. Here they
paint portraits of golden-haired spring with her various flowers,
and there make mention of groves made green by sparkling
fountains. Frequently they stroll on the shady banks of streams, of
Venetian Eridanus, it may be, or Aetolian Achelous, and people
the scene with Pans and Fauns and Dryad maids, and the
hundred sisters from the sea, the daughters of
Nereus.[41]

   Remember, however, to include often in the midst of your
festive passages a memorable saying which in its brevity will move
men's hearts, something touching on the proper conduct of
human life—the sort of maxim which parents may some day
commend to their children's remembrance.[42] But I should not
discourage you from treating even negligible things, should you
wish to compare great things to small [43]—Tyrians to bees, for
example, or Troy's exiles rushing to leave Libya's shores to ants.[44]

Sed non Aufonii recte fœdiffima mufca
Militis æquarit numerum, quum plurima mulctram
Pervolitat; neque enim in Latio magno ore fonantem
Arma, ducefque decet tam viles decidere in res.
Nec dictis erit ullus honos, fi quum actus ab urbe   290
Daunius hoftili Teucris urgentibus heros
Vix pugna abfiftit, fimilis dicetur afello,
Quem pueri læto pafcentem pinguia in agro
Hordea ftipitibus duris detrudere tendunt
Inftantes, quatiuntque fudes per terga, per armos: 295
Ille autem campo vix cedere, & inter eundum
Sæpe hic atque illic avidis infiftere malis.
Omnia conveniunt, rerumque fimillima imago eft,
Credo equidem; fed turpe pecus, nec Turnus afellum
Turnus avis, atavifque potens dignabitur heros.   300
Aptius hanc fpeciem referet leo, quem neque terga
Ira dare, aut virtus patitur, neque fufficit unus
Tendere tot contra, telifque obftare fequentum.
Hoc quoque non ftudiis nobis levioribus inftat
Curandum, ut, quando non femper vera profamur   305
Fingentes, faltem fint illa fimillima veris.
Vidi aliquos, qui, quum Glauco medio æquore belli
Tydides ferus occurrit, vix credere poffunt
Tot traxiffe moras longis fermonibus ufos
Inter fe fe ambos, dum fervent omnia cæde.   310
Alter enim diri narrat fera fata Lycurgi;
Crimine damnati falfo alter Bellerophontis
Facta refert, magna domitam virtute Chimæram,
Et victos pariter Solymos, & Amazonas armis.
Nam quæ multa canunt ficta, & non credita vates,   315

It would not be proper, however, to have the number of filthy flies which hover around a milk pail used as a comparison for the number of Ausonia's soldiery. For when intoning the arms and leaders of Latium it is unfitting that the poet should descend to such base creatures.[45] Nor will the poet's words gain much esteem if, when the Daunian hero has been driven back from the enemy's city and is retreating inch by inch from the fight, pushed back by the Teucrians, he is said to be "like a donkey which youngsters are chasing and trying to beat away with thick clubs as it grazes on fat ears of barley in a fertile field, but which, though its back and its sides are belabored with the cudgels, deserts the pasture as slowly as possible, and in going, pauses often, and hungrily crops the grass." [46] Every detail of the simile fits the situation; the analogy is precise, in my best estimation, but the animal is a base one. An ass will not be considered a worthy comparison for Turnus—Turnus, a hero mighty in his fathers and forefathers. The lion represents this sort of man more justly, for its anger and courage forbid it to turn tail and run, though it cannot make headway alone against so many or withstand its pursuers' spears.[47]

There follows now another matter to be dealt with which demands of us no trifling effort. Since in composing we at times present things which are not factually true, we must at least make them perfectly plausible.[48] I have seen some who can scarcely believe that when savage Tydides met Glaucus in the full flow of battle, with slaughter raging all about, they whiled away so many delays in lengthy conversations with each other. For one tells of the harsh fate of cruel Lycurgus; the other spins tales of Bellerophon, who was condemned on a trumped-up charge, of how the Chimera was vanquished by his great valor and the Solymaeans and Amazons were alike overthrown by his arms.[49] As for the many fictional and uncredited tales which the poets tell,

Dulcia quo vacuas teneant mendacia mentes,
Illis nulla fides, quam nec sibi denique aperti
Expofcunt, nec diffimulant, licet omnia obumbrent
Relligione deûm, quæ non credenda ptofantur.
Iccirco Solis perhibent armenta locuta   320
Mortua, & in verubus Vulcano tofta colurnis,
Ut minus acris equos itidem miremur Achillis,
Verbaque veliferas roftris fudiffe carinas:
Omnia quæ porta veniunt infomnia eburna.
Difce etiam, pulchri tibi fi cura ordinis ulla eft,   325
Res tantum femel effari. repetita bis aures
Ferre negant, fubeunt feffas faftidia mentes.
Quamquam etiam hic noftris cernes differre Pelafgos;
Nam tibi non referent femel illi fomnia Atridæ,
Nec fat erit fi rettulerint, quid fortis Achilles   330
Mente dolens Danaûm fe fe fubduxerit armis,
Ipfe iterum Æacides nifi folo in litore ponti
Flens eadem æquoreæ narraverit omnia matri.
Quin etiam reges quum dant mandata ferenda,
Cuncta canunt prius ipfi, eadem mox carmine eodem   335
Miffi oratores repetunt nihil ordine verfo.
Non fic Aufonius Venulus, legatus ab Arpis
Quum redit Ætoli referens refponfa tyranni.
Altum aliis affurgat opus: tu nocte, dieque
Exiguum meditator, ubi fint omnia culta,   340
Et vifenda novis iterumque, iterumque figuris.
Quod fi longarum cordi magis ampla viarum
Sunt fpatia, anguftis quum res tibi finibus àrcta,
In longum trahito arte. viæ tibi mille trahendi,
Mille modi. nam ficta potes multa addere veris,   345

                                                          Et

the honeyed lies, devised to take possession of minds at leisure: the
poets ask no one to give credence either to the stories or, indeed, as they
make perfectly clear—to themselves. Nor are they being deceptive,
even though they shelter everything they say which is not to be believed
behind an awe of the gods. Thus it is that they claim that the sun's dead
oxen spoke—even after being roasted on Vulcan's hazel spits. How
much less, then, should we wonder that the horses of hot-tempered
Achilles likewise spoke and that the beaks of sailboats uttered words;
for all these are dreams which come by the ivory gate.[50]

You must learn as well, if you are at all concerned for the attractive
disposition of your material, to say a thing once only. Our ears will not
tolerate repetition; it wearies our minds and produces distaste. You will
note, however, that the Pelasgians differ from our poets in this matter
too. For they do not stop with reporting Atreus' son's dreams to you
once,[51] nor will it suffice if they tell why valiant Achilles, sulking
inwardly, withdrew himself from the Danaan troops; but Aeacides
himself, alone on the beach of the ocean, must weep and report the
very same things all over again to his mother, whose home is the sea.[52]
Indeed, even kings, when they give commands to be conveyed, first
recite everything themselves; and then the orators they have sent
repeat the very same matter in the very same meter in the very same
order.[53] Such is not the case with the Ausonian Venulus, sent as legate
from Arpi, when he returns carrying the replies of the Aetolian
tyrant.[54]

Let others project a lofty undertaking. For yourself, lay plans night
and day for a short work, one in which everything is highly polished
and ornamented constantly with new figures.[55] But if the broad vistas
which long journeys allow please you more, after you have compressed
your material within narrow limits, lengthen it out by art. There are a
thousand courses for drawing it out, and a thousand ways [of following
them]. You may, for instance, add many fictional things to the true

Line: 319: should read *profantur*.

Et petere hinc illinc variarum femina rerum.
Nonne vides, ut noftra deos in proelia ducant,
Hos Teucris, alios Danais focia arma ferentes,
Certantefque inter fe odiis, donec pater ipfe
Concilium vocet, atque ingentes molliat iras?   350
Quum fecura tamen penitus natura deorum
Degat, & afpectu noftro fummota quiefcat.
Addunt infernafque domos regna invia vivis,
Tartareofque lacus, Ditemque, & Erinnyas atras.
Tum volucrum captant cantus, atque omina pennæ.   355
Sæpe etiam hofpitibus convivia læta receptis,
Regalefque canunt epulas, ubi multa repoftis
Narrantur dapibus vario fermone viciffim.
Nunc ludos celebrant magnorum ad bufta virorum,
Annua nunc patriis peragunt diis facra periclo   360
Servati quondam: laudefque ad fidera tollunt
Aut Phœbi, monftro ingenti Pythone peremto,
Aut magni Alcidæ, Cacum ut videre jacentem.
Rege fub Euryftheo tulerit quos ille labores,
Alterni repetunt cantu. fuper omnia Caci   365
Speluncam adjiciunt, fpirantemque ignibus ipfum.
An memorem, quandoque omnes intendere nervos
Quum libuit, verbifque ipfam rem æquare canendo,
Seu dicenda feri tempeftas horrida ponti,
Ventorum & rabies, fractæque ad faxa carinæ   370
Aut Siculo angufto, aut impacato Euxino?
Sive coorta repente lues, quum multa ferarum,
Corpora multa hominum leto data, five Sicana
Dicendum quantis terra tonet Ætna ruinis
Prorumpens atram cæli ufque ad fidera nubem   375

or search here and there for the origins of various phenomena.[56] You
surely have noticed how poets draw the gods into our battles and
make them bear arms as allies, some to the Teucrians and others to
the Danaans, fighting in bitter animosity amongst themselves, until
the Father himself calls a council and calms their passionate
quarrels.[57] The gods' nature, however, lives on in complete serenity
and dwells in peace far removed from our gaze.[58] The poets sing, too,
of the houses of Hell, the realms which no one living can enter,
Tartarus' lakes, and Dis, and the black Erinyes.[59] Then they take
delight in the songs of birds, and the omens which a feather implies.[60]
Often, too, they sing of joyous feasts given for the reception of guests
and of kingly banquets, where, when the sumptuous foods have been
taken away, many tales are spun in turn in discourse diverse.[61] Now
they celebrate games at the tombs of mighty men; [62] now those once
saved from danger carry out the annual rites sacred to the gods of
their fathers. They extol to the stars the praises either of Phoebus, for
he slew the great monster Python, or of mighty Alcides, for they saw
Cacus stretched on the ground; they sing in antiphonal song of those
labors which Hercules bore under King Eurystheus; and above all
others they include "The Cave of Cacus" and "Cacus Breathing
Fire." [63]

Shall I describe here the times when the poet puts all his powers on
the stretch, and attempts to compose a work in which his words will
emulate the thing itself? [64] Perhaps he will tell of a fearful storm on the
savage sea, or the roar of the winds, or of keels splintered on rocks in
the Sicilian straits or the turbulent Euxine; [65] or he may sing of a
plague which suddenly broke out and delivered to death countless
bodies of men and wild beasts.[66] Perhaps his tale will be of the appalling
disasters which Sicilian Aetna thundered out on the earth as she erupted;
how she belched an ink-black cloud high as the stars in the heavens,

Turbine fumantem piceo, & candente favilla.
Vidifti quum bella canunt horrentia, & arma
Arma fremunt, mifcentque equitum, peditumque ruinas.
Ante oculos, Martis fe fe offert triftis imago,
Non tantum ut dici videantur, fed fieri res;   380
Unde ipfis nomen Graji fecere poetis.
Armorum fragor audiri, gemitufque cadentum,
Cædentumque ictus, & inania vota precantum.
Quis quoque, quum captas evolvunt hoftibus urbes,
Temperet a lacrimis? tectorum ad culmina fævas   385
Ire faces, paffimque domos involvere flammas
Cernere erit, trepidofque fenes, puerofque parentes
Amplexos, flentefque ipfas ad fidera matres
Tollentes clamorem hoftes inte rque, fuofque
Abftractafque nurus adytis, arifque deorum   390
Et crinem laniare, & pectora tundere palmis;
Hos fugere, aft illos ingentem abducere prædam.
Perque domos, perque alta ruunt delubra deorum,
Atque huc, atque illuc tota difcurritur urbe.
Quid quum animis facer eft furor additus, atque potens vis? 395
Nam variant fpecies animorum, & pectora noftra
Nunc hos, nunc illos multo difcrimine motus
Concipiunt, feu quod cæli mutatur in horas
Tempeftas, hominumque fimul quoque pectora mutant:
Seu quia non iidem refpondent fæpe labore   400
Senfus effœti, atque animus cum corpore languet:
Seu quia curarum interdum, vacuique doloris,
Interdum triftes cæco intus tundimur æftu.
Dii potius noftris ardorem hunc mentibus addunt
Dii potius, felixque ideo qui tempora quivit,   405
                                                          Ad-

as smoke shot up in a pitch-black swirl, studded with glowing ash.[67]
You have seen, when the poets sing of fearful war and clatter arms
upon arms and mix in a common destruction soldiers both ahorse
and afoot, how the baleful figure of Mars appears before your very
eyes, so that it seems that the dire events you behold are not merely
being described but actually taking place. (From this ["making" a
creation of their own], the Greeks gave "poets" their name.) [68] You
seem to hear the clash of weapons, the groans of the slain, the slayer's
strokes, and the useless vows of those who pray. And who, then,
would hold back his tears as poets tell of cities captured by enemy
hands? They will show you savage flames towering over the rooftops,
flames everywhere enveloping houses, old men palsied with fear, boys
clutching their parents, the mothers themselves in tears, raising their
clamor to the stars as they stand between the enemy and their
children. Look! Young women are dragged from the gods'
sanctuaries and altars, tearing their hair and beating their breasts with
their hands. The victims flee, while their conquerors drag off a huge
booty, rolling [like a torrent] through houses and the gods' lofty
temples, while everywhere people rush wildly about the city.[69]

And what of the times when our minds are imbued with the sacred
madness and its mighty powers? [70] For the cast of our souls varies,
and at one time our minds conceive greatly different impulses from
those at another—perhaps because heaven's aspect is altered from
hour to hour, and men's minds change, too, in accord with it; or
because one's senses when wearied often do not react with wonted
vigor, and the spirit grows listless with the body; or because at times
we are free from worries and useless sorrow, and at others buffeted
with hidden anxiety. But above all it is the gods who infuse this ardor
into our minds, the gods above all; he is fortunate, therefore, who can
wait for the divinely favored times,

Line 389: should read *interque*.

Adventumque dei, & facrum exfpectare calorem,
Paullifperque operi pofito fubducere mentem,
Mutati donec redeat clementia cæli.
Sponte fua veniet juftum (ne accerfite) tempus.
Interdum & filvis frondes, & fontibus humor   410
Defunt, nec victis femper cava flumina ripis
Plena fluunt, nec femper agros ver pingit apricos.
Sors eadem incertis contingit fæpe poetis.
Interdum exhauftæ languent ad carmina vires,
Abfumtufque vigor, ftudiorumque immemor eft mens. 415
Torpefcunt fenfus, circum præcordia fanguis
Stat gelidus. credas penitus migraffe Camœnas;
Notaque numquam ipfum rediturum in pectora Phœbum.
Nil adeo Mufæ, nil fubvenit auctor Apollo.
Ah quoties aliquis fruftra confueta retentat   420
Munera, nec cernit cælum fe tendere contra,
Adverfofque deos, atque implacabile numen!
Quidam autem inventus qui fæpe reduceret auras
Optatas veterum cantando carmina vatum,
Paullatimque animo blandum invitaret amorem,   425
Donec collectæ vires, animique refecti,
Et rediit vigor ille, velut poft nubila, & imbres
Sol micat æthereus. unde hæc tam clara repente
Tempeftas? deus ecce deus jam corda fatigat,
Altius infinuat venis, penitufque per artus   430
Diditur, atque faces fævas fub pectore verfat.
Nec fe jam capit acer agens calor, igneaque intus
Vis fævit, totoque agitat fe corpore numen.
Ille autem exfultans jactat jam non fua verba,
Oblitufque hominem, mirum fonat. haud potis ignem 435
                                              Excu-

for the god's visitation, and the sacred fire; who can switch his
attention for a little time from the work he has begun until
heaven reverses itself and its good will returns. The proper time
will come spontaneously; no use to summon it. For at times
forests lose their leaves, and the water in fountains dries up. Deep
rivers do not always run full to overflowing, nor does spring
always adorn sun-drenched fields. A similar fate often befalls
poets and perplexes them. From time to time their exhausted
powers falter over their poems, and their energy disappears; they
grow absent-minded about their studies; their senses become dull,
and the blood lies cool in their breasts. You would think that the
Muses had fled them entirely, and that Phoebus himself never
intended to return to his home in their hearts, so adamantly do
the Muses, and Apollo, their leader, deny aid. Alas, how often a
poet vainly attempts to exercise the powers he normally possesses,
and is not aware that he is striving against heaven, the will of the
gods, and their implacable power! I knew of a man, however, who
would often woo back the inspiration he longed for by reciting
the poems of the ancient bards; little by little he would suffuse his
mind with the sweet love [of their works], until his energies were
recruited, and his spirits revived, and his vigor returned, like the
sun flashing forth in its brilliance after clouds and a drenching
rain. How is it that the sky is suddenly so sparkling now? The god
comes! See, already the god assaults his heart, slips deep through
his veins, spreads everywhere through his frame, and sets a
blazing fire under his heart. Now the harsh flame rages out of
control and drives him on; the fiery force sears him within as the
god surges through his whole body. In an ecstasy he shouts forth
words no longer his own and, oblivious to his human limitations,
sings with marvelous power. He is helpless to shake off the fire,

Line 431: should read *Deditur*.

Excutere. invitum miratur se ire, rapique
Præcipitem te, Phœbe, vocans, te, Phœbe, prementem
Vociferans, plenufque deo, ftimulifque fubactus
Haud placidis. non ille dapum, non ille quietis,
Aut fomni memor hanc potis eft deponere curam .   440
Sæpe etiam in fomnis memores Phœbeïa verfant
Munera, & inventi quidam qui fæpe fopore
In medio Mufis cecinere, & Apolline digna.
Tantus amor famæ, præfentis tanta dei vis.
Ne tamen ah nimium, puer o, ne fide calori.   445
Non te fortuna femper permittimus uti,
Præfentique aura, fævum dum pectore numen
Infidet: at potius ratioque, & cura refiftat;
Freno fifte furentem animum, & fub figna vocato,
Et premere, & laxas fcito dare cautus habenas.   450
Atque ideo femper tunc exfpectare jubemus,
Dum fuerint placati animi, compreffus, & omnis
Impetus. hic recolens fedato corde revife
Omnia, quæ cæcus menti fubjecerint ardor.
Præterea haud lateat te nil conarier artem,   455
Naturam nifi ut affimulet, propiufque fequatur.
Hanc unam vates fibi propofuere magiftram:
Quicquid agunt, hujus femper veftigia fervant.
Hinc varios morefque hominum, morefque animantum,
Aut ftudia imparibus divifa ætatibus apta   460
Effingunt facie verborum; & imagine reddunt
Quæ tardofque fenes deceant, juvenefque virentes,
Femineumque genus; quantum quoque rura colenti,
Aut famulo diftet regum alto e fanguine cretus.
Nam mihi non placeat, teneros fi fit gravis annos   465
                                                      Tele-

and astonished that he moves when he has not willed to, astonished to
be drawn headlong away, as he calls to you, Phoebus, shouts, Phoebus,
as you drive him on, and calls you by name. For the poet is filled with
the god and goaded by those restless spurs, forgetting to eat, to relax,
or to sleep, unable to escape this obsession. Often, even in their dreams,
poets pore over Phoebus' gifts; and some have been found who, in the
midst of sleep, have frequently sung verses worthy of the Muses and
Apollo, so great is the love of fame, so powerful the presence of the
god. But young bard, trust not, ah, trust not too much to poetic ardor.
We cannot allow you always to adopt the suggestions of fortune and the
bursts of inspiration which come to you while the raging god dwells in
your breast. Rather let reason and care oppose their power. Bridle in
your frenzied soul, and recall it to [reason's] colors; be cautious and
learn when to restrain your mind and when to give it free rein. Hence
we insist that you must invariably pause at this point until your spirits
are calmed and every impulse is curbed. Then return and, with your
emotions well under control, revise everything that blind frenzy cast up
in your mind.[71]

You are surely aware, too, that art functions only by imitating
nature, and conforms to it closely. For the poets have set Nature
before them as their sole mistress, and in whatever their
undertaking they always follow her footsteps.[72] Thus, using
words as their medium, they create likenesses which depict the
varied habits of men and animals or the different interests suited
to the various stages of life, and so present an image [73] of what
is appropriate to sluggish old men, and vigorous youths, and
women [for example], and of the extent to which a scion of
the lofty blood of kings differs from a servant or rustic. For
I am displeased by depictions in which Telemachus is
grave beyond his years

Line 454: *subjecerit.* Rome, 1527, et al.

Telemachus fupra, fenior fi Neftor inani
Gaudeat & ludo, & canibus, pictifve pharetris .
Et quoniam in noftro multi perfæpe loquuntur
Carmine, verba illis pro conditione virorum ,
Aut rerum damus, & proprii tribuuntur honores,   470
Cuique fuus, feu mas, feu femina, five deus fit .
Semper enim fummus divûm pater, atque hominum rex
Ipfe in concilio fatur, fi forte coorta
Seditio, paucis. at non Venus aurea contra
Pauca refert, Teucrûm indignos miferata labores.   475
Ingreditur furiis, atque alta filentia rumpit
Acta furore gravi Juno, ac fœta ufque querelis .
Quumque etiam juveni glifcat violentia major,
Ardens cui virtus, animufque in pectore præfens,
Nulla mora in Turno, nec dicta animofa retractat.   480
Stat conferre manum, & certamine provocat hoftem
Defertorem Afiæ. verum quantum ille feroci
Virtute exfuperat, tanto eft impenfius æquum
Et pietate gravem, & fedato corde Latinum
Confulere, atque omnes metuentem expendere cafus. 485
Multum etiam intererit, Dido ne irata loquatur,
An pacato animo. Libycas fi linquere terras
Trojanus paret, & defertum fallere amorem,
Sæviet, ac tota paffim bacchabitur urbe.
Mentis inops, immanis, atrox verba afpera rumpet,   490
Confufafque dabit voces incertaque, & anceps
Quæ quibus anteferat. quantum ah diftabit ab illa
Didone, excepit Teucros quæ nuper egentes
Solvere corde metum, atque jubens fecludere curas,
Invitanfque fuis vellent confidere regnis!
                                                495
                                        Nec

or old Nestor delights in empty sports and dogs and painted
quivers. And since often a large number of characters speak in
our poems, we assign them language appropriate either to the
nature of the speaker or to the circumstances under which he
is speaking; marks of distinction are allotted, each receiving his
own, whether he be a male, a female, or a god.[74] Should it
happen that dissension has broken out in heaven, the most high
father of the gods and king of men invariably speaks few words
in the council. But not so golden Venus: pitying the Trojans'
unmerited sufferings she replies with words more than a few.
And Juno, veritably teeming with complaints and driven by her
heavy anger, advances in a rage and shatters the silence on
high.[75] Since violence blazes with more fury in a youth whose
courage is hot and whose spirit is ready, Turnus neither brooks
delay nor retracts his spirited boasts. He insists on doing battle,
and challenges his enemy, "the deserter from Asia," to combat.
But the more Turnus excels in headstrong courage, the more
imperative it is that Latinus, unprejudiced and grave in his
piety, should take counsel with a calm mind, pondering with
dread every pitfall.[76] It will also matter greatly whether Dido is
speaking in anger or with her mind at peace. If the Trojan
should prepare to leave Libyan soil and desert and deceive his
love, she will run mad and play the Bacchante the length and
breadth of the city. She will burst out with bitter words, raving,
inhuman, and savage, babbling, and wavering in uncertainty as to
what to say first. Oh, how greatly will she differ from that Dido
who once received the Trojans when they were in need and
bade them free their hearts of fear and throw off their care,
asking them if they might not wish to settle in her kingdom! [77]

Nec te oratores pigeat, artifque magiftros
Confuluiffe, Sinon Phrygios quo fallere poffit
Arte dolis, quocumque animos impellere doctus;
Quove tenere queat Grajos fandi auctor Ulyffes
Stante domum Troja tandem difcedere certos.   500
Quid tibi nunc dulcem præ cunctis Neftora dicam,
Qui toties inter primores Argivorum
Ingentes potuit verbis componere lites,
Et mulcere animos, & mollia fingere corda?
Artibus his certe Cytherea inftructa, dolifque   505
Arma rogat nato genitrix, & adultera læfum
Vulcanum alloquitur, dictifque afpirat amorem.
Nam cauffas petit ex alto indeprenfa, virique
Circuit occulta verborum indagine mentem.
Difcitur hinc etenim fenfus, mentefque legentum   510
Flectere, diverfofque animis motus dare, ut illis
Imperet arte potens (dictu mirabile!) vates.
Nam femper, feu læta canat, feu triftia mœrens,
Affectas implet tacita dulcedine mentes.
Quem non Threicii quondam fors afpera vatis   515
Molliat, amiffam dum folo in litore fecum,
Eurydice, folans ægrum teftudine amorem,
Te veniente die, te decedente vocaret?
Quid, puer Euryalus quum pulchros volvitur artus,
Ah dolor! inque humeros lapfa cervice recumbens   520
Languefcit moriens, ceu flos fuccifus aratro?
Ardet adire animus lectori, & currere in ipfum
Volfcentem, puerique manum fupponere mento
Labenti, ac largum fruftra prohibere cruorem
Purpureo niveum fignantem flumine pectus.   525

Poftre-

Do not be above consulting those orators who are masters of their art
in order to learn by what skill Sinon, experienced in impelling minds
through trickery in any direction whatever, could dupe the Phrygians
with his tricks; [78] and how Ulysses, the father of eloquence, could
succeed in restraining the Greeks determined to leave for home at last
with Troy still standing.[79] What need to remind you now of Nestor,
most amiable of men, who so often was able to compose mighty
quarrels among the Argive chieftains, soothe passions, and soften and
mold tempers with his words alone? [80] Cytherea, mother of Aeneas,
was certainly versed in these arts and employed her wiles when she
sought weapons for her son, making her plea, adulteress that she was,
to Vulcan, her injured husband, breathing love in all her words. For
she referred her motives to long-past events and went undiscovered,
ensnaring her husband's mind in the hidden net of her words.[81] The
orator's art, then, is the source whence the poet may learn how to direct
the minds and feelings of his readers and to plant in their souls various
sympathies, so that, powerful through his art in a way marvelous to tell,
the poet is able to command them at will. For whether he sings glad
songs or laments and sings of gloom, he invariably touches their souls
and fills them with silent sweetness.[82] Who would not be moved by the
bitter fate of the Thracian poet as he stands alone on the solitary shore
and eases the ache of his love with his lute, and, as the day dawns, calls
to you, Eurydice, though you are lost to him, and, as the day dies, calls
out your name? [83] What more shall I say? When the youth Euryalus
thrashes his handsome limbs about in agony (ah, sorrow!), and
his head falls to rest on his shoulders, and sinking to the ground, he
droops in death like a flower nipped off by the plow, the reader's
mind takes fire to rush to the field and attack the Volscian who killed
him, to place his hand under the lad's chin as it sinks down, and to
stanch (though in vain) the thick flow of blood which stains his
white chest in a purple stream.[84]

Poſtremo, tibi ſiqua inſtant dicenda, ruborem
Quæ tenerum incuterent Muſis adaperta, choriſque
Virgineis, molli vel præterlabere tactu
Diſſimulans, vel verte alio, & rem ſuffice fictam.
Si pater omnipotens tonitru cælum omne ciebit,   530
Speluncam Dido, dux & Trojanus eamdem
Deveniant, pudor ulterius nihil addere curet.
Nam ſat erit, tellus ſi prima, & conſcius æther
Connubii dent ſignum, ululentque in vertice Nymphæ.
Neve aliis impar nimium ne Troilus armis   535
Ah puer infelix facito concurrat Achilli,
Quam quibus in Libyco conſpexit litore pictum
Illum Anchiſiades heros, dum victus anhelis
Fertur equis, curruque hæret reſupinus inani:
Nec pueri veros congreſſus dicere cures.   540
Quid deceat, quid non, tibi noſtri oſtendere poſſunt.
Inventa ex aliis diſce: & te plurima Achivos
Conſulere hortamur veteres, Argivaque regna
Explorare oculis, & opimam avertere gazam
In Latium, atque domum lætum ſpolia ampla referre. 545
Haud minor eſt adeo virtus, ſi te audit Apollo,
Inventa Argivûm in patriam convertere vocem,
Quam ſi tute aliquid intactum inveneris ante.
Aſpice ut inſignis peregrino incedat in auro
Fatidicæ Mantus, & Mincî filius amnis,   550
Fulgeat ut magni exuvias indutus Homeri,
Nec pudet. egregias artes oſtenderit eſto
Græcia, tradiderit Latio præclara reperta,
Dum poſt in melius aliunde accepta Latini
Omnia rettulerint, dum longe maxima Roma   555

Tom. II.   F   Ut

Finally, if you find yourself faced with an episode whose telling
would bring even a faint blush [to the cheeks of] the virgin
chorus of the Muses, conceal it, and either glide by it with a light
touch only, or turn your narrative elsewhere and put fictitious
material in its place. If the omnipotent father is to shake all
heaven with his thunder, let Dido and the prince of Troy take
shelter in the same cave; but modesty must take care to add
nothing further. For it will suffice if primal Earth and the
witnessing Air give the signal of the marriage, and the Nymphs
keen on the peaks of the hills. Do not arrange a battle between
Achilles and Troilus—poor youngster, he was no match for the
Greek—unless you show him arrayed in the same way as the hero,
Anchises' son, saw him depicted in Libya, already beaten, being
dragged by his panting horses, face upward, stuck to his empty
chariot. Avoid describing the [details of] the actual clashes in
which the boy was involved.[85]

Our [Latin] poets can show you what is appropriate and what is
not: learn your inventions from others.[86] I especially urge you to
consult the ancient Achaeans and to explore the Argive kingdoms,
to divert their rich treasure into Latium, and to carry home
joyfully an abundant booty. For your glory is no whit less, if
Apollo hears your prayers, should you rework Argive material
into your native tongue than if you had devised something which
had never before been touched upon.[87] See how the son of the
prophetess Manto and the stream Mincio advances, gloriously clad
in foreign gold. How splendid he appears, dressed in the spoils of
the great Homer! [88] Nor is there any cause for shame in this.
Greece showed the way in the excelling arts: so be it. Grant her
that she transmitted illustrious material to Latium. But thereafter
the Latins reproduced and improved upon everything which they had
received from elsewhere, until Rome, greatest by far of the nations,

Ut belli ftudiis, ita doctis artibus omnes,
Quod Sol cumque videt terrarum, anteiverit urbes.
Dii Romæ indigetes, Trojæ tuque auctor Apollo,
Unde genus noftrum cæli fe tollit ad aftra,
Hanc faltem auferri laudem prohibete Latinis.   560
Artibus emineat femper, ftudiifque Minervæ
Italia, & gentes doceat pulcherrima Roma,
Quandoquidem armorum penitus fortuna receffit ;
Tanta Italos inter crevit difcordia reges.
Ipfi nos inter fævos diftringimus enfes,   565
Nec patriam pudet externis aperire tyrannis.
Spes tamen Italiæ proftratæ affulferat ingens
Nuper, & egregiis animos erexerat aufis
Heu fruftra. invidit laudi fors læva Latinæ,
Nec dum fata malis Italûm exfaturata quierunt.   570
Jam gentes longe pofitæ trepidare, ducefque
Externi. jam dives Arabs, jam Nilus, & Indus
Audierant longe Tufci decora alta LEONIS,
Audierant Medycumque genus, ftirpemque deorum.
Jam tum ille egregias curas accinxerat ardens   575
Pro patriæ decore, pro libertate fepulta
Antiquæ Aufoniæ germano fretus Iulo,
Quicum partitus curarum ingentia femper
Pondera, commiffas rerum tractabat habenas
Idem regnatorque hominum, divûmque facerdos.   580
Jamque illum Europæ reges, genfque omnis in unum
Converfique oculos, converfique ora tenebant.
Jamque duces animis illum concordibus omnes
Velle fequi trepidos in Turcas arma parantem.
Illum quadrijugo invectum per mœnia curru,   585
                                             Roma,

surpassed in the arts of learning as she had in the pursuits of war
every city in every land the sun sees.

Native gods of Rome, and you, Apollo, protector of Troy,
whence our race lifted itself to the stars of the sky, let this glory,
at least, never be taken from the Latins: let Italy always excel in
the arts and the pursuits of learning, and Rome, loveliest of all
things, always teach the nations.[89] For fortune in arms has
departed entirely, so great is the discord which has grown among
Italy's princes. We draw violent swords, and war upon one
another, and feel no shame in laying our homeland open to
foreign tyrants.

A great hope, however, shone over prostrate Italy a short time
past and roused our minds to extraordinary endeavors.
But—bitter sorrow—it came to nothing; for a perverse fortune
grudged the Latins their glory, and the fates, though gorged with
Italy's ills, still have not ceased to vex her. Already far-flung
nations and foreign princes were trembling with fear; already
sumptuous Arabia, and the Nile, and the Indus had heard from
afar of the high and distinguished abilities of Leo of Tuscany, had
heard of the line of the Medici, the offspring of the gods. Already
Leo had eagerly set in motion brilliant projects for his homeland's
glory, for ancient Ausonia's entombed liberty, leaning for support
on his cousin Giulio, with whom he always shared the crushing
burdens of state affairs, [and thus] guided the reins of
government entrusted to his skill, at once ruler of men and priest
of the gods. Already Europe's rulers and the peoples of every
nation had turned their gaze to Leo, looking to him alone.
Already military commanders were one in their desire to follow
him as he prepared arms against the trembling Turks.—O Rome,
you would soon have seen him, triumphant over the world,

Roma, triumphato vidiſſes protinus orbe.
Illum, Tybri pater, lætanti ſpumeus alveo
Exciperes Tuſcus Tuſcum, veherefque per undas
Miratus habitufque novos, hominumque figuras.
Iſſent poſt currus capti longo ordine reges,   590
Oblitufque minas minor iret barbarus hoſtis,
Qui victis Solymis nunc, atque Oriente ſubacto
Exſultat fidens, orbiſque affectat habenas
Efferus, atque Italæ jam jam (ſcelus!) imminet oræ.
Viſendi ſtudio paſſim Romana juventus   595
Per fora, perque vias feſta diſcurreret urbe.
Ipſe ſuos ſolio fulgens pater aureus alto
Aſpiceret cives longo poſt tempore viſos,
Barbaricumque aurum, prædæque juberet acervos
Sacratis adytis, penitufque alta arce reponi.   600
Verum heu (dii, veſtrum crimen) ſpes tanta repente
Italiæ abſumta, ac penitus fiducia ceſſit.
Egregius moriens heros ſecum omnia vertit .

borne about your walls in a chariot and team of four. And you, father
Tiber, yourself a Tuscan, would have received the Tuscan and foamed
between your glad banks as you bore him through your waves and
marveled at the exotic dress and the features [of the prisoners he led
home]. A long line of captive kings would have followed his chariots;
our barbarous enemies would have forgotten their threats, their pride
brought low.—But now they have taken Jerusalem and conquered the
East, and, boasting self-confidently, are making a savage grasp at the
reins of the world. Now at this very moment (hideous crime!) they
threaten the shore of Italy.—In their eagerness to see [Leo's triumph],
the youth of Rome would have thronged and milled through the public
squares and the streets while the city made festival. The Father himself,
splendid in gold, would have gazed from his uplifted throne on the
citizens he had not seen for so long and issued commands that the
barbarians' gold and the high-piled spoils he had won be laid in the
holy temples and the vaults of the towering citadel. But, alas (the
blame, O gods, is yours), Italy's so great hope was taken suddenly away
and all our confidence fled. For when he died that surpassing hero
toppled all things with him.[90]

M. HIERONYMI VIDÆ
CREMONENSIS
ALBÆ EPISCOPI
POETICORUM
AD FRANCISCUM FRANCISCI REGIS F.
FRANCIÆ DELPHINUM
LIBER TERTIUS.

 Unc autem linguæ ſtudium, moremque loquendi,
Quem vates, Muſæque probêt, atq; auctor Apollo,
Expediam, curam extremam, finemque laborum.
Diſcendum, indicia, & verborum lumina quæ ſint
Munere Pieridum luſtrandis addita rebus.   5
Ne te opere incœpto deterreat ardua meta,
Audendum, puer, atque invicto pectore agendum.
Jam te Pierides ſumma en de rupe propinquum
Voce vocant, viridique oſtentant fronde coronam
Victori, atque animo ſtimulos hortatibus addunt.   10
Jamque roſas calathis ſpargunt per nubila plenis
Deſuper, & 'florum placido te plurima nimbo
Tempeſtas operit, gratumque effuſus odorem
Ambroſiæ liquor aſpirat divina voluptas.
Verborum in primis tenebras fuge, nubilaque atra.   15

                                         Nam

THE THIRD BOOK

OF

❧ THE POETICS ❧

OF

M. HIERONYMUS VIDA
OF CREMONA
BISHOP OF ALBA

[*Dedicated*]

To Francis, Son of King Francis of France
& Dauphin of France

AND NOW I SHALL SET FORTH THE STUDY OF LANGUAGE AND THE
style which the poet, the Muses, and their leader, Apollo, would
approve—for this is my final concern, the end point of my labors.[1] One
must learn the figures and embellishments of expression which, by gift
of the Pierians, may be added to material one wishes to ornament.[2] Do
not lose courage for the task you have begun because the goal is
difficult to achieve; you must be daring, lad, and press on with
undaunted bravery. Look! Already the Pierians are calling to you from
the mountain peak nearby, holding out to the victor a crown of verdant
leaves and spurring on your spirit with their encouragements. From
high above they scatter through the clouds the roses with which their
baskets are brimming; a thick shower of blossoms envelops you in a
pleasing cloud, and a liquid essence flows down, breathing (oh,
pleasure fit for the gods!) the sweet fragrance of ambrosia.

As your first care, avoid the black clouds of obscure expression.[3]

Nam neque (fi tantum fas credere) defuit olim
Qui lumen jucundum ultro, lucemque perofus
Obfcuro nebulæ fe circumfudit amictu;
Tantus amor noctis, latebræ tam dira cupido .
Ille ego fim cui Pierides dent carmina Mufæ　　　　　20
Lumine clara fuo, externæ nihil indiga lucis.
Nec tamen id votis optandum denique magnis .
Ipfe volens per te poteris; vis dædala fandi
Tot fe adeo in facies, tot fe convertit in ora,
Mille trahens varia fecum ratione colores .　　　　　25
Mille modis aperire datur mentifque latebras,
Quique latent tacito arcani fub pectore motus.
Si tibi, dum trepidas, non hac fuccefferit, & lux
Non datur hinc, te verte alio, lumenque require
Nunc hac, nunc illac, donec diffulferit ultro,　　　　30
Claraque tempeftas cælo radiarit aperto .
Quin, etiam anguftis fi non urgebere rebus,
Quum fandi tibi mille viæ, tibi mille figuræ
Occurrent, tu mille vias, tu mille figuras
Nunc hanc, nunc aliam ingredere, & mutare memento, 35
Jamque hos, jamque alios haud fegnis fumere vultus.
Nempe inde illectas aures immenfa voluptas
Detinet, & dulci pertentat pectora motu .
Ergo omnem curam impendunt, ut cernere nufquam
Sit formas fimiles, naturæ exempla fequuti,　　　　　40
Diffimili quod fint facie quæcumque fub aftris
Vitales carpunt auras, genus omne ferarum,
Atque hominum, pictæ volucres, mutæque natantes.
Nonne vides, verbis ut veris fæpe relictis
Accerfant fimulata, aliundeque nomina porro　　　　45

Tranf-

For if one can believe so much, there was a poet of old who, willfully
hating an agreeable clarity and lucidity, wrapped himself in an
obfuscating mantle of cloud, so great was his love of darkness, so
pernicious his fondness for the covert.[4] But let me be one to whom
the Pierians grant verses illustrious in their own clarity, in no need of
elucidation from another source. In fact, you need not make this wish
the object of great vows. Should you yourself wish it, the power is
yours. The power of speech is variable and assumes numberless
shapes and aspects involving a thousand shades of utterance of
varying significance. There are a thousand ways in which you may lay
bare the hidden recesses of your mind and those secret impulses
which lie concealed deep in your silent breast. If, despite anxious
attempts, one mode of expression has failed and light is not to be
achieved in that quarter, turn your attention elsewhere and seek for
clarity first in one place, and then another, until clear weather shines
forth spontaneously and gleams across the open sky. Again,
since a thousand modes and figures of speech are at your disposal, if
you are not hard-pressed by narrow limitations, introduce those
thousand modes and figures, each in its turn; remember to practice
variety by diligently adopting first one set of expressions and then
another. For thus a boundless pleasure holds our ears in your power
and pervades our breasts with an impulse of delight. Poets therefore
bend every effort to ensure that, as among the examples which nature
supplies, one may never find [in their works] two forms quite alike,
since all things which breathe the living winds beneath the
stars—every species of beasts and men, the gorgeously plumed birds
and the silent swimmers in the sea—all are of varying appearance.[5]

Do you not observe how the poets frequently abandon literal
language and introduce figurative expressions by transferring names
from sources far removed

Tranfportent, aptentque aliis ea rebus, ut ipfæ
Exuviafque novas, res, infolitofque colores
Indutæ, fæpe externi mirentur amictus
Unde illi, lætæque aliena luce fruantur,
Mutatoque habitu; nec jam fua nomina mallent?   50
Sæpe ideo quum bella canunt, incendia credas
Cernere, diluviumque ingens furgentibus undis.
Contra etiam Martis pugnas imitabitur ignis,
Quum furit accenfis acies Vulcania campis.
Nec turbato oritur quondam minor æquore pugna.   55
Configunt animofi Euri certamine vafto
Inter fe, pugnantque adverfis molibus undæ.
Ufque adeo paffim fua res infignia lætæ
Permutantque, juvantque viciffim, & mutua fe fe
Altera in alterius transformat protinus ora.   60
Tum· fpecie capti gaudent fpectare legentes.
Nam diverfa fimul datur e re cernere eadem
Multarum fimulacra animo fubeuntia rerum.
Ceu quum forte olim placidi liquidiffima ponti
Æquora vicina fpectat de rupe viator,   65
Tantum illi fubjecta oculis eft mobilis unda:
Ille tamen filvas, interque virentia prata
Infpiciens miratur, aquæ quæ purior humor
Cuncta refert, captofque eludit imagine vifus.
Non aliter vates nunc huc traducere mentes   70
Nunc illuc, animifque legentum apponere gaudet
Diverfas rerum fpecies, dum tædia vitat.
Res humiles ille interea non fecius effert
Splendore illuftrans alieno, & lumine veftit:
Verborumque fimul vitat difpendia parcus.   75

                                                    Hunc

and applying them to other things, so that those objects themselves,
dressed in new garments and unfamiliar hues, often wonder whence
these foreign robes came, and delighted, vaunt themselves in their
unaccustomed radiance and changed array, no longer preferring
their proper names? [6] Often, therefore, when poets sing of wars, you
would believe that you were seeing a conflagration or a mighty deluge
on the surging waves. The converse is true also: fire will imitate Mars'
battles when Vulcan's battle line rages across fields fanned to fury.
Nor is the war which breaks forth intermittently on the roiled deep
any less tumultuous: for the violent East Winds struggle against each
other in tremendous combat, and waves do battle with the swells
which rise to oppose them. For everywhere things signified take
constant pleasure in changing the tokens [which distinguish them]
and delight [the reader] through a constant alternation or
interchange in which one object straightway transforms itself into the
appearance [characteristic] of another. Then, enthralled by this
pageant, the readers are pleased to gaze on. [7] For it is possible for one
to perceive, while looking at one object only, diverse images of many
things simultaneously entering his mind. It is as though a traveler
should chance on a time to gaze into the transparent waters of a placid
sea from a lofty crag near the shore: only the flowing wave is really
beneath his eyes; but gazing on the waters he marvels to see at the
same time forests and verdant meadows—for the water's crystal dew
reflects them all and deceives his entranced gaze with an image of the
real. Just so, the poet enjoys directing his readers' attention first to
one point and then to another, placing in their minds the diverse
images of what he is presenting, and, in doing so, he prevents tedium.
Similarly he elevates lowly subjects by adorning them with a splendor
not their own and clothes them with the ornaments [of style],[8] at the
same time cautiously avoiding prolixity.

Hunc fandi morem (fi vera audivimus) ipfi
Cælicolæ exercent cæli in penetralibus altis,
Pieridum chorus in terras quem detulit olim,
Atque homines docuere, deûm præclara reperta.
Illæ etenim Jovis ætherea dicuntur in aula   80
Immixtæ fuperis feftas agitare choreas,
Et femper canere alternæ, Phœbique fruuntur
Colloquio, vatumque infpirant pectora ab alto.
Nec tamen haud folis fugit hæc me nota poetis,
Verum etiam auctores alii experiuntur, & audent,   85
Præcipue orantes cauffas, fandique magiftri,
Seu fontes tendant legum compefcere habenis,
Seu caros cupiant atris e mortis amicos
Faucibus eripere, & defletos reddere luci.
Quin etiam agricolas ea fandi nota voluptas   90
Exercet, dum læta feges, dum trudere gemmas
Incipiunt vites, fitientiaque ætheris imbrem
Prata bibunt, ridentque fatis furgentibus agri.
Hanc vulgo fpeciem propriæ pænuria vocis
Intulit, indictifque urgens in rebus egeftas.   95
Quippe ubi fe vera oftendebant nomina nufquam,
Fas erat hinc, atque hinc transferre fimillima veris.
Paullatim accrevere artes, hominumque libido;
Quodque olim ufus inops reperit, nunc ipfa voluptas
Poftulat, hunc addens verborum rebus honorem.   100
Sic homines primum venti vis afpera adegit,
Vitandique imbres ftipulis horrentia tecta
Ponere, & informi fedem arctam claudere limo:
Nunc altæ æratis trabibus, Pariifque columnis
Regifico furgunt ædes ad fidera luxu.   105

Par-

This is the mode of speaking (if what we have heard is true) which the sky-dwellers themselves use in heaven's lofty halls and which the chorus of Pierians brought down to earth long ago and taught to men—the gods' splendid inventions. For it is said that in Jove's shining courts in the air, the Muses mingle with the gods above and dance festal choruses, sing ever in antiphonal song, enjoy converse with Phoebus, and inspire from on high the breasts of the poets.[9]

I am aware that figurative language is not known to the poets alone; indeed, other authors make bold use of it as well. Particularly is this true of those masters of eloquence, the men who plead causes, whether their attempt is to curb the guilty by the restraints of the law or their desire is to snatch dear friends from the black jaws of death and return them, much mourned, to the light of day. Indeed, one common ornament of speech imposes itself even on farmers, when they speak of "happy" crops, of vines beginning to "push out" their "gems," of "thirsty" fields "drinking in" heaven's shower, and of fields "smiling" on their "growing offspring." [10]

A lack of appropriate terms and a pressing need to express things as yet inarticulable introduced this style everywhere. Indeed, in cases where literal terms were nowhere to be found, one had a perfect right to transfer from one source or another the terms closest to the literal fact. But little by little the arts flourished, and too men's urge for gratification; what once a pauper usage devised was now demanded by a certain delicacy which added this verbal ornament to the object. Thus the bitter force of the winds and the need to avoid downpours first drove men to build roofs bristling with straw and to wall in their sheltered dwellings with crude mud. Now, lofty mansions of regal opulence soar to the stars with brazen beams and columns of Parian marble.[11]

Parcius ifta tamen delibant, & minus audent
Artifices alii, nec tanta licentia fandi
Cuique datur, folis vulgo conceffa poetis.
Nempe pedum hi duris cohibentur legibus, & fe
Sponte fua fpatiis angufti temporis arctant.   110
Liberius fas campum aliis decurrere apertum.
Sacri igitur vates facta, atque infecta canentes
Libertate palam gaudent majore loquendi,
Quæfitique decent cultus magis, atque colores
Infoliti, nec erit tanto ars deprenfa pudori.   115
Crebrius hi fando gaudent fuper æthera miris
Tollere res (nec fit fas tantum credere) dictis.
It cælo clamor, tremit omnis murmure olympus.
Nec mora, bis vocem ingeminant, urbifque ruinas,
Fataque, prœliaque, & fortem exfecrantur iniquam,   120
O pater, o patria, o Priami domus inclyta quondam,
Clamantes, cecidit proh Juppiter! Ilion ingens.
Quid quum Neptunum dicunt mare, vina Lyæum,
Et Cererem frumenta, patrumque e nomine natos
Significant, memorantque urbes pro civibus ipfis?   125
Atque ideo timor attonitos quum invaferit Afros,
Africa terribili tremet horrida terra tumultu.
Nec deerit, tibi pro fluviis, proque omnibus undis,
Pocula qui preffis Acheloïa mifceat uvis.
Ecce autem fubitis converfi vocibus ultro   130
Sæpe aliquem longe abfentem, defertaque, & antra,
Et folos montes affantur. fæpe falutant
Silvafque, fluviofque, & agros, fenfuque carentes
Speluncas, velut hæc fint refponfura vocata:
Et vos, o vacui, compellant nomine, faltus.   135

                                                              Præ-

Other artists indulge in these luxuries more sparingly and are less daring, for not everyone is allowed so sweeping a freedom of expression; [on the contrary], this liberty is commonly conceded to poets alone. For poets are limited by strict prosodic laws; of their own will they confine their expression within narrow limits of [metrical] time, while other artists are permitted to roam more freely over an unrestricted field. Therefore, whether singing of deeds either actual or fictive, the sacred bards plainly enjoy a greater liberty of expression; special ornaments and uncommon figures are more suitable [in their compositions], nor is their art to be confined by so great attention to conventional usage.[12]

As they compose, poets often enjoy using awe-inspiring language to lift their argument above the skies—even though one is not to accept the language as literal. The din "hits heaven"; "all Olympus shakes with a tumultuous sound." [13] Without pause they doubly redouble their voices to curse a city's sack, its devastation, its battles, and its unjust fate: "O father!" "O my country!" "O house of Priam, once glorious!" they cry out; "O Jupiter, Ilium the mighty has fallen!" [14]

[How suggestive, too, is the effect] when poets call the sea "Neptune," wine "Lyaeus," and crops "Ceres"; when they call sons by patronymics, and use the names of cities when they are referring rather to the citizens! And thus, when terror has astounded and seized the Africans, one may say that "savage Afric land trembles, thrust into terrible tumult." And there will be no lack of a poet who, instead of rivers' waters or any other waters, would mix "Acheloian draughts" with pressed grapes for you.[15]

Note as well that poets turn from those to whom they are speaking and in an unprompted and sudden cry often address someone a great distance off, and deserts, and caverns, and solitary mountains; often they salute forests, and streams, and fields, and insensible caves, as though they might answer when called to. And you, too, O peopleless woodlands, you, too, they call on by name.[16]

Præterea verbis inimicos addere senfus
Oppofitis, dum diffimulant, aliudque videbis
Sæpe loqui, atque aliud fimulata condere mente.
Egregia interea conjux ita nocte fuprema
Deiphobo fidam capiti fubduxerat enfem.   140
Nec minus infignis Drances, quum ftragis acervos
Tot dedit, & claris infigniit arva trophæis.
Quid fequar ulterius, quanta dulcedine captas
Detineant aures, vocem quum rurfus eamdem
Ingeminant, modo non verborum cogat egeftas?   145
Pan etiam Arcadia neget hoc fi judice præfens,
Pan, etiam Arcadia dicam te judice vanum.
Hæc adeo quum fint, quum fas audere poetis
Multa modis multis, tamen obfervare memento
Siquando haud propriis rem mavis dicere verbis,   150
Translatifque aliunde notis, longeque petitis,
Ne nimiam oftendas, quærendo talia, curam.
Namque aliqui exercent vim duram, & rebus iniqui
Nativam eripiunt formam indignantibus ipfis,
Invitafque jubent alienos fumere vultus.   155
Haud magis imprudens mihi erit, & luminis expers
Qui puero ingentes habitus det ferre gigantis,
Quam fiquis ftabula alta, lares appellet equinos,
Aut crines magnæ genitricis gramina dicat.
Præftiterit vero faciem, fpolia & fua cuique   160
Linquere, & interdum propriis rem prodere verbis,
Indiciifque fuis, ea fint modo digna Camœnis.
Res etiam poteris rebus conferre viciffim,
Nominibufque ambas verifque, fuifque vocare.
Quod faciens, fuge verborum difpendia, paucifque   165

You will observe also that as a verbal ruse poets suggest an
incongruous meaning for words whose obvious sense is quite the
opposite, thus often saying one thing [explicitly] and covertly
harboring another in their mind. It is thus that "the most excellent wife
on the supreme night had drawn from under Deiphobus' head his
faithful sword" and that similarly "Drances, that grace of manhood,
bestowed high-piled carnage, and graced the plains with his noble
trophies." [17]

Why need I insist at length how sweet is the charm by which the poets
hold our ears enthralled when they repeat the same phrase—provided
that poverty of vocabulary has not compelled them to do so?

> Should even Pan in person, Arcadia being our judge, deny this,
> I should even, Pan, Arcadia being our judge, proclaim you a fool. [18]

Although poets have such sweeping prerogatives and may try
numerous daring experiments involving a variety of techniques,
whenever you choose to express your meaning in figurative rather
than literal language, in terms both characteristic of another object and
fetched from afar, you must be careful not to show too much effort in
seeking such things out. For some poets employ a harsh constraint, and
though the objects themselves are inimical to it, unjustly strip from
them their innate appearance and force them, even against their bent,
to assume incongruous characteristics. [19] In my opinion, a poet who
would name tall stables "equine home-shrines" or call grassy pastures
"our mighty mother's locks" is scarcely less inept and lacking in lucidity
than a man who would give a boy the ungainly garments of a giant to
wear. [20] Indeed, one will have done better if he leaves each of these
objects its own appearance, dress, and properties, and from time to
time speaks of a matter in literal language and in terms of its own
characteristics—provided only that they be worthy of the Muses. [21]

You may, moreover, compare one subject with another in sequence,
referring to both by their proper names. When you use this
technique avoid prolixity;

Includas numeris, unde illa fimillima imago
Ducitur, & breviter confer. ne forte priorum
Oblitus fermonum alio traducere mentem,
Inque alia ex aliis videare exordia labi.
Jamque age verborum qui fit delectus habendus,   170
Quæ ratio; nam nec funt omnia verfibus apta,
Omnia nec pariter tibi funt uno ordine habenda.
Verfibus ipfa etiam divifa, & carmina quantum
Carminibus diftant, tantum diftantia verba
Sunt etiam inter fe, quamvis communia multa   175
Interdum invenies verfus diffufa per omnes.
Multa decent fcenam quæ funt fugienda canenti
Aut divûm laudes, aut heroum inclyta facta.
Ergo alte veftiga oculis, aciemque voluta
Verborum filva in magna, tum accommoda Mufis   180
Selige, & infignes vocum depafcere honores,
Ut nitidus puro verfus tibi fulgeat auro.
Rejice degenerem turbam nil lucis habentem,
Indecorefque notas, ne fit non digna fupellex.
Quo fieri id poffit, veterum te femita vatum   185
Obfervata docebit. adi monimenta priorum
Crebra oculis, animoque legens, & multa voluta.
Tum quamvis, longe fi quis fupereminet omnes,
Virtutem ex illo, ac rationem difcere fandi
Te jubeam, cui contendas te reddere femper   190
Affimilem, atque habitus greffufque effingere euntis,
Quantum fata finunt, & non averfus Apollo;
Haud tamen interea reliquûm explorare labores
Abftiteris vatum moneo, fufpectaque dicta
Sublegere, & variam ex cunctis abducere gazam.   195

Nec

confine your notice of the source of this exact resemblance to a few
measures, and draw your comparisons concisely, lest perhaps it
should appear that you have forgotten what you presented earlier
and are leading your reader's mind elsewhere by simply passing
insensibly from one set of ideas to new ones.[22]

Consider now the choice to be made in vocabulary and the principle
governing that choice. Not all words are suitable for verse, nor should
you consider all which are as of equal rank, for they are also
differentiated by the measures to which they are suited; [23] indeed,
words differ as widely one from another as do poems, although here
and there you will find a number of words which are common to all
types of verse. Much diction suitable for the stage should be shunned
by one singing the gods' praises or heroes' illustrious acts.[24]
Therefore examine closely as you read, and, gazing sharply about in
the vast forest of words, choose diction which is suited to the Muses,
selecting thus the words' best glories, so that your polished verse may
glitter for you in pure gold. Discard the base mass of words which are
devoid of all splendor and are mere unseemly ciphers,[25] lest your
vocabulary be undistinguished. That you may reach this goal, follow
the path of the old poets: it will lead you aright.[26] Let your eyes
journey often to the monuments of the ancients; read eagerly, and
ponder a large number of works. Then if one author should far
surpass all the others, I should direct you to learn excellence and the
principles of expression from him, and to strive always to make
yourself like him, copying his characteristics and manner of proceeding so far as the fates will allow and Apollo grants you his favor.[27]

I should scarcely discourage you, however, from exploring at the
same time the productions of the rest of the poets and, by collecting
noteworthy phrases from their works, drawing from all authors a
diverse treasure.[28]

Nec dubitem verſus hirſuti ſæpe poetæ
Suſpenſus luſtrare, & veſtigare legendo,
Sicubi ſe quædam forte inter commoda verſu
Dicta meo oſtendant, quæ mox melioribus ipſe
Auſpiciis proprios poſſim mihi vertere in uſus   200
Deterſa prorſus priſca rubigine ſcabra.
Flumina ſæpe vides immundo turbida limo:
Haurit aquam tamen inde frequens concurſus, & altis
Important puteis ad pocula. deſuper illa
Occultis diffuſa canalibus influit, omnemque   205
Illabens bibulas labem exuit inter arenas.
Nil adeo incultum quod non ſplendeſcere poſſit,
Præcipue ſi cura vigil non deſit, & uſque
Mente premas, multumque animo tecum ipſe volutes.
Atque ideo ex priſcis ſemper quo more loquamur   210
Diſcendum, quorum depaſcimur aurea dicta,
Præcipuumque avidi rerum populamus honorem.
Aſpice ut exuvias, veterumque inſignia nobis
Aptemus. rerum accipimus nunc clara reperta,
Nunc ſeriem, atque animum verborum, verba quoque ipſa: 215
Nec pudet interdum alterius nos ore loquutos.
Quum vero cultis moliris furta poetis,
Cautius ingredere, & raptus memor occule verſis
Verborum indiciis, atque ordine falle legentes
Mutato. nova ſit facies, nova prorſus imago.   220
Munere (nec longum tempus) vix ipſe peracto
Dicta recognoſces veteris mutata poetæ.
Sæpe palam quidam rapiunt, cupiuntque videri
Omnibus intrepidi, ac furto lætantur in ipſo
Deprenſi, ſeu quum dictis nihil ordine verſo   225

Nor would I personally hesitate to survey frequently and attentively the verses of a rude poet, searching as I read to see if some phrases might not occur here and there which would be suitable if rendered in my own verse and which I with better auspices might turn to my own purposes so soon as I had quite polished away the rust of ages with which they were encrusted.[29] One often sees rivers thick with filthy slime from which constant crowds of people draw liquid nonetheless which they then take up to the high cisterns which hold their drinking water. There they pour in the water, and down it flows into hidden channels, divesting itself of every impurity as it seeps below through thirsty sands. Similarly there is nothing so unpolished that it cannot become lustrous, particularly if there is vigilant effort on your part and you apply your mind energetically to the task, turning your thoughts again and again to a thorough consideration of your problem.

As these observations indicate, it is from the ancient poets that we ought always to learn how to express ourselves. Their golden words are our food [30] and their best ornaments of style our eagerly sought plunder. Note how, that we may fit to our own use the spoils and noble trappings of the ancients, we appropriate in one instance their brilliant inventions, in another the order they employ, in others yet the spirit of their words, and even the words themselves—for one need not be ashamed of having sometimes spoken with another's tongue.

But when you are attempting thefts from the polished poets, proceed with particular caution; remember to conceal what you have stolen by altering the forms of the words and to escape detection by switching word order. Give everything a new countenance and a wholly new form. Once this task is complete (and it will not occupy you long), you yourself will scarcely recognize the altered words of the ancient poet.

Certain authors frequently commit their theft quite in the open and, intrepid as they are, wish their action to be noticed by all; when caught, they glory in the very theft: in some cases, they have made no change in the order of the words,

Longe alios iiſdem ſenſus mira arte dedere,
Exueruntque animos verborum impune priores.
Seu quum certandi priſcis ſuccenſa libido,
Et poſſeſſa diu ſed enim male condita victis
Extorquere manu juvat, in meliuſque referre: 230
Ceu ſata, mutatoque ſolo felicius olim
Cernimus ad cælum translatas ſurgere plantas.
Poma quoque utilius ſuccos oblita priores
Proveniunt. ſic regna Aſiæ, Trojæque penates
Tranſtulit, auſpiciis Phrygius melioribus heros   235
In Latium, quamvis (nam divûm fata vocabant)
Invitus, Phœniſſa, tuo de litore ceſſit;
Nec connubia læta, nec incœpti hymenæi
Flexerunt immitem animum. tu victa dolore
Occidis, & curæ vix ipſa in morte relinquunt.   240
Numquam o Dardaniæ tetigiſſent veſtra carinæ
Litora, fors nulli poteras ſuccumbere culpæ.
Ergo agite o mecum ſecuri accingite furtis
Una omnes, pueri, paſſimque avertite prædam.
Infelix autem (quidam nam ſæpe reperti)   245
Viribus ipſe ſuis temere qui fiſus, & arti,
Externæ quaſi opis nihil indigus, abnegat audax
Fida ſequi veterum veſtigia, dum ſibi præda
Temperat heu nimium, atque alienis parcere crevit;
Vana ſuperſtitio, Phœbi ſine numine cura.   250
Haud longum tales ideo lætantur, & ipſi
Sæpe ſuis ſuperant monimentis, illaudatique
Extremum ante diem fœtus flevere caducos,
Viventeſque ſuæ viderunt funera famæ.
Quam cuperent vano potius caruiſſe labore,   255

Eque

but with impunity have stripped them of their former significance and given them a wholly different meaning; [31] in others, aflame with a desire to compete with the ancients, they delight in vanquishing them by snatching from their hand even material which has long been their peculiar possession, but which is, however, ill-fashioned, and improving it.[32] So it is with seedlings: when shoots have been transplanted we note that thereafter they stretch heavenward with richer growth; fruits, too, develop more successfully when they have forgotten the saps which formerly nourished them. Thus the Phrygian hero with auspices of better fortune transferred the sovereignties of Asia and the tribal gods of Troy into Latium, although—the destiny pronounced by the gods summoning him on—he left your shore unwillingly, lady of Phoenicia, nor did the joys of married love nor Hymen's rites begun dissuade his inflexible mind. You, lady, perished, overwhelmed with sorrow, and your griefs scarce deserted you even in death. Oh, had the Dardanian keels never touched your shores, you might perhaps have never succumed to the fault of unchastity.[33]

Therefore, my pupils, let each of you follow my example; commit your thefts fearlessly and draw your booty from every quarter. For he is a hapless poet (though there are many to be found) who trusts rashly in his own powers and skill and, as though he stood in no need of another's aid, brashly refuses to follow the trustworthy steps of the ancients, abstaining, alas, too much from taking booty, having decided to spare "others' property"—a vain scrupulosity this, an effort not sanctioned by Phoebus.[34] Their rejoicing on that account is pitiably short-lived, however, and often they survive their own monuments; unpraised, they have wept ere their final day for their dead offspring, and, yet living, have seen the funeral of their own fame. How they might wish that they had avoided vain labor,

Eque fuis alias didiciffe parentibus artes!
Sæpe mihi placet antiquis alludere dictis,
Atque aliud longe verbis proferre fub iifdem.
Nec mea tam fapiens per fe fe prodita quifquam
Furta redarguerit, quæ mox manifefta probabunt   260
Et nati natorum, & qui nafcentur ab illis.
Tantum abiit, pœnæ metuens infamis ut ipfe
Furta velim tegere, atque meas celare rapinas.
Non tamen omnia te prifcis fas fidere, qui non
Omnia fufficient. quærenti pauca labore   265
Attentanda tuo, nondum ulli audita, fuperfunt.
Nos etiam quædam iccirco nova condere nulla
Relligio vetat, indictafque effundere voces.
Ne vero hæc penitus fuerint ignota, fuumque
Agnofcant genus, & cognatam oftendere gentem   270
Poffint, ac ftirpis nitantur origine certæ.
Ufque adeo patriæ tibi fi pænuria vocis
Obftabit, fas Grajugenûm felicibus oris
Devehere informem maffam, quam incude Latina
Informans patrium jubeas dedifcere morem.   275
Sic quondam Aufoniæ fuccrevit copia linguæ:
Sic auctum Latium, quo plurima tranftulit Argis
Ufus; & exhauftis Itali potiuntur Athenis.
Nonne vides, mediis ut multa erepta Mycenis
Graja genus fulgent noftris immixta, nec ullum   280
Apparet difcrimen? eunt infignibus æquis
Undique per Latios & civis, & advena tractus.
Jamdudum noftri ceffit fermonis egeftas.
Raro uber patriæ, tibi raro opulentia deerit.
Ipfe fuis Cicero thefauris omnia promet,   285

Au-

and learned other arts from their parents!

Often I enjoy playing with phrases from the ancients and, while using precisely the same words, expressing another meaning.[35] Nor shall anyone (however wise) prove my self-betrayed thefts guilty ones, for soon my borrowings will be obvious to all, and our sons' sons and their descendants will approve them. Heaven forbid that I should wish to conceal my thefts or hide my spoils because I feared the punishment of disrepute!

You may not entrust yourself to the ancients entirely, however, since they will not supply you with everything you need.[36] For, if you inquire well into [even] a few matters, [you will find that] there will remain things as yet unheard by any man which you must attempt [to express] through your own efforts. For this reason, we also are under no sanction forbidding us to fashion certain new locutions and publish freely words never spoken before. That these may elicit a measure of recognition, however, let them declare their origin, be able to show the family to which they are cognate, and rely [for acceptance] on their descent from a well-known lineage.

If the poverty of your native language is a sufficiently serious hindrance, it is quite legitimate for you to import a formless mass [of linguistic ore] from the prosperous lands where the Greeks dwell, and by shaping it on the Latin anvil, compel it to renounce the characteristics of its [verbal] forebears. It was thus that anciently the riches of the Ausonian tongue grew. Thus, too, Latium flourished, whither contact transferred an overwhelming variety of usages from Argos, as the Italians took up their inheritance from prostrate Athens. Note how many Greek expressions there are which have been lifted from their Mycenaean milieu and now shine brightly, mingled with our own, with no apparent distinction made between the two sorts of vocabulary; both citizen and foreigner pass everywhere through Latian lands with like marks of honor.[37] Our language ceased to be poor a long time since; only rarely will the plenty and splendor of your native land fail you. Cicero himself will provide all that you require from his own riches,

Auctorefque alii nati felicibus annis
Omnia fufficient, nec folis crede poetis .
Sæpe etiam vidi veterum inter carmina vatum
Barbarico verfus cultu, gazaque fuperbos:
Belgicaque immifit trans alpes effeda Gallus   290
In Latium, & longæ Macedûm venere fariffæ.
Et metuam, ne deficiat me larga fupellex
Verborum, anguftique premat fermonis egeftas?
Quin & victa fitu, fi me pænuria adaxit,
Verba licet renovare: licet tua, fancta vetuftas,   295
Vatibus indugredi facraria. fæpius olli
Ætatis gaudent infignibus antiquai,
Et veterum ornatus induti incedere avorum.
Non tamen ille veter fqualor fuat undique, & ater
Verborum fitus. his modus adfit denique, quando   300
Copia non defit quorum nunc pervius ufus.
Tum quoque fi deerunt rebus fua nomina certa,
Fas illas apta verborum ambire corona,
Et late circumfufis comprendere dictis.
Verba etiam tum bina juvat conjungere in unum   305
Molliter inter fe vinclo fociata jugali.
Verum plura nefas vulgo congefta coire,
Ipfaque quadrifidis fubniti carmina membris.
Itala nec paffim fert monftra tricorpora tellus.
Horrefco diros fonitus, ac levia fundo   310
Invitus perterricrepas per carmina voces.
Argolici, quos ifta decet conceffa libido,
Talia connubia, & tales celebrent hymenæos,
Tergeminas immane ftruant ad fidera moles
Pelion addentes Offæ, & Pelio Olympum.   315

At

and other artists born in those years of felicity (and do not rely on the poets alone) will fully suffice for your needs.

Moreover, I have often seen among the songs of the ancient bards verses which, though barbarous in style, are a splendid hoard: Gaul has sent its Belgian "war-wains" across the Alps into Latium, and long Macedonian "pikes," too, have come. And shall I fear lest I find myself without a copious stock of words, and the poverty of a confined language limit me? [38] "Sholde" want of diction "bringe" me to it, however, it is permissible to revive even words quite vanquished by neglect. It is granted to poets, O hallowed antiquity, "to fare foorth" into thy shrines. Oft "thei" take pleasure in the trappings of "elden" times, and delight in proceeding with pomp, dressed in the adornments of their "sires" of old. "Lat nat" this ancient uncouthness and dark mustiness of language "sprede" everywhere, however; in fact, restrict sharply the use of these words when there is no shortage of current diction. [39]

Then, too, if precise terms are lacking for those things one wishes to convey, one may encompass them in a circlet of words, expressing them broadly in language which embraces their meaning. [40]

Moreover, it produces a pleasing effect if one joins together two words, uniting them smoothly to each other in a marriage bond. Generally, however, there must not be more words than two piled together and combined: verse lines must not be propped up on quadripartite limbs. Similarly, Italian soil will not everywhere support three-bodied monsters. I shudder at the wretched roar they make and am unwilling to spread these high-terror-rumbling words about through my smooth-flowing verses. Let the Argolians, to whom this fancy is permitted and becoming, celebrate such unions, such marriages as these, and immoderately heap threefold mounds as high as the stars, piling Pelion on Ossa, and Olympus on Pelion. [41]

At verbis etiam partes ingentia in ambas
Verba interpofitis profcindere, feque parare;
Deterere interdum licet , atque abftraxe fecando
Exiguam partem, & ftrinxiffe fluentia membra.
Iccirco fiquando ducum referenda, virûmque   320
Nomina dura nimis dictu, atque afperrima cultu,
Illa aliqui, nunc addentes , nunc inde putantes
Pauca minutatim, levant, ac mollia reddunt,
Sichæumque vocant mutata parte Sicarbam.
Hinc mihi Titanum pugnas, & fæva gigantum   325
Bella magis libeat canere, Enceladique tumultus,
Quam populos Itala quondam virtute fubactos ,
Atque triumphatas diverfo a litore gentes.
Sed neque verborum cauffa vis ulla canentem,
Confilium præter, cogat res addere inanes,   330
Nomina fed rebus femper fervire jubeto ,
Omnia perpendens verfus refonantia membra .
Verba etenim quædam ignarum te fallere poffunt,
Ni vigiles, mandatum & munus obire recufent,
Furenturque operi clam fe fe, & inertia ceffent,   335
Cætera dum labor exercet concordia juffus
Quæque fuus. tantum illa dabunt numerumque, fonumque.
Atque ideo quid ferre queant, quid quæque recufent,
Explorare prius labor efto, & munera jufta
Mandato, ac proprium cunctis partire laborem .   340
Obfcuros aliter crepitus, & murmura vana
Mifcebis, ludefque fonis fallacibus aures.
Nec tamen interdum vacuas, animoque carentes
Addubitem ipfe volens incaffum fundere voces,
Verbaque, quæ nullo fungantur munere fenfus,   345
                                                    Dives

Indeed, one may even from time to time cleave and separate large words, diminishing them into their two constituent parts, and then inter—between those parts—pose words, or shorten them by excising a particle and then drawing the disjoin'd parts together again.[42]

Therefore, whenever poets must recount the names of chieftains and famous men, names too difficult to pronounce and exceedingly harsh in style, they polish them by now adding, now deleting one by one, a few letters, and thus render the names more agreeable. "Sicharbas," when they have altered one part, they call "Sichaeus." Hence I should rather sing of the battles the Titans fought, the savage wars the giants waged, and the tumults Enceladus caused, than of the peoples conquered long ago by Italian valor, and the nations from many a shore whom their arms laid low.[43]

But as you compose, let no force impel you to add empty material irrelevant to your plan for the sake of words alone; rather compel your words without exception to subserve your subject matter, weighing with care every sonorous section of your verse. For certain words can deceive you in an unmindful moment unless you are vigilant, and will refuse to perform your bidding and their function, will withdraw secretly from their task, and idle in utter indolence. While the other words working in harmony fulfill each their appointed task, these words supply only meter and sound. And therefore make it your task to investigate first what each word will and will not convey; then assign all words equable functions and apportion to each a fit task. Otherwise you will simply be mixing obscure clatterings and empty murmurs and cheating our ears with deceptive sounds.[44] I personally, however, should not hesitate from time to time to utter willingly, though to no particular purpose, empty words which are void of significance and fulfill no semantic function,

Dives ut egregio tantum, & confpectus amictu
Verfus eat, dulcique fono demulceat aures.
Atque adeo quæ fint ne vero quære profecto
Illa: tibi fe fponte dabunt per fe obvia paffim.
Sæpe autem ruptis vinclis exemta volutes   350
Membra, & compactum quæfitor disjice verfum,
Poft iterum refice, & partes in priftina redde
Partibus avulfas. numquam te libera vinclis
Incautum fallent refoluto carmine verba.
Huc ades. hic penitus tibi totum Helicona recludam. 355
Te Mufæ, puer, hic faciles penetralibus imis
Admittunt, facrifque adytis invitat Apollo.
Principio quoniam magni commercia cæli
Numina conceffere homini, cui carmina curæ,
Ipfe deûm genitor divinam noluit artem   360
Omnibus expofitam vulgo, immeritifque patere.
Atque ideo, turbam quo longe arceret inertem,
Anguftam effe viam voluit, paucifque licere.
Multa adeo incumbunt doctis vigilanda poetis.
Haud fatis eft illis utcumque claudere verfum,   365
Et res verborum propria vi reddere claras:
Omnia fed numeris vocum concordibus aptant,
Atque fono quæcumque canunt imitantur, & apta
Verborum facie, & quæfito carminis ore.
Nam diverfa opus eft veluti dare verfibus ora,   370
Diverfofque habitus, ne qualis primus, & alter,
Talis & inde alter, vultuque incedat eodem.
Hic melior motuque pedum, & pernicibus alis
Molle viam tacito lapfu per levia radit:
Ille autem membris, ac mole ignavius ingens   375

Incedit

so that my rich verse, striking by reason of its splendid vesture, may roll on in opulence and caress our ears with its sweet music. You obviously need not inquire what these words are, for they will surely occur to you spontaneously, being everywhere to hand by their very nature.[45]

To return to our point on concision: break frequently the bonds which connect your line, consider the disjunct parts: then reconstitute the line, restoring to their original position the sundered members. Words will never deceive you in a heedless moment if the meter has been destroyed and the words are thus free from the links which join them.

Draw near: at this point I shall reveal all Helicon to its very depths to you. Now the compliant Muses admit you, young poet-to-be, to their inmost sanctuaries, and Apollo invites you into his sacred courts.[46]

In the first place: since the gods granted that he who should make poetry his study might know the discourse of great heaven, the father of the gods himself was unwilling that this divine art should be commonly exhibited to all and exposed to the unworthy. And therefore, in order to keep far off the indolent crowd, he willed that the way should be narrow and accessible to few. For this reason, poets who are skilled in their art must devote their attention to a multitude of tasks.[47] It is scarcely sufficient for them to compose verse in simply any fashion whatever, and to use only the semantic force of words in making their meaning clear. Rather, they fit their conceptions to words whose rhythmic flow is appropriate, and through sound and words whose appearance is apt and through the carefully selected likeness they give their verse, imitate whatever it is of which they are singing. For they must give varied faces, as it were, and varied garb to their verses, lest the second line plod along just like the first, and so the third after the second, each identical to the other in appearance.[48]

One verse, with spurn of feet and swift wings, skims more easily over the road in silent flight through the plains. That one, however, with vast limbs and massive bulk

Incedit tardo molimine fubfidendo.

Ecce aliquis fubit egregio pulcherrimus ore,

Cui lætum membris Venus omnibus afflat honorem:

Contra alius rudis informes oftendit & artus,

Hirfutumque fupercilium, ac caudam finuofam   380

Ingratus vifu, fonitu illætabilis ipfo.

Nec vero hæ fine lege datæ, fine mente figuræ,

Sed facies fua pro meritis, habitufque, fonufque

Cunctis, cuique fuus, vocum difcrimine certo.

Ergo ubi jam nautæ fpumas falis ære ruentes   385

Incubuere mari, videas fpumare reductis

Convulfum remis, roftrifque tridentibus æquor.

Tunc longe fale faxa fonant, tunc & freta ventis

Incipiunt agitata tumefcere: litore fluctus

Illidunt rauco, atque refracta remurmurat unda   390

Ad fcopulos, cumulo infequitur præruptus aquæ mons.

Nec mora, Trinacriam cernas procul intremere omnem

Funditus, & montes concurrere montibus altos.

Quum vero ex alto fpeculatus cærula Nereus

Leniit in morem ftagni, placidæque paludis,   395

Labitur uncta vadis abies, natat uncta carina.

Hinc etiam folers mirabere fæpe legendo,

Sicubi Vulcanus filvis incendia mifit,

Aut agro, ftipulas flamma crepitante cremari.

Nec minus exfultant latices quum teda fonore   400

Virgea fuggeritur coftis undantis aheni.

Carmine nec levi dicenda eft fcabra crepido.

Tum, fi læta canunt, hilari quoque carmina vultu

Incedunt, lætumque fonant haud fegnia verba,

Seu quum vere novo rident prata humida: feu quum   405

Tom. II.   H   Pan-

lags along more sluggishly, slouching to a halt from ponderous exertion. Now there follows one of supremely lovely and exquisite countenance on all whose limbs Venus breathes a grace which charms. Facing it is another, a crude one, which flaunts its formless limbs, shaggy brow, and coiling tail, repulsive to the sight, and disagreeable even to the ear. Nor indeed are these figures given without rule and rational order; to the contrary: because every word is clearly different from every other word, each figure has its own characteristic visage suited to its excellences, its own peculiar garb, and its own sound.[49]

Hence, when sailors have flung themselves into the salt-sea breakers in their bronze-prowed boats, and have launched their ships on the main, you will see the roiled deep dashed into spray by their oars' backward sweep and their trident prows. Listen! with a roar the rocks resound to the crash of the salt flood; listen! driven by the winds the sea begins to rise in billows; breakers smash on the grating shore, and a surging swell, split into spray, groans beneath granite crags, as hard behind it looms a sheer mountain of water. Instantly—though far from its shores—you will see all Sicily rocked to its foundations as its lofty mountains jostle together. But when Nereus has once glanced up from his depths, he quells the azure sea till it resembles a marsh or a placid pond. The pitched craft glides gently along, lapped by ocean streams; its pitched keel swims smoothly.

Thus as you read, even should you be a sophisticate, you will often be seized with admiration at passages in which Vulcan has flung his fire through forests or field and consumed the stubble with a crackling flame. And when pine brush is heaped roaring beneath the sides of a cauldron filled to the brim, the seething waters, too, leap high.

A rough rock ledge should not be described in delicate verse. But then, should your measures sing of joyful things, they, too, trip on with merry face, and lilting words laugh out the joy—be it when with spring's return the meadows smile all drenched with dew, or when,

Panditur interea domus omnipotentis olympi.
Contra autem fe fe triftes inamabile carmen
Induit in vultus, fi forte invifa volucris
Nocte fedens ferum canit importuna per umbras,
Ut quondam in buftis, aut culminibus defertis.   410
Verba etiam res exiguas angufta fequuntur,
Ingentefque juvant ingentia. cuncta gigantem
Vafta decent, vultus immanes, pectora lata,
Et magni membrorum artus, magna offa, lacertique.
Atque ideo, fi quid geritur molimine magno,   415
Adde moram, & pariter tecum quoque verba laborent
Segnia; feu quando vi multa gleba coactis
Æternum frangenda bidentibus, æquore feu quum
Cornua velatarum obvertimus antemnarum.
At mora fi fuerit damno, properare jubebo.   420
Si fe forte cava extulerit mala vipera terra,
Tolle moras, cape faxa manu, cape robora, paftor.
Ferte citi flammas, date tela, repellite peftem.
Ipfe etiam verfus ruat, in præcepfque feratur,
Immenfo quum præcipitans ruit Oceano nox,   425
Aut quum perculfus graviter procumbit humi bos.
Quumque etiam requies rebus datur, ipfa quoque ultro
Carmina paullifper curfu ceffare videbis
In medio interrupta. quierunt quum freta ponti,
Poftquam auræ pofuere, quiefcere protinus ipfum   430
Cernere erit, mediifque incœptis fiftere verfum.
Quid dicam, fenior quum telum imbelle fine ictu
Invalidus jacit, & defectis viribus æger?
Nam quoque tum verfus fegni pariter pede languet.
Sanguis hebet, frigent effœtæ in corpore vires.   435

For-

the while, all powerful Olympus' home shines clear to view on high.

But a verse which presents something repugnant assumes, on the contrary, disagreeable looks—if it describes, for instance, a hated bird which sits late at night and discordantly rasps a song through the shadows, as once it did on tombs or ruined turrets.

Note, too, that concise themes imply the use of brief words to express them, while huge words support huge themes; it is fitting that a giant be vast in every part—that his features be enormous, his chest broad, his joints immense, his frame prodigious, and his arms mighty. And therefore if anything involving exceptional exertion is afoot, pause, and let your lagging words do equal labor with you—when, for instance, we must turn up a meadow, furrow after furrow, by forcing the plowshare through the soil with enormous effort, or when on the sea we turn the ends of sail-laden yardarms.

But if to hesitate will mean disaster, my command will be to make haste. If, for example, an underground hole has spewed forth mischievous vipers, away with delays, seize stones in your hand, shepherd, seize staves of oak, hurry, bring flaming brands, hurl your darts, repulse the plague. So, too, when night descends with a rush to the measureless sea, or a man strikes an ox a huge blow and it falls with a crash to the ground, let the verse which describes it race swift, wrought to precipitous haste. But when rest descends, a gift to all the world, you will see

> Your very verses too—no need of force—
> Delay a little while their headlong flight
> And at the mid-point rest. And when the winds
> Have died, and ocean's streams have calmed in peace,
> Your verse itself will straight—as you may note—
> Repose, and at the mid-line halt its flow.

What language should I use when an aged and weak man, sick and worn out, throws a powerless spear which will not strike? Then the verses too must shuffle along at an equally lagging pace, for the old man's blood is sluggish, and his strength is exhausted and grows cold in his body.

Line 419: should read *antennarum*.

Fortem autem juvenem deceat prorumpere in arces,
Evertiffe domos, præfractaque quadrupedantum
Pectora pectoribus perrumpere, sternere turres
Ingentes, totoque ferum dare funera campo.
Nulla adeo vatum major prudentia, quam se   440
Aut premere, aut rerum pro majestate canendo
Tollere. nunc illos animum summittere cernas
Verborum parcos, humilique obrepere greffu,
Textaque vix gracili deducere carmina filo:
Nunc illos verbis opulentos, divite vena   445
Cernere erit fluere, ac laxis decurrere habenis
Fluxofque, ingentefque. redundat copia læta
Ubere felici, verborumque ingruit agmen
Hibernarum inftar nivium, quum Juppiter alpes
Frigidus aereas, atque alta cacumina veftit.   450
Interdum vero cohibent undantia lora.
Non humiles, non fublimes media inter utrumque
Litus arant veluti fpatia, & confinia radunt.
Sic demum portu læti conduntur in alto.
Quod fupereft, quæ poftremo peragenda poetæ   455
Expediam. poftquam cafus evaferit omnes,
Signaque perpetuum deduxit ad ultima carmen,
Exfultans animo victor, lætufque laborum
Non totam fubito præceps fecura per urbem
Carmina vulgabit. ah ne fit gloria tanti,   460
Et dulcis famæ quondam malefuada cupido.
At patiens operum femper, metuenfque pericli
Exfpectet, donec fedata mente calorem
Paullatim exuerit, fœtufque abolerit amorem
Ipfe fui, curamque alio traduxerit omnem.   465

H 2   Inte-

But it would be in character for a strong youth to burst into
citadels, overthrow houses, smash and rip with the might of his
chest through the breasts of four-footed beasts, lay huge towers in
ruins, and, implacably fierce, load the whole field with his slaughters.

There is no greater mark of discretion in poets than that they
know how to restrain themselves or, conversely, how to soar when
the majesty of the universe must be their theme. Now you may
see them curb their mind, chary of words, and creep along at a
humble gait, barely spinning out with a slender thread the fabric
of their verses. And now you may see them flow on, with a rich
vein, wealthy in words, and course ahead with loosened reins,
exuberant and mighty. Their prodigal riches flow out in
sumptuous abundance, and the host of their words assails us like
the wintry snows when Jupiter blows cold and clothes the lofty
peaks of the high-soaring Alps.

At times, indeed, the poets draw in the flowing reins. Then,
neither creeping low on the ground nor soaring aloft, they till the
beach and strip the border territories—the middle regions, as one
might say, between the other two lands.[50] And thus at length they
come rejoicing to haven in a deep harbor.

I shall now canvass in brief what remains—the concluding tasks
which the poet must perform. After he has escaped all the pitfalls
and elaborated the entire poem down to the colophon at the
end,[51] though he exult in his soul as the victor and rejoice in his
labors, the poet must not be overhasty and immediately publish
his self-confident verses abroad through the whole city. Ah, may
he never hold glory or an ill-advised greed for sweet fame so
dear. Rather, always patient with his works and apprehensive of
hazards, let him wait until, his mind stilled, he has extinguished
the poetic ardor, has thoroughly effaced his fondness for his
own progeny, and transferred all his attention elsewhere.

Interea fidos adit haud fecurus amicos,
Utque velint inimicum animum, frontifque feveræ
Dura fupercilia inducre, & non parcere culpæ
Hos iterum atque iterum rogat, admonitufque latentis
Grates lætus agit vitii, & peccata fatetur   470
Sponte fua, quamvis etiam damnetur iniquo
Judicio, & falfum queat ore refellere crimen.
Tum demum redit, & poft longa oblivia per fe
Incipit hic illic veterem explorare laborem.
Ecce autem ante oculos nova fe fert undique imago,   475
Longe alia heu facies rerum, mutataque ab illis
Carmina, quæ tantum ante recens confecta placebant.
Miratur tacitus, nec fe cognofcit in illis
Immemor, atque operum piget, ac fe fe increpat ultro.
Tum retractat opus, commiffa piacula doctæ   480
Palladis arte luens. nunc hæc, nunc rejicit illa,
Omnia tuta timens, melioraque fufficit illis,
Attondetque comas ftringens, filvamque fluentem,
Luxuriemque minutatim depafcit inanem
Exercens durum imperium, dum funditus omnem   485
Nocturnis inftans operis, operifque diurnis
Verfibus eluerit labem, & commiffa piarit.
Arduus hic labor. hic autem durate, poetæ,
Gloria quos movet æternæ pulcherrima famæ.
Tum fiqua eft etiam pars imperfecta relicta,   490
Olim dum properat furor, ingeniique morari
Tempeftas renuit, fuppletque, & verfibus affert
Invalidis miferatus opem, claudifque medetur.
Nec femel attrectare fatis: verum omne quotannis
Terque quaterque opus evolvendum, verbaque verfis   495

                         Æter-

In the meantime, he should approach his loyal friends with trepidation, and beg them to be willing to assume a hostile attitude and a critic's unbending brow, and urge them again and again not to spare a fault. He extends his thanks cheerfully when warned of a hidden flaw, and admits his errors freely, even when he is condemned by an unjust evaluation and could easily refute the erroneous accusation.

Then, finally, he returns to his writings, and long after he has blotted memory of them from his mind begins to examine here and there his former work. But lo! an image which is everywhere new presents itself to his gaze; its features appear different (alas!) from before; his verses seem changed from those which he had composed only a short time earlier and which had pleased him so much. He marvels in silence and, not remembering, does not find himself in them; he is ashamed of his works, and of his own accord censures himself roundly. Then he atones for the sins he committed. Apprehensive of everything settled, he rejects one passage after another, and substitutes for them better ones, clipping and shearing off locklike excrescences, and rooting out little by little dense verbal wood and empty extravagance. In doing so he exercises his authority sternly, and pursues his work energetically by night and by day until he has quite freed his verses of all flaws and has atoned for his errors. This task is arduous, but, poets, persist at it nonetheless if the most fair glory of eternal fame is for you a motive force.

Then if any part of his work remains still imperfect, the poet makes use of the times when the poetic ardor slips away and his period of full creative power will stay no longer to take pity on those verses which are ailing, to mend and succor them, and to heal the lame ones. And it will not suffice for him to redact the poem once only; indeed, he must work through the whole composition three or four times a year,

Æternum immutanda coloribus. omne frequenti
Sæpe revifendum ftudio per fingula carmen.
Quod non una dies, fors afferet altera, & ultro
Nullo olim ftudio, nulla olim in carmine cura
Deprenfæ per fe prodentur tempore culpæ,   500
Quæque latent variæ denfa inter nubila peftes.
Quin etiam doctum multum juvet ille laborem,
Qui varias cæli creber mutaverit oras.
Namque etiam mutant animi, genioque locorum
Diverfas fpecies, diverfos pectora motus   505
Concipiunt, noftrifque novæ fe mentibus offert
Ultro aliquid femper lucis, tenebræque recedunt:
Atque novos operi femper fas addere flores.
Verum efto hic etiam modus. huic imponere curæ
Nefcivere aliqui finem, medicafque fecandis   510
Morbis abftinuiffe manus, & parcere tandem
Immites, donec macie confectus, & æger
Aruit exhaufto velut omnis fanguine fœtus,
Nativumque decus pofuit, dum plurima ubique
Deformat fectos artus inhonefta cicatrix.   515
Tuque ideo vitæ ufque memor brevioris, ubi annos
Poft aliquot (neque enim numerum, neque tempora pono
Certa tibi) addideris decoris fatis, atque nitoris,
Rumpe moras, opus ingentem dimitte per orbem;
Perque manus, perque ora virûm permitte vagari.   520
Continuo læto te dulces undique amici
Gratantes plaufu excipient. tua gloria cælo
Succedet, nomenque tuum finus ultimus orbis
Audiet, ac nullo diffufum abolebitur ævo.
Et dubitamus opes animo contemnere avari,   525

Nec

continually changing the words and altering the figures. He must review every verse frequently and individually with constant zeal. What one day does not afford, perhaps the next will, and quite of their own accord, with no further attention, no further effort over the poem on his part, his faults and the various pestilences which lie hidden amidst dense clouds will discover and betray themselves with time.

Indeed, the poet would much forward this learned labor should he frequently change his place beneath heaven's varied zones. For minds, too, vary, and through the peculiar genius of differing places our breasts conceive diverse images and diverse impulses; some fresh light always dawns of its own accord on our minds, and the shadows recede. And one may always add new ornaments to his composition.

But let there be moderation in the matter of revision as well. For some have not known how to call a halt to this task or how to restrain their healing hands from cutting out diseases which apparently need to be excised nor, pitiless as they are, how to extend mercy at last, until, exhausted and sick from the diminution it has suffered, with its blood, if I may so put it, quite drained away, their whole child has shrunk to a shadow and has forfeited the beauty it had at its birth, since masses of ugly scars deform its lacerated limbs.

Bear constantly in mind, therefore, that life's span is all too brief; and after several years (though I do not set down a definite number of years or fixed periods to wait), when you have endowed your work with sufficient beauty and polish, cease all delay, send your poem abroad through the far-reaching earth, and let it roam through the hands and lips of men. Straightway your loving friends everywhere will congratulate you, and will swell your praises with happy applause. Your glory will ascend to the sky; earth's utmost land will hear your name, and, spread abroad, it will not be destroyed to the world's end.[52]

And in our greed we hesitate to disdain riches from the very depths of our souls

Nec potius fequimur dulces ante omnia Mufas.
O fortunati, quibus olim hæc numina dextra
Annuerint præcepta fequi, quæve ipfe canendo
Juffa dedi plenus Phœbo, attonitufque furore!
Quando non artes fatis ullæ, hominumque labores,   530
Et mea dicta parum profint, ni defuper adfit
Auxilium, ac præfens favor omnipotentis olympi.
Ipfe viam tantum potui docuiffe repertam
Aonas ad montes, longeque oftendere Mufas
Plaudentes celfæ choreas in vertice rupis,   535
Quo me haud ire finunt umquam fata invida, & ufque
Abfterrentque, arcentque procul, nec fumma jugi umquam
Fas prenfare manu faftigia. fat mihi, fiquem
Siquem olim longe afpiciam, mea fida fequutum
Indicia, exfuperaffe viam, fummoque receptum   540
Vertice, & hærentes focios juga ad alta vocantem.
Sed nonnulla tamen noftri quoque gratia facti
Forfan erit. me fida olim præcepta canentem
Stipabunt juvenes denfo circum agmine fufi,
Et vocem excipient intenti fenfibus omnes.   545
Tum vitæ fi jufta meæ procedere luftra
Fata finent, nec me viridi fucciderit ævo
Impia mors, olli gelida tardante fenecta
Languentem, & fera defeffum ætate magiftrum
Certatim prenfa fuper alta cacumina dextra   550
Sæpe trahent, ultroque ferent per amœna locorum,
Et fummi invalidum fiftent ad limina Phœbi
Cantantem Mufas, vatumque inventa piorum.
Virgilii ante omnes læti hic fuper aftra feremus
Carminibus patriis laudes. decus unde Latinum,   555

Unde

and fail to follow the sweet Muses rather than all things else. Oh, happy the men to whom these gracious goddesses shall have granted to follow these precepts, their laws, which I, filled with Phoebus and smitten with the poetic furor, have set forth in my song! Nonetheless, no skills or mortal toilings will suffice, and my teachings will profit but little, unless aid from on high [53] and the sustaining favor of almighty Olympus be present.

For myself, I have only been able to teach others a path already discovered to the Aonian mountains and to show from afar the Muses dancing choruses at the summit of their lofty mountain. Thither my grudging fates never allow me to go, always deterring me and keeping me far from my goal, never permitting me to place my hand on the mountain's peak. It will suffice for me if, even from afar, I should someday catch sight of one student who by following my sure guidelines has conquered the path, is received on the highest pinnacle, and calls his lagging friends to the lofty peaks.

Yet there may be some personal reward as well for my achievement. In days to come boys will crowd around me, circling me about in a dense throng as I sing my sure precepts, and, intent on my words, all shall listen eagerly to my teachings, every sense on the stretch. Then, if death has not cut me off in the spring of life; then, though I languish in cold, slow old age; though I am faint and weary since well-stricken in years, my students shall eagerly grasp my right hand and take their master often over the lofty peaks and lead me through the lovely places and set me, though feeble, before the portals of most high Phoebus, as I sing of the Muses and the inventions of the sacred bards.[54]

Now let us in exultation praise Vergil above all poets else, bearing his praises above the stars in the songs of his native land.[55] From him flows the Latins' glory,

Unde mihi vires, animus mihi ducitur unde.
Primus ut Aoniis Mufas deduxerit oris
Argolicum refonans Romana per oppida carmen :
Ut juvenis Siculas filvis inflarit avenas,
Utque idem, Aufonios animi miferatus agreftes,   560
Extulerit facros ruris fuper æthera honores
Triptolemi invedus volucri per fidera curru:
Res demum ingreffus Romanæ laudis, ad arma
Excierit Latium omne, Phrygumque inftruxerit alas
Verba deo fimilis. Decus a te principe noftrum   565
Omne, pater. tibi Grajugenûm de gente trophæa
Sufpendunt Itali vates tua figna fequuti.
Omnis in Elyfiis unum te Græcia campis
Miraturque, auditque ultro, affurgitque canenti.
Te fine nil nobis pulchrum. omnes ora Latini   570
In te, oculofque ferunt verfi. tua maxima virtus
Omnibus auxilio eft. tua libant carmina paffim
Affidui, primis & te venerantur ab annis.
Ne tibi quis vatum certaverit. omnia cedant
Secla, nec invideant primos tibi laudis honores.   575
Fortunate operum! tua præftans gloria fama,
Quo quemquam afpirare nefas, fe fe extulit alis.
Nil adeo mortale fonas. tibi captus amore
Ipfe fuos animos, fua munera lætus Apollo
Addidit, ac multa præftantem infigniit arte.   580
Quodcumque hoc opis, atque artis, noftrique reperti
Uni grata tibi debet præclara juventus,
Quam docui, & rupis facræ fuper ardua duxi,
Dum tua fida lego veftigia, te fequor unum,
O decus Italiæ, lux o clariffima vatum.   585

Te

from him my powers, from him my strength of mind. When first he had drawn the Muses from Aonia's shores, he made Argolian song echo through the cities of Rome. Yet a youth, he piped in the woodlands on Sicilian reeds. Young still, and pitying in his spirit the rude Ausonians, he exalted above the heavens the hallowed rites of the countryside, borne through the stars in Triptolemus' swift chariot. At last taking up the task of singing Rome's praise, he set all Latium aflame with war, and drew up the Phrygian array, a man in language like a god. All our glory, father, is ours because you are our leader. Italy's poets have followed in your steps, and have hung as votive offerings in your praise the trophies they have won from the Greeks. And in the Elysian Fields, you alone are he at whom all Greece wonders; to you alone she listens uncompelled; in your honor she rises as you sing. Without you we are bereft of beauty. To you have all Latins turned, their gaze intent on you. Your surpassing excellence is their common help; they drink constantly of every part of the river of your songs, and revere you from their earliest years. Let no poet ever dispute your supremacy: let all ages give way, nor let them envy you your absolute eminence in praise. O man blessed in your works! The excelling glory of your fame, to which it were sacrilege for anyone to aspire, has taken wing and soared aloft. For you sing a more than mortal song. Caught with love, Apollo himself joyfully grants you his power and marks your eminence with a boundless art. Whatever worth and art and invention are ours in this work come from you; my pupils whom I have taught and led over the steeps of your holy mountain owe these most excellent gifts to you alone; for I tread in your sure footsteps; I follow you alone, O glory of Italy, O supreme splendor of the poets!

Te colimus: tibi ferta damus, tibi tura, tibi aras,
Et tibi rite facrum femper dicemus honorem
Carminibus memores. falve, fanctiffime vates.
Laudibus augeri tua gloria nil potis ultra,
Et noftræ nil vocis eget. nos afpice præfens,   590
Pectoribufque tuos caftis infunde calores
Adveniens, pater, atque animis te te infere noftris.

F   I   N   I   S.

To you we give our reverence; to you give garlands; yours is this incense, and yours the altars we make: to you we shall ever sing with fitting rites a sacred litany, remembering you in our songs. Hail, holiest of poets! Your glory cannot be increased by praise, nor does it need my voice. Be present, and look with favor upon us; come, father, pour into our pure minds your fire, and infuse yourself through our souls.

COMMENTARY TO BOOK ONE

1. The title given in the index of the 1527 edition is simply "De Arte Poetica Lib[ri] III"; the heading to Book 1 reads: "M[arci] Hier[onymi] Vidae Cremonen[sis] / Poeticor[um] Ad Franciscum / Francisci Regis F[ilium] / Franciae Delfinum / Liber Primus": "The First Book of the Poetics of Marcus Hieronymus Vida of Cremona, [written] to Francis, the son of King Francis and Dauphin of France."

Francis (1518–36) was son of Francis I, and Dauphin. In 1525 Francis I was defeated and captured at Pavia by the emperor Charles V. Under the terms of the Treaty of Madrid (1526), Francis was released, but the Dauphin and his brother Henry were to be left in Spain as hostages. They were finally ransomed in 1529, but the Dauphin never did hold "the scepter of Gaul's monarchs," for he died at the age of eighteen while his father was still alive.

The dedication is in no way integral to Vida's poem—any more than is Horace's mention of the Pisos central to his *Ars poetica*. After the paternal admonitions and optimistic encouragements which Vida addresses to Francis at the beginning of the poem, the Dauphin is not mentioned again by name, and Vida directs his advice largely to a rhetorical audience of boys and their parents and tutors.

The 1527 Stephanus edition of the poem is dedicated to Angelo Dovizio, as is the earliest extant version of the poem (see p. 201).

2. As Scaliger (*Poetices libri septem* [Lyons, 1561], p. 310) disapprovingly notes, Vida here combines the invocation and the proposition of his poem. The invocation echoes Vergil in *Aeneid* 6.266–67: "Sit mihi fas audita loqui, sit numine vestro / pandere res alta terra et caligine mersas." Note that Vida wishes to educate a poet who will write epic indeed, but epic understood as hymns and encomia, the two poetic types which Plato (*Rep.* 10.607a) proposes to allow into the polis of the idea.

It is curious that Vida's extraordinarily sensitive ear seems to have failed him in the first line of his poem: "Vulgare arcana," though the words present a fine contrast in meaning, is a rather unpleasant combination of sounds.

The "springs" ("fontes") sacred to the Muses are the Castalian (on Mt. Parnassus), Aganippe and Hippocrene (on Mt. Helicon, and the Pierian (on Mt. Pierus, near Mt. Olympus).

3. See Vida's slightly more elaborated comments on the origins and history of poetry below (1.27–38, 129–203). That poetry came from the gods and was first used as a form of religious expression is an old *topos* in the humanists' discussions—and defense—of poetry: see, for example, Boccaccio in Book 14 of the *De genealogia deorum gentilium,* chapter 8. (Books 14 and 15 of the *Genealogia* have been translated by Charles G. Osgood as *Boccaccio on Poetry;* see that version *in loco,* and Osgood's notes, particularly note 1, p. 160.)

Vida's classification of the various *genera* of poetry by both verse measure and subject matter is also traditional. Aristotle refers to the fact that each of the various types of poetry had a name based on the verse measure in which it was written and/or one based on its content; one could write a "lampoon," but the same activity was ἰαμ-βίζειν, "to write iambics on someone." To write an epic was also to write "in hexameters" (*Poetics* 1448b–1449b). Vida, it appears, did not know Aristotle, but he might have found similar distinctions almost anywhere; in Horace *Ars poetica* 73 ff., for example, or in Quintilian, or in any handbook used in the schools. Sidney, approximately sixty years later, notes the same phenomenon in his *Apology for Poetry* when he lists types of poetry: "The most notable be Heroic, Lyric, Tragic, Comic, Satiric, Iambic, Pastoral, and certain others, some of these being termed according to the matter they deal with, some by the sorts of verses they liked best to write in."

4. The preeminence of epic over all other forms was scarcely in question in the quattrocento and early cinquecento. Vergil was *the* poet and his *Aeneid* the great poem of all times. Only Homer could approach him, and Homer, indeed, was the father of the epic. The question was reopened, of course, when the full influence of Aristotle's *Poetics* began to be felt in the second third of the cinquecento.

5. Dactylic hexameters were commonly known as ἡρωικοί in Greek and *versus heroici* in Latin. English prosody has its own "heroic" couplets.

6. Phemonoe was a daughter of Apollo and priestess at the temple of Delphi. She is mentioned by Pausanias (second century A.D.) in his *Description of Greece* 10.5.7: "I have heard that as men were tending their flocks the power of prophecy came upon them and they became inspired by the vapor and prophesied by Apollo's power. But the greatest and most far-spread renown belongs to Phemonoe, for Phemonoe was the first priestess of the god, and first chanted the hexameter." Isidore (*Etymologiae* 8.8.4) also mentions her.

7. These lines (39, 40) echo Horace's famous dictum:

> sumite materiam vestris, qui scribitis, aequam
> viribus, et versate diu, quid ferre recusent,
> quid valeant umeri.
>
> (*Ars poetica* 38–40)

8. Vida mentions several of the most common poetic genres, but, according to his own precept (2.40–50), by elegant circumlocution rather than by name. The genres are, of course, the epic, the drama, the elegy (note Vida's pun on "elegis," "choose," and the technical term which he does not write, "elegi," "elegies"), and the pastoral. The "Sicilian poet" is Theocritus, regarded as the father of the pastoral, and Vergil's "model" in the *Eclogues.*

Vida is quite justified in his claim: Book 1 of his poetics is concerned with the nurture of a poet—any poet—and Book 3 with poetic techniques which by and large might be used in a number of genres. Book 2 is primarily directed at the epic, but even there general rules of decorum are enunciated which would prove widely applicable. Finally, the whole poem involves not only sustained technical instruction but equally importantly a celebration of the life of the poet.

9. Vida later speaks with some bitterness of the burden he felt when he himself was "composing on command." See Introduction, p. xix.

10. The *topos* of the poem as a ship, the poet as pilot, and composition as a voyage is a common and old one. See, for example, the passage in Vergil (*Georgics* 2.39, 41) which Vida is imitating here.

> tuque ades inceptumque una decurre laborem. . .
> Maecenas, pelagoque volans da vela patenti.

Cf., too, Dante's lines (*Purgatorio* 1.1–3):

> Per correr miglior acque alza le vele
> omai la navicella del mio ingegno
> che lascia dietro a sè mar sì crudele.

Petrarch, Boccaccio, and Ariosto are among the virtually endless list of Renaissance authors who also use the *topos*.

11. To acquire words and *topoi* was standard advice in all the ancient works on rhetoric, and part of the Renaissance schoolboy's— and poet's—activity; witness the plethora of "commonplace" books of one sort and another (notable examples are Erasmus' *Adagia* and *De copia*), and passages in the poets which are almost wholly composed of *topoi;* Hamlet's speech beginning "What a piece of work is man . . ." is a superlative example. Sister Miriam Joseph's *Rhetoric in Shakespeare's Time* (New York, 1962) discusses English rhetorical practice, including instructions on how to elaborate one's material by the use of "topics." The passage in question here echoes Quintilian's advice in *Institutio oratoria* 10.1.5: "Num ergo dubium est, quin ei velut opes sint quaedam parandae, quibus uti, ubicumque desideratum erit, possit? Eae constant copia rerum ac verborum."

12. Cf. Quintilian 10.3.33: "Debet vacare etiam locus, in quo notentur quae scribentibus solent extra ordinem, id est ex aliis, quam qui sunt in manibus loci, occurrere. Irrumpunt enim optimi nonnunquam sensus, quos neque inserere oportet neque differre tutum est, quia interim elabuntur. . . ."

13. Vida's metaphors are curiously mixed here. Note, too, that the first part of his comment echoes Horace's advice:

> vos exemplaria Graeca
> nocturna versate manu, versate diurna.
> (*Ars poetica* 268–69)

For one of Quintilian's repeated uses of the military metaphor, see 7.10.13.

14. This precept conforms to the practice of Vergil in writing the *Aeneid*, at least as Suetonius reports it: "[Vergil] first drafted the *Aeneid* in prose and disposed it into twelve books; then he began to put each of the books into verse separately as the fancy moved him, taking them up in no particular order at all" (Suetonius *Vita Vergili* 23).

15. From this point to nearly the end of Book 1 (to line 485) Vida discusses the education of the poet. The precepts are ones common to Renaissance humanist pedagogues such as Vittorino da Feltre and Guarino; for a still useful discussion of this topic, see William H. Woodward, *Studies in Education during the Age of the Renaissance* (Cambridge, 1906). The principal ancient sources for Vida's advice are Quintilian, above all, and Plutarch's *De liberis educandis* (available to Vida in Guarino's Latin translation, and in common circulation in the Renaissance). If Vida indeed knew St. Basil's *De legendis antiquorum libris* in Bruni's translation, as Nicola Salvatore thinks (*L'arte poetica di Marco Girolamo Vida* [Foligno, 1912], pp. 12–40, cited in Di Cesare, p. 307, n. 3), the fact has little or no importance for the *De arte poetica,* for Vida seems nowhere to refer to the work or to owe any specific intellectual debt to it.

Those who may wish either to examine precept for precept Vida's indebtedness to Quintilian or simply to gain a close notion of Vida's use of this source will find most helpful a reading of Books 1 and 2 of the *Institutio oratoria,* now easily available in a separate English translation edited by J. J. Murphy as *On the Early Education of the Citizen-Orator* (New York, 1965). Quintilian often discusses at length points which Vida merely touches upon; one has the impression that Vida's references are in some sense a shorthand which he could assume would be filled in by his readers' detailed knowledge of the text. A complete text of Quintilian had been available since 1416, when it was discovered by Poggio, and the *Institutio* had the widest currency in the quattrocento.

Specific references to Quintilian below are extensive, though limited to those which might be significant for an understanding of Vida's text; further parallels might have been suggested from time to time, but I have omitted those which would have been of minimal use to the reader either because similar passages had already been cited, or because the parallel was so vague as to be without value.

16. Cf. Quintilian 1.1.15–19 on when the youth should be introduced to literature.

17. For a full discussion of the point see Quintilian 1.1.4–11. Plutarch (*De liberis educandis* 6) makes a similar requirement for the youth's servants and companions. In the Latin, note at line 92 Vida's pun on "nefandi" ("of what ought not to be said"); "nefas" also

means "that which is not sanctioned by the gods," and therefore something abhorrent and to be avoided.

18. The Getae were a Thracian tribe living along the Danube; it was the Getae, one remembers, among whom Ovid was exiled and of whose barbarism he complained. On ignorant and bombastic instructors, see Quintilian 2.3.7–9.

19. The "poet" is, of course, Vergil; the Mincio, a tributary of the Po, flows past Mantua near Andès, where Vergil was born. Compare Quintilian 1.8.5 on the molding of youths' sensibilities.

Pitt's version of this passage is particularly misleading. It was not for "fire" that the Renaissance gave Vergil preeminence, but for his "gravitas," his painstaking art, and, as Pitt does translate correctly, his "invention." "Invention," a category borrowed from rhetoric, is the first of the major concerns in composing and presenting a speech: invention, disposition, elocution, memory, and delivery. The first three activities were obviously paralleled by poetic concerns; hence the same terminology came early to be used for both. Invention involves the searching out, the "discovery" of one's material, disposition its proper arrangement, and elocution its proper expression. Invention and disposition will be the chief topic of Book 2; elocution the main concern of Book 3.

20. Note that the youth is especially moved by the characters and episodes in Vergil which deal with "youths [the pupil's] own age." The power of Vergil's "art" and "invention" is attested by the student's intense reactions. Ascanius, or "Julus," was Aeneas' son by his wife Creusa: the Julians claimed descent from him; see *Aeneid* 2.650 ff., 6.756–90, and numerous other passages. For the story of Lausus' death, and an excellent illustration of Vergilian sensibility, see *Aeneid* 10.794 ff. Note that Vida echoes Vergil's words (10.839) "Multa super Lauso rogitat. . . ." Pallas was the only—and dearly loved—son of Evander, a Latin chieftain who allied himself with Aeneas. Aeneas made special promises for the safety of the youth, but Pallas was slain by Turnus nonetheless. It was the sight of Pallas' belt on Turnus that roused Aeneas to kill him even as he begged for mercy; see *Aeneid* 10.495 ff. and 12.938 ff. The story of Euryalus and Nisus is told in *Aeneid* 9.176 ff. The death of Euryalus is particularly moving and is described in sensitive and suggestive language,

some of which Vida echoes here. The "parent" is Euryalus' mother, whose despair is described at 9.473 ff.

21. It is inevitable that Vida should reverse the advice of Quintilian (1.1.12) that the pupil learn Greek before Latin. Quintilian suggests that a lad would learn Latin "whether we wish him to or not" since he would hear it all about him. In Vida's day both Latin and Greek were obviously learned languages. Latin, of course, was a basic requirement for any scholar; Greek might come later. Vida himself did not know Greek (see Giraldus' comment, p. xvii).

22. Cf. Quintilian 2.4.20, 21.

Aeacides is Achilles: "Aeacides" is a patronymic—"descendant of Aeacus" (a son of Zeus).

23. The short literary history which follows draws on details from Horace and Quintilian, among others. See Horace *Epistulae* 2.1, and the *Ars poetica,* and Quintilian 10.1.46 ff. For an analysis of literary history as Vida presents it, see Introduction, pp. xxxviii ff. The pattern is no doubt factitous and does little justice to fifth- and fourth-century Athens, for example, but the Greek works of the "classical age" were still so little known generally that they could be safely slighted, especially in comparison with Homer. Though "it would be blasphemous for poets to hope for anything excelling [Vergil]," might not Vida hope that this new cycle would produce an epic (perhaps one written by himself) to equal those of the cycles in the ancient world? For an extended discussion of Renaissance conceptions of cultural history, see Wallace K. Ferguson, *The Renaissance in Historical Thought* (Boston, 1948), pp. 7–28.

24. Vida refers to the Turks' incursions into Greece and their stunning victories. See Wallace K. Ferguson, *Europe in Transition* (Boston, 1962), pp. 406–9, or Myron P. Gilmore, *The World of Humanism* (New York, 1962), pp. 6 ff., for a concise discussion of the Turkish threat until 1520.

25. These lines echo Lucretius *De rerum natura* 1.117 ff. Quintus Ennius (239–169 B.C.), called by Horace—if a little condescendingly—"pater Ennius" (*Epistulae* 1.19.7), was a man of versatile genius; he wrote tragedy and comedy, but he is primarily remembered as the author of the epic *Annales.* Originally the work contained eighteen books; of these some six hundred lines or partial

lines are extant. Ennius had an immense influence on the development of the epic; Vergil in particular is frequently indebted to him. Note in the Latin, incidentally, that the words "sylvai frondosai" are archaic in form; indeed, the whole phrase is a fragment of Ennius preserved by Macrobius in his *Saturnalia* 6.2:

> Omne sonabat
> Arbustum fremitu sylvai frondosai.

The reference to rustic poetry resounding "among forest-dwelling fauns" probably recalls Ennius' slighting remark on Naevius' Saturnians (recorded in Cicero *Brutus* 18.71):

> quos olim Fauni vatesque canebant
> cum neque Musarum scopulos
> nec dicti studiosus quisquam erat ante hunc. . .

26. Vida is here referring to Lucretius (c. 99–55 B.C.) and his poem *De rerum natura;* Vergil knew his Lucretius well, and it is widely noted that Vergil's triumphs with the hexameter grew out of the earlier poet's achievement.

27. This paean to Vergil is only a prelude to the magnificent hymn which Vida addresses to him at the end of Book 3 (ll. 554 ff.). The exaltation of Vergil must be understood and appreciated in its cultural context; see Introduction, pp. xlii–lii. Cf., too, note 61, pp. 146–47. Angelo Poliziano (1454–94) had written earlier a somewhat less extended and effective but still beautiful encomium to Vergil at the end of his poem *Manto* (see ll. 319 ff., part of the passage is quoted below, p. 142, note 56).

28. As is well known, the Renaissance humanists' contempt for the "barbarian" Middle Ages and for medieval Latin was virtually boundless (see Ferguson, *The Renaissance in Historical Thought,* pp. 7–28). The concept of "dark ages" from which they, the humanists, were just extricating themselves to enter into their true and glorious inheritance was a major point of the humanists' cultural faith and part of their understanding of history and their mission within its pattern. See, for example, in Rabelais, Gargantua's famous letter to Pantagruel on education:

"Mais encores que mon feu père, de bonne mémoire, Grandgousier, eust adonné tout son estude à ce que je proffitasse en toute perfection et sçavoir politique et que mon labeur et estude correspondit très bien, voire encores oultrepassast son désir, toutefoys, comme tu peulx bien entendre, le temps n'estoit tant idoine ne commode ès lettres comme est de présent, et n'avoys copie de telz précepteurs comme tu as eu. Le temps estoit encores ténébreux et sentant l'infélicité et calamité des Gothz, qui avoient mis à destruction toute bonne litérature. Mais par la bonté divine, la lumière et dignité a esté de mon eage rendue ès lettres, et y voit tel amendement que de présent à difficulté seroys-je receu en la première classe des petitz grimaulx, qui en mon eage virile estoys (non à tord) réputé le plus sçavant dudict siècle" (*Pantagruel* 8).

If Vida is referring to specific poets in lines 180–83, one could think of numerous candidates; the man who trusts in his genius and spurns art is probably Ovid (43 B.C.–A.D. 18): the charge most often laid against him is that of uncontrolled facility. Ovid himself claims:

> sponte sua carmen numeros veniebat ad aptos
> et quod temptabam scribere, versus erat.
> (*Tristia* 4.10.25–26)

Quintilian, whom Vida may be echoing here, remarks that Ovid was "nimium amator ingenii sui" (10.1.88). Horace frequently comments that mere facility does not in itself suffice for a poet:

> ego nec studium sine divite vena
> nec rude quid prosit video ingenium. . .
> (*Ars poetica* 409–10)

See, too, *Sermones* 1.4.9–13.

The poet who "thunders endlessly through all his verses" is perhaps Lucan (A.D. 39–65), the author of the epic *Pharsalia*. Quintilian remarks (10.1.90): "Lucanus ardens et concitatus et sententiis clarissimus et, ut dicam quod sentio, magis oratoribus quam poetis imitandus." The remark is pregnant with good sense. Lucan is tireless—and often tiresome—in his use of rhetorical devices.

The "others" who "offer vapid songs" are legion: one would be happy to suggest Silius Italicus (c. A.D. 25–100), author of the epic *Punica,* and Statius (c. A.D. 45–96), author of the *Thebaid*.

29. The Medici, of course, are the great Florentine banking,

merchant, and political family: their power was consolidated by Cosimo de' Medici (1389–1464) who put the family fortune on a solid basis and subtly gained political control of Florence, and continued, if weakly, by Piero (1414–69). The most illustrious member of the family during the quattrocento was that immensely intelligent, vital, and cultured man, Lorenzo the Magnificent (1448–92). The Medici most prominent in Vida's day were Lorenzo's son Giovanni (1475–1521), later Pope Leo X (1513–21), and Giovanni's bastard cousin Giulio (c. 1477–1534), afterward Clement VII (1523–34). Leo was perhaps the greatest of the humanist popes; certainly under his papacy humanism was nurtured at Rome as never before; not only literary activities, but also painting (he was patron to Raphael among others), sculpture, and architecture flourished under his patronage. It was Leo who commissioned Vida's magnum opus, the *Christiad*, though he never lived to see it completed. The Medici interest in preserving Greek manuscripts and in bringing Greek scholars into Italy was responsible for retrieving much that might otherwise have been lost. For the notion of a "scholar's leisure" ("otium") see Cicero *De oratore* 1.1.3, and *Disputationes Tusculanae* 5.36.105. See below, Book 2.572 ff. and note 90, for Vida's lament on Leo's death.

The "barbarian" refers to the Turks.

30. This impassioned and somewhat despairing cry refers to the constant competition and hostility among the Italian states and to the negotiations and alliances which various of them made with the French and the Hapsburgs. It was as a result of this disunity among the states of Italy, and of the meddling which Venice and the papacy particularly encouraged, that the French had first invaded Italy and that Italy was the prize in the Franco-Hapsburg struggles over the following decades. Finally, in 1527, an imperial "army" of marauders took Lombardy and then in a march south sacked Rome as few cities had ever been sacked. Though the scourge passed, humanism at Rome was never again the same, in some measure because of the irretrievable loss suffered by the private collections of humanist prelates. For the complex history of the period see J. C. L. de Sismondi, *History of the Italian Republics* (London, 1906), pp. 665–737.

31. That is, in the Augustan Age; as Vida has noted above, "silver" Latinity represented a great decline from the peak reached with Vergil. Cf. Quintilian 10.1.20.

32. This whole passage, including the simile, echoes advice given by Plutarch in De liberis educandis 7; cf., too, Quintilian 2.2.5: "Sumat igitur ante omnia parentis erga discipulos suos animum. . . ."

33. See Quintilian 1.1.20 and 1.3.13–18, and Plutarch De liberis educandis 12 for extended passages giving the same advice.

34. Vida frequently makes extraordinarily graceful use of the associative value of the language of the author whom he is echoing. Here he chose Vergil Aeneid 5.517–18: "decidit exanimis vitamque reliquit in astris/ aetheriis . . ." The language is used of a dove which had been fixed to the top of a tall pole as a shooting mark. One of the archers had come close to hitting it, but instead snapped the bond which held it. The bird winged away, free, but just as it was about to enter a cloud, another archer, Eurytion, struck it with an arrow, and it fell to the earth. The parallel between the bird's moment of freedom and death and the boy's is extraordinarily poignant. Note, too, the tolerance and sympathy which this personal reminiscence implies.

The Serio is a tributary of the Po, the great river of northern Italy.

35. Apollodorus is the source of this tale; see Bibliotheca 2.4.9.1–3 (Vida, however, undoubtedly found the story in some more contemporary collection): "Heracles was taught to drive a chariot by Amphitryon, to wrestle by Autolykos, to shoot a bow by Eurytos, to fight in full armour by Kastor, and to play the lyre by Linus. This Linus was a brother of Orpheus; he came to Thebes and became a Theban, but was struck with a lyre by Heracles, and died. For Heracles became angry when Linus hit him a blow, and he killed him. When certain parties put him on trial for murder, he cited the law of Rhadamanthus which stipulates: 'whoever defends himself against one who begins to assault him unjustly shall not be punished,' and thus he was freed. But Amphitryon was afraid lest he might do the same sort of thing again, and sent him down to the herds."

The "singing tortoise shell" is, of course, the lyre, the first lyre having traditionally been made of a turtle's shell.

Vida is obviously smiling a little here, but note that he catches himself up by remarking immediately that lads ought really to obey their teachers' instructions.

36. See Quintilian 1.2 for an extended discussion of the merits of having a private tutor rather than having a boy taught in a school.

37. As is well known, Petrarch's father, for example, had precisely this problem; the following rather amusing anecdote is recorded in *Rerum senilium epistulae* 15.1: Petrarch was studying (or was supposed to be studying) the law at Montpellier according to his father's directions, but was in fact spending most of his time reading the ancient poets and Cicero. Ser Petracco made a trip to Montpellier, and finding a cache of books "lucrativo velut studio adversi" as Petrarch says, threw them into the fire, whereat Petrarch began to roar most wonderfully, as though, he reports, he himself had been thrown into the fire. Apparently unprepared for such vehemence, Ser Petracco snatched two books out of the flames, one Vergil's works, the other Cicero's *Rhetoric,* and handed them to his tearful son, saying that the first he might have as "an occasional—very occasional—diversion for his mind and the second as an aid in his studies."

38. Tusculum was a town in Latium, built on a hill just a few miles southeast of Rome. Tibur is modern-day Tivoli.

39. Quintilian discusses the ways for a teacher to ascertain the pupil's abilities and characteristics: see 1.3.1–5; the passage includes a discussion of precocity, and contains a crop simile.

40. See Quintilian 1.3.8 ff. and Plutarch *De liberis educandis* 13 for much the same advice.

41. Faunus, according to myth, was a grandson of Saturn and the father of King Latinus. He was responsible for the introduction of agriculture and sheep raising and was deified after his death as the god of farmers and of shepherds. When Pan-worship was introduced into Italy, Faunus was assimilated to Pan and given the latter's horns and goats' feet; hence, too, the name

"faunus" came to be used in the plural, after the pattern of "Panes." Thus "Fauns" are simply rustic, sylvan deities.

42. Seneca has the same comparison in his *De tranquillitate animi* 15: "Danda est remissio animis: meliores acrioresque requieti surgent. Ut fertilibus agris non est imperandum; cito enim exhauriet illos nunquam intermissa foecunditas; ita animorum impetus assiduus labor frangit. Vires recipient paulum resoluti et remissi."

"Albunea" is a fountain at Tibur which gushes up near the location of Horace's villa. Vida undoubtedly has in mind Vergil's lines in *Aeneid* 7.81 ff:

> At rex sollicitus monstris oracula Fauni
> fatidici genitoris, adit lucosque sub alta
> consulit Albunea, nemorum quae maxima sacro
> fonte sonat saevamque exhalat opaca mephitim.

and Horace *Odes* 1.7.10–14:

> Me nec tam patiens Lacedaemon
> nec tam Larisae percussit campus opimae
> quam domus Albuneae resonantis
> et praeceps Anio ac Tiburni lucus et uda
> mobilibus pomaria rivis.

The Anio is a stream, tributary to the Tiber, that flows by Tibur.

43. These lines obviously echo Anchises' words to Achilles in the underworld (*Aeneid* 6.847–50):

> excudent alii spirantia mollius aera
> (credo equidem), vivos ducent de marmore vultus,
> orabunt causas melius, caelique meatus
> describent radio et surgentia sidera dicent.

See Quintilian's full discussion of the varying abilities of youths at 2.8.

44. Plutarch discusses this point at length; see *De liberis educandis* 2.

45. Machaon, the son of Aesculapius, was with the Greeks at Troy; see *Iliad* 4.192 ff. and *Aeneid* 2.263.

46. This is an instance of Vida's not infrequent dry humor: another is the passage already noted on the homicide which Heracles committed on his tutor. Quintilian advises that boys not be allowed to read love elegies (see 1.8.6), and Horace remarks

> qui studet optatam cursu contingere metam
> multa tulit fecitque puer, sudavit et alsit,
> abstinuit Venere et vino.
>
> (*Ars poetica* 412–14)

Note the much more extended comment in the Cremona text (1.485 ff.) on the necessity of remaining unmarried if one is to have the *otium* necessary for composition.

47. The advice to read both poetry and prose is paralleled in Quintilian 1.4.4.

The position of Cicero as the greatest of ancient prose authors and orators was secure for most Renaissance humanists. Petrarch had practically worshiped him: "I confess, I admire Cicero as much or even more than all whoever wrote a line in any nation. . . . If to admire Cicero means to be a Ciceronian, I am a Ciceronian. I admire him so much that I wonder at people who do not admire him. . . . I even feel sure that Cicero himself would have been a Christian if he had been able to see Christ and to comprehend his doctrine" (cited from *On His Own Ignorance,* in Ernst Cassirer and Paul O. Kristeller, eds., *The Renaissance Philosophy of Man* [Chicago, 1948], p. 15). See, too, the anecdote quoted above in note 37, and Petrarch's epistle to Cicero. Cicero's civic humanism was the pattern for the civic humanism of the Renaissance; his *De officiis* particularly was read and admired. For Quintilian's estimate of Cicero, see 10.1.105 ff.

The question of the use of Cicero as a strict model for modern (Latin) eloquence was hotly debated at various points in the quattrocento and cinquecento. Vida, like Bembo and Longolius, asserts the peremptory value of Cicero's example. For further notice of this controversy, see Introduction, pp. xlvi–xlviii, and the bibliography listed in note 64 *in loc.*

48. The first part of this sentence (lines 391–93) echoes *Odyssey* 1.3,4. Ulysses' voyage had since classical times been used as a type

of the proper *paideia* (see W. B. Stanford, *The Ulysses Theme* [Oxford, 1954]). Cf. Cicero *De finibus* 5.18.48–49, and Horace *Epistulae* 1.2.17 ff: "Rursus, quid virtus et quid sapientia possit/ utile proposuit nobis exemplar Ulixen,/ qui domitor Troiae multorum providus urbis/ et mores hominum inspexit, latumque per aequor,/ dum sibi, dum sociis reditum parat, aspera multa/ pertulit."

The "wall paintings" are maps.

49. Cf. Horace *Odes* 1.11, 2.3, and 4.7.

50. Plutarch makes these points in much the same way; see *De liberis educandis* 10.

51. Vida's *De arte poetica* is most noted for the bravura section on imitative harmony in Book 3.355–454, but the poem is everywhere filled with an amazing mastery of verbal and metrical effects, and Vida constantly exemplifies in practice what he has been (or will be) advising. This simile is an excellent example of imitative harmony, as is the paragraph following, and Book 2.367 ff. The whole passage preceding clearly—and amusingly—reflects Vida's own experiences in composition.

52. Vergil's practice was normative for Vida; hence, besides the obvious pedagogical sense in having a boy begin with small rather than large tasks, it is natural that Vida should advise that pupils try such topics as those he suggests here. Among Vergil's juvenilia is the *Culex*—a *jeu d'esprit* which tells "the fearsome fates of a gnat," written, according to Suetonius (*Vita Vergili* 17, 18), when Vergil was sixteen years old. Similarly appropriate subjects, Vida feels, are those of the *Batrachomyomachia,* a pseudo-Homeric mock-epic (303 lines in length), and the *Arachnomachia* (not now extant but mentioned by Proclus [second century A.D.] and others as Homeric, though certainly it was not). Aside from being amusing subjects for composition, each of these topics would give the student practice with epic diction, conventions, and tone. Cook's groping suggestion (*The Art of Poetry* [Boston, 1892], p. 255) that the reference to the spider alludes to the story of Arachne as told in Ovid's *Metamorphoses* misses not only the allusion but the point of Vida's remark as well.

53. Quintilian elaborates on this topic in much the same terms; see 2.4.10–14.

54. Nymphs of the woods; see Vergil *Eclogues* 5.58–59:

> ergo alacris silvas et cetera rura voluptas
> Panaque pastoresque tenet Dryadasque puellas.

55. For the phrase, see Dido's rebuke to Aeneas at *Aeneid* 4.365–67:

> nec tibi diva parens, generis nec Dardanus auctor
> perfide, sed duris genuit te cautibus horrens
> Caucasus. . . .

56. This paean to the retired life of the poets is carefully patterned upon Vergil's praise of the life of the rustic and the poet in the countryside. See *Georgics* 2.458–542, and cf. Horace *Odes* 3.1, *Epode* 2, and *Epistulae* 2.2.65–86. Renaissance humanists never tired of praising the charms of country retreat and telling the delights a poet could find in rusticating; most seemed to have found pleasure in the city and the courts as well, however. Petrarch, for instance, protests frequently his love of being alone at his house at Vaucluse, but his need for adulation—and patronage—frequently drew him to the centers of ecclesiastical and political power. Boccaccio has an important discussion of the topic in his *De genealogia deorum gentilium* 14.11 (and see Osgood's note on the passage, p. 168). Poliziano delivers an encomium which is rather like Vida's and likewise based on the passage from the *Georgics;* see the end of his *Manto:*

> O vatum preciosa quies! O gaudia solis
> Nota piis, dulcis furor, incorrupta voluptas,
> Ambrosiaeque deum mensae! Quis talia cernens,
> Regibus invideat? Mollem sibi prorsus habeto
> Vestem aurum gemmas, tantum hinc procul esto malignum
> Vulgus. Ad haec nulli perrumpant sacra profani.
>
> *(Manto* 368–73)

Doubtless Vida knew the passage from Poliziano. Note, too, that Vida is carefully and artfully following Vergilian practice by ending each of the books of his "didactic" poem with magnificent set pieces patterned after Vergil's which Vida hopes will "revive [the] readers' weary minds. . . . [and make them] eager to return again and again" (2.240–44, 251). See, as well, the end of Book 2 (ll. 558–603, and note 90) and Book 3 (ll. 554–92).

57. There are two chief ancient stories connected with Prometheus (the "Forethinker"), both told by Hesiod; the first concerns his theft of fire from heaven and his taking it back to earth after Zeus had withdrawn it from men. The second is the tale of the punishment Prometheus suffered chained to a mountain peak in the Caucasus, his liver eaten out every day by an eagle, only to have it renewed each night. See *Theogony* 42–53, 507–69. Prometheus is, of course, the central character in *Prometheus Bound,* the one play extant of Aeschylus' Promethean trilogy. Prometheus' name and acts supported wonderfully an allegorical interpretation of his identity and significance; Boccaccio happily canvasses the possibilities in his *De genealogia deorum gentilium* 4:44, reviewing in doing so the views held by the chief ancient and patristic authors.

If Vida has a "source" for the conceit that Prometheus stole the Muses from the spheres, I have not identified it. Certainly Prometheus was credited with bringing men the arts; see (although Vida did not know him directly) Aeschylus *Prometheus Bound* 443–44, 460–61:

> Hear now, how I [Prometheus] made mortals, who were before like infants
> Creatures of wisdom and possessors of counsel.
> I showed them . . . the art of arranging letters—
> The mother of the Muses, the servant which remembers all.

See, as well, Plato *Protagoras* 321c, where Prometheus is described as stealing simultaneously both fire and the "arts of Athena."

The idea of the "music of the spheres" is an old one; Pythagoras put forward the theory; Plato in the *Timaeus* and *Republic* incorporates the idea into his cosmology; Aristotle denied that the music exists. Cicero (*Somnium Scipionis* 5) expatiates on the theory, and Macrobius (*Commentarii in Somnium Scipionis*) develops a lengthy exegesis of Cicero's meaning. Macrobius refers to passages in Hesiod and Plato, and stretches the limits of interpretation (particularly in equating Plato's "Sirens" with the Muses, *Republic* 10.617b) to show that the Muses are the tutelary spirits of the spheres, each possessing and tuning her own (see *Commentarii* 2.1–3).

This whole passage in Vida not only is admirable in its power of expression but shows remarkable capabilities in "invention" as well, coupling as it does the cosmic vision of the Muses whirling and turning the vast spheres of heaven with the old myth of Prometheus' theft from heaven on behalf of men. The phrase "the mighty music of Olympus as it whirled" ("sonitum circumvolventis Olympi/ Ingentem") is particularly audacious in conception yet stately in expression, and is, so far as I know, Vida's own. Less splendidly expressed the concept might be amusing; as Vida presents it, it is impressive.

58. Rather than stopping the reader every few words with a gloss, I shall list and explain here the names or phrases likely to puzzle him in the next two sentences.

Dodona was a city in Epirus (a province in the north of Greece) famous for its ancient oracle of Zeus, whose responses were given by the rustling of the sacred oaks; see Ovid *Metamorphoses* 7.623 and 13.716.

Libyan groves: There was an oracle of Zeus Ammon in Libya, at the oasis of Siwah.

The cave at Phocis: Themis, goddess of justice and prophecy, had an oracle on Mount Parnassus in Phocis; see Ovid *Metamorphoses* 1.313 ff. and 7.762, where Themis is described by the same epithet as in Vida, "kindly" ("alma").

Delphi: Perhaps the most famous of the ancient oracles was that of Apollo, at Delphi in Phocis; there, it was supposed, was the *omphalos,* the "navel" of the universe.

Faunus: See note 41, above. Faunus also was a giver of oracles; see *Aeneid* 7.81 ff.

Solyma: Solyma is an abbreviated form of Hierosolyma, or Jerusalem. It is interesting that Vida gives the pagans pride of place over the Hebrews in the matter of when each received the gift of poetry; earlier humanists had often been driven to assimilate Musaeus to Moses, for instance, in order to show that pagan poetry had respectable origins. The question was still an issue when Russel wrote his notes to Vida's text in 1732. In a comment on Book 1.28, Russel, following the tack taken by Tristram in his commentary, takes Vida's part against an objection of Scaliger's, but in doing so (apparently forgetting this passage) asserts that the Hebrews had poetry before the Greeks: "For the glory of having discovered poetry belongs not to the Greeks but to the Hebrews, who antedated not only the Trojan war but the arrival of Cadmus in Boeotia. For there are no poems by the Greeks which can snatch the palm of antiquity from the hymns in the Holy Scriptures—particularly that of Moses and Miriam in Exodus 15 (which Josephus . . . testifies was chanted in a hexameter rhythm)."

Sibyls: A sibyl was a prophetess. The most famous of these was the Sibyl of Cumae who served Apollo; see *Aeneid* 6.10, 98. Another sibyl provided Tarquinius Superbus (an early king of Rome) with books of prophecies; these were put in the Capitol and consulted in times of crisis.

Divine fury: The idea that the prophet or poet is possessed by the god and composes or prophesies in a "divine fury," or μανία, or "furor" is common both to Greco-Roman and—at least as far as prophets are concerned—to Hebrew culture. Plato discusses the notion in some detail, notably in the *Ion,* the *Phaedrus,* and the *Laws* (719c). The concept was an ancient poetic convention by the time of Vergil and Horace.

59. For such recitals, see the song of Demodocus in Homer's *Odyssey* 8.62 ff., or 8.470–520, where he sings of the fortunes of the Achaeans during the Trojan War, or the accounts of his own deeds and fortunes which Aeneas gave (*Aeneid* 2 and 3) after the feast Dido held in his honor.

60. The phrase "[you] draw above the heavens the minds which you have inspired" is perhaps a reminiscence of Plato's famous passage at *Phaedrus* 246–48 where the soul is likened to a charioteer and his team. If the charioteer (the rational function of the soul, the λογιστικόν) has his horses (the spirited and the appetitive faculties—τὸ θυμοειδής and τὸ ἐπιθυμητικόν) well under control he will be able to soar above the heavens with the god in whose train he is numbered and contemplate the realm of the forms.

The sentence "without you . . . amiable" that follows echoes Lucretius' magnificent hymn to Venus:

> nec sine te quicquam dias in luminis oras
> exoritur neque fit laetum neque amabile quicquam.
>
> (*De rerum natura* 1.22–23)

61. See note 56, above, on the whole section of which this hymn is the climax. The final paean is to the god who inspires poetry; as will be noted below (p. 194), the language of the praise of Vergil (3.554–92) is of much the same character as the jubilant but reverent praise here. The rhetorical structure of this passage follows closely that of the ancient Latin and Greek prayer or hymn. The god is addressed carefully; here as so often the suppliant does not presume to know the ultimate name for the god ("Quisquis es," "whoever you are"); then the suppliant praises the god's characteristics and mighty deeds ("Your gifts move hard rocks and draw forests . . . in their train"); next comes the mention of self and one's relation to the god ("a poet and a priest"); and finally, if a prayer for help is involved, a request: here, an implicit one for benediction and aid, a request which will be made explicit in the lines which begin the next book.

The phrase "your gifts move hard rocks and draw forests now here and now there in their train" refers to Orpheus, who was said to have been able to charm trees and wild beasts and even stones into doing his bidding simply by playing on his lyre and singing. Amphion, it was told, built the walls of Thebes with his music; rocks heard, moved, and ordered themselves spontaneously (see Horace, Ars poetica 391 ff.). "Cursed Tartarus," the "keeper of hell gate" (Cerberus), and the Erinyes felt the power of song when Orpheus descended to rescue Eurydice. The whole story is told with graceful art by Vergil in Georgics 4.453–527.

Those who have read Vida's De arte poetica most closely have remarked with pleasure that his personality reveals itself through his lines; Symonds (The Renaissance in Italy: The Revival of Learning [New York, 1935], p. 345) notes Vida's "good sense" and "kindly feeling." Vida's contempt for pretentious pedantry (see 1.95 ff. and 2.191 ff.), his fervent patriotism (1.206–7; 2.58 ff.), his genuine love for Vergil and poetry and a simple life (1.161 ff., 486 ff.; 3.554–92), his genial tolerance and sympathy (1.230 ff., 340 ff.), and his occasional humor (1.265 ff.; 2.175 ff.) infuse into the poem a sense of both urbane good-nature and deep-felt concern. In the passage before us there is more than rhetorical excellence; the extent of Vida's exaltation of the god who gives poetic inspiration is evidenced not only by majestic cadences but by the remarkable equivalence which closes the hymn. Vida is both poet and priest, a claim he could make more literally than could Vergil (*Georgics* 2.475–76) or Horace (*Odes* 3.1.3); in his role as priest he administers the sacraments to those who come to learn and worship at the altar of God. But the role of poet in the *De arte poetica* is also that of a priest, and as poet-priest at the altar of the god whose praise he is now hymning he is giving to the "novices" an analogous sacrament, those "gifts" which will instruct them and enable them to lead the life of the poet. This passage, then, gives both rhetorical and conceptual focus to the frequent references Vida makes to the fact that he is imparting "mysteries" to the young, and that only initiates may follow and succeed in the path he is pointing out. For in his poem Vida is presenting the paradigm of the life of the poet, a life with a calling, an *ascesis,* a *doctrina,* a sacred text (Vergil), and a rhetoric of its own. And through his choice of diction and the equivalence he makes here he shows the loftiness of that paradigm by equating it with the life-paradigm of the Christian priest. One realizes, then, the majesty of the Christian humanist's concept of the life of the poet, for finally the god who inspires the poet is the God who inspires the priest, and as the latter distributes the wisdom and Word of God at the altar, so the former proclaims the wisdom and word of God through his poems. For the early humanists, Petrarch and Boccaccio, for example, the paradigm was intensely compelling and its rhetoric unjaded. By Vida's time, both pattern and rhetoric were for many, though they continued to exalt them, empty; but Vida both in concept and in expression seems still to preserve the vision. See Introduction, pp. xlix ff.

COMMENTARY TO BOOK TWO

1. The phrase "Pergite Pierides"—"Press on, Pierians"—is borrowed from Vergil *Eclogues* 6.13. Vida's use of this second invocation

is in accordance with the advice he gives at ll. 25 ff.: "Nor is it sufficient to invoke the Muses and implore their bounty once only. You may call on the gods as often as, like crags at sea, things exceptionally difficult to express . . . obstruct your course." That advice is of course based on Vergil's practice; note that at the structural and thematic turning point of his work, for example, Vergil reinvokes the Muse and outlines what is to come (see *Aeneid* 7.37–45).

2. The metaphor of the "mountain fastnesses" is frequent in Vida. This passage echoes the opening lines of Book 1, especially lines 5 and 8; Book 3 will begin with the same image (line 8). Note, too, that difficulties encountered in composition are like "crags at sea."

3. Note that Vida is again following his own advice and Vergil's practice: "At the very entrance, just at the threshold of their works, the [poets] prudently skim lightly over the highlights of their material. . . ." (ll. 17 ff.).

"Invention" and "disposition" are discussed and defined above, p. 132, note 19. Vida has completed his discussion of the education of the poet-to-be and now proceeds in a carefully structured manner to set forth "the first rules for the composition of the work" (1.81).

4. The distinction made here is that invention, which involves the ability to find excellent material and select what is best for one's use (see Quintilian 3.3.1–6), seems often to come by gift of the gods, while "disposition," the ability to structure one's material in an orderly and cogent fashion, comes by art. Vida's remark that it is in the area of the disposition of their material that "poets chiefly hope to gain glory" is more significant than might be realized at first reading, for the comment points directly at what Renaissance humanists considered the *sine qua non* of great poetry. Modern critics accustomed to the notion that art at Rome by the time of Leo X was beginning to descend toward mannerism, and that Italian literary achievement was long on its way into a sort of third sophistic, will probably understand this remark of Vida's as a general endorsement of form to the neglect of content; and those who assume Vida to be a precursor of all that they dislike in "neoclassical" criticism will be likely to pass over the remark altogether and concentrate on Vida's stylistic pyrotechnics as symptomatic of an intense, but precious and unhealthy

concern with style. Both will be wrong. In order to understand with some degree of sympathy what Vida is saying we must try to set aside our indignation that he did not indicate "invention" or "genius" or "imagination" as the one quality indispensable to good poetry, or our perplexity that he did not insist that "elegance" was most central. Whether we agree with him or not, Vida is here expressing a point which he consistently maintains both in statement and in practice in his poem: that meaning, and the clear and effective presentation of meaning, are of the first importance to a poem, and that the basic means of achieving this lucidity is the significant, artful deployment of one's material. Outstanding invention is of vast importance for Vida, to be sure, and the ability to express one's meaning so eloquently that "it seems that the . . . events you behold are not merely being described but actually taking place" (2.380) is perhaps the most marvelous of all the poet's acts of creation; nonetheless, Vida is convinced that both of these qualities result in mere copiousness or preciousness in a major work unless a significant structure gives them form. One can indeed construct a perfectly articulated but lifeless skeleton, though one can hardly accuse Vida of encouraging such a course. All three tasks, invention, disposition, and elocution, are important; proper structure is simply for Vida *primum inter paria;* it above all, he feels, will both gain and hold the reader's attention, and justify that attention. Horace mentions, but does not develop significantly, his similar conception of "lucidus ordo":

> ordinis haec virtus erit et venus, aut ego fallor,
> ut iam nunc dicat iam nunc debentia dici
> pleraque differat et praesens in tempus omittat.

(*Ars poetica* 42–44)

5. Much of what follows in Book 2, though from time to time based on earlier dicta, represents an extrapolation from Vida's practical criticism of Vergil's—and to some extent Homer's—works. Thus, for the "skim[ming] lightly over the highlights of their material," one might refer to Vergil *Aeneid* 1.1–2 and 12–33, or Homer *Iliad* 1.1–7.

6. The poets call on various gods or goddesses for aid. At the beginning of the *Iliad* and *Odyssey* it is simply the "goddess" or

"Muse" who is invoked; at *Iliad* 2.484 ff. Homer addresses "the Muses of Olympia, the daughters of Zeus of the aegis." Lucretius invokes Venus (*De rerum natura* 1.1–43). Vergil calls on the "Muse" (*Aeneid* 1.8) and Erato (*Aeneid* 7.37 ff.); at 6.264 ff. he prays:

> Di quibus imperium est animarum umbraeque silentes
> et Chaos et Phlegethon, loca nocte tacentia late
> sit mihi fas audita loqui. . . .

Petrarch takes out a rather remarkable amount of poetic insurance at the beginning of his *Africa:* first he invokes the "Muse," then "the Muses," and then God both as redeemer and as "summus parens."

In ancient Greek and Roman prayers it was considered essential that one address the god by his proper name, call to him in his proper habitation, and recount his mighty deeds—particularly those germane to one's request (see above, p. 146); note the practice of Homer (*Iliad* 2.484 ff.) and Vergil (*Aeneid* 6.264 ff.). Vida himself (*Christiad* 1.1 ff.) calls on the Holy Spirit:

> Qui mare, qui terras, qui caelum numine comples,
> Spiritus alme tuo liceat mihi munere regem
> Bis genitum canere. . . .

7. See the note immediately above for instances of repeated invocation of the Muse. The poet will call for special aid when, for example, human memory would be insufficient—as Homer prayed for help with the so-called Catalogue of the Ships (cf. Vergil's imitation of this prayer at *Aeneid* 7.641 ff.); or when the poet has something especially fearsome, secret, or difficult to tell—as when Vergil called on "the gods who rule over the shades" before he recounted Aeneas' experience in Hades; or when he passes to more exalted (*Aeneid* 7.44–45) or to improbable (*Aeneid* 9.77 ff.) material.

8. Horace gives related advice in a passage famous for its wit and pithiness:

> nec sic incipies ut scriptor cyclicus olim;
> 'fortunam Priami cantabo et nobile bellum.'
> quid dignum tanto feret hic promissor hiatu?
> parturient montes, nascetur ridiculus mus.
>
> (*Ars poetica* 136–39)

The opening lines of Lucan's *Pharsalia* may be taken as an example of a tumid proposition. The tone is from the beginning shrill and high-flown, and the pace agitated:

> Bella per Emathios plus quam civila campos,
> Iusque datum sceleri canimus, populumque potentem
> In sua victrici conversum viscera dextra
> Cognatasque acies, et rupto foedere regni
> Certatum totis concussi viribus orbis
> In commune nefas, infestisque obvia signis
> Signa, pares aquilas et pila minantia pilis.
>
> (*De bello civili* 1.1–7)

Contrast with Lucan the restrained vigor of style, tone, and diction of the opening of the *Iliad* and *Aeneid*.

9. The "desire to read on" is based on suspense, but suspense not so much as to what the end will be but as to *how* the event will be reached. Hence Homer tells us at the beginning of the *Iliad* that he will tell of the "wrath of Achilles." We are told the general results of that wrath; we know the outcome of the Trojan War. The question uppermost in the reader's mind, then, is how one gets from "A" to "B." How does the tale unfold? What are the details in the chain of events? In the proposition to the *Odyssey* we are told that Ulysses left Troy and arrived home. But what trials, what delays, what marvels did he meet on the way? Aeneas will reach Italy, if not precisely found his city ("dum conderet urbem"), but what were the divine and human purposes and passions involved in that vast undertaking ("tantae molis erat Romanam condere gentem" 1.33)? At these the poet simply hints, and so whets our curiosity.

10. See *Odyssey* 1.1–5; Odysseus' name is not mentioned until line 21.

11. This line echoes Horace *Ars poetica* 151–52:

> atque ita mentitur, sic veris falsa remiscet,
> primo ne medium, medio ne discrepet imum.

12. Vida is again echoing Horace (*Ars poetica* 146–50):

> nec reditum Diomedis ab interitu Meleagri,
> nec gemino bellum Troianum orditur ab ovo:
> semper ad eventum festinat et in medias res

> non secus ac notas auditorem rapit, et quae
> desperat tractata nitescere posse, relinquit. . . .

The "in medias res" is, of course, one of the most famous of epic devices, designed first to capture the reader's interest by its vividness and vigor and then to make him eager to hear the antecedent events, even though they should be a little less spectacular.

13. Vida outlines in the following passage Homer's ordering of his material in the *Iliad*. The "shepherd of long ago" is, of course, Paris, who earned Hera's hate by deciding against her in favor of Aphrodite in the famous beauty contest. Aphrodite's reward to Paris was the love and possession (at least temporary) of the loveliest of women—Helen.

"Aeacides" is a patronymic for Achilles; the "captive maiden" was Achilles' war-prize, Briseis (*Iliad* 1.184 f.); Xanthus is another name—the name used by the gods—for the river Scamander (*Iliad* 20.74); the Simois is a stream which flows down from Mount Ida across the plain by Troy into the Scamander (*Iliad* 5.773–74). For the description of the bodies floating in the waters, see *Iliad* 21.300 ff. Though the swearing of the oath is not described, Nestor vaguely mentions "oaths" at 3.339; but that is all. Dido, in explaining to Anna how innocuous she has been to Aeneas, refers to the incident and mentions the oath:

> non ego cum Danais Troianam exscindere gentem
> Aulide iuravi. . . .
>
> (*Aeneid* 4.425–26)

For further references see Ovid *Metamorphoses* 12.24 ff. and 13.181 ff. The "thousand ships borne through the sea" refers to the "Catalogue of the Ships" at *Iliad* 2.493 ff. Paris recounts briefly the abduction of Helen (*Iliad* 3.441–46). Menelaus actually "rages" seldom, if ever, and can even show circumspect anxiety (*Iliad* 17.89 ff.), though he can speak bravely and proudly on occasion (see *Iliad* 3.95 ff., 349 ff.,and 17.18 ff.). The afflictions of Troy are hinted at here and there throughout the *Iliad:* Hector's rebuke to Paris and the subsequent scene with Andromache (see *Iliad* 6.325–529) as well as references *passim* to the slaughter inflicted on the Trojans and their allies point up their sufferings during the earlier part of the war. Vida's references throughout this whole section are sufficiently oblique, however, to show that his knowledge of Homer, whom he could not read in the original, was weak and derivative indeed in comparison with his complete mastery of Vergil.

14. Vida here gives a sketchy description of the plot structure of the *Odyssey,* Books 1–12. The "wandering son of Laertes" is, of course, Odysseus. (Note Vida's repeated use of the patronymic: cf. *De arte poetica* 3.124–25.) "Ida" is the name of a mountain range which ends near Troy; hence "shores of Ida" is here a metonymy for Troy. Odysseus tells of the raid on the Cicones (Thracian allies of the Trojans) in *Odyssey* 9.39 ff. The *Odyssey* opens with Odysseus on Ogygia (see Book 1.11 ff.; Ogygia is first mentioned at line 85). Calypso is the daughter of Atlas. Odysseus arrives at the kingdom of the Phaeacians after a series of misfortunes described in Book 5. King Alcinous is induced, partly by the good offices of his lovely daughter, Nausicaa, to welcome Odysseus; a feast is held in the stranger's honor, and after the feast Odysseus tells of his wanderings (Books 9–12). Most of Odysseus' companions were either eaten by the Cyclops or smashed in their boats by rocks hurled by the Laestrygonians (10.80–135). Cf. Macrobius' comment in *Saturnalia* 5.2.

15. These lines, which echo Vergil *Aeneid* 1.8 ff.: "Musa, mihi causas memora . . . ," describe Vergil's and Homer's practice (see *Iliad* 1.8–56 and *Aeneid* 1.8–33).

16. Note again that the suspense is directed not at the final outcome of a story, as in a modern novel, but at the outcome of episodes, or at the nature of the events which lead from one situation to another. The gifts to Achilles are listed in *Iliad* 19.242 ff.; Odysseus' escape from Polyphemus' cave is told in *Odyssey* 9.316 ff.

17. The impudent (or "inferior") poet is, of course, Homer, whom Vida is quite willing to take to task for lapses of decorum, whether formal (as here) or stylistic (2.282–99, 304–24, 325–38). The purpose of Vida's criticism of Homer is to demonstrate Vergil's superiority over his greatest rival. The particular reference here is to *Iliad* 3 where Homer prepares elaborately for a duel between Menelaus and Paris (3.1–120), and then delays the action and switches the scene while Helen ("the lady of Lacedemonia") is brought before us (ll. 121–60). At the request of Priam Helen proceeds (ll. 161–242) to

point out the leaders of the Greeks—after they had been fighting before Troy for nine years. "Lacedemonia" is another name for Sparta.

The critic who appreciates Homer more than Vergil is likely to cite Homer's vigor, his "naturalness," and his quick-paced and gripping narration as the reasons for his preference. The reader who prefers Vergil will emphasize the Vergilian seriousness expressed in his profound sensitivity to the problems of order in human life and the constant and polished artistry involved in his adaptation of language to subject matter. Part of the problem (apart from the fact that in this instance the authors' purposes are significantly different and hence the tone of their works must differ, too) is that notions of "decorum" change, and the "realism" which will be prized by one audience will be dismissed as vulgar by another; the conventions and literary techniques which will be readily accepted by one period will be stumbling blocks to the next. One could write a tolerable history of modern literary taste by following the comparative reputations of Homer and Vergil since the Renaissance.

Vida, of course, and much of the Renaissance with him, preferred Vergil to Homer. They could read him more easily for one thing, but the reasons for their preference go deeper than that. The problems of disorder in the state and the need for a civic and moral "virtus" which would not be anti-Christian, and for an eloquence which would allow one to express himself in a language and with an art which would not be ephemeral, made Vergil the most profoundly relevant of authors. Further, tastes formed by a rhetorical education in which decorum was highly prized and intricately analyzed would be ill-satisfied with what, by their standards, could only seem lapses in Homer's artistry.

18. The story of the archery contest is told in *Odyssey* 21. Vida may refer to Homer's lengthy description of how Odysseus had come to acquire the bow in question when he mentions Penelope's "innumerable delays," or he may be confusing with the bow episode Penelope's famous delaying tactic with the loom.

19. The reference is to *Aeneid* 6.77 ff. and 756 ff. Vida echoes the Sibyl's words, "bella, horrida bella" (6.86) and "alius Latio iam partus Achilles" (6.89). Compare Vergil 6.889 and 1.205 with Vida 2.132–33. See, too, Helenus' warning in *Aeneid* 3.458–60.

20. See *Aeneid* 10.287 ff., esp. 310–13.

21. "Menoetius' son" is Patroclus, Achilles' much-loved companion; his death at the hands of Hector was the proximate cause of Achilles' reentrance into the fighting. Achilles is, of course, the "greater adversary." See *Iliad* 16.784 ff. Vida refers specifically here to ll. 851–54.

22. See *Aeneid* 12.843–68; the bird was one of the Dirae, the fates. Vida echoes especially ll. 865–68.

23. Vida echoes *Aeneid* 10.503–5; for the story of Paullas' death see ll. 457 ff. Turnus' death is described at 12.915–52. It was the sight of Pallas' belt on Turnus that prompted Aeneas to disregard Turnus' appeals and to kill him.

24. Note again Vida's emphasis on care in structuring a work; see note 4, pp. 148–49.

25. As will become clear below, Vergil sets the standard for relevance of material and economy of means for Vida; Homer again serves as a bad example. The half-humorous reference here is to the description of Hera's chariot at *Iliad* 5.719 ff. Homer's passage is undoubtedly splendid verbally, but Vida sees it as an irritating and inartful interruption.

26. Vida refers to Thersites, the "ugliest man who came to Troy," adding a few details to Homer's account to strengthen his point; see *Iliad* 2.211 ff., esp. ll. 216–19.

27. Drances speaks in *Aeneid* 11.343 ff.; the description to which Vida alludes occurs at ll. 336–43. The point is obvious; Homer not only allows a base character in his epic but introduces him inartfully. Vergil, on the contrary, makes even his most minor characters of some significance, both personally and artistically. Needless to say, one might quibble with Vida, particularly on the point of the artistic merit of Thersites' appearance; one would soon become aware, however, of the profound difference in taste which would give rise to the quibble. Vida is aware of the difference in criteria: "There are . . . many things which the laxness of the Greek tongue allows . . ." but his evaluation breathes a quiet assurance of the superiority of Vergil's decorum.

28. In this passage Vida is almost certainly referring to Lucretius and probably Lucan and Statius.

29. "Cruel Mars' combats" refers to the epic, and "the varying

characteristics of soil or techniques of cultivation" to Vergil's
Georgics, particularly *Georgics* 1 and 2 where the subjects are agricul-
ture and viticulture. Vergil speaks of the "courses of the sun" at
Georgics 1.231–56 and the "eclipses of the moon, the risings of the
stars" at ll. 276 ff., for example; for this whole passage cf.
Georgics 2.475 ff. which Vida is echoing almost verbatim.

30. Vida's point is well taken. The *Georgics,* for example, is surely
among the most artfully structured of poems.

31. Vida half-quotes, half-paraphrases Anchises' famous speech
de rerum natura to Aeneas; *Aeneid* 6.719 ff; in the phrase "blandique
luminis ad auras" Vida seems to be playing with Lucretius' oft repeated "ad luminis oras" (cf. *De rerum natura* and Vida's advice at ll.
213–63).

32. The precept to "be various" was common in rhetorical theory;
indeed, Horace's complaint was that an excessive desire to be
"various" led poets to juxtapose material ludicrously:

> qui variare cupit rem prodigialiter unam,
> delphinum silvis appingit, fluctibus aprum.
>
> (*Ars poetica* 29–30)

Vida's phrase "cunctamque potens labor occulat artem" seems to be
a variation on the familiar phrase "ars est celare artem"; the precise
origin of the latter *sententia* is unknown.

33. Aeneas' shield, wrought by Vulcan ("the mighty fire god") at
Venus' request (cf. below ll. 505–9), is described at *Aeneid* 8.625 ff.
Note Vida's *Romanitas;* the shield of Aeneas depicted Roman history
with its culmination in Roman world conquest. Vulcan, the *artifex,*
knew ("haud inscius") what Aeneas did not ("rerumque ignarus,"
Aeneid 8.730); Vida chooses his example to remind the reader of
Rome's rightful place in history.

As Vulcan the *artifex* depicted Rome's glory, and as Vergil used
the description of the shield to vary his poem, so the new Latin poet
is to vary his own poem and in so doing praise Italy; hence the consecutive "tum" which begins l. 232.

34. Vida refers here to *Georgics* 2.83 ff., and echoes particularly
ll. 136 ff.

35. See Vergil's description of the portents which accompanied
Julius Caesar's death at *Georgics* 1.466 ff.

36. Vergil's resonant praiue of the rural life begins at *Georgics* 2.458: "O fortunatos nimium sua si bona norint/ agricolas. . . ."

37. See *Georgics* 4.315–558 for the story of Aristaeus. The central part of the Aristaeus episode is the story of Orpheus ("the Thracian poet"); Vida echoes especially ll. 461–63 and 511–12. For the story of Philomela, who was changed into a nightingale, see Ovid *Metamorphoses* 6.438 ff. Rhodope is a mountain range in Thrace; Pangaea is a mountain, also in Thrace; Rhesus was the son of a Muse and a king of Thrace; the Getae are a Thracian tribe; the Hebrus is the chief river of Thrace; and Orithyia is a daughter of Erechtheus, king of Athens.

38. The story of the metamorphosis of "the Ligurians' king" is told at *Aeneid* 10.185 ff. Phaëthon, the son of Helios, attempted to drive the sun's chariot for a day, but lost control of it and was struck down by Zeus to prevent the destruction of the earth.

39. For Hippolytus' resurrection, see *Aeneid* 7.761 ff., esp. ll. 768–69; Paeonia is part of Macedonia.

40. See *Aeneid* 7.655–69.

41. "Cool Tempe" echoes *Georgics* 2.469; for Vergil's exquisite description of spring, see *Georgics* 2.323–45; "groves made green by sparkling fountains" and "shady banks of streams" might refer to a number of passages: see *Aeneid* 1.162 ff. and 441 ff., 6.673–75, 8.95–96, and *Georgics* 4.333 ff. The phrases "Venetian Eridanus" and "Aetolian Achelous" both occur in Propertius (1.12.4 and 2.34.33), but there seems to be no significance to the echoes other than a verbal reminiscence: see, too, *Georgics* 4.371–73; *Aeneid* 6.659; and *Georgics* 1.9. For the Pans and Fauns and Dryad maids, see *Georgics* 1.10–11, 16–18. The phrase "the hundred sisters from the sea, the daughters of Nereus" echoes *Georgics* 4.382–83.

42. These sayings are, of course, *sententiae*. The sort of *sententia* which Vida refers to here is the aphorism, a pithy phrase which expresses concisely a piece of traditional wisdom—"what oft was thought, but ne'er so well-expressed," to use Pope's phrase. For Vida's injunction in general, cf. Horace *Epistulae* 1.1.10 ff. On *sententiae* see Quintilian 8.5. Glaucon delivers this sort of *sententia* during his dialogue with Diomedes:

> As is the generation of leaves, so is that of men:
> For the wind whirls the leaves to the ground, but the timber

Swells and gives birth again when the season of spring returns:
Even so is the generation of men: one grows; another dies.
(*Iliad* 6.146–49)

43. This phrase is a witty turn on *Georgics* 4.176: ". . . si parva
licet componere magnis."

44. The Tyrians building Carthage are compared to bees at *Aeneid* 1.430 ff.; Aeneas' men preparing to leave Libya are compared
to ants at *Aeneid* 4.402 ff.

45. Vida again praises Vergil at the expense of Homer by indicating what he feels are improprieties in Homer's similes, and by illustrating how Vergil avoids indecorous comparisons even when dealing with the same situations as Homer. Homer compares the
multitudes of the Greeks at Troy to the swarms of flies which gather
about the milk pails in spring (see *Iliad* 2.469 ff.; the same simile is
used in a different context at *Iliad* 16.641 ff.). When telling of the
Latins' forces, Vergil excludes the fly simile, though he does parallel
Homer's bird simile (cf. *Iliad* 2.459 ff. and *Aeneid* 7.699 ff.).

46. The famous comparison of the hero Ajax to a donkey is presented at *Iliad* 11.555 ff. The "Teucrians" are, of course, the Trojans; Teucer was an early king of Troy.

47. When Turnus is beleaguered as was Ajax, Vergil compares
him to a lion; see *Aeneid* 9.791–96. For the phrase "a hero . . . forefathers," see *Aeneid* 7.56.

48. Verisimilitude is an old problem in literary criticism. Renaissance discussions of the concept became infinitely more complex
with the diffusion of Aristotle's *Poetics* later in the cinquecento (the
first widely circulated text was published in 1536). Vida speaks here
simply of what is credible or probable; cf. Horace *Ars poetica* 338–40:

> ficta voluptatis causa sint proxima veris
> ne quodcumque volet poscat sibi fabula credi,
> neu pransae Lamiae vivum puerum extrahat alvo.

49. The passage to which Vida refers is *Iliad* 6.119–236: "Tydides" is Diomedes, the son of Tydeus. Lycurgus attacked and beat off
the nurses of Dionysus and so frightened that god that he dove into
the ocean. The Olympians took umbrage at this audacity and
blinded Lycurgus and arranged that he die shortly thereafter. The

story of Bellerophon which Glaucon recounts begins with an episode rather like that of Joseph and Potiphar's wife. Anteia, wife of Proetus, attempted to seduce Bellerophon, and when her attempt failed, she accused Bellerophon of making attempts on her virtue. Proetus exiled Bellerophon to Lycia and sent along instructions that he be killed. The tasks set Bellerophon, in which it was assumed he would be killed, were that he kill the Chimera (a creature formed by the gods, part-lion, part-snake, and part-goat) and that he fight against the Solymaeans (a Lycian tribe) and the Amazons. Bellerophon, as one might suspect, conquered them all.

Homer's point in recounting these stories, apart from their intrinsic interest, was that in these speeches Glaucon and Diomedes discovered that they were bound by *xenia,* "guest rights," from the days of their fathers.

50. Vida's exculpation of the poets from the old charge that they are liars is general and brief. One senses, moreover, that the humanists' struggle is won; Vida's explanations show nothing of the tension and heat of real battle, as had Petrarch's, Boccaccio's, and Salutati's, for example. The ancient discussion of poetic "fictions," particularly Hesiod's implicit (see *Theogony* 29–34) and Plato's explicit (see especially *Republic* 2 and 3) condemnations of the poets' "lies," was picked up by Christian authors and used to buttress specifically Christian objections to pagan literature. Vida's explanations are typical humanist replies to such objections: the "lies" are so obvious that no one is fooled, nor do the poets intend that anyone should be; the fictions are merely designed to excite wonder and maintain attention; no one really believes that the gods do such things, but the actions are attributed to their intervention for the sake of verisimilitude and to give the poem an elevated tone.

The spitted oxen "speak" at *Odyssey* 12.395–96; Achilles' horses weep for Patroclus at *Iliad* 17.426 ff. and prophesy Achilles' death at *Iliad* 19.404 ff. Aeneas' ships were changed to nymphs by Cybele, and one of them, Cymodoce, made a lengthy speech warning Aeneas of the peril in which Ascanius and the Trojans stood (*Aeneid* 10.228 ff.).

Echoing *Odyssey* 19.562 ff., Vergil closes Book 6 of his *Aeneid* with a reference to the "gates of sleep." "Twin," says Vergil, "are the gates of sleep, of which one they say is horn, and through it ready exit is granted to true shades; the other gleams flawless in pure ivory, but through it the shades send false dreams to the world." Dreams which come by the ivory gate are then false ones, fictitious.

51. Vida here sets up another invidious comparison between Homer and Vergil. Vida had, of course, no notion of the "oral-formulaic" theory of the composition of the *Iliad* and *Odyssey* (see G. F. Else on "Homer and the Homeric Problem" in *Lectures in Memory of Louise Taft Semple* [Princeton, 1967], pp. 319–65) and hence thought the frequent repetitions unartful and rather tiresome. For Agamemnon's dream, see *Iliad* 2.16–34, 56–70.

52. In recounting his woes to his mother, Thetis, Achilles repeats largely verbatim the account at the beginning of the poem. See *Iliad* 1.9–67 and 365–85.

53. See Agamemnon's promises of gifts to Achilles, *Iliad* 9.121–61; his messengers repeat his speech virtually word for word, changing only the forms of the verbs: *Iliad* 9.262–306. Note that the messengers are prudent enough not to repeat Agamemnon's final words about Achilles' giving place to him since he is the kinglier and elder, but rather refer to the kudos Achilles might win by slaying Hector.

54. Venulus was sent to ask Diomedes (a Greek hero of the Trojan War) for advice and help (*Aeneid* 8.9). Upon his return, Venulus gives a summary report (11.225–30) and then quotes in full Diomedes' reply (11.252–93). The two reports are complementary rather than repetitive.

55. Note that Vida's advice here is consonant with his injunction earlier (1.459–65 and note 52) to begin with the smaller genres, and with his constant emphasis on variety (2.220 ff.; 3.32 ff.) and polish (2.155 ff.; 3.473 ff.).

56. For adding "fictional things to the true" cf. Horace *Ars poetica* 151–52:

> atque ita mentitur, sic veris falsa remiscet,
> primo ne medium, medio ne discrepet imum.

To "search here and there for the origins of various phenomena" refers to the etiologies which occur frequently in longer classical poems. Ovid's *Metamorphoses,* of course, contains numerous etiologies; for examples in Vergil, see the Aristaeus episode (*Georgics* 4.315 ff.: note the beginning question: "Quis deus hanc, Musae, quis nobis extudit artem?/ unde nova ingressus hominum experientia cepit?"); and the story of Hippolytus (*Aeneid* 7.761 ff.), which contains an etiology. See, too, *Aeneid* 8.313–58.

57. Homer's gods constantly interfere on behalf of their favorites; for the chief divine protagonists on either side, see *Iliad* 5 and 20 (the "Theomachy"); the council at which Zeus threatens reprisals on the Olympians if they do not keep out of the fighting is recorded at *Iliad* 8.1–40. Zeus' injunction was constantly disregarded. So, too, in the *Aeneid* the gods are in conflict. Hera opposes Aeneas; Venus, his mother, protects him. In both epics, of course, "the will of Zeus was—[finally]—accomplished."

58. The language of this description of the gods' state sounds rather more Neo-Platonic or Epicurean than specifically biblical. Whether Vida's use of such terms as "secura," "penitus . . . degat," "summota," and "quiescat" might derive from Cicero (see, in *De natura deorum,* Veilleius' speech), Augustine (note some of the language of *Confessions* 1.4), or the Renaissance interpreters of Plato and Plotinus, Ficino and Pico, it is difficult to say.

Alternatively and more probably, Vida may be referring to the famous passage in Book 3.18–27 of the *De rerum natura:*

> apparet divum numen sedesque quietae
> quas neque concutiunt venti nec nubila nimbis
> aspergunt neque nix acri concreta pruina
> cana cadens violat semperque innubilus aether
> integit, et large diffuso lumine ridet.
> omnia suppeditat porro natura neque ulla
> res animi pacem delibat tempore in ullo.
> at contra nusquam apparent Acherusia templa
> nec tellus obstat quin omnia dispiciantur,
> sub pedibus quaecumque infra per inane geruntur.

Note that at 3.211 Vida echoes a line of Lucretius' (3.12) which almost immediately precedes this passage: "omnia nos itidem depascimur aurea dicta."

59. The primary reference here is obviously to *Aeneid* 6, which

recounts Aeneas' journey through the underworld; Ulysses (*Odyssey* 11) had converse with the dead, but he did not see the sights Vida indicates—the dead came to him rather than vice versa. Note, however, that Circe (12.21–22) refers to Ulysses' having gone into the "houses of Hades."

The Erinyes are goddesses who carry out curses—especially those of mothers—and wreak revenge for crimes; see *Odyssey* 11.280.

60. For auguries and "omens" see *Iliad* 10.274–82, *Aeneid* 1.393–401, 12.853–70. The phrase "omina pennae" is borrowed from *Aeneid* 3.361.

61. See the feast for Odysseus at Alcinous' palace, and Demodocus' and Odysseus' tales (*Odyssey* 8–12); see, too, Dido's feast for Aeneas, and his narration of the fall of Troy and of his wanderings thereafter (*Aeneid* 1; 2; 3).

62. Cf. the funeral games for Patroclus, *Iliad* 23.257 ff., and the games for Anchises, *Aeneid* 5.104 ff.

63. Vida refers here to tales told after banquets in Statius' *Thebaid* and Vergil's *Aeneid*. In the *Thebaid*, Adrastus tells of the annual feasts held in honor of Apollo who slew the monster Python, and leads in the hymn to Apollo which closes Book 1: see *Thebaid* 1.557–720. At the conclusion of the feast which he gives for Aeneas, Evander tells of how Hercules delivered his people from the depredations of Cacus, and the Salii (here, priests of Hercules) dance and sing of Hercules' labors under Eurystheus and chant hymns on Hercules' conquest of Cacus (see *Aeneid* 8.184–305). Vida echoes the *Aeneid* passage extensively.

64. Vida is referring here not only to imitative harmony and onomatopoeia, though these are of course included in his meaning, but to the poet's total abilities, through vivid description and metrical and verbal sound-effects, to reproduce in the readers' minds a precise image of what he is describing; the technique is called "ecphrasis."

65. The storm in the Sicilian straits refers to the tempest Juno raises; see *Aeneid* 1.34–123, especially ll. 81 ff. I have not located a description of a storm on the Euxine; Valerius Flaccus describes a tempest and the churning of the sea at the Cyanean rocks just at the

entrance to the Euxine, but there we find no "carinae" "fractae ad saxa."

66. See *Aeneid* 3.137–42 and *Georgics* 3.478–566.

67. An eruption of Aetna is described at *Aeneid* 3.570–82. Here, as in virtually all his examples, Vida illustrates his point by citing in detail relevant passages from an ancient author, generally, if the reference is favorable, Vergil.

68. That the poet, like God, presides over a creation of his own is an old *topos* in Renaissance humanist criticism. Here Vida points out that the poets' words, like God's, are fraught with power; when the poet tells you of war, the events seem not merely to be described ("dici") but to be actually taking place ("fieri"). At creation, God said ("dixit") "fiat lux—et facta est lux" ("Let there be light and there was light"). Similarly, here the poet virtually says "bellum fiat" ("let there be war") and his words create the illusion to complete the parallel—res fieri videntur. Thus the poets' works will be replete with all the appeals which the external world presents to the senses—particularly appeals to sight and hearing.

Vida's reference to the Greek word for "poet" is also traditional; the word is *poiētēs* (ποιητής, "maker"), a noun formation from the verb *poiein* (ποιεῖν, "to make," "to do").

69. Many of the details of this description—including the "torrent" simile—are drawn from Aeneas' narration of the sack of Troy. See *Aeneid* 2.298–558, particularly lines 486–99. See, too, Quintilian 8.3.67–69 for a similar passage which Vida doubtless had in mind.

70. In the long section which follows, Vida canvasses the reasons why at one time a poet writes with ease, and at another with the greatest difficulty. Perhaps, he says, it is because of the stars— "heaven's aspect is altered from hour to hour"—perhaps because of exhaustion or worry. He rejects these reasons, however, and states that only "the god" can enable one to write well and that he will do so only at his own good time.

Note throughout this whole section how Vida carries out his own precepts on imitative harmony (cf. Book 3.365 ff.): lines 400–3 and 414–17 are made heavy with almost constant spondees to emphasize the languor the poet feels; ponderous alliteration also helps to slow the pace to a crawl. With lines 247 ff. the rhythm picks up sharply; dactyls almost tumble over one another, and lines such as 429 and 436 with their multiple caesuras and repetitions indicate both the agitation of the poetic furor and the precipitate nature of the inspiration which seizes him.

The "quidam . . . inventus" ("I knew of a man . . .") of line 423 is almost certainly a personal reference, rather like St. Paul's "I knew a man . . ." (2 Corinthians 12:2), particularly since the unnamed person found such powerful help in the "ancient bards."

The description of the poetic furor is reminiscent of that in Plato's *Ion,* or of the Neo-Platonic ecstasy as it is described at the end of Castiglione's *Courtier.* Vida indeed nowhere makes direct reference to. Plato or his dialogues in the *De arte poetica* (though lines 622–25 of the Cremona version make a clear reference to *Republic* 10; see p. xxix, note 45), but Plato had been available for almost half a century; Ficino (1433–99) had translated his works into Latin, and artists and poets at Rome during Vida's years there were deeply imbued with the Neo-Platonic aesthetic. From Giraldus' comment (see Introduction, p. xviii) we gather that Vida was acquainted with Castiglione. For the idea that people have received inspiration in dreams, see Plato *Timaeus* 71c–72b, and a comment in Giraldus (cited in Russel's note *in loco*):

"Illud tamen mihi magis mirandum videtur, quod est a *Synesio* proditum, per somnium posse etiam aliquem poetam fieri, idque per sua tempora contigisse affirmat. Idem ait et Plutarchus de Socrate, quem per insomnia quaedam poeticae aptum inventum scribit" ("But, more marvelous still seems to me what Synesius reported, that someone can also become a poet through a dream, affirming that it happened in his own time. And Plutarch says the same thing of Socrates who, he writes, found material fit for poetry through dreams").

Finally, one may wish to note the *sententiae* (cf. 2.278–81 and note 42) at lines 410–12: "For at times forests lose their leaves, and the water in fountains dries up. Deep rivers do not always run full to overflowing, nor does spring always adorn sun-drenched fields."

71. Vida's advice here parallels closely both in matter and in expression Quintilian's at *Institutio oratoria* 10.3.4–10.

72. That the poet "imitates" nature is one of the oldest concepts in literary criticism. Plato (*Republic* 3 and 10) discusses at some length the nature of the poetic imitation, finding it defective and pernicious, at least as it was generally practiced. Aristotle makes "imitations" the class of which the various types of *poieseis* (ποιήσεις) are species: " Ἐποποιία δὴ καὶ ἡ τῆς τραγῳδίας ποίησις, ἔτι δὲ κωμῳδία καὶ ἡ διθυραμβοποιητική . . . πᾶσαι τυγχάνουσιν οὖσαι μιμήσεις τὸ σύνολον" (*Poetics* 1447a 13–15), though one should again note that Vida almost surely did not know Aristotle's *Poetics*. Horace counsels the Pisos (*Ars poetica* 317–18; see too ll. 108–11):

> respicere exemplar vitae morumque iubebo
> doctum imitatorem et vivas hinc ducere voces,

and Quintilian in discussing vividness (ἐνάργεια) writes in *Institutio oratoria* 8.3.70, 71: "Consequemur autem, ut manifesta sint, si fuerint verisimilia. . . . Naturam intueamur, hanc sequamur. Omnis eloquentia circa opera vitae est, ad se refert quisque quae audit, et id facillime accipiunt animi, quod agnoscunt."

73. Vida's phrases "using words as their medium, they create likenesses" and "present an image" (l. 461) are based in the old conception that poetry is like painting (see Horace *Ars poetica* 361: "ut pictura poesis").

74. Vida's discussion of decorum largely parallels that of Horace in *Ars poetica* 153–78 and 112–24.

Odysseus is an excellent example of one whose speech shows his station even when—as among the Phaeacians or his own swineherds —he is stripped of every outer dignity. Telemachus is Odysseus' young son; Nestor, the most aged of the Greek warriors before Troy.

75. Vida refers to—and echoes verbally—*Aeneid* 10.1–117.

76. Turnus was the firebrand leader of the Latin forces opposed to Aeneas; Latinus, the aged king of the Latins whose daughter Lavinia was—before Aeneas' intervention—to have been married to Turnus. For the passage which Vida here partly paraphrases, partly quotes, see *Aeneid* 12.11–21.

77. Vida here weaves together passages from *Aeneid* 4.300–74, 2.274–75, and 1.561–74. The choice of passages is skillful. The first

shows Dido in her distraction at Aeneas' departure, the central phrase recalls the radical change which Aeneas told Dido he noted in the dead Hector, and the third shows Dido at her most gracious and regal; the contrast gained through the reversion is striking.

78. Sinon duped the Trojans by convincing them that he had deserted the Greeks, that the Greeks had truly gone home, and that the horse, if brought inside Troy's walls, would bring a victory for the Trojans over the Greeks. As Aeneas remarks: "Through lying Sinon's craft, the story was believed, and we whom neither Tydides nor . . . Achilles nor ten years nor a thousand ships had mastered were captured by tricks and forced tears." See *Aeneid* 2.57–198.

79. Just after his quarrel with Achilles, Agamemnon, in order to test his soldiers, rather foolishly suggested that the expedition be given over and they all go home. The soldiers were only too ready to do so, but Ulysses' eloquence persuaded them to remain. See *Iliad* 2.5–210, 278–332.

80. Nestor was the oldest of the warriors who came to Troy. For his ancestry and characteristics, see *Iliad* 1.247 ff.; his speeches are generally rambling, repetitive, and full of personal reminiscences: see, for example, *Iliad* 1.253–84 and 2.336–68.

81. Cytherea (Venus) charmed Vulcan into providing weapons, including the marvelous shield, for Aeneas; *Aeneid* 8.370–406. The weapons themselves are described at 8.608–728. It is quite clear that Vulcan was seduced rather than overwhelmed by Venus' oratory.

Notice the *équivoque* on "injured" ("laesum") and Vida's sly echo of the binding of Aphrodite; Demodocus recounts the tale in *Odyssey* 8.266 ff. As he has it, Aphrodite and Ares were caught in a net, a trap set by Hephaestus to catch the adulterers. Here Aphrodite (Venus) gets her revenge on her susceptible and rather beef-witted lord by—according to Vida—trapping him in a net of words.

82. The study of the orators (see Vida's encomium on Cicero at 1.385–90 and note 47) was designed to provide the poet with the persuasive tools of the successful rhetorician: see pseudo-Cicero *Rhetorica ad Herennium* 2.1 and Quintilian 10. The care with which Quintilian emphasizes that the orator must first and foremost be a good man is an indication of how widespread was the notion that rhetoric was "amoral," concerned only with successful persuasion. This argu-

ment over rhetoric's "morality" was commonplace by the time of Plato (see the *Georgias*) and Aristotle (see Aristotle's discussion in *Rhetoric* 1.1).

Horace, too, advises that a poet know how to lead his readers' minds at will (*Ars poetica* 99–105):

> non satis est pulchra esse poemata: dulcia sunto
> et quocumque volent animum auditoris agunto.
> ut ridentibus arrident, ita flentibus adsunt
> humani vultus: si vis me flere, dolendum est
> primum ipsi tibi: tunc tua me infortunia laedent,
> Telephe vel Peleu; male si mandata loqueris
> aut dormitabo aut ridebo.

The "silent sweetness" felt by those who hear grief well told, as well as by those who hear "glad songs," frequently perplexed critics. Plato laid the pleasure to the delight felt by the appetitive nature when the passions were indulged (see *Republic* 605d–606d); Aristotle felt that its source was in the natural pleasure which all find in well-executed imitation (*Poetics* 1448b4–19), and, when the poem was a tragedy, in the specific "tragic pleasure" (*Poetics* 1453a35; see G. F. Else, *Aristotle's Poetics: The Argument* [Cambridge, Mass., 1963], *in loco*). Vida seems to imply here that the pleasure is both a psychological one, based on the artist's skillful manipulation of the reader's sensibilities, and an aesthetic one, based on the power and beauty of his language.

83. The Thracian poet is Orpheus. Vida echoes here Vergil's telling of the story of Orpheus and Eurydice: see *Georgics* 4.453–527, especially ll. 465–66.

84. For Euryalus' death at the hand of Volcens ("the Volscian"), see *Aeneid* 9.431–37.

85. It is interesting that Vida indicates not only the immodest but the gruesome too as matter likely to bring a blush "to the cheeks of the virgin chorus of the Muses." For Dido and Aeneas' tryst, see *Aeneid* 4.160–68. The bas-relief of Troilus' fate is described at *Aeneid* 1.474–78.

86. Decorum, whether involving the disposition of one's material or the language chosen to express that material, was felt to be preeminently the grace of Latin literature—with Vergil being the prime

exemplar of that excellence. Preeminence in invention, at least insofar as it involves what we should call originality of subject matter, was generally conceded to the Greeks. The dependence of even Vergil on Greek literature for material was too obvious and great to do otherwise. See Quintilian 10.1.85 for an ancient comparison between Vergil and Homer. Renaissance commentators were ready to exalt Vergil even more and to place him unequivocally above Homer. For a discussion of quattrocento Vergilianism, see Di Cesare, pp. 40–86.

87. See Horace's comment on the derivative nature of Latin literature (*Epistulae* 2.1.156–57):

> Graecia capta ferum victorem cepit et artis
> intulit agresti Latio. . . .

and his advice in *Ars poetica* 268–69:

> vos exemplaria Graeca
> nocturna versate manu, versate diurna.

Vida's remark beginning "For your glory is no whit less . . ." is significant for an understanding of Renaissance humanist literature; what was prized was not originality or uniqueness of material but the excellence with which it was handled; see note 4, pp. 148–49.

88. Manto was an Italian nymph who had the gift of prophecy; she was said to have given her name to the city of Mantua, the place of Vergil's birth (see *Aeneid* 10.198–200). The Mincio, a tributary of the Po, runs by Mantua.

89. The language of this prayer is Vergilian—the passage echoes *Georgics* 1.498–514. As I have discussed briefly above (see note 56, p. 142), Vida's closest model for the structure of his poem and its stylistic features is Vergil's *Georgics*, not, as one might suppose, Horace's *Ars poetica*. Vida is, as was Vergil, writing a "didactic" poem. The work is unusually carefully planned as to disposition of material (see Introduction, pp. xxxi ff.); the language is most frequently didactic to epic in tone; while ostensibly setting out to instruct, both Vergil's and Vida's poems are really more celebrations of their subjects than technical handbooks on a profession; both poems have a strong thread of political commentary running through them; and finally, both make use of artful digressions to make their political

point ("you would believe that the subject itself required their inclusion . . . for they aim above all at ease of development," Vida
2.213–14) and to charm and relax the reader by varying the tone
and content ("[they] spin out long passages whose wonderful sweetness [makes] weary minds eager to return again and again"). As does
each book of the *Georgics,* each book of Vida's *De arte poetica* ends
with a bravura set piece.

The relationship between the content of Vida's prayer and thren-
ody at the end of Book 2 and its "model" in the *Georgics* and *Aeneid*
(see note 90 below) is striking and significant. Critics even of Renaissance literature are too prone to think their task finished when once
they have discovered a "source" for a passage at hand, to assume
that "imitation" is somehow a mindless task. With authors of the
subtlety of Vida, however, one's task is just begun when he has
recognized the model: the writer assumes that his readers will have
the ancient text as well in mind as he. The mark of excellence is how
artfully the poet has used his source, and the meaning of the later
passage or poem may be best—and sometimes may be only—understood in relation to the earlier one.

At the end of Book 1 of the *Georgics* Vergil tells of the portents
which took place at Caesar's death and then prays that somehow
Augustus may bring peace—a Roman peace—to a war-weary world.
Despite the terrifying metaphor of a chariot careening out of control, one has a sense of the extent of Rome's power: the battles range
from the Euphrates to Germany; "Mars impius" rages over all the
world. Power is not what is lacking; what *is* needed is that firm control be exercised over that power and that it be directed for rational
and humane ends.

Vida's prayer recognizes that Rome's political power is gone; his
plea is that Rome might at least retain its *magisterium* in the arts since
its political *imperium* has been lost. Symonds cites this passage as
proof that Italy was "content to accept the primacy of culture in
exchange for its independence," but this is nonsense: as the re-
mainder of this book and another passage (Book 1.205–6) which I
have remarked upon above indicate, Vida longed ardently for the
secular power of Rome to be restored. He is not blind to circumstances, however, and seeing the reality of the situation, he laments

it. The "Augustus" in whom he and "the people of every nation" had placed their hope for political revival is dead. The *imperium* is surely gone, and just as historically *magisterium* replaced *imperium,* just as Peter's Rome replaced Augustus', so Vida prays that since cinquecento Rome has no political power, it still be left the humanist *magisterium:* "let Italy always excel in the arts and the pursuits of learning, and Rome, loveliest of all things, always teach the nations." The pathos of Vida's prayer lies in the fact that not only is the chariot out of control but the reins are not even in Rome's hands (the Turks "are making a savage grasp at the reins of the world"); that the heavens so grudged Leo to the earth that they took him hence, and in consequence there is then no "Augustus" remaining to seize the reins for Rome.

90. Vida throws the agony and peril of Italy into relief by counterposing real conditions against an ecstatic vision of what might have been. A brief notice of the de' Medici family is given in note 29, p. 135. Italian politics after the death in 1492 of Lorenzo the Magnificent became more and more chaotic. Whether one credits Lorenzo with maintaining a "balance of power" among the major Italian city-states or feels that other factors combined to produce the same result, the main states were at least in some measure of uneasy peace during most of Lorenzo's lifetime. After his death the papacy and Venice in particular intrigued with the French and the Spanish, and the French invasion under Charles VIII in late 1494 showed just how vulnerable the immensely wealthy city-states were to outside intervention. Italy was scarcely at peace thereafter; there was almost constant internal strife, punctuated by invasions by the French and Spanish. The sack of Rome by an imperial army of marauders and fanatics in 1527 climaxed the horrors of the previous years. "Discord among Italy's princes" was indeed a major cause of the ease with which the French and Hapsburgs meddled in Italian politics; one must remember that "Italy" was more a rhetorical fancy and political aspiration of the humanists than a political fact. "Italy" did not really exist except as a geographical term: Florence existed, the Papal States existed, Venice existed, Milan existed, Naples existed, but not "Italy"; the states were too bitterly competitive and hostile to unite, and they suffered the consequences.

"Italy" shared in a pan-European problem at the same time, however. The Turks under Mohammed II and Selim I had consolidated control of the East, and by 1517 when the conquest of Egypt and Syria was complete and the caliphate had been transferred to Constantinople, the Muslims had procured a solid base of power. By 1520 with the accession of Suleiman the Magnificent, the Muslims did indeed seem ready to make "a savage grasp at the reins of the world." Leo X apparently had far-reaching plans for uniting all of Europe under the papacy's banner in wiping out this threat to Christendom (see Vida's poem "Leoni X Pontifici Maximo") but he died abruptly in 1521 and his plans came to nothing (for a concise but comprehensive discussion of the Turkish threat, see Myron P. Gilmore, *The World of Humanism,* pp. 6–21).

Vida's vision here is impassioned, vivid, and detailed (cf. 2.380). Leo is called "father," both father of his country and the Holy Father. Note 89 immediately above presents in some detail the significance of Vida's "imitation" of *Georgics* 1.466–514; that passage dealt with the death of Caesar and included Vergil's prayer for Rome. The passage which Vida draws upon for the triumphal scene is *Aeneid* 8.714 ff., the description of Augustus' triumphs as depicted on Aeneas' shield. All about Augustus are scenes of disorder and carnage, but he is depicted in glory (note the strength of the disjunctive "at"):

> at Caesar, triplici invectus Romana triumpho
> moenia, dis Italis votum immortale sacrabat,
> maxima ter centum totam delubra per urbem.
> laetitia ludisque viae plausuque fremebant;
> omnibus in templis matrum chorus, omnibus arae;
> ante aras terram caesi stravere iuvenci.
> ipse sedens niveo candentis limine Phoebi
> dona recognoscit populorum aptatque superbis
> postibus; incedunt victae longo ordine gentes,
> quam variae linguis, habitu tam vestis et armis.
> hic Nomadum genus et discinctos Mulciber Afros,
> hic Lelegas Carasque sagittiferosque Gelonos
> finxerat; Euphrates ibat iam mollior undis,
> extremique hominum Morini, Rhenusque bicornis,
> indomitique Dahae, et pontem indignatus Araxes.

The parallel makes the destruction of modern Rome's hopes seem more bitter; the Augustus who might have brought control and the majesty of settled order and power is gone; the leader who might have ridden in triumph is dead, and all that remains is the chariot careening out of control.

COMMENTARY TO BOOK THREE

1. Vida here takes up the third of the poet's concerns, "elocution" (cf. note 19, p. 132, and Book 2.11–16). Book 2 has already canvassed the subjects of "invention" and "disposition"; Quintilian, too, had treated both these subjects in one section. See *Institutio oratoria* 1.Pr.22: "Quinque deinceps [libri] inventioni (nam huic et dispositio subiungitur) . . . dabuntur." Elocution involves, as we shall see, what we should call style, including diction, the choice of figurative language, and, to some extent, prosody. In the original, *indicia verborum* means "figurative expressions," particularly metaphor. See Quintilian 5.9.9: "Signum vocatur . . . σημεῖον quanquam id quidam indicium, quidam vestigium nominaverunt, per quod alia res intellegitur. . . ."

2. One should note here again the pervasive influence of the rhetorical distinction between "res" and "verba"; indeed, "elocution" is here primarily considered an art of ornamentation.

3. Quintilian in speaking of style comments (8.2.22): "Nobis prima sit virtus perspicuitas, propria verba, rectus ordo, non in longum dilata conclusio, nihil neque desit neque superfluat: ita sermo et doctis probabilis et planus imperitis erit. Haec eloquendi observatio. . . ." Cf. *ibid.* 2.3.

4. One might guess that Pindar and Aeschylus (whom he did not know directly) and certainly Persius are among the poets whom Vida would accuse of unnecessary obscurity.

5. Vida has advised the poet earlier to practice variety in his choice and disposition of material (see 2.220 ff., and note 32);

here he advises variety of "copiousness" of expression. This advice, as well as a description of the means to attain that goal without turgidity or obscurity, is central to ancient, medieval, and Renaissance rhetoric; see, for examples, Quintilian, Books 8 and 9, and the *artes* of the twelfth and thirteenth centuries which Edmond Faral edits in his *Les Artes poétiques du XIIe et du XIIIe Siècle* (Paris, 1924), particularly the sections on the "ornatus difficilis" and the "ornatus facilis" in Geoffroi de Vinsauf's *Poetria nova.* Erasmus' *De copia* is a full Renaissance discussion of how to achieve copiousness; particularly apt for understanding Vida's conduct of Book 3 is Erasmus' comment at *De copia* 2. fol. lxxiiii: "Et ubique taedium varietate, incunditate, risuque levandum. Varietas potissimum petitur a figuris, et ab eisdem incunditas." Beside the minute and exhaustive discussions of Quintilian, Geoffroi de Vinsauf, and Erasmus, it will be clear that Vida's discussion is highly selective indeed, including as it does only the chief figures.

Throughout this whole book, as in the poem at large and not simply in the famous section on imitative harmony in ll. 355–454, Vida exemplifies in practice what he is discussing. The extreme "copiousness" of language in the passage before us is startling until one realizes precisely what Vida is about.

Note the appeal to Nature again as the poets' guide: here Vida observes that the *plenum* is unique in each of its parts; if it follows Nature, the poet's creation should therefore display this quality (cf. note 72, p. 165, and note 68, p. 163). Verbally, the latter part of this section echoes Quintilian 10.2.10: "Tantam enim difficultatem habet similitudo, ut ne ipse quidem natura in hoc ita evaluerit, ut non res quae simillimae, quaeque pares maxime videantur, utique discrimine aliquo discernantur," and Vergil *Georgics* 3.242–43:

> Omne adeo genus in terris hominumque ferarumque
> et genus aequoreum pecudes pictaeque volucres. . . .

6. Vida is referring to metaphor; note that in doing so he employs personification and metaphor as well: words "vaunt themselves" and are the "garments" of things.

Almost all of the illustrations which Vida uses below are drawn from Vergil or, from time to time, another ancient author; only those which are extraordinarily interesting or lengthy will be annotated for source, since an exhaustive list would simply present a mass of citations of doubtful usefulness. Anyone wishing to search out a source which is not listed here should consult first M. N. Wetmore's *Index verborum Vergilianus* (New Haven, 1911). Note that Vida employs periphrasis in presenting each of the figures below, never actually giving them their technical names.

7. Cicero refers to this delight in *De oratore* 3.39.159: "Hoc in genere [orationis] persaepe mihi admirandum videtur quid sit quod omnes translatis et alienis magis delectentur verbis quam propriis et suis."

For discussions of metaphor which Vida parallels in many instances, see Quintilian 8.6.4–19, and Cicero *De oratore* 3.38.155–42.168.

8. Cf. Quintilian 8.6.8 for the use of metaphor to give dignity to a lowly subject:

"Quaedam etiam parum speciosa dictu per hanc explicantur:

Hoc faciunt, nimio ne luxu obtunsior usus
Sit genitali arvo et sulcos oblimet inertes."

9. I have not found a source for Vida's comment that according to report the gods speak in metaphors and that oracles were so given; perhaps he simply refers to metaphors used in the councils of the gods described in the epics, and to well-known metaphoric oracles.

Homer describes the music which Apollo and the Muses provide for the gods' enjoyment after a banquet on Olympus (*Iliad* 1.601–4), and Hesiod describes in lengthy detail how the Muses dance and sing on Olympus and inspire the poets (*Theogony* 1–115).

10. The "common ornament of speech" is metaphor. Cf. Quintilian 8.6.6 and Cicero *De oratore* 3.38.155 for much the same comment and examples as in Vida.

11. Cf. Cicero *De oratore* 3.38.155. Cicero's analogy is drawn from clothing, first used to protect men from the cold and then refined into garments of ornament and dignity.

12. In speaking of archaisms, Cicero comments that they are "more freely allowed to the license of poets than to our profession" (*De oratore* 3.38.153). Quintilian comments more fully, in passages which Vida surely has in mind: "In illo vero plurimum erroris, quod ea, quae poetis, qui et omnia ad voluptatem referunt et plurima vertere etiam ipsa metri necessitate coguntur, permissa sunt, convenire quidam etiam prosae putant" (*Institutio oratoria* 8.6.17). See, too, 10.1.28–29: "Meminerimus tamen, non per omnia poetas esse oratori sequendos nec libertate verborum, nec licentia figurarum; genus ostentationi comparatum et praeter id, quod solam petit voluptatem eamque etiam fingendo non falsa modo sed etiam quaedam incredibilia sectatur, patrocinio quoque aliquo iuvari, quod alligata ad certam pedum necessitatem non semper uti propriis possit, sed depulsa recta via necessario ad eloquendi quadam deverticula confugiat, nec mutare quaedam modo verba, sed extendere, corripere, convertere, dividere cogatur. . . ."

13. The figure here described is hyperbole; see Quintilian 8.6.67–76; Vida's examples are from *Aeneid* 5.451 (11.192) and *Aeneid* 9.106.

14. When "cursing," the poets are using the figure "exsecratio" (execration); the staccato phrases "O father!" "O my country!" etc., are examples of "exclamatio" (exclamation). Vida draws his examples from Cicero *De oratore* 3.58.217 (Cicero is citing Ennius) and Vergil *Aeneid* 2.241–42.

15. As Cicero notes (*Orator* 26.93), the rhetoricians call this figure "hypallage" and the grammarians call it "metonymy." See, too, Cicero *De oratore* 3.42.167–68 and Quintilian 8.6.23–27 for elaboration and the same examples as in Vida. Metonymy involves "the substitution of one word for another" (see Quintilian, *loc. cit.*); the substitution may obviously take numerous forms, as Vida's examples suggest, though the relationship between the word substituted and the common name must be close enough to allow immediate identification.

"Lyaeus" is a surname of Bacchus. The Achelous is a river in Greece; Vida is referring in this instance to *Georgics* 1.9: "poculaque inventis Acheloia miscuit uvis."

16. Apostrophe is meant; see Quintilian 9.2.38–39 for a length-

ier but similar treatment of the subject. Note that Vida's last sentence itself contains an apostrophe.

17. Irony is meant. See Quintilian 8.6.54 and 9.2.44–46 for his definition and examples of irony. Vida's examples are from *Aeneid* 6.523–24 and 11.384–86.

18. Vida refers to "repetitio" (see Quintilian 9.1.33 and cf. 9.3.29 ff.). The example he gives is modeled on Vergil *Eclogues* 4.58–59:

> Pan etiam, Arcadia mecum si iudice certet
> Pan etiam Arcadia dicat se iudice victum.

Ovid seems extraordinarily fond of the figure: cf. *Metamorphoses* 1.325–26, 481–82.

19. See similar warnings in *Institutio oratoria* 8.6.14–18 and Cicero *De oratore* 3.40.162–64: "Quo in genere primum fugienda est dissimilitudo . . . : Deinde videndum est ne longe simile sit ductum. . . . Nolo esse aut maius quam res postulet. . . ."

20. The phrase "lares equinos" perhaps echoes Ovid's phrase, used of a bird's building its nest: "nunc avis in ramo tecta laremque parat" (*Metamorphoses* 3.242; cf. Statius *Thebaid* 8.616–17: "sic Pandioniae repetunt ubi fida volucres/ hospitia atque larem . . . relictum . . ."). The phrase "crines magnae genitricis" I have not found elsewhere. Saintsbury has a rather amusingly intemperate defense of the latter phrase: "What has Reason to say (more than she has to say against poetic transports altogether) against the exquisite and endlessly suggestive metaphor of 'tresses of the Mighty Mother' for the grass, with its wave, and its light, and its shadow, and the outline of the everlasting hills and vales as of a sleeping body beneath it? In all these cases, and in a hundred others, we may boldly answer 'None and Nothing!' The true Reason—the Mind of the World—has not a word to say against any of these forbidden things, or in favour of any of those preferred ones."

21. The tone of this comment is a little ironic. Quintilian (*Institutio oratoria* 8.6.14) gives similar advice: "Ut modicus autem atque opportunus eius usus illustrat orationem, ita frequens et obscurat et taedio complet, continuus vero in allegorias et aenigmata exit."

Note that the proviso that the language "be worthy of the Muses" points to a well-defined conception of the various "levels" of language; for an elaboration of this conception in rhetorical theory, see Cicero *Orator* 20.69–28.99.

22. Vida's rather complicated periphrasis refers to simile. The warning he gives is an indirect slap at Homer, whose epic similes seemed to some Renaissance arbiters of decorum to go on to quite an indecent length, to take on life of their own, and to introduce irrelevant material.

Quintilian discusses simile at 5.11.22 ff. and 8.3.72 ff. (see particularly 8.3.81).

23. "Decorum" in the choice of one's language was studied in as great detail by theorists of poetry as by rhetoricians (for the latter, see Quintilian 8.1.2–24). Vida's point that verses are "differentiated by the measures to which they are suited" is twofold. As mentioned above (see note 3, p. 128), various poetic genres were traditionally written in a particular rhythm and meter— *"tragici versus,"* for example, were iambic trimeters; "epic verses" were dactylic hexameters. It follows naturally that the metrical characteristics of certain words would make them more suitable for inclusion in a basically iambic than in a basically dactylic pattern, for example. The second implication of his statement is that words are differentiated by whether or not they are of the proper dignity for certain types of "verses." Obviously, as Vida notes, some words will be suitable in a variety of poems.

24. Horace *Ars poetica* 89–98 and 231–39 makes the same point with numerous illustrative references. See, too, Quintilian 10.2.22, though his passage is in a slightly different context: "Sua cuique proposita lex, suus cuique decor est. Nam nec comoedia in cothurnos adsurgit, nec contra tragoedia socco ingreditur," and 11.1.38–39.

25. Quintilian makes a similar remark at 8.3.17: "In universum quidem optima simplicium creduntur, quae aut maxime exclamant aut sono sunt iucundissima. Et honesta quidem turpibus potiora semper nec sordidis unquam in oratione erudita locus. . . ."

Cf. Erasmus *De copia* 1.10 (fol. vii) where he is speaking of synonymies: "Tum ut demus in significatu nihil omnino discriminis esse, tamquam sunt alia [sc. verba] aliis honestiora, sublimiora, nitidiora, iucundiora, vehementiora, vocaliora, ad compositionem magis concinna. Proinde dictura delectus adhibendus, ut ex omnibus optima sumat."

26. From this point (l. 185) to approximately line 328, Vida discusses the ways in which one may profitably imitate the language and style of the ancients, just as he has discussed in Book 2 how one may profit by their excellence in invention and disposition. His advice at this point is particularly vulnerable to trivialization and attack; certainly its attitude toward the use of language in writing poetry is far removed from our own. For a full discussion of this passage, see Introduction, pp. xlii–xlix.

27. The language which the poet is to choose for the epic is to be splendid, "suited to the Muses"; the model to follow in this style is, of course, Vergil, the "one author" who "far surpass[es] all the others." Cf. Cicero's dictum on "models," which is rather closer to Vida's than is Quintilian's: "Ergo hoc sit primum in praeceptis meis, ut demonstremus, quem imitetur atque ita ut, quae maxime excellant in eo, quem imitabitur, ea diligentissime persequatur. . . . Qui autem ita faciet, ut oportet, primum vigilet necesse est in deligendo; deinde, quem probarit, in eo, quae maxime excellent, ea diligentissime persequatur" (*De oratore* 2.22.90, 92).

28. Cf. Quintilian's similar statement on the imitation of Cicero: "Quid ergo? non est satis omnia sic dicere, quomodo M. Tullius dixit? Mihi quidem satis esset, si omnia consequi possem. . . . Nam praeter id quod prudentis est, quod in quoque optimum est, si possit, suum facere, tum in tanta rei difficultate unum intuentes vix aliqua pars sequitur. Ideoque cum totum exprimere quem elegeris paene sit homini inconcessum, plurium bona ponamus ante oculos, ut aliud ex alio haereat, et quod cuique loco conveniat aptemus" (10.2.25–26).

29. Cf. Quintilian 2.5.23: "Firmis autem iudiciis iamque extra periculum positis suaserim et antiquos legere, ex quibus si assumatur solida ac virilis ingenii vis, deterso rudis saeculi squalore, tum noster hic cultus clarius enitescet. . . ."

30. Vida here, as not infrequently, echoes Lucretius; see *De rerum natura* 3.12: "omnia nos itidem depascimur aurea dicta."

31. Vida himself uses this device; see, for instance, his imitation of Vergil's *Eclogue* 4 at 3.146–47 (cited above, p. 176). In the last line of each verse, the wording and grammar are sufficiently changed so that the whole meaning is quite different, though certain phrases are identical and the whole is parallel.

32. In the constant comparisons which were made between Vergil and Homer, much is made of the way in which Vergil took over lines from Homer and improved them. Russel quotes from Macrobius' *Saturnalia* 6.1:

"Si haec societas et rerum communio poetis scriptoribusque omnibus inter se exercenda concessa est; quis fraudi Virgilio vortat, si, ad excolendum se, quaedam ab antiquioribus mutuatus fit? Cui etiam gratia habenda est, quod nonnulla ab illis in opus suum, quod aeterno mansurum est, transferendo fecit, ne omnino memoria veterum deleretur. Quos, sicut praesens aetas ostendit, non solum neglectui, verum etiam risui habere coepimus. Denique et judicio consecutus est, ut quod apud illum legerimus alienum, aut aliud esse malimus aut melius hic, quam ubi natum est, sonare miremur."

Book 5 of the *Saturnalia* is given over to a detailed comparison between the two great epic poets and includes passages which were typically juxtaposed.

33. Vida illustrates here the "borrowing" of passages for one's own use. The transferring of the gods into Latium (see *Aeneid* 1.6) parallels the poet's transfer of material from a less fortunate to a more auspicious milieu. Aside from phrasal reminiscences of *Aeneid* 3.374–75, the rest of this passage is quoted or paraphrased from various parts of *Aeneid* 4 (see ll. 361, 316, 474, 657–58, 19) and from a passage which immediately precedes the brief reappearance of Dido in Book 6 (see l. 444).

34. Vida's advice here closely echoes Quintilian's at 10.1.2, 8: "Nam neque solida atque robusta fuerit unquam eloquentia nisi multo stilo vires acceperit, et citra lectionis exemplum labor ille carens rectore fluitabit. . . . Id autem consequemur optima

180   C o m m e n t a r y   t o   B o o k   T h r e e

legendo atque audiendo; non enim solum nomina ipsa rerum cog-
noscemus hac cura, sed quod quoque loco sit aptissimum." See,
too, 10.2.1, 2.

35. See, immediately above, note 31, and ll. 437–38 (cf. *Aeneid*
11.614–15). Note Vida's *équivoque* on "alludere," both "to play
with" and "to allude to."

36. Lines 264–87 parallel discussions in Horace (*Ars poetica*
48–72) and Quintilian 1.5.71, 72. Horace is particularly apposite:

> si forte necesse est
> indiciis monstrare recentibus abdita rerum,
> fingere cinctutis non exaudita Cethegis
> continget, dabiturque licentia sumpta pudenter;
> et nova fictaque nuper habebunt verba fidem si
> Graeco fonte cadent, parce detorta. . . .
>
> (*Ars poetica* 48–53)

37. Cf. *Institutio oratoria* 1.5.58 and Erasmus *De copia* 1.7; both
stress the contribution of Greece (for which Mycenae, a city in
Argos, is here a metonymy) to Latin usage.

38. The foreign—"barbaric"—words which Vida employs to illustrate his point are "gaza" ("treasure," here translated as
"hoard"), a Persian word mediated through Greek (γά'ζα) but
common enough in classical Latin (Vida has already used it at
3.195); "esseda" ("war-wains"), a Celtic word which Vergil uses in
Georgics 3.204 ("Belgica vel molli melius feret esseda collo"); and
"sarissae" ("pikes"), a "Macedonian" word (Greek σαρίσα) used,
for example, by Ovid in *Metamorphoses* 12.466–67 ("qui clipeo gla-
dioque Macedoniaque sarisa/ conspicuus . . ."").

On foreign words, see Quintilian 1.5.55–64. Erasmus' *De copia*
10 gives two of the same examples as Vida, and several others;
Erasmus comments, "Dicam enim graece quo dicam melius."

39. In this passage "adaxit" (1527 "adassit"), "indugredi," "olli,"
"antiquai," "avorum," and "fuat" are all archaic in form.
Cf. Quintilian 1.6.39 on archaic words: "Verba a vetustate repetita non solum magnos assertores habent sed etiam adferunt ora-
tioni maiestatem aliquam non sine delectatione; nam et auctorita-
tem antiquitatis habent et, quia intermissa sunt, gratiam novitati
similem parant. Sed opus est modo, ut neque crebra sint haec

neque manifesta, quia nihil est odiosius adfectatione. . . ." See also 8.3.24–28 for a longer discussion with examples.

40. The technique is periphrasis; note that Vida presents it periphrastically. Cf. Quintilian 8.6.59–61 for further discussion of the topic.

41. Vida here alludes to compounds; Quintilian has an extended discussion of the topic at 1.5.65–70, mentioning many of the same points as Vida: that Latin allows easily composites formed of two, but not more than two, "whole Latin words" (68) and that Greek is more congenial to compounds.

The passage in Vida contains several composite words in perfectly good usage, "quadrifidis" and "tricorpora" among them, and one which Vida indicates offends his ear, "perterricrepas"; this last compound is used by Lucretius (*De rerum natura* 6.129), but comes beneath Vida's censure because it is made up of three constituent parts and is harsh-sounding; cf. Cicero's comment on the word at *Orator* 49.164.

The piling of "Pelion on Ossa, and Olympus on Pelion" refers to the hybristic act of the giants in their war with the gods; verbally, the line echoes Vergil *Georgics* 1.281–82.

42. The technique of separating the constituent parts of a word and interposing other words between them is called tmesis ("cutting"); the figure is not used in English, though it is common enough in the classical authors. Ennius has a startling example, "saxo cere comminuit brum" (for "saxo cerebrum comminuit"), but Vergilian—and general—usage is rather more graceful. See, for example, *Aeneid* 9.115–16: ". . . maria ante exurere Turno/ quam sacras dabitur pinus. . . ."

Vida himself makes repeated use of the technique; see, for example, 1.62, 64. In the passage at hand the tmesis is at l. 317, ". . . seque parare"; in the translation I attempt to reproduce some of the effect of the figure without making it seem too bizarre—hence I chose to make the tmesis on a word which seemed rather more apt for the attempt.

Shortening words by excising a particle, called "syncope," is not an uncommon figure in classical Latin. The pluperfect form of the verb is particularly amenable to being shortened for metrical reasons. Vida here follows Lucretius 3.650 in shortening the pluperfect infinitive "abstraxisse" to "abstraxe" (l. 318).

Vida's "fluentia membra" is a slightly precious image which might be rendered by "bleeding limbs," were that not so wildly baroque in this context in English; hence I chose the rather less concrete meanings of each word, since not to have done so would, I think, have betrayed more the qualities of the original.

43. Sichaeus (Sychaeus) is the name uniformly given in the *Aeneid* for Dido's husband (see *Aeneid* 1.343, 4.632, etc.). In a comment to *Aeneid* 1.343, Servius notes: "Huic coniunx Sychaeus erat[:] quotiens poeta aspera invenit nomina vel in metro non stantia, aut mutat ea aut de his aliquid mutilat. nam Sychaeus Sicarbas dictus est; Belus, Didonis pater, Methres; Carthago a cartha, ut lectum est et in historia Poenorum et in Livio . . ." (Servius, *In Vergilii carmina commentarii*, ed. George Thilo and Hermann Hagen [Leipzig, 1881], I, 121; Cook's cryptic reference to Servius on *Aeneid* 1:347 is simply a slip).

The Titans were the children of Heaven and Earth, Kronos being their leader. To Kronos and Rhea was born Zeus, who with his brothers and sisters overcame the elder gods after a terrible struggle, the *Titanomachia* (see Hesiod *Theogony* 207–10, 453–505, 617–818).

The giants were the children of Gaea (Earth) by the blood which dropped from Uranus when he was castrated by his son Kronos; they attacked the Olympians and were repulsed by the help of Heracles. Among the giants was Enceladus, who was believed to have been buried under Aetna. Apollodorus *Bibliotheca* 1.43 ff. has an account of the battle, whence the story passed into the encyclopedists.

Vida's point is that the names of the Titans, gods, and giants are euphonious and hence more pleasing in verse than would be those of barbarous tribes and nations in an epic on Rome's conquests; the latter comment is perhaps a glance at Ennius' *Annales*.

44. Vida's advice here is solid, but he is seldom given credit either for giving the precept or for following it. The primacy of matter over expression is an old *topos* in rhetorical literature:

"Rem tene," counsels Cato the Censor, "verba sequentur," and Horace echoes him (*Ars poetica* 311): "verbaque provisam rem non invita sequentur." Cicero warns, ". . . oratio, si res non subest ab oratore percepta et cognita, aut nulla sit necesse est, aut omnium irisione ludatur. Quid est enim tam furiosum, quam verborum, vel optimorum atque ornatissimorum, sonitus inanis, nulla subiecta sententia, nec scientia?" (*De oratore* 1.12.50–51). And Quintilian delivers a lengthy and warm lecture on the fact that words are ancillary to material; see 8.Pr.18–33 and 8.3.17 ff., particularly the final sentences of the former section: "Sit igitur cura elocutionis quam maxima, dum sciamus tamen nihil verborum causa esse faciendum, cum verba ipsa rerum gratia sint reperta. . . ."

45. This passage may seem to negate the previous strong injunction to make words serve matter; in fact, Vida only enters a significant exception. The wording in which he makes his comment is again suited to the sense; the diction is copious to the point of prolixity, yet without making any extravagant claims for the lines, the verse is sonorous enough. Note for instance the frequent alliteration and resonant vowels. Even the best poets, of course, do precisely what Vida is speaking of; Milton's line describing the infernal thunder "which bellow[ed] through the vast and boundless deep" is redundant enough, though no one but a fool would delete a syllable of it.

Vida's comment that "you obviously need not inquire what these words are . . ." is made in a tone of wry humor; most writers find redundancy all too hard to control. Indeed, Vida's line "Illa tibi se sponte dabunt per se obvia passim" is surely intended to provoke a laugh of recognition from both writers and readers who use and meet "fillers" all too frequently.

46. This passage, from line 355 to line 454, is the most famous in the *De arte poetica*. Boileau and Pope pay Vida the ultimate compliment of imitation, the latter rather more openly and fully than the former; see Boileau, *L'art poétique* 1.165 ff.:

> Un style si rapide, et qui court en rimant
> Marque moins trop d'esprit, que peu de jugement.
> J'aime mieux un ruisseau qui sur la molle arène

Dans un pré plein de fleurs lentement se promène,
Qu'un torrent debordé qui, d'un cours orageux,
Roule, plein de gravier, sur un terrain fangueux.

Cf. Pope, *An Essay on Criticism* 337–73, especially ll. 364 ff.:

'Tis not enough no Harshness gives Offence,
The *Sound* must seem an *Eccho* to the *Sense*.
Soft is the Strain when *Zephyr* gently blows,
And the *smooth Stream* in *smoother Numbers* flows;
But when loud Surges lash the sounding Shore,
The *hoarse, rough Verse* shou'd like the *Torrent* roar.
When *Ajax* strives, some Rocks' vast Weight to throw,
The Line too *labours,* and the Words move *slow;*
Not so, when swift *Camilla* scours the Plain,
Flies o'er the unbending corn, and skims along the Main.

(The notes to the Twickenham Edition of Pope's poems, Volume I, pp. 280–82, make the appropriate references to Vida and cite the letter in which Pope mentions his borrowings from the *De arte poetica.*)

Even Saintsbury, though he scarcely refers to this passage other than with an oblique mention of "extensive Virgilian illustration," does admit, if with some ill temper, that the poem "deserves perhaps less grudging praise for the extreme fidelity and ingenuity with which it illustrates its own doctrines."

It is generally considered that Vida is the first to illustrate his own precepts by the language in which those precepts are given and by set pieces illustrative of imitative harmony. Certainly both the ancient rhetorics and the medieval *artes* discuss imitative harmony and give examples, but Vida's elegant tour de force seems to be the first of its kind. As is often mentioned earlier in the notes (see, for example, note 70, p. 163, and note 51, p. 141), Vida frequently illustrates through the language and meter of his exposition precisely the point he is making, though—as Vida himself is aware (see *Cr.* 3.588—"intactus labor hactenus")—none had before attempted so full a presentation as he of the effects available.

The Muses are described as admitting the lad to their "inmost sanctuaries" at this point because the ability to so write that "the events you [narrate seem] not merely being described but actually [to be] taking place" (2.380), while not the most essential element of a poem, is the final test of a poet's power over words; see note 4, p. 149.

47. Like the way to eternal life, "strait is the way" to poetic excellence and "few there be that find it." The notion of the poet as polymath and initiate into mysteries which are not given to the vulgar crowd is old. Pindar, even though he insists that a poet must have natural gifts, emphasizes the mastery a poet must have over his art; Plato is convinced, on the contrary, that the poet and rhetorician of the polis of the present have no art or peculiar function (οἰκεοπραγία), and that pretensions to universal knowledge must be presumptuous and disastrous (see *Ion* and *Republic* 2, 3). The allegorizers of Homer from the sixth century B.C. onward emphasize his role as a hierophant with an encyclopedic knowledge which he perforce covered beneath charming fictions both to delight the *cognoscenti* and to keep such knowledge as lay beneath the surface of his tales from the ignorant and undeserving. Vergil, of course, was thought to contain final knowledge as to man's place and function in the universe; Fulgentius (c. 6th century) did a full allegorical interpretation of the *Aeneid* based on this conviction. Dante paid unparalleled tribute to Vergil as the guide to the highest moral perfection man can achieve through his own powers, and quattrocento humanists like Salutati constantly defended against pietistic critics such as Domenici Vergil's eminence both as teacher of moral excellence and as guide to inimitable eloquence. One must remember too that from the time of the Church Fathers there was combined with the ancient pagan formulations on the wisdom of the poets the authority of the Gospels that God the Son himself at times spoke in parables, that the impious "seeing . . . [might] see, and not perceive, and hearing . . . [might] hear and not understand" (Mark 4:12).

This whole tradition and controversy, whose complexities are barely indicated in the outline above, lies just beneath the surface of Vida's words. In the context here, Zeus was presumably unwilling that the ignorant and indolent have a gift of creation analogous to his own and speak the language of the gods (see 2.76 ff.).

48. Quintilian discusses in detail the rhetorical means by which one "imitates," or presents clearly before the auditors' or readers'

eyes whatever it is that one is describing; see *Institutio oratoria*
8.3.61 ff. Vida's techniques for imitative harmony naturally involve
metrical effects as well as vivid and apt-sounding diction. As Quintilian notes, the use of words for euphony and copiousness, quite
apart from rhythm, produces variety, and such variety has a pleasure of its own ("suo nomine solet esse iucunda," 9.4.58).

The effects which Vida attempts in the following section are superbly achieved; lines 373 and 374 present racing dactyls and
frequent alliteration on liquid consonants, and line 374 in particular
skips along almost without a pause. Lines 375 and 376 are exceedingly "heavy" and slow-paced; note the predominance of spondees
and the especially plodding character of line 376 with its four ponderous words. Lines 377 and 378 are pleasing in a rather general
way; note the emphasis which their comparative length produces for
the tetrasyllabic "egregio" and "pulcherrimus" and the graceful end
rhyme on "ore" and "honorem." Lines 379 to 381 are harsh; the
sibilants produce a constant hissing, and the rhythm of lines 379 and
381 is unattractively choppy, especially so in the latter line where it is
combined with slack-paced spondees. Even the frequent rhymes are
distasteful: the effect of the "-um" and "-um" and "-am" "-am" of
line 380 is strikingly displeasing, almost competing with Cicero's
famous "O fortunatam natam me consule Roman" in this respect.

Lines 385–93 echo the tumult of the sea with constant sibilants
and alliteration on "r," with a succession of resonant "o's" ("aequor,"
"longe," "sonant," "litore," "rauco," "scopulos," "mons," "mora,"
"montibus," "altos"), and with emphasis by position given significant
words (whether by placing them first or last in the line or just preceding or following the caesura). Certain word combinations are
superb—"sale saxa sonant" (1.388) for example; or "litore fluctus
illidunt rauco" with its liquid consonants and the onomatopoeic
"rauco"; or "refracta remurmurat," again onomatopoeic and alliterative, the like metrical characteristics of the two words echoing the
sense of the repeated "re-"; and "praeruptus aquae mons" with the
onomatopoeia of "praeruptae" and the assonance on "ae." Note, too,
the numerous dactyls in such lines as 390 and 391. Especially effective is the way the flowing dactyls "break up" on the spondee at
"praeruptus" (1.391) and the sense of conflation which the elision in
both lines 390 and 391 gives.

Lines 394 to 396 represent an obvious quieting of the tempest raised in the previous passage; the verses are full of liquids, and the total regularity of the dactyls in line 396 emphasizes order and calm restored. The repetition here is not on resonant words but on "uncta" with its lush vowel sounds. A neat touch is the way the word order of "ex alto speculatus" recapitulates the motion of Nereus' glance.

Notable in lines 397 to 401 are the reappearance of the sibilants to imitate the hissing of the fire, the onomatopoeia of "crepitante cremari," and the way the rhythm and sound of "undantis aheni" captures the heaving of the boiling liquid. In line 402 the melody of the first part of the verse breaks up on the ugly words "scabra crepido," a transition which precisely echoes the sense of the line. The skipping rhythm, pleasant alliteration, and easy liquids of lines 403–6 capture exactly the lilting tone Vida wishes, while the pleasing pomp of "domus omnipotentis Olympi," with its polysyllabic "omnipotentis" and careful procession of "m's" and "p's," brings the passage to a majestic close which supports the grandeur and spaciousness of the concept being expressed.

The "hated bird" and his song (lines 407–10) are made unpleasant through the reintroduction of frequent sibilants, through the alliteration on "c" ("contra," "carmen," "canit," "culminibus"), and through the unpleasant repetition of the plosive syllable "-bus" in "bustis" and "culminibus." Suitably little words express the need for little words in line 411, while the diction which expresses the need for large words and describes the giant in lines 412–14 is not only most often polysyllabic ("ingentesque," "ingentia," "gigantem," "immanes," "membrorum," "lacertique") but metrically ponderous as well—note, for example, the number of spondees in line 414.

The organization of this section is by now obvious; Vida chooses characteristics which he wishes to emphasize, and then illustrates the extremes of expression possible by incorporating them in contrasting passages. Lines 415–19 and 420–23 are among the most clever of the contrasting pairs. The ponderous tasks described in the former passage are emphasized by the alliterative "molimine magno," by the clever use of a caesura immediately following the words "adde moram" and "segnia," by the piling up of numerous words in one line to form a staccato chain ("adde moram, et pariter tecum quoque verba laborent"), by composing a line (419) with only four necessarily heavy and polysyllabic words, and by frequent use of spondees (note that verse 419 is a rare "spondaic" line, having a spondee at the fifth foot).

The contrasting passage is a study in frenetic activity; dactyls now predominate, and the words are almost all mono- or bisyllabic. The elision at "cava extulerit" (l.421) emphasizes the hurry; and line 422, composed wholly of tumbling dactyls which roll on in counterpoint to the staccato effect of the triple caesura, is a masterpiece of agitated haste.

Lines 424–26 and 427–31 again contrast neatly. The forward thrust of the earlier passage is produced by such devices as the elision in line 424 ("ipse etiam") and by the fact that the subject of the clauses which compose lines 425 and 426 is placed at the very end of each verse. Note, too, that the ambiguous relationship of "graviter" in line 426 discourages one from making a definite caesura (are we to read ". . . cum perculsus // graviter procumbit . . . ," or ". . . cum perculsus graviter // procumbit . . ."?); one's tendency is to minimize the presence of a caesura and read directly to the end of the line—precisely the effect Vida wishes. At line 427, with its repeated "re-s" sounds ("requies," "rebus") and numerous words, we are slowed significantly, and in the following verse the triple alliteration on the stopped "c" ("carmina . . . cursu cessare") and the plosives ("paullisper . . . videbis") almost bring us to a halt. We do finally come to a full stop syntactically and metrically at the middle of line 429 (aptly enough, after the words "in medio interrupta"). The following two lines with their frequent spondees, their quadruple alliteration on the plosive "p" ("ponti," "postquam," "posuere," "protinus"), and their *adnominatio* ("quierunt," "quiescere") shuffle toward another major caesura after "erit" (l.431) and just before the words "mediisque incoeptis." The line ends, fitly, with the words "sistere versum."

The penultimate matched pair contrast the sorts of verses suitable for describing old men and youths. In the first passage (lines 432–35) the rhyme on "telum" and "imbelle" emphasizes the paradox involved in the phrase itself, and lines 434 and 435 are sluggish with their weight of spondees. The youth, on the other hand, is heralded with resounding polysyllables ("prorumpere," "praefractaque," "quadrupedantum," "pectoribus," and "perrumpere"), explosive "p's," and frequent alliteration (besides the "p's," "deceat" and "domos," "ferum" and "funera").

Finally, the last set—a triplet this time—illustrates the style of the three "levels" of writing. The primary distinction between the two extremes is made neatly by contrasting the stark "aut premere" with the sonorous and majestic cadence and diction of "aut rerum pro majestate canendo/ tollere" (ll.441–42). The language which further delineates the "low style" is plain, with only a modest metaphor (l.444) allowed; in all, three (rather stark) lines suffice for its description (ll.442–44). The "high" or "florid" style is described in six copious and image-laden lines; we have sonorous cadences ("fluxosque, ingentesque; redundat copia laeta"), a plethora of words signifying "rich" or "abundant" ("opulentos," "divite," "fluere," "laxis," "fluxosque," "ingentesque," "redundat," "copia," "laeta," "ubere," "felici," and several more), and a resonant simile well on its way to the proportions of an epic simile. Finally, the passage describing the "middle" style does indeed "rein in" the exuberance of the earlier lines. The figures are more modest, confined to lines or half-lines (ll.452b, 453, 454), though they are more numerous than in the passage on the low style. Note, too, that this passage as a whole is between the other two in length. The exact nature of the middle style is defined by a contrast made by placing words of opposite meaning in parallel positions ("non humiles, non sublimes"), but it will be noted that the diction conveys concept as much as spatial image. A modestly presented version of an ancient *topos* of the conclusion ("sic demum portu laeti conduntur in alto") brings the whole bravura passage to a close.

In preference to constantly interrupting the reader to remind him that Vida echoes Vergil at every line in this section, I shall list here in continuous order the chief passages on which Vida draws.

One verse . . . plains (373–74): See the description of the young boxer Dares (*Aeneid* 5.430) and of Fama (*Aeneid* 4.180).

That one . . . exertion (375–76): Cf. the description of the "man-mountain" Entellus, Dares' opponent (*Aeneid* 5.431–32).

Now there follows . . . charms (377–78): See the description of Aeneas at *Aeneid* 1.561–91 and 4.149–50.

Facing it . . . ear (379–80): One may catch verbal echoes of Vergil

Eclogues 8.34, *Georgics* 1.245, and *Aeneid* 11.753; see, too, *Aeneid* 12.619.

Hence, when sailors . . . jostle together (385–93): Vida is echoing various passages of sea description in Vergil; see *Aeneid* 1.35; 1.84; 8.689–93 (cf. 5.143); *Georgics* 1.356–59; *Aeneid* 10.291; 1.105; 3.581–82. A brief textual note is in order at this point; line 387 is an exact quotation of Vergil 8.690 (5.143) and is printed here correctly. Most, though not all, editions after at least the 1536 edition of the collected works (including Cook's but not the Cominiana) read "stridentibus" for "tridentibus"; there is no reason to think this other than an unusually persistent misprint.

But when . . . smoothly (394–96): Cf. the description of Neptune calming the storm in *Aeneid* 1.124–27; *Aeneid* 8.87–91 and 4.398 are the other sources for the language of this section.

Thus . . . high (397–401): *Georgics* 2.303–11 describes a forest fire in vivid detail; for the rest of Vida's passage cf. *Georgics* 3.99 and *Aeneid* 7.74, 462–64.

A rough . . . verse (402): Such a ledge is described at *Aeneid* 10.653: "Forte ratis celsi coniuncta crepidine saxi. . . ."

But then . . . high (403–6): For a magnificent description of spring which Vida may have in mind here, see *Georgics* 2.323–45; the last clause is a quotation of *Aeneid* 10.1. Note how, in accordance with his remark at 3.257 ff., Vida has expressed a different meaning while using the same words as an ancient author.

But . . . turrets (407–10): One of the Dirae took on the form of such a bird and appeared as an omen to Turnus; see *Aeneid* 12.863–64.

Note, too . . . mighty (411–14): Vida alludes again to the description of Entellus; see *Aeneid* 5.422.

And . . . yardarms (415–19): Cook, misunderstanding a note of Russel's, suggests that "si quid geritur molimine magno" "probably refers to Od[yssey] 2.593–600"; probably it does not. Vida gives below the examples to which he wishes to refer, and although the Sisyphus anecdote is relevant, there is no evidence that Vida had it in mind.

See *Georgics* 2.399–400 and *Aeneid* 3.549 for the lines on plowing and sailing.

But if to hesitate . . . plague (420–23): At *Georgics* 3.414 ff., especially line 420, Vergil gives his advice on how to discourage snakes from lurking in stalls, and tells shepherds when and how to kill them. Amusingly enough, the command to "bring flaming brands, [and] hurl your darts" echoes Dido's raging words at *Aeneid* 4.594.

So, too . . . haste (424–26): For the "night" figure see *Aeneid* 2.250; for Entellus' slaughter of a bull with one blow, *Aeneid* 5.481 (the Entellus episode seems to have made a considerable impression on Vida; this is the third time he has quoted from it—the other instances are at ll.375 and 414—and he does so again below, l.434).

But when . . . flow (427–31): The lovely "Quumque etiam requies rebus datur" is probably patterned after *Aeneid* 2.268: "Tempus erat quo prima quies mortalibus aegris/ incipit. . . ."

Vida, of course, does not shift his medium from verse to prose, though the translation shifts briefly from prose to verse at this point; it is impossible, however, to reproduce in prose the effect of the caesuras in the original.

The phrases "quierunt . . . posuere" include reminiscences of *Aeneid* 10.103, 7.6–7, 27–28, and *Georgics* 1.356.

What language . . . body (432–35): This passage refers in the first instance to Priam, who, goaded to fury by the sight of his son Polites' death, hurled a spear at the man (Pyrrhus) who had killed him; see *Aeneid* 2.526 ff., especially line 544, which Vida quotes here. The last line of the portrait of an old man is drawn, ironically enough, from Entellus' characterization of his own condition, *Aeneid* 5.396.

But it would be . . . slaughters (436–39): Though much of this description only vaguely resembles particular lines or phrases in Vergil, two recognizable passages stand out, one from *Aeneid* 11.614–15 and another from *Aeneid* 12.383. In connection with the former passage, Vida again illustrates his pleasure (3.257 ff.) in using the same words as the ancient poets but putting them in a context which changes their meaning; cf. ll.146–47 and 406, and note 18.

There is . . . Alps (440–50): The phrase "with a rich vein" ("divite vena") echoes Horace *Ars poetica* 409–10:

> ego nec studium sine divite vena
> nec rude quid prosit video ingenium.

The simile "Hibernarum instar nivium" would seem to echo Homer's description of Odysseus' eloquence; see *Iliad* 1.249. If Vida did not get the simile from a translation into Latin of this passage itself, he might have gotten the gist of it from Quintilian 12.10.64: "sed summam expressurus [Homerus] in Ulixe facundiam et magnitudinem illi vocis et vim orationis nivibus hibernis et copia verborum atque impetu parem tribuit."

At times . . . harbor (451–54): Various phrases here echo Vergil; "undantia lora," for example, is drawn from *Aeneid* 5.146, and the line "Sic demum . . . alto" is patterned on 5.243. That Vida should use the phrase "litus arant" is rather curious, for "to till the beach" was proverbial for "to perform a useless task." Perhaps Vida gives here his evaluation of the usefulness of the "middle style" in poetry, though it must be admitted that considered spatially, the metaphor is well chosen and justifies itself without our insisting on irony.

By all accounts, citations from Vergil in this whole section themselves "assail us like the wintry snows when Jupiter . . . clothes the lofty peaks of the high-soaring Alps." One may well ask then, "What, after all, is Vida's achievement here?" His achievement on the first level, of course, may be measured by those parts of almost every line which are his own, and those more extended sections which are original with him. That they are not mere patchwork is obvious from the fact that usually one simply cannot tell, unless he knows Vergil's "alta . . . tragedia . . . tutta quanta," which words and phrases are Vergil's, which Vida's. Moreover, not only can Vida write with true Vergilian style, but he can even suggest an improvement on his original here and there; he can touch in an effective alliteration, for example (note the addition of "re-" to the phrase "fracta remurmurat" to produce the lovely "refracta remurmurat" in l.390 or the inclusion of "perculsus graviter" just before "procumbit humi bos" in l.426).

But more important than the fact that phrases or whole lines are Vida's own (see, for instance, ll.416, 427–28, 441, 449–50) is the fact that the conception itself and its superbly successful implementation are Vida's. He wishes to show how one may use the ancients' diction without making one's work seem a cento—and he has done so. He wishes to illustrate the vivid effect of imitative harmony—and the images and his music together create the clearest of impressions. For the startling fact is that this passage, read on its own terms, is poetically brilliant. True, all its verbal effects are not "original" with Vida, though some exceedingly fine ones are, but what is original with him is the "invention" of this material in Vergil for his purposes, and its magnificent disposition into the passage before us—and it is in the disposition of one's material, we remember, that poets, according to Vida, "chiefly hope to gain glory" (see 2.16 and note 4).

49. Quintilian, too, is at great pains to emphasize that one must exercise propriety in his use of figures; see 8.1.1–3.15. As he remarks pungently, "sciamus nihil oratum esse quod sit improprium" (8.3.15). Much of Books 8 and 9 describes how various figures are to be used.

50. Quintilian, drawing upon Cicero (*Orator* 20.68–28.99) and his own resources, describes the three styles concisely at *Institutio oratoria* 12.10.58 ff.

51. From this point through line 524 Vida speaks of painstaking and prolonged but responsible revision, the poet's last task and hence the last concern on which Vida must give his pupil instructions. The chief classical bases for his comments are Horace *Ars poetica* 386–90 and 438–52, and Quintilian *Institutio oratoria* 10.4; from the latter in particular, Vida draws much—the metaphor of the child, for example. Vida pointedly ignores Horace's "nonumque prematur in annum" and refuses to state precise periods to be set aside for correction.

52. Two passages of note in this paragraph echo classical sources; the phrase "vitae . . . memor brevioris" reminds one of numerous passages in Horace (see *Odes* 1.11; 2.3; and 4.7, for example) and of the proverb "Ars longa, vita brevis"; line 520 ("Perque manus, perque ora virum permitte vagari") echoes Ennius' epitaph "volito vivu' per ora hominum" (see Cicero *Disputationes Tusculanae* 15.34).

53. Cf. Vida's statement on natural ability above (2.12 ff. and note 4) and Horace's at *Ars poetica* 408–10:

> natura fieret laudabile carmen an arte
> quaesitum est: ego nec studium sine divite vena
> nec rude quid prosit video ingenium.

54. This vision in one form or another appears to be the universal dream of the pedagogue. One is not expected to take Vida's self-depreciations too seriously, however; they are rather a *topos* of modesty.

The "lustrum" (see l. 546) was a religious rite performed every five years.

55. The praise of Vergil which begins this passage modulates into a prayer. Vida first echoes Vergil's own words on his poetry ("Ascraeumque cano Romana per oppida carmen," *Georgics* 2.176), changing the line slightly to indicate the general Greek influence on Vergil's verse. Then follows quick reference to the *Eclogues* (the "Sicilian reeds" points to Theocritus, Vergil's "model"), the *Georgics* (Triptolemus was the supposed inventor of agriculture), and finally the *Aeneid*.

Vida then slips with dignity and elegance into the majestic hymn to Vergil. The modulation is made smooth by the reference to Vergil's godlike language, a suggestion then strengthened by the statement that the poets perform a rite to Vergil which the reader knows is one performed to a god in gratitude for his aid and grace (cf. Horace *Odes* 1.5). The lines of the hymn are not only magnificent poetry whose sonorous melody is both powerful and graceful, but they constitute a conceptual coda to the whole work. The poet-priest who is the author addresses Vergil in the language of invocation, recalling the diction and cadences he used earlier (at the end of Book 1) to address the god of poetry. The parallel is unmistakable and compelling; Vergil is for Vida what he was for Dante, "lo mio maestro e'l mio autore" and what Epicurus was for Lucretius (cf. ll.584–85 with *De rerum natura* 3.1–6)—and still more: Vida is audacious enough to equate Vergil with the god of poetry. Rather it is perhaps more correct to say that Vergil and the god of poetry become assimilated each to the other and that it is for this reason that Vida is not made uneasy by the tenor of his prayer.

The phrase "to you have all Latins turned, their gaze intent/ on you" (ll.570–71) recalls the observation Vida made in his lament on Leo:

> Iamque illum Europae reges, gensque omnis in unum
> Conversique oculos, conversique ora tenebant.

Now it is not *imperium* for which the Latins must look; for in their disunited state, they cannot. But they can and must, if Rome is to "always teach the nations," maintain their allegiance to the supreme artist of their culture. Vergil, or rather the religio-cultural life paradigm which he represents (Introduction, p. xxxviii), is presented then not only as the focus of the poet's aspiration but as the focus of "national" life. And as Vida contemplates the poet who has become assimilated to the God who is poet-creator, his language takes on the cadences of the litany and in Christian Neo-Platonic fashion he gives praise and contemplates, and prays that the Poet and his priests be made one.

APPENDIX
THE TEXT OF
c. 1517

INTRODUCTION

I think it important to include here what I take to be, for all practical purposes, the first version of Vida's poem which he shared with the public, the same as that which he sent to the *patres* of Cremona to be used in the schools of that city.[1] The text has never before been published; Vida never intended that it should be.[2] The edition put out at Rome in May of 1527 is considered the definitive text, and is apparently the only one whose publication Vida authorized.

Aside from these two versions, the "Cremona" and Rome edition of 1527, there is a third, discovered by Professor Di Cesare in the Harvard Library, which was published in Paris by Stephanus in July of 1527.[3] This would seem to have been an unauthorized printing. While close to the text of the Rome edition, it is obviously earlier (see below), and it is highly unlikely that Vida would authorize the publication of an earlier version of his poem after the later had already appeared.[4]

[1] See Vida's letter to the *patres,* below, pp. 212–13. I shall hereafter refer to this manuscript as "Cr."

[2] See the letter to the *patres,* p. 212.

[3] Professor Di Cesare has found copies of this text in Leiden, Rome, Venice, and the Vatican as well.

[4] Tiraboschi apparently knew nothing of the Stephanus text of 1537. He did, however, have access to the text of c. 1517; the Baron Vernazza, who owned it, lent it to Tiraboschi while the latter was preparing his *Storia della letteratura italiana.* Tiraboschi refers to it numerous times, chiefly because it contains frequent references (see below, p. 201) to figures contemporary with Vida. The reader interested in a discussion of the literary production of those whom Vida mentions is referred to Tiraboschi's monumental work.

Tiraboschi observes in passing the numerous differences between, and the relative merits of, the two versions: "one who has not seen [the early text] could not understand the diversity between it and the edition [Rome, 1537] which we possess. Not only are the verses often changed, but the order is not infrequently quite other than that which we now have; and one may clearly see in reading it that it was a work of Vida while still a young man, by him later more maturely polished and corrected" (*Storia della letteratura italiana* [Milan, 1824], tome 7, pt. 4, p. 2112).

The Vernazza codex (now lost), which Tiraboschi (*loc. cit.*) speculates is the copy sent by Vida to Cremona, is the exemplar from which (see below, pp. 210–11) the codex Venturi, which I have transcribed, was copied. Tiraboschi quotes liberally from the Vernazza codex. I have collated his citations with Venturi's text, and find a few variants. These are either nonsignificant matters of orthography, or involve readings, both good Latin and good sense, which give one no reason to choose between them. Only in one case was it clear that Venturi ought to be emended: at 2.365 Venturi reads "virtus," Tiraboschi "virtutis"; "virtutis" is needed syntactically, and I emend Venturi.

In a valuable paper delivered to the First International Congress of Neo-Latin Studies in Louvain in August of 1971 and printed in the transactions of that Congress,[5] Professor Di Cesare does a statistical analysis of the readings of the Stephanus text in relation to the earlier and later versions. His figures bear out well that on the whole the major revisions are complete by the time of the Stephanus text; while the number of differences in readings between the Stephanus and the authorized version is considerable, consecutive reading of the two texts reveals little difference in substance between them. It is clear, however, that the Stephanus antedates the authorized text: the change in the passage at 2.565 ff. from a lament on the death of Giuliano to one on the death of Leo X gives us a *terminus a quo* of 1521; the fact that the dedication of the Stephanus is still to Angelo Dovizio, as in the earlier version which I shall tentatively date 1517,[6] and the fact that the stylistic changes between Stephanus and the Rome text are without doubt improvements indicates that the version published by Stephanus is earlier than the text published by Vicentino at Rome.

If the differences between the Stephanus text and the authorized version, though significant, are not major, the case is quite different with the earliest text we possess. Professor Di Cesare's figures, which coincide with my own, are illuminating and bear rehearsing: "Of the 2507 lines in [the earliest text], more than 1000 are not at all in the [authorized version]. Only 600 of the original lines survive unchanged, though not necessarily in the same place in the poem. To put it another way: over half the lines of the [earliest] text were cut out or heavily revised; only one-quarter of the original stayed unchanged."

The effect of the revisions between the 1517 and the authorized version is to produce a poem quite recognizable as the same work, but different in its proportions. The first version is fairly dropsical: its illustrations go on to intolerable lengths, it introduces personages of marginal relevance to the poem or at least unnecessary in its economy, and moralizing passages are

---

[5] Mario A. Di Cesare, "The *Ars poetica* of Marco Girolamo Vida and the Manuscript Evidence," in *Acta Conventus Neo-Latini Lovaniensis, Proceedings of the First International Congress of Neo-Latin Studies, Louvain, 23–28 August 1971* (Louvain and Munich, 1973), pp. 207–18.

[6] The best clues to the date of the Cremona version are these:

a) It must have been written before Leo's death in 1521 (cf. 2.800–1). Indeed, if we assume that this version is that sent to Cremona, it must antedate the letter of 1520 by some time, since Vida claims (see p. 213) that he had "long since put [his] final hand to [his] work in this branch of poetry."

b) The reference to the death of Leo's brother Giuliano gives us a *terminus a quo* of 1516, at least for that section of Book 2. Note the suggestion that a tomb be built for Giuliano.

c) The elevation of Ercole Langone to the cardinalate, to which Vida refers (2.358–59), took place in 1517.

This information suggests 1517 as the earliest date for our MS.

frequent and rather heavy-handed; in short, the poem is so full as to be tiresome. And the problem grows worse as the poem proceeds: Book 1 has 653 lines; Book 2, 842; and Book 3, fully 1012.

The revisions Vida makes change the effect of the poem markedly. The pace of the authorized version is graceful and leisurely rather than ungainly. The parts of the poem are of almost equal length (the books contain 563, 603, and 592 lines respectively). Much unnecessary material has been omitted, and along with some truly lovely lines, a host of infelicitous words or passages. Where a line is altered, the change is almost invariably for the better. In a very few places, the excision of material resulted (as we shall see below) in a certain jaggedness in the Latin, but this is very infrequent indeed.

To illustrate: certain types of material are systematically dropped after the Cremona version. Almost all explicit reference to contemporary figures disappears; the sole exceptions remaining in the authorized version are the passages on the Medici at 1.192 ff. and at the end of Book 2 and the dedication (to Francis, not Angelo, in the later version). The overt references to Angelo Dovizio (*Cr.* 1.13 ff., 2.13 ff., 3.11 ff.), Ghiberti (1.383), Annibale, Ercole, Guido, and Lodovico Rangone (1.512, 2.344 ff., 2.365–66), Giraldus (1.573), Bibienna (2.19), Lipomanus (3.25 ff.), and Accolti (3.946–50) are deleted, as are certain references to the Medici themselves (2.347, 355, 356–57, 362). The revised poem, in short, is much less "occasional."

Also deleted are two passages which might titillate (cf. Vida's own precept on the maintenance of modesty at 2.525 ff.). One concerns the mating of animals (*Cr.* 3.130–35):

> Ceu ubi jam in venerem pecuaria solvere tempus
> Pastores macie tenuant armenta volentes—
> Quam semper vitare alias ante omnia tendunt—
> Tunc autem nimio ne luxu obtusior usus
> Sit genitali arvo et sulcos oblimet inertes
> Sed rapiat sitiens venerem interiusque recondat.

Another describes the near-rape of Venus (*Cr.* 3.592–620).: [7]

> Illa olim tereti spumosa per aequora concha
> Vecta ibat, bijugi mordebant aurea frena
> Delphines curvisque secabant marmora caudis,
> Lora regebat amor. Pulchram maria humida alumnam
> Excipere plausu laeto, susidere fluctus
> Undaeque iratique Euri tumidaeque procellae,

---

[7] Note that the continuation of this story (3.628 ff.) also contradicts the explanation given in the Prometheus story (*Cr.* 1.22 ff.) of the coming of poetry to men. The passage contains much fine verse, however, and it is rather a pity that it was dropped wholly.

Littora laetari. Liquidi gens squammea ponti
Undique visendi studio fluit omnibus antris
Et turpes phocae et dorso horrentia cete.
Ecce autem dictu horrendum mirabile monstrum
Prima hominis facies cui, desinit alvus in anguem,
Terribilis visu ponti fera deserit antra
Capta deae forma, subitoque fit obvia et illi
Vim parat. Exclamat dea turpi exterrita monstro
Luctaturque deosque implorat voce marinos.
Desuper aligerum frustra trepidum agmen amorum
Tendere curvatos arcus pavidaequa parenti
Auxilium levibus nequicquam ferre sagittis.
Instabat fera et hirsutis nivea ora lacertis
Oraque collaque vexabat, scelus, oscula captans.
Et vim passa foret monstro supposta Dione
Aurea deformi, socio ni ex agmine Triton
Ter spumante cava insonuisset ab aequore concha.
Audiit excitus fundo Neptunus ab imo;
Exciti affluxere dei Inousque Palaemon
Nereusque Glaucusque et Phorci exercitus omnis
Una omnes Veneri auxilio. Pater ipse tridentem
Neptunus dextra quatit exitiumque minatur
Absterretque feram et pontum deturbat in imum.

Likewise modified or dropped are two passages in which the divine furor
is made to seem mad indeed; the description in the first (*Cr.* 2.591–614) is
excessively shrill:

Unde haec tam clara repente
Tempestas? Deus, ecce Deus jam corda fatigat,
Altius insinuat venis penitusque per artus
Deditur atque faces acres sub pectore versat.
Nec se jam capit ille ardens calor asperaque intus
Vis agit attonitumque rapit mirabile vatem.
Huc atque huc furit ille animumque ad sydera tollit
Igneus exultantem animum atque exercet anhela
Oraque pectoraque et jactat jam non sua verba
Oblitusque hominem mirum sonat; haud potis ignem
Excutere invitum miratur se ira rapique
Praecipitem, te, Phoebe, vocans, te te evhoe Bacche,
Evohe Bacche, fremens; cadit ars visque illa gerit rem
Omnipotens. Non ille dapum, non ille quietis
Aut somni memor absistit noctemque diemque
Indulget cantu moraque omnis iniqua videri.
Qualis ubi quondam pastorum lusus in arvis

Subjecit stipulas caudae tedamve flagrantem
Aut canis aut vulpis, rapidis fugit ocyor Euris
Atque huc atque illuc juga per deserta, per agros
Territa quacunque illa fugit trahit inscia secum
Pestem inimicam, eadem trepidi sibi causa furoris;
Talis Phoebeus vates rapiturque furitque
Incensus plenusque Deo stimulisque subactus.

The second passage (*Cr.* 2.643–51) presses an analogy between the orgiastic rites of Cybele and poetic inspiration; it is likely that Vida latterly found it too enthusiastic and sensual:

Non aliter Phrygiae matris post acta furentes
Sacra chori postque gelidi juga Dindymi et Idae
Frondosae lucos atque avia lustravere
Timpana tundentes tenta et cava cymbala palmis
Procumbunt lassosque artus in gramine ponunt.
Interea fessi permulcent pectora alumni
Pierides gremioque fovent placidumque soporem
Artubus infundunt lapsis sparguntque salubres
Largius ambrosiae succos atque oscula jungunt.

Conversely Vida also omits in the authorized version two passages which emphasize the *ascesis* required of the poet; one (*Cf.* 1.457–68) remarks that some teachers restrict, not only food and drink, but maternal influence:

Quid procul a patria qui in extera regna relegant
Foemineis matrum illecebris blandoque favori
Subductos humilesque docent dediscere curas?

The other (*Cr.* 1.485–92) describes amusingly enough the debilitating effects of marriage and, in contrast, the freedom of the celibate:

Fortunatus at ille et diis gratissimus ipsis
Cui licuit fugisse thorum et connubia, semper
Laeta prius, mox foeta malis et plena laborum.
Fas illi longos cantando claudere soles
Liberius curis vacuo atque impendere noctem
Cunctam operi insigni studiisque intendere mentem;
Quippe Venus vires non tantum carpit et artus,
Mentem hebetat simul, egregiis contraria curis.

Finally, passages of plodding moralization likewise disappear; see for example, *Cr.* 1.270–78 on our bent to evil:

Quid dicam amisso qui dictu obscoena pudore
Obliti divum ac divini muneris ore
Immundo cecinere inhonestaque carmina vulgo

Spargentes Musis tenerum incussere ruborem?
Sancte puer, sancti si qua est cura pudoris,
Sacrilegos horum versus ne quaere doceri
Nec te discendi capiat tam dira libido.
Semper enim in pejus proni sumus et mala quae nos
A teneris olim coepere tenacius haerent.

Vida also relieves his poem of much tedious illustration of the points he is
making. The reader of the Cremona text is likely to mutter "Odysseus and
no end!" during the early lines of Book 2 (cf. 97–206). In revising for the
later version Vida cut these lines heavily: a consecutive reading of the passages in question in both the Cremona text and the authorized version will
demonstrate just how radical these excisions were. Book 3, even more than
Book 2, is pared down for the final text: illustrations and technical elabora-
tions are frequently deleted or shortened; see, for example, *Cr.* 3.139–49,
155–58, 170–80, 249–50, 273–75, 281–83, 292–98, 321–23, 338–42, 369–85,
517–26, 570–73, and 578–673. Citation here of two or three passages from the
Cremona text will underscore the inflated nature of that version. At Book
1.69–97 Vida mentions either by name or circumlocution virtually all of the
poetic genres:

Ast alii intrepidi crudelis munera Martis
Pleni animis fera bella canunt caedesque cruentas
Prostratosque duces eversasque hostibus urbes;
Nec desunt qui ficto ineant proscenia versu
Aut ausi grandi suras operire cothurno
Funera dum populo referunt indigna, parentem
Ferro obtruncantem natos epulasve nefandas
Aut humili plebis fandi de more loquuti
Et cupidos juvenes captas et amore puellas
Delususque senes. Quid qui execrantur iniqua
Temporaque et populi mores carpuntque tyrannos
Versibus inque omnes effundunt triste venenum?
An memorem dulcem Siculi pastoris avenam
Quique canunt pastorales sub tegmine fagi
Aut lites aut auditas per rura querelas?
Nec vos transierim caros qui in funere amicos
Ad tumulum ploratis inaequalesque cietis
Per numeros lacrymas, nec vos quos nocte sub atra
Non exauditos ad limina fundere questus
Immitis dominae circumque operire superbos
Floribus ac sertis et olenti gramine postes
Cogit durus amor ruptis cum nubibus imbres
Praecipitant pugnantque noti transversa frementes.
Adde illos quos perpetui non carminis orsa

Longa juvant sed enim paucis concludere gaudent
Uno multa die sub versibus argumenta.
Tum qui ruri opes quantae, qui flumina pisces
Aequorave alta natent: adeo nil jam prope inausum
Nil intentatum Ausoniae liquere sorores.

This leisurely catalogue is entirely omitted in the later version; the whole topic is there represented only by *Cr.* 1.119–27 (= authorized version 1.41–49).

Nam licet hic divos, ac diis genitos heroas
In primis doceam canere, et res dicere gestas,
Haec tamen interdum mea te praecepta juvabunet.
Seu scenam ingrediens populo spectacula praebes,
Sive elegis juvenum lacrimas, quibus igne medullas
Urit amor, seu pastorum de more querelas,
Et lites Siculi vatis modularis avena,
Sive aliud quodcumque canis, quo carmine cumque,
Numquam hinc (ne dubita) prorsum inconsultus abibis.

Similarly, at *Cr.* 3.369–85 Vida gives us examples of the sorts of proper nouns which are suited and ill-suited to verse; the list goes on and on:

Titanas minor hinc labor Enceladique tumultus
Coeumque Iapetumque Othumque ferumque Ephialtem
Et socios canere ingentem rescindere Olympum
Atque Iovem astrifera conatos pellere ab arce
Quam Gallorum acies Itala virtute subactas
Cedentum nuper Latioque iterumque ruentum
Alpibus (Ausonidum sic vos voluistis inertes
Primores scelere immani) et turbantia regna
Insubrum, Eridani gentes, Venetosque togatos.
Quandoquidem minor est libertas nomina vana
Fingere, vera autem oderunt plerumque Camoenae;
Tunc vero si falsa tibi inducenda, Pelasgum
Aut aliquem referant aut non indicta profare;
Insolita oderunt aures nec nomina agrestum
Pastorumve indigna placent. Quid enim Ciceriscus
Faburnusque mihi cantet quae Mopsus et ipse
Tityrus aut Damon quondam cantare solebant?

In the authorized version (3.320–28) this list is much more economical:

Iccirco siquando ducum referenda, virumque
Nomina dura nimis dictu, atque asperrima culta,
Illa aliqui, nunc addentes, nunc inde putantes
Pauca minutatim, levant, ac mollia reddunt,
Sichæumque vocant mutata parte Sicarbam.

> Hinc mihi Titanum pugnas, et saeva gigantum
> Bella magis libeat canere, Enceladique tumultus,
> Quam populos Itala quondam virtute subactos,
> Atque triumphatas diverso a litore gentes.

Just before he begins the famous passage on imitative harmony in Book 3, Vida invokes the Muses. In the Cremona version it goes thus:

> Sit mihi fas, divae, vestros nunc prodere cantus
> Tam varios quales suspensis auribus haurio
> Admirans vestraeque loqui discriminia vocis
> Arcanos numeros tacitasque in carmine leges.
> Illa quidem divina animis illapsa voluptas
> Oblectat varie sensus, sed pandere verbis
> Difficile; intactus labor hactenus. Hic mihi, divae,
> Este bonae. Favet ipsa altro dea mater amorum,
> Alma Venus, perquam (nisi vana est fama) repertum est
> Quodcumque humanas aures dulcedine tangit.
>
> (3.582–91)

The invocation then modulates into the long passage on the near-rape of Venus before going on to present examples of imitative harmony. The authorized version (3.355–57) is much simpler; the invocation has been modified into the assurance of the Muses' favor:

> Huc ades. his penitus tibi totum Helicona recludam
> Te Musae, puer, hic faciles penetralibus imis
> Admittunt, sacrisque adytis invitat Apollo.

The passage concerning the attack on Venus is wholly deleted as we noted, and the imitative harmony section, while remaining lush, is much more economical and coherent.

The effect of all these deletions is to make the final version by and large both more sober than the earlier text and more graceful. Certain of the passages had at any rate only an episodic, or local, interest—the Venus passage, for example—while others simply represent in an early and overwrought form what Vida handles in a much more controlled fashion in the later text. With the exception of certain lines in the Venus passage, none of these deletions is likely to arouse regret.

The benefits Vida gains by his greater concision in the authorized version are increased by the added grace of individual lines and whole passages. Let a comparison of *Cr.* 1.325 ff. with 1.257 ff. of the authorized version stand for the literally hundreds of such instances one could adduce to illustrate this observation. The 1517 text reads:

> Ecce furens animis multa increpat ille minacique
> Insurgens nimium pavitantem territat ore,

Horrendum, et dextram loris immanibus armat
Terribilem poenisque iras crudelibus explet.
At puer implorare Deos carosque parentes,
Ah frustra, miseroque locum clamore replebat,
Donec fessam animam moriens post verbera liquit.
Heu nimium miserande puer, tua fata sorores
Flerunt Castaliae, flerunt Libetrides undae;
Te pater Eridanus, toto te Serius amne
Seriadesque nigro velatae tempora moro
Et turres te per noctem patriae ulularunt.

The authorized version is significantly altered:

Ecce furens animis multa increpat ille, minisque
Insurgens, saevo pavitantem territat ore
Horrendum, et loris dextram crudelibus armat.
Quo subito terrore puer miserabilis acri
Corripitur morbo. Parvo is post tempore vitam
Crescentem blanda cæli sub luce reliquit.
Illum populifer Padus, illum Serius imis
Seriadesque diu Nymphae flevere sub undis.

Note, first, that the Cremona version is twelve lines long, the authorized
eight. The lines omitted, it will be observed (*Cr.* 328, 332, 333, 336), are all
either repetitive or a little overdone (the "wailing towers" of 336 is a particularly inept phrase). The story is made less melodramatic by the rewriting of
Cr. 329–31; in the revised version the student dies, not under the whips, but
later, as a result of the terror and the shock he received. The alterations in
lines 325–26 make for easier reading, and get rid of the colorless "nimium"
in favor of the more expressive "saevo." "Loris crudelibus" (l. 259 of the authorized version) is clearly more apt than the "loris immanibus" of *Cr.* 327.
The music of lines 263 and 264 of the authorized version is at least as great
as that of the Cremona version, lines 332–36; the repetition of the "illum" in
line 263 and the rhyming "imis" and "undis" are particularly effective. And
most importantly, the whole effect is not overdone.

But not only are whole passages modified; they may be transposed as well.
For example, in the Cremona text the story of Prometheus occurs at the
very beginning of Book 1. In the authorized version it is shifted to the end
of the book where it provides a splendid introduction to the praise of the
god of poetry, which, as we have seen (pp. 146 f.), is so important to the meaning of the poem as a whole. Another artful transposition is the removal of
Cr. 3.416–62 (the description of the struggle to achieve an apt and ornate
verse) to a place in the authorized version (1.424–58) where it is used more
appropriately to describe the throes of the fledgling poet.

At times, as suggested above, the excision of lines results in a certain

jaggedness in the style or progression of the authorized version. In the
Cremona text at 1.270 ff. Vida moralizes on the need for boys to abstain
from prurient literature. A general reflection on the human bent to sin
(cited above, p. 204) leads at this point rather naturally into a warning to
parents to choose the boys' tutors carefully. The analogous passage in the
authorized version has no such moralizing passage, but goes directly from
advice that a boy read only the Augustans at first (for stylistic reasons) to the
warning to the parents on the matter of the tutor. The transition is rather
harsh (see the authorized version, 1.207–20).

Similarly, 2.20–25 in the final text seems rather peculiar, particularly the
seeming contradiction of line 22 ("Quos ores autem non magni denique
refert") by lines 24–25 ("Iovis neque enim nisi rite vocato/ Numine fas quicquam ordiri mortalibus altum"), until one examines the early form of the
passage and sees that Vida originally intended quite another point and revised with minimal thoroughness. The two passages follow:

> dehinc coelestia divum
> Auxilia implorant propriis haud viribus ausi
> Fidere. Contra alii prius atque ante omnia versi
> Supplicibus dictis ad coelum in vota secundas
> Musasque Phoebumque vocant hilaremque Lyaeum;
> Post subito quae mente agitant dicenda recludunt
> Aut utrumque simul. Nec magni denique refers
> Fiat utrum prius, auspiciis modo cuncta deorum
> Aggrediare: Iovis siquidem nisi rite vocato
> Numine nil fas est ordiri.
>
> (*Cr.* 2.24–33)

> simul cælestia Divum
> Auxilia implorant, propriis nil viribus ausi.
> Quos ores autem non magni denique refert,
> Dum memor auspiciis cujsquam cuncta Deorum
> Aggrediare. Jovis neque enim nisi rite vocato
> Numine fas quicquam ordiri mortalibus altum.
>
> (authorized version, 2.20–25)

Note in particular the different function of the "Nec ["non" 1527] magni
denique refers ["refert" 1527]" in the two passages.

Odd, too, is the syntax of 2.575–80 in the authorized version (the estimate
of Leo's importance and Giulio's importance to him):

> Iam tum ille [Leo] egregias curas accinxerat ardens
> Pro patriae decore, pro libertate sepulta
> Antiquae Ausoniae germano fretus Iulo,
> Quicum partitus curarum ingentia semper

Pondera, commissas rerum tractabat habenas
Idem regnatorque hominum, divumque sacerdos.

But one can understand how Vida came to write such a strained syntactic
structure if one sees that Vida is revising (minimally again) *Cr.* 2.798–802:

Iam tum ille [Julianus] insignes curas accinxerat ardens
Pro patriae decore, pro libertate sepulta
Antiquae Ausoniae, germani [Leonis] fretus amore,
Germani, qui nunc immenso praesidet orbi
Idem regnatorque hominum divumque sacerdos.

As is quite clear, the whole difficulty of the "Qui cum" clause (ll. 578–80 in
the 1527 version) is a result of the change of the reference of the "ille" in
line 575 (*Cr.* 798) from Giuliano to Leo.

It remains to note two or three passages which were added between the
time of the Cremona and the authorized versions to see if we may not observe further something of the development of Vida's attitudes and interests
during the period of revision. Quite in keeping, for example, with the dele-
tion we noted above of passages which might titillate is Vida's addition of a
pious reminder (in Lucretian language) of the true nature of the "gods" as
over against the poets' representation of them; see 2.351–52: "Quum secura
tamen penitus natura deorum/ Degat, et aspectu nostro summota quiescat."

On the matter of poetic practice, Vida apparently came under continued
attack during this period for his "borrowings" from the ancients. His rather
sharp self-defense is unique to the authorized version; see 3.259 ff.:

Nec mea tam sapiens per se se prodita quisquam
Furta redarguerit, quae mox manifesta probabunt
Et nati natorum, et qui nascentur ab illis.

He adds to these lines ones which occur in a slightly different form at
2.761–62 of the Cremona version:

Tantum absit poetae metuens infamis ut ipse
Furta velim tegere atque meas celare rapinas.

But by far the most telling additions have to do with two passages of the
highest significance for appreciating Vida's purpose in the final version: the
evaluative history of poetry in Book 1 and the exploration at the end of
Book 2 of Italy's place in world culture and politics. The history of poetry
contained in Book 1 of both the Cremona and the authorized versions is
capped in the authorized text as it is not in the earlier version with a fine
praise of the Medici for instituting a resurgence in culture through their liberal patronage (see 1.192 ff. of the 1527 poem). This pride and hope in
"Italy's" cultural resurgence is to be seen in the context of the praise of and
prayer for Rome which Vida adds (at 2.555 ff.) in his later text. The caustic

comment of *Cr.* 2.781 ff. on the relationship between the political cowardice of Italian rulers and the poor verse being written is changed to a reminiscence of Italy's great past and a pathetic prayer for continuing preeminence in culture. In the authorized version, too, the references to the "barbarus hostis" who threatens Italy are much more precise (see 2.591 ff.). Finally, the effect of the very end of Book 2 is more bitter in the authorized than in the Cremona version: whereas in the earlier text there was the healing suggestion of building a tomb for Giuliano, the 1527 version ends with the bleak line, "Egregius moriens heros secum omnia vertit." In short, the authorized version emphasizes much more than the 1517 text the loss of political power and hope because of the death of the great Medici "hero" and refers with greater insistence to what is left—the cultural resurgence and the *magisterium* which is Italy's heritage from the past, the Medici gift to the present age, and Italy's only hope for the future. This reinforcement of emphases already present in the Cremona text is of the first importance for a proper understanding of the final poem (see Introduction, pp. xxxvii–xli).

Of such nature, then, are the revisions which Vida so painstakingly made in his text between the 1517 version and the version which he authorized to be published in 1527. It remains now to consider briefly the transmission of Vida's early text. Our present knowledge of the 1517 version of the poem derives solely from the Codex Venturi, which is a copy made in 1819 from Vida's manuscript (known as the Codex Vernazza, from its owner in the mid-eighteenth century, Giuseppe Vernazza, Baron of Freney). We know nothing of the transmission of Codex Vernazza from Vida's own time to the 1770s. Di Cesare's description of the nature and fate of the Venturi manuscript, which, through the help of the omnipresent Kristeller and others, he finally located, is interesting and useful:

"In December 1818 Giovanni Battista Venturi borrowed [Vida's] manuscript from the Baron Vernazza and made a copy of it, for use on a projected quarto volume to supplement the Cominiana edition. Unfortunately, Venturi did not succeed in publishing the volume before his death a few years later. In 1922, the copy which Venturi made of the Codex Vernazza, along with his other papers, was deposited in the Biblioteca Municipale de Reggio nell'Emilia (Ms. Regg. A. 46). I located this copy after long and frustrating searches, with the help and cooperation of Paul Kristeller and Dottore Bruno Fava, director of the library.

"The Codex Venturi consists of 42 folios (the last one blank) 31 x 21 cm. Folios 1–16 are in Venturi's own hand; ff. 17–41, in the hand of an amanuensis. Folio 16r is blank; f. 16v contains 36 lines in Venturi's hand: 'Versus ab amanuensi meo omissi, atque inserendi in pagina sequenti ad locum X (Venturi).' The lines in question are Codex II.357–392. Though highly reliable, the manuscript has at least a few flaws. In the second half, particularly, there are dubious renderings of some words; apart from these, there are two substantial copyist errors corrected by Venturi: on f. 19, where the copyist garbled the text of Codex II.496 f., omitting most of 496 and the first word of 497, and on f. 20, Codex II.576–577.

"The Codex Vernazza, from which the Venturi Codex was copied, was destroyed by fire in 1904. One other copy of the Codex is known to have been made; Francesco Novati copied the manuscript and made notes on it around 1900, but this copy has not been found, though his notes based on it are among his papers."

I have transcribed the Codex Venturi from a photocopy of the codex lent me by Professor Di Cesare, and have given the text modern punctuation in lieu of the troublesomely misleading punctuation it had. I have otherwise left the text, which is both readable and accurate, much as I found it, with the exception of one or two regularizations of spelling which I have done silently. I was finally able to solve most of the textual problems to which Di Cesare makes reference above, though his description of the manuscript is otherwise accurate; three places only seemed to demand emendation. At line 139 of Book 2 the text clearly reads "Eccinuet"; neither I nor colleagues at the University of Michigan and elsewhere could make sense of this, and I emend, without much conviction, to the "Evadat" of the authorized version. The second difficulty was more straightforward: line 162 of Book 1 was metrically defective; it seems clear that the "fors" contained in the other texts was inadvertently omitted, and I restore it. For the third, see p. 199, note 4.

The letter which immediately precedes the text of the poem is my translation of Vida's letter to the *patres* of Cremona as that letter appears in the Cominiana edition of Vida's works.

Note: On pp. 283 ff. the reader will find a listing of passages peculiar to each text and common to both. One interested in a fuller comparison of the two versions is invited to make use of it.

As will be observed, the third book is the most heavily revised. Not only is much material excised (e.g., *Cr.* 3.577–745) or transferred in large blocks (e.g., *Cr.* 3.416–62); a large number of individual lines or half-lines are deleted or shifted about. The final version of that book in particular is strikingly more compact and coherent than the Cremona version, with tedious elaboration and inelegant repetition deleted.

One final observation: Vida inserted in the later version a passage (*A.V.* 2.315 ff.) assuring the reader that poetic fiction is not "lie." The tack is that taken by Sidney later: the poet "nothing lieth for he nothing affirmeth." Of like import is Vida's revision of a line (*Cr.* 2.748) in which he might have seemed cavalier about the importance of telling the truth. Perhaps he was replying to pietistic objections? Whatever the specific situation, the revisions coincide with the greater attention to orthodox piety noted above (pp. 201–2, 209) as characteristic of the 1527 version.

VIDA'S LETTER

OF 1520 TO

THE *PATRES* OF CREMONA

M. Hieronymus Vida sends greeting to the Senate of the People, and to the Populace of Cremona:

If you and your children are in health, I am pleased; I myself am so. I have never, most noble Fathers, felt that I have gained richer reward for my studies than I have just now received from the letter which you have sent to me publicly, requesting by the authority you bear that I might forward to you my books in hexameters on the art of poetry, so that by reading them your children might either become more learned or, encouraged by the example of one from their own city, be the more enflamed to take up these studies.

Though I had long since put my final hand to my work in this branch of poetry, I had determined—following what I myself consider was the best advice—not to publish it yet, for I know how perilous it is to write on a topic so various, difficult, and demanding, particularly in these times, when a multitude of brilliantly talented men, encouraged by the liberality of the Pontifex Maximus, Leo X, have emerged and are emerging to notice every day. Indeed the arts, which were long ago brought to ruin by the destructive power of time, seem to me to be somehow coming to life again under his auspices. But what would I dare deny to you, or to my homeland, the object of my earliest memories? I prefer that others think me rash and inept than that you should think me ungrateful and obstinate.

I entrust these books to you with this stipulation, however: that wherever they are kept while in your possession—whether in a public place or private—the location be one to which our citizens alone have access. For if the books should happen to be stolen and fall into the hands of foreigners, venal men, encouraged by the avarice of booksellers, might publish them without my consent—and nothing more damaging, heaven knows, could happen to me than this.

Let no one suppose that I am trying to gain from this any glory or the trifling praise of the crowd; I shall be satisfied if I learn that the youth of our city have derived some small benefit from what I have written. But these books will not, I think, be wholly useless, for aside from the fact that the subject is therein developed as fully as may be, our youth are also made more cautious in the matter of the authors whom they are to read, since we point out to them those whom they should study assiduously, and whom avoid, lest they happen to learn such literary habits as they will later have to spend an equal effort unlearning. Indeed, if only they do not fail to exercise that self-discipline which is the first necessity in all arts and studies, they will shortly master all those things which I, who was dedicated to these studies from my childhood on, barely achieved with the labor and vigils of many years. They will realize, too, how much ornament and light Virgil conferred on this art through his preeminent genius; indeed, of all poets (and I am speaking not of our Latin authors only, but of the Greeks as well) I consider him easily the first. For, most noble Fathers, each time I read his divine poem I am struck by the idea that this preeminent poet was not simply writing history, but wished quite beyond this to give instructions on the poetic art itself, doing so to demonstrate how much the Greeks, from whom we received this study, were wanting, and to show that whatever might be claimed for all other nations in this pursuit, our poets, for their part, always transformed and improved what they received from others.

One further point: you will perhaps find a certain number of passages in our poem comparatively obscure, since we have dealt in a complex and subtle way with many subjects which youths are incapable of understanding without some commentary. But there will be tutors to fill this need, for our city above all others is most rich in masters superlatively learned in both Greek and Latin.

Farewell. *Rome, February 7, 1520.*

M. HIERONIMI VIDAE

POETICORUM LIBER PRIMUS

AD ANGELUM DIVITIUM.

Sit mihi fas vatum sanctos recludere fontes
Et sacra Pieridum vulgare arcana per orbem,
Nam juvenem egregium teneris educere ab annis
Heroum qui facta canat laudesve deorum
Mente agito sacrique in vertice sistere montis. 5
Huc si saepe tuos casti libavimus amnes,
Phoebe pater, vosque o vatum praesentia semper
Numina ferte pedem, Musae; mihi munera vestra
In manibus, vestri mihi rite novantur honores.
Ecquis erit juvenis igitur qui plebe relicta . 10
Sub pedibus pulchrae accensus virtutis amore
Ausit inaccessae mecum se credere rupi?
Ante alios mihi te comitem subjungere crevi,
Angele, Divitiae decus et spes altera gentis
Post patruum praestans quem tollit ad aethera virtus; 15
Ante alios te Pierides, te pulcher Apollo
Atque Helicon atque antra vocant Cyrrhaea, voluptas
Solis nota piis; te verae praemia laudis
Indubitata manent, puer, et pulcherrima merces;
Laetus adi et dulci jam nunc assuesce labori. 20
Dona deum Musae; vulgus procul esto malignum.
Has coelo magni natas Iovis attulit olim
Callidus in terras insigni fraude Prometheus
Cum liquidos etiam mortalibus addidit ignes.
Quippe rudes hominum mentes et pectora dura 25
Ipse sagax animi miseratus, ubi astra per aurea
Ire datum ac superum mensis accumbere divum
Miratus sonitum circumvolventis Olimpi
Ingentem magnique argutos aetheris orbes
Quos sua quemque cient certo discrimine Musae, 30
Continuo utilius ratus est mortalibus addi
Post ignem nil posse animumque ad callida movit
Furta vigil. Dii mox coelestia dona volentes
Concessere, doni licet audentissimus ipse
Autor Caucaseo diras det vertice poenas. 35

Atque ideo multo nisi post hinc tempore inertes
Haud ausi dias homines accedere Musas.
Sed ventura prius pandebant carmine divi
Coelicolae dubiisque dabant oracula rebus:
Ipse pater divum Dodonam carmine primus   40
Et Libyes lucos sacravit, Phocidis antro
Insonuit Themis alma, suos Thymbreus Apollo
Responsis monuit Delphos, nec defuit olim
Antiquis Faunus caneret qui fata Latinis.
Tum Solymum prisci vates, tum sacra Sibyllae   45
Nomina sublimes coeli in penetralia mentes
Arripuere deumque animis hausere furentes.
Paulatim tum deinde homines lucem addere rebus
Versibus atque novos invenit Graecia cultus
Atque pios castas docuit sibi nectere lauros.   50
Principio ne te fugiat genus esse canendi
Haud unum, quamvis fuerint ad sacra reperti
In primis olim versus laudesque deorum
Dicendas, ne relligio contempta jaceret;
Sed res diversis divisae versibus omnes   55
Carminibus, neque enim dici omnibus omnia dignum est.
Apta sed invenit solers industria rebus
Carmina cuique suum et numeros et tempora certa
Praescripsit, quippe ingeniis non omnibus aequa est
Conditio mentesque movet non una libido.   60
Sunt quibus est cordi semper sacra dicere versu
Divinasque Deum laudes natosque Deorum
Heroas magnos ad sydera tollere cantu;
Hi vero rerum naturam pandere adorti
Scrutari immensum gaudent ab origine mundum   65
Et causas rerum haud dubia ratione requirunt
Tollentesque aciem divum super aurea templa
Sydera dinumerant picto fulgentia coelo;
Ast alii intrepidi crudelis munera Martis
Pleni animis fera bella canunt caedesque cruentas   70
Prostratosque duces eversasque hostibus urbes;
Nec desunt qui ficto ineant proscenia versu
Aut ausi grandi suras operire cothurno
Funera dum populo referunt indigna, parentem
Ferro obtruncantem natos epulasve nefandas   75
Aut humili plebis fandi de more loquuti
Et cupidos juvenes captas et amore puellas
Delususque senes. Quid qui execrantur iniqua
Temporaque et populi mores carpuntque tyrannos

Versibus inque omnes effundunt triste venenum? 80
An memorem dulcem Siculi pastoris avenam
Quique canunt pastorales sub tegmine fagi
Aut lites aut auditas per rura querelas?
Nec vos transierim caros qui in funere amicos
Ad tumulum ploratis inaequalesque cietis 85
Per numeros lacrymas, nec vos quos nocte sub atra
Non exauditos ad limina fundere questus
Immitis dominae circumque operire superbos
Floribus ac sertis et olenti gramine postes
Cogit durus amor ruptis cum nubibus imbres 90
Praecipitant pugnantque noti transversa frementes.
Adde illos quos perpetui non carminis orsa
Longa juvant sed enim paucis concludere gaudent
Uno multa die sub versibus argumenta.
Tum qui ruri opes quantae, qui flumina pisces 95
Aequorave alta natent: adeo nil jam prope inausum
Nil intentatum Ausoniae liquere sorores.
Sed nullum tamen ex numero praestantius omni
Unde queat major sperari gloria carmen
Quam quo Smyrna tuus Teucrorum funera vates 100
Aut Danaum varios casus canit atque labores
Fatidici Phoebi et sacrae venerabile donum
Phoemonoes quae prima dedit, si vera minores
Accipimus, tali responsum carmine Grajis.
Ipse equidem fandi mihi si foret ulla facultas 105
Hoc uno heroum canerem facta inclita versu.
Tu vero ipse tuas vires metitor et aptum
Semper onus impone humeris ne pondere victus
Haud aequo in medio succumbas forte labore.
Nam licet hic divos et diis genitos heroas 110
In primis doceam canere et res dicere gestas,
Fors tamen interea labor hic te multa juvabit
Seu scaenam ingrederis fictoque est carmine agendum
Seu juvenum lacrymas durus quibus igne medullas
Urit amor seu pastorum de more querelas 115
Sive aliud quodcumque canis, quo carmine cumque,
Nunquam hinc (ne dubita) prorsum inconsultus abibis.
Atque ideo quodcumque audes quodcumque paratus
Aggrederis, tibi sit placitum atque arriserit ultro
Ante animo; nec jussa canas nisi forte coactus 120
Magnorum imperio regum, si quis tamen usquam est
Primores inter nostros qui talia curet.
Omnia sponte sua quae nos elegimus ipsi

Proveniunt, multo assequimur vix jussa labore,
Libertas adeo in rebus valet illa legendis.   125
Sed neque quamprimum tibi menti inopina cupido
Aut repens calor inciderit subito aggrediendum
Magnum opus; adde moram tecumque impensius usque
Consule quicquid id est partesque expende per omnes
Mente diu versans donec nova cura senescat.   130
Ante etiam quam vela voces et coerula verras
Incumbasque operi incipiens, tibi digna supellex
Verborum rerumque paranda est proque videnda
Multa prius quorum proprius vatum indiget usus;
Illis tempus erit mox cum laetabere partis.   135
Saepe ultro dum forte etiam nil tale putamus
In mentem quaedam veniunt quae, forsitan ultra
Si semel exciderint, numquam revocata redibunt
Sponte sua et studio frustra expectabis inani.
Nec mihi non placeant qui fundamenta laborum   140
Cum jaciunt veterum explorant opera inclyta vatum
Atque hinc atque illinc passim praesentia cogunt
Auxilia intentique aciem per cuncta volutant.
Quin etiam effigiem rudibus numerisque solutis
Totiusque operis simulacrum fingere primum   145
Proderit atque omnes ex ordine nectere partis
Et seriem rerum et certos praescribere fines
Per quos tuta regens vestigia tendere pergas.
Iamque hic tempus erat dare vela vocantibus Euris
Et tibi jam primos ostendere carminis orsus   150
Condendique operis sit qualibus ingrediendum
Scilicet auspiciis vatumque recludere leges.
At prius aetati tenerae quae cura colendae
Dicendum, quantus puero labor impendendus;
Nulli etenim dabitur viridem sibi nectere laurum   155
Aonios teneris nisi fontes norit ab annis.
Postquam igitur primas fandi puer hauserit artes,
Iam tunc incipiat sanctos invisere fontes.
Ille autem tenerum qui primis artibus ante
Imbuit atque notas docuit legesque loquendi   160
Quam vellem vocis non insyncerus et oris
Contigerit, fandi ne [fors] puer atque nefandi
Nescius imbiberit male gratae semina linguae,
Quae post infectis animis radicitus olim
Haud facili poterunt evelli impressa labore.   165
Ne mihi ne quaeso quisquam persuadeat unquam
Ut placeant qui, se dum tentant numine levo

Tollere humo, veterum spernunt monimenta virorum
Inclyta et insolito penitus de more loquendi
Obscuras gaudent in vulgum spargere voces   170
Irrisi, diram illuviem, atque immania monstra,
Argolica enixi non aequo foedere nostris
Iungere verba, novas adeo juvat edere voces.
Non minus a recta mentis ratione feruntur
Decepti quam qui liquidi cum pocula fontes   175
Sufficiant malunt limosam haurire paludem.
Ne mihi ne tenerae talis se admoverit auri,
Sed procul o procul ista ferat placitura Britannis
Aut si qua est usquam gens toto obtusior orbe.
Iamque igitur mea cura puer penetralia vatum   180
Ingrediatur et Aonia se proluat unda,
Iamque sacrum teneris vatem veneretur ab annis
Matre satum Musa ad liquidi vada coerula Minci,
Atque olim similem poscat sibi numina versum
Admirans artem, admirans praeclara reperta,   185
Quem sese ore ferat, quam dulci carmine, quanto
Numine magnanimos Latiis Phrygas advehit oris.
Iamque favet puero Ascanio tactusque dolore
Aequales legit impubes quos impius hausit
Ante diem Mavors et acerbo funere mersit;   190
Multa super Lauso, super et Pallante perempto
Multa haeret dolor illachrymans raptumque parenti
Cum miserae videt Euryalum pulchrosque per artus
Purpureum leto dum volvitur ire cruorem.
Nec tamen interea Graii moremque loquendi   195
Et varias fandi facies divina reperta
Deficient; magno Aeneae jam conferet igneis
Aeacidem flagrantem animis variosve legentem
Dulichium deserta ducem per inhospita casus.
Huc venerande puer, spes o certissima vatum,   200
Huc geminas nunc adde aures, huc dirige mentem.
Nam quia non paucos parte ex utraque magistros
Nostrosque Grajosque tibi se offerre videbis,
Quos hic evites, quibus idem fidere tutus
Evaleas referam ne quis te fallere possit.   205
Nec multus labor est Grajos tibi dicere vates:
Hos inter potitur sceptris insignis Homerus
Cujus quanto alius sancto mage distat ab aevo
Abjunctus tanto ille minor plerumque; adeo usque
Degenerant Danai magis ac magis, alta parentum   210
Mentibus obliti prorsus decora illa suorum.

Iamque adeo Inachiae praestans ea gloria linguae
Subsedit, paulatim ipsi quoque donec avitis
Sunt pulsi reges soliis civesque coacti
Diversa exilia atque alienas quaerere sedes.   215
Huc illuc inopes errant, habet omnia victor
Barbarus et versis nunc luget Graecia fatis.
Nostri autem ut sanctum divas Helicona colentes
Ceperunt primum in Latium transferre, fluebant
Versu incomposito informes atque artis Pelasgae   220
Vix memores musa fundebant carmina agresti
Sylvicolas inter Faunos; tunc omne sonabat
Arbustum fremitu silvai frondosai.
Arma aciesque rudi nondum pater Ennius ore
Tentarat, Grajo qui mox de vertice primus   225
Est ausus viridem in Latio sibi poscere laurum.
Tum rerum causas naturae arcana latentis
Explorare ausi, paulatim inducere versus
Coeperunt nitidi formam nostrique poetae
Agrestem exuerunt animum liquidissima donec   230
Coeli tempestas velut post nubila et imbres
Extulit os sacrum summi certissima Olympi
Progenies Maro, qui veterum squalore situque
Deterso in melius mira omnia rettulit arte
Vocem animumque Deo similis (date lilia plenis   235
Naiades calathis). Praestanti hic gentis Acheae
Ingenio vates longe superavit et omnes
Restinxit stellas exortus uti auricomus Sol.
Nil adeo mortale sonat; stupet ipsa pavetque
Quamvis Ascraeos miretur Graecia cultus.   240
Haud alio Latium se tantum tempore jactat:
Tunc linguae Ausoniae potuit quae maxima virtus
Esse fuit caeloque ingens se gloria vexit
Italiae; sperare nefas sit vatibus ultra.
Nulla mora, ex illo in pejus ruere omnia visa,   245
Degenerare homines, retro et res lapsa referri.
Hic etenim ingenio confisus posthabet artem;
Ille furit strepitu vulgique sonoribus aures
Silvifragis quatit et clamoribus omnia terret.
Hi sine mente sonum et sopito pectore voces   250
Effundunt suaves dum plebis dulcibus aures
Illecebris captant vacuas plausumque coronae.
Tum magis atque magis successit decolor aetas,
Pierides donec penitus Tiberina fluenta
Deseruere Italis expulsae protinus oris   255

Atque iterum terris petierunt astra relictis.
Tanti causa mali Latio gens aspera aperto
Saepius irrumpens; nam jussi vertere vocem
Ausonidae victi durumque reducere morem.
Cessit amor Musarum omnis, clarae illic et artes   260
Cesserunt; nunc tot veterum monimenta virorum
Amissa incassum flemus quae barbarus igni
Tradidit, ah ferus, ah duris e cautibus ortus.
Et tentamus adhuc sceptris imponere nostris
Externum, necdum civiles condimus enses?   265
Haec aetas omnis, vatum haec fortuna priorum.
At meus ille puer, Phoebi justissima cura,
Virgilii magni haud longe discedat ab aevo
Felici si forte Maro non sufficit unus.
Quid dicam amisso qui dictu obscoena pudore   270
Obliti divum ac divini muneris ore
Immundo cecinere inhonestaque carmina vulgo
Spargentes Musis tenerum incussere ruborem?
Sancte puer, sancti si qua est cura pudoris,
Sacrilegos horum versus ne quaere doceri   275
Nec te discendi capiat tam dira libido.
Semper enim in pejus proni sumus et mala quae nos
A teneris olim coepere tenacius haerent.
Hic vos o moniti, vos hic audite parentes:
Quaerendus custos de millibus aeque legendus   280
Sicubi Musarum studiis insignis et idem
Egregius morum culpaeque et criminis experts
Qui curas dulces carique parentis amorem
Induat atque velit blandum perferre laborem.
Illa suis niti nondum ausit viribus aetas,   285
Externae sed opis alienaeque indiga curae est;
Nam puerum ni praesentis vis fida regentis
Obstet et Aonium paulatim infundat amorem
Illecebrae sacris avertant mille Camoenis,
Deceptum falsa melioris imagina curae.   290
Sic quoque ubi invalidas oleas in collibus olim—
Aut oleas certe aut coniferas cupressus—
Telluri agricola primum mandavit alendas,
Fraxineos contos juxta erigit et sua cuique
Robora ut innixae ventos coelique ruinam   295
Contemnant tutaeque altas spatientur ad auras.
Ille autem pueri cui credita cura colendi
Artibus egregiis in primis optet amari
Atque odium cari placidus devitet alumni

Ne forte et sacras simul oderit ille Camoenas   300
Imprudens et, adhuc tantae dulcedinis expers,
Deficiantque animi studiorum in limine primo.
Ponite crudeles iras et flagra, magistri,
Foeda ministeria atque minis absistite duris.
Ne mihi ne puerum indignos quis rumpere fletus   305
Ah cogat, neque enim lachrymas aut dulcis alumni
Ferre queunt Musae gemitus flentisve dolorem,
Illiusque cadunt animi, nec jam amplius audet
Sponte sua quicquam egregium ingratumque laborem
Invitus trahit aegre et sese ad verbera durat   310
Degener indecorique remittit corda pavore.
Vidi ego qui pueros levia ob commissa vocabat
Ad poenas semper furiis insurgere et ira
Terribilem invisos veluti saeviret in hostes.
Hinc semper gemitus audiri, hinc dura sonare   315
Verbera; regna putes furiarum immania sontes
Cum jussae torquent animas Acheronte sub imo.
Atque equidem memini cum formidatus iniquis
Urgeret poenis solitoque immanior ille
Terreret turbam invalidam, miserabile visu,   320
Forte puer prima signans nondum ora juventa,
Insignis facie ante alios, exegerat omnem
Cum sociis ludens lucem oblitusque timorum
Posthabuit ludo jussos ediscere versus.
Ecce furens animis multa increpat ille minacique   325
Insurgens nimium pavitantem territat ore,
Horrendum, et dextram loris immanibus armat
Terribilem poenisque iras crudelibus explet.
At puer implorare Deos carosque parentes,
Ah frustra, miseroque locum clamore replebat,   330
Donec fessam animam moriens post verbera liquit.
Heu nimium miserande puer, tua fata sorores
Flerunt Castaliae, flerunt Libetrides undae;
Te pater Eridanus, toto te Serius amne
Seriadesque nigro velatae tempora moro   335
Et turres te per noctem patriae ulularunt.
Tempore jam ex illo vatem cum dura monentem
Phoebigenam Alcides animo indignante peremit
Immanem quassans super utraque tempora concham
Debuit immites ultro monuisse magistros.   340
Vos tamen o jussi juvenes parete regentum
Imperiis monitique animos submittite vestros.
Si quem igitur clari formandi gloria vatis

Digna movet, verbis puerum compellat amicis,
Saepe rogans, laudisque animum pertentat amore   345
Egregiae. Proinde hunc postquam semel ossibus ignem
Implicuit, labor inde levis; sese excitat ille
Sponte sua, duros ardens non ille labores
Noctes atque dies nixus praestantibus ausis
Horrescit, vivit tacito sub pectore flamma.   350
Quid memorem (socium nam mos aequalibus annis
Iungere cui paribus studiis contendat alumnus)
Aemula cum virtus stimulis agitarit honestis?
Praesertim si victori tunc praemia rector
Pollicitus volucremve canem pictamve pharetram.   355
Continuo videas studio gestire canendi
Ardentem trahere et sera sub nocte laborem
Dum timet alterius capiti spectare coronam.
At cum sponte sua studia haec assuerit amare,
Iam non laudis amor, non illum gloria palmae   360
Sollicitat, sed enim sola dulcedine captus
Musarum nequit avelli; coelestia tantum
Gaudia Musae animos humanaque pectora tangunt.
Nonne vides duri natos dum saepe parentes
Dulcibus ammorunt studiis et discere avaras   365
Impellunt artes, mentem si quando libido
Nota subit solitaque animum dulcedine movit,
Ut laeti rursum irriguos accedere fontes
Ardescant studiis et sueta revisere Tempe,
Exultantque animis cupidi pugnantque parentum   370
Imperiis, nequit ardentes vis ulla tenere.
Qualis equus si forte viam secus agmen equarum
Non procul errantum notis inspexerit arvis,
Ire cupit, veterum neque enim ille oblitus amorum
Huc obnixus et huc haeretque et pugnat habenis.   375
Quo magis instat eques loris, hoc acrius ille
Effurit insultatque solo et cervicibus alte
Arrectis micat; it tandem vix verbere victus
Ceptum iter, ipsa tamen respectans crebra moratur
Pascua et hinnitu late loca complet acuto.   380
Pierides, quantum vobis invidit honorem,
Heu quantum sors laeva decus cum vestra reliquit
Sacra puer quondam vestris Gibertus ab aris
Ereptus, jam tum ingentes qui pectore curas
Conciperet dominoque in magnis rebus adesset!   385
Ah quoties sacros lachrymans reminiscitur amnes
Infelix juvenis, saltus secretaque vatum

Secum aeger nemora et fontes suspirat amatos
Pana ubi cornigerum et Faunos audire canentes
Assuetus Dryadumque ultro spectare choreas.   390
Quam vellet mecum gelido sub Tusculo iniquam
Pauperiemque pati et ventos perferre nivales!
Fata vetant durusque parens dominique potentes.
Illum Pierides, illum tu pulcher Apollo,
Vester honos vobis, si vestra et munera curae,   395
Sistite sub Helicone, sub aerio Parnaso,
Et juvenem ingratis tam sanctum exolvite curis.
Contra autem cassum multi effudere laborem
Quos sero excoluisse solum male pinguis arenae
Poenituit frustra: quod ne tibi forte docenti   400
Eveniat, poteris certis presciscere signis.
Continuo nullis puer ipse hortatibus usque
Sponte sua exercetur amatque rogatque docentes
Submittitque animum imperiis ac jussa facessit
Primus inardescitque ingenti laudis amore   405
Scitaturque auditque libens monimenta priorum;
Provocat et socios pulchra ad certamina primus
Exultatque animo victor, superatus amaris
Mordetur stimulis, latebras et sola requirit
Infelix loca, ad aequales pudet ire, gravesque   410
Vultus ferre nequit cari rectoris inultus,
Mente putans ignominiam, amissamque coronam
Suspirans lachrymis pulcher lavit ora decoris.
Hic mihi se divis fatisque volentibus affert,
Huic Musae se se indulgent, hunc poscit Apollo.   415
At nullam prorsus tibi spem frustra excitet ille
Quem non ulla movet praedulcis gloria famae
Et praecepta negat duras demittere in aures
Degeneresque animos obtusaque pectora gestans
Immemor auditi, cui turpis inertia mentem   420
Pressat humo languentque hebetes in pectore sensus;
Huic curam moneo ne quisquam impendat inanem.
Nec placet ante annos sapiens puer; omnia justo
Tempore proveniant. Ah ne mihi olentia poma
Mitescant prius Autumnus bicoloribus uvis   425
Quam redeat spumetque cadis vindemia plenis.
Ante diem nam lapsa cadant ramosque relinquent
Maternos, calcabit humi projecta viator.
Nec ludos puero abnuimus: subducere mentem
Interdum liceat studiis; defessus amoena   430
Rura petat saepe et mores exploret agrestum

Et venator agat de vertice Tyburtino
Veloces capreas aut tendat retia cervis.
Non ille interea prorsum patietur inanem
Ire diem ac comitum coetu se subtrahet ultro   435
Interdum et sola secum meditabitur umbra
Sylvestrem Faunis laudem Musasque sub alta
Consulet Albunea vitreas Anienis ad undas.
Proinde etiam alternis requiescere foetibus arva
Permittunt gnari agricolae ac cessare novales   440
Attonsas magno ut reddant cum foenore frugem.
Verum non eadem tamen omnibus esse memento
Ingenia; inventus saepe est cui carmina cordi,
Cui placeant Musae, cui sit non laeva voluntas,
Nititur ille tamen frustra et contendit inani   445
Delusus studio vetitisque accingitur ausis;
Numina laeva obstant frustraque vocatus Apollo.
Orabit melius causas fors ille vel altam
Naturam et caecos rerum scrutabitur ortus.
Saepe tamen cultusque frequens et cura docentum   450
Imperat ingeniis, quae tu quocumque vocabis,
In quascumque artes tandem expectata sequentur
Mitescentque animi; quid non mollire colendo
Vis humana queat? Mitescunt fera leonum
Semina, mansuescunt ursique et pessima tigris,   455
Admittitque hominem dorso immanis elephantus.
Nil intentatum linquunt fidique docentes
Omnibus invigilant studiis atque omnia porro
Experiuntur et impendi nihil est satis unquam.
Hi puerum ante diem aurora surgenti minaci   460
Voce vocant dulcesque invisi rumpere somnos
Non dubitant ventrisque avidi tum protinus arcent
Ingluviem paucisque docent ultroque paratis
Vivere; vix illi sitienti Acheloia tingunt
Pocula rore levi insperso Lenaeidos aurae.   465
Quid procul a patria qui in extera regna relegant
Foemineis matrum illecebris blandoque favori
Subductos humilesque docent dediscere curas?
Est etiam labor ille alius non ultimus acres
Incauto juveni stimulos avertere amoris   470
Donec crescentem doceat maturior aetas
Ferre jugum atque faces saevique cupidinis iras.
Saepe etenim duros immitis in ossibus ignes
Versat amor mollesque perurit cura medullas,
Nec miserum patitur vatum meminisse nec undae   475

Castaliae, tantum suspirat vulnere caeco.
Ante oculos simulacra volant noctesque diesque,
Nuncia virginei vultus quem perditus ardet.
Huic uni invigilat studio speratque timetque
Nec potis est aegras alio traducere curas   480
Saucius. Ignari frustra miscere parentes
Poeonios succos medicasque Machaonis artes
Consulere. Interea mentem calor ille relinquit
Pierius; vexant alii corda aegra calores.
Fortunatus at ille et diis gratissimus ipsis   485
Cui licuit fugisse thorum et connubia, semper
Laeta prius, mox foeta malis et plena laborum.
Fas illi longos cantando claudere soles
Liberius curis vacuo atque impendere noctem
Cunctam operi insigni studiisque intendere mentem.   490
Quippe Venus vires non tantum carpit et artus,
Mentem hebetat simul, egregiis contraria curis.
Pierius vero juvenis cum jam altius hausit
Musarum dulcem sanctique Heliconis amorem
Et sese Phoebo addixit propriumque sacravit,   495
Haud tantum vatum exploret monimenta sacrorum;
Consulat ille alios etiam observetque magistros
Nulla sit ingenio quam non libaverit artem
Ut sciat assimiles ex cunctis ducere rebus
Effigies quantum ostendens siet instar in illis.   500
Proderit et linguam interea Ciceronis ad unguem
Fingere et eloquii per campos ire patentes;
Ille decus Latii et magnae lux altera Romae
Ore effundit opes fandi certissimus autor.
Nec nocuit varios mores hominumque locorumque   505
Explorasse situs multas terraque marique
Aut vidisse ipsum urbes aut narrantibus illas
Ex aliis didicisse aut pictum in pariete mundum.
Quid memorem qui ut saeva queant aequare canendo
Proelia non horrent Martis certamina inire   510
Per mediasque acies vadunt et bella lacessunt?
At secus Annibali Rangonum e gente vetusta
Evenit. Nam cum puer olim accensus amorem
Musarum solum coleret sanctosque poetas,
Hanc unam ob causam belli se vertit ad artes   515
Unde pedem mox non longum detentus in armis
Rettulit; arma placent Martisque ante omnia curae
Quamvis Pieridum irriguos accedere fontes
Interdum juvat et sacris requiescere in antris.

Nec fuit omnino vobis non utile, Musae,   520
Esset ut imbelles vates aliquando piosque
Qui justis ultro praesens defenderet armis.
Quod si forte Leo late qui praesidet orbi
Egregias iras Turcam convertet in hostem,
Hic juvenis quantas strages, quae funera campis   525
Externis dabit Ausonio late agmine septus?
Quae quondam nostri vates facta inclita fama
Una omnes paribus studiis aequare canendo
Contendent; nil non illo promittitur ense.
Vos ideo sat erit tantum omnes isse per artis,   530
Felices pueri, quarum fastigia saltem
Summa sequi fas est, neque enim omnia scire jubemus
Sed nescire veto: princeps tamen haereat illa
Cura animis noctemque atque diem vos excitet una
Omnem quam propter libuit perferre laborem   535
Quando vetant dura in cunctis nos fata morari
Longius angustique monet nos terminus aevi.
Nec refert rate qui varias legit aequoris oras
Mercis ut in patriam referat se dives opimae
Si non cuncta oculis lustraverit oppida late   540
Et circumfusis passim terat ocia terris:
Sat fuerit portus extremaque littora tantum
Explorasse, secus toto miser exulet aevo
Et serus dulces natosque domumque reviset.
Nulla dies tamen interea, tibi nulla fluat nox   545
Quin aliquid vatum sacrorum e fontibus almis
Hauseris et dulcem labris admoveris amnem.
Non hic te quibus aut gradibus pedibusve monebo
Nitantur ducti versus; labor iste regentum
Postulat haud multum curae qui saepe morando   550
Ipsa minutatim metiri carmina sectis
In partes membris numerosque et certa docebunt
Tempora. Nulla mora est, jam tum Phoebeus alumnus
Incipiat certas sub leges cogere verba.
Iam tum submissa meditetur carmina voce   555
Sermonum memor antiquis quos vatibus hausit
Nec dubitet capiti insignem sperare coronam.
Iamque ausit Faunos et Pana lacessere cantu,
Gaudeat et graciles pastorum inflare cicutas,
Iam culicis (primos lusus) fera funera dicat   560
Aut quanto excierit certamina fulmineus mus
Argutas contraque et amantes humida turmas

Aut quae bella grues vigiles quae proelia miscent
Orditurque dolos et retia tenuis Aranei.
Consiliis etiam hic nostris vobisque, docentes,   565
Est monitis opus; ingeniis nam parcere multa
Fas teneris donec paullatim attollere sese
Incipiant animi videantque in carmine labes
Per se ipsi tacitique notent ultro ora rubore.
Nam si forte omnes maculas in carmine monstret   570
Quaesitor ferus, abjicient spem protinus omnem
Atque alias ultro potius vertentur ad artis.
I, puer, atque fores Lili pulsare docentis
Ne dubita et vatis sacratum insistere limen;
Excipiet facilis teque admiretur ab annis   575
Spesque avidas ultro dictis accendat amicis.
Felices qui te talem genuere parentes
Macte acri, puer, ingenio et felicibus ausis;
Perge animi intrepidus, tibi enim favet altus Apollo,
Se tibi se indulgent Musae et numina poscunt.   580
Post tamen hos stimulos, postquam te junxeris illi
Captus et infuso paulatim tactus amore
Castalii laticis, parcens si forte quis inter
Claudus eat veluti tardus de vulnere versus,
Haud medicas adhibere manus aegroque mederi   585
Abstineat culpam rescindens et tibi semper
Ostendet meliora; juvabit saepe redire
Teque ultro imperiis placidi supponere vatis.
Postremo hic etiam moneo semperque monebo:
Neu quisquam nisi curarum liberque laborum   590
Inchoet egregium quicquam; verum procul urbis
Attonitae fugiat strepitus et amoena silentis
Accedat loca ruris ubi Dryadesque puellae
Panesque Faunique et monticolae Sylvani
Laeti habitant nemoris per amica silentia opaci.   595
Est Tibur gelidum haud longe egredientibus urbe
Et placidae liquidi valles Anienis ad amnem;
Quod si forte tibi gelido sub Tibure coelum
Non placet, est alto collis sub Tusculo amoenus
Atque antrum Phoebo ac Musis accomoda sedes.   600
Hic laeti haud magnis opibus, non divite cultu
Vitam agitant vates; procul hinc sceleratus habendi
Est amor, insanae spes longe atque impia vota
Absistunt, curae non ingrediuntur atroces;
Dulcis et alma quies, ac paucis nota voluptas.   605

At ferus ille nimis durisque e rupibus ortus
Qui sanctos genus innocuum gentemque Deorum
Aut audet ferro vates aut laedere voce.
Parcite mortales sacros vexare poetas;
Ultores sperate Deos, sub numine quorum   610
Semper vita fuit vatum. Non litibus illi
Immiscent sese mortalibus; omnia laeti
Fataque fortunasque hominum posuere volentes
Sub pedibus regnumque et opes et sceptra superba
Ingenti vincunt animo ac mortalia rident   615
Ex alto. Non unquam illis mens conscia caecos
Horrescit coeli crepitus ignemve coruscum
Cum pater omnipotens jaculatus fulmina turres
Ingeminans quatit et montes diverberat altos;
Securi terrorum hilares ad sydera mentes   620
Arrexere deumque agitant sine crimine vitam.
Ne mihi tam duros quisquam laudaverit unquam
Sanctarum autores legum morumque magistros,
Qui nullam ob culpam sacros damnare poetas
Quondam ausi atque hominum sancto depellere coetu.   625
Hi tamen et rerum causas ortusque latentes
Scitantur morumque canunt exempla priorum
In melius semper referentes commoda vitae
Mortalis hominumque arcent oblivia rebus.
Quis deus Argolicas acies longosque labores   630
Troiugenum aut versas Argivo milite Thebas
Perpetua nostrum fama traxisset in aevum?
Quis natos divum prius ausos per freta ponti
Ire iter insolitum et curvo se credere ligno?
Nulla ducis Phrygii Latio qui Pergama vexit   635
Et tibi Roma deos eversae numina Trojae
Fama foret vatum nisi praesens cura fuisset.
Quid mirandum aeque coelo divinitus unquam
Concessum est homini? O divum venerabile donum,
Quisquis es ille, deus certe, qui pectora vatum   640
Accolis afflatasque rapis super aethera mentes,
Te sine nil nobis laetum nec amabile quicquam;
Aeriae volucres vario tua numina cantu
Testantur, pecudesque ferae mutaeque natantes
Ad tua jussa citae properant; tua munera surda   645
Saxa movent sylvasque trahunt hinc inde sequentes.
Tu Iovis ambrosiis das nos accumbere mensis,
Tu nos diis aequas superis, tu blanda laborum
Sufficis et durae praesens solatia vitae.

Salve hominum dulcis requies divumque voluptas;   650
Ipse tibi egregios nunc ultro laudis honores
Ingredior vates idem templique sacerdos
Sacraque dona fero dulci comitatus alumno.

MAR HIERONYMI VIDAE

POETICORUM LIBER SECUNDUS

AD ANGELUM DIVITIUM

Pergite Pierides natae Iovis; en mihi totum
Nunc fas venturis Helicona recludere seclis.
Inspirate animos; ego templa in vestra sacerdos
Sacra ferens juvenes lauro capita apta tegentes
Duco audens durum per iter. Vos mollia divae,   5
Si qua latent vobis tantum divortia nota,
Praesentes monstrate novosque ostendite saltus
Quos teneam. Vos en omnis vos Itala pubes
Quae juga sub nostris nunc tendit ad ardua signis
Supplicibus poscit votis facilesque precatur.   10
Nam mihi nunc reperire apta atque reperta docendum
Digerere in partes atque in sua reddere membra.
Tu modo sub mediis ne fessus defice ceptis,
O cui praecipue noster labor excubat uni,
Sancte puer, non te sacris vis ulla Camoenis   15
Angele, non te fortunae indulgentia laetae
Avertat; placeant dulces ante omnia Musae.
Forsan erit te cum tanto laetissima partu
Audiet ad ripas Arni Bibienna canentem
Laurenti decora et Medicum facta ampla tuorum.   20
Vestibulum ante ipsum rerumque in limine primo
Prudentes operum vates fastigia summa
Libant et parcis attingunt omnia dictis
Quae canere instituere; dehinc coelestia divum
Auxilia implorant propriis haud viribus ausi   25
Fidere. Contra alii prius atque ante omnia versi
Supplicibus dictis ad coelum in vota secundas
Musasque Phoebumque vocant hilaremque Lyaeum;
Post subito quae mente agitant dicenda recludunt
Aut utrumque simul. Nec magni denique refers   30
Fiat utrum prius, auspiciis modo cuncta deorum
Aggrediare: Iovis siquidem nisi rite vocato
Numine nil fas est ordiri. Scilicet illum
Mortales nunquam tacitum indictumve relinquunt;
Omnia plena Iovis, coelum, mare, sydera, tellus.   35
Tu vero poteris Musarum atque aetheris alti

Poscere opem primis non tantum ingressibus olim,
Sed quoties veluti scopuli durissima dictu
Obiicient sese tibi non superanda labore
Mortali, toties divum implorare memento   40
Auxilium. Sed principiis labor usque sub ipsis
Impendendus erit major studiumque adhibendum.
In primis odium fugito facilesque legentum
Nil tumidus devinci animos; nec grandia fari
Convenit aut passim nimium ostentantia cultum,   45
Omnia sed nudis prope erit fas tangere verbis
Ne si magna sones cum nondum ad proelia ventum
Deficias medio irrisus certamine cum res
Postulat ingentes animos viresque valentes:
Pollicitis potius semper majora sequantur.   50
Exin mira avidas succende cupidine mentes
Ac desiderio studiumque immitte legendi
Aut placita aut nulli spondens libata priorum.
Cumque etiam promissa dabis rem nomine nunquam
Prodere conveniet manifesto: semper opertis   55
Indiciis longe et verborum ambage petita
Significant umbraque obducunt; inde tamen ceu
Fulgenti e nebula rerum tralucet imago
Clarius et certis datur omnia cernere signis.
Ut si dura mihi passus dicendus Ulisses,   60
Non illum vero praemittam nomine, sed qui
Multorum mores hominum conspexit et urbes
Naufragus eversae post saeva incendia Trojae;
Addam alia angustis praelibans omnia signis.
Iamque age quae vates servandi cura fatiget   65
Ordinis intentos operi cum carmine aperto
Rem tempus memorare vocat quo quaeque decenti
Cernere sit disposta loco ne meta laborum
Ultima dissideat primis ingressibus unquam:
Hoc magnum artis opus, laudem hinc optate poetae.   70
Principio invigilant non expectata legenti
Promere suspensosque animos novitate tenere
Atque per ambages seriem deducere rerum
Pene indeprensam et narrandi quaerere causas.
Nec quacumque viam suadet res ipsa sequuntur,   75
Plerumque a mediis arrepto tempore fari
Incipiunt fictisque juvant primordia causis;
Inde minutatim gestarum ad limina rerum
Descendunt revocantes omne ab origine factum.
Haud sapiens quisquam Trojana incendia et Ilii   80

Inchoet excidium veteri pastoris ab usque
Iudicio memorans ex ordine singula et olim
Quicquid apud Trojam cessatum est Hectore duro
Annales ac si referat nullumque solutis
Pandere rem numeris an ficto carmine gestam   85
Intersit discrimen, eo quo est acta canendo
Ordine opusque decem totos proferre per annos.
Conveniet potius prope finem proelia tanta
Ordiri atque graves iras de virgine rapta
Aversi Aeacidae praemittere; tum fera bella   90
Consurgunt, tum pleni amnes Danaumque Phrygumque
Simoisque Xantusque et inundant sanguine campi.
Haud tamen interea quae praecessere silendum,
Aulide jurantes Danaos vectasque per aequor
Mille rates raptusque Helenes et conjugis iras   95
Quaeque novem Troja est annos perpessa priores.
Quare etiam in patriam si quis deducere adortus
Errantem Laertiadem post Pergama capta,
Non illum Idaeo solventem e littore primum
Cum sociis classem memoret Ciconesque subactos   100
Sed jam tum Ortygiam delatum sistat ad alta
Amissis sociis nymphae Atlantidos antra.
Exin post varios Pheacum tecta labores
Inferat; hic positis demum ipse miserrima mensis
Erroresque suos narret casusque suorum,   105
Ut Ciconum post congressus victumque Ciclopa
Venerit Aeoliam caecisque incluserit austros
Carceribus, retro ut mox tempestatibus actus
Rursum iter emensus longasque relegerit oras
Vectus ad immites Lestrigonas, utque Aeaeae   110
Virginis arte dolos evaserit, inde per amplum
Elysium egregias sociorum agnoverit umbras,
Post hinc Sirenum voces Scyllamque Caribdimque
Arte canet victas, tum quanti armenta perempta,
Heu, steterint Solisque boves, brevibusque Calypsus   115
Hospitium repetet—dapibus quae cuncta repostis
Conveniunt magis. Haec autem si ex ordine vates
Ipse velit memorare, dolor non pectora tantus
Corripiet, sed enim minus et miserebitur hospes.
Qui vero praecepta canunt rurisve colendi   120
Naturasve docent rerum nulla ordine ferri
Ipse putes, nunc hac temere, nunc protinus illac
Quo mentem arripuit furor et discurrere passim,
Cum tamen hi seriemque et leges ordinis ultro

Dissimulent, vinclo occulto tenuique cathena 125
Omnia nectentes ut rem res usque sequatur.
Primus at ille labor sero tenuisse legentem
Suspensum cupidumque diu ne tedia menti
Irrepant, ne crebra animus subsistat et usque
Respiciens suspiret adhuc, heu, tot mala fesso 130
Et tantum superesse viae tantumque laboris.
Verum illum ex longo collecta cupido fatiget
Et semper desiderium succrescat aventi
Cernere quo res cumque cadat dubiosque videre
Eventus rerum: quo tandem durus Achilles 135
Munere placatus regi rursum induat arma
In Teucros, cujusve deum Laertius heros
Auxilio quave arte feri Cyclopis ab antro
Evadat seseque epulis subducat iniqui
Hospitis; ardescunt animi durantque volentes 140
Nec perferre negant superest quodcumque laborum.
Instant saepe licet fessos sopor avocet artus
Aut epulis placanda fames Cererisque libido,
Hoc studium hanc operam sero dimittimus aegri
Intenti cupidique quibus cognoscere tandem 145
Indiciis se pastori natoque suisque
Exul inops qui bisdenos erraverat annos
Detegat atque ultro pateat manifestus Ulisses
Post ludibria longa, domus post damna paternae
Explorata, procris cum sese callidus ultro 150
Immiscet poenasque illis letumque sagaci
Mente parat crudele procacibus, omnia versans.
Scilicet in mediis poteris requiescere dictis
Absistesque prius nisi facti videris omnem
Eventum et quod res fuerit sortita periclum? 155
Quid dicam quoque qui victor nimis arte superbit
Improbus et captis animis illudere gaudet
Et nunc hac deinde hac mentes deducit hiantes
Suspenditque diu miseras pariterque volentes
Nolentesve trahit? Si te certamen anhelum 160
Atridae et Paridis promissum senserit ille
Expectare avidum talique cupidine captum,
Longas usque moras trahit ultro et proelia difert,
Sacrorum longos memorans prius ordine ritus.
Ipsa procos postquam accendit certare sagittis 165
Penelope optatas victori callida tedas
Promittens, per quanta morae dispendia mentes
Suspensas trahet ante viri quam proferet arcum

Thesauris clausum antiquis penitusque repostum.
Namque prius scalas conscendet et ardua tecti   170
Corripietque manu clavem candente recurvam
Cui capulum labor artificum subjecit eburnum,
Tum secreta domus late stipata ministris
Interius subit; hic aurum ferrumque latebat
Arte laboratum multa fulgentiaque aera   175
Cumque arcu insignis pharetra aerataeque sagittae
Quae dona hospitio dederat bonus Iphitus olim,
Iphitus Euritides. Sat erat hucusque nec ultra
Cunctandi ratio ulla, sed arcum prodere tandem
Fas fuerat pulchrumque viros certamen inire.   180
Tu tamen invitus prius hic cogeris Ulisses
Scire quid Orchilochi sedes, cur Iphitus ipse
Venerit, annales longos, casumque perempti
Euritidae indigna longo post tempore morte.
Quin etiam tibi se limenque foresque superbae   185
Obiicient quas praeteriit regina, ubi longum
Artificumque manus doctas variumque laborem
Atque hic atque illic spectans mirabere, quamvis
Non hoc ista sibi tempus spectacula poscat.
Adde serae ingentem sonitum, mirabile dictu,   190
Quantum olim taurus mugitum rumpit in agris.
Hic vero patuere fores, tum regia conjux
Thesauros aperit quibus omnis condita gaza.
Verum illic ne cuncta putes discrimine nullo
Servari interius sine more, sine ordine passim   195
Indiscreta quibus vestes quibus arma jacebant
Accipies secreta locis; tum protinus arcum
Coritumque una accepit quo conditus arcus
Pendebat longus longa demissus ab hasta;
Tum sedet et tristis monimentum insigne doloris   200
Humectat lacrymis arcumque affatur et ultra
Multa virum super infelix rogat et tenet udis
Impositum genibus donec saturata dolore
Et gemitu ad proceres tandem descendit in aulam
Dextra arcum pharetramque gerens, nam tela ministrae   205
Caetera portabant ingenti fasce secutae.
Haec si cuncta pati prius et quae multa sequuntur
Non refugis nec te deterrent tedia longa,
Tandem tantorum merces haud parva laborum
Indubitata manent; procerum certamina cernes,   210
Cui laudem optatasque ferat victoria tedas.
Haud tamen egregii artifices sub nube relinquunt

Obscura incertas mentis penitusque futuri
Ignaras donec seriem perduxerit omnem
Expletus labor; immo inter persaepe canendum 215
Indiciis porro ostendunt in luce maligna
Venturos rerum eventus sortemque futuram.
Hinc pater Aenean multique instantia vates
Fata docent Latio bella, horrida bella manere
Atque alium partum Trojanis rebus Achillem. 220
Spem tamen usque addunt animo firmantque labantem
Spondentes meliora et res in fine quietas.
Ipse etiam novit per se cum in limine belli
Navibus egressus turmas invasit agrestes
Atque (omen pugnae) prostravit Marte Latinos 225
Occiso ante alios qui se se objecerat hoste.
Fata Menoetiades etiam praedixerat olim
Victori moriens majore instare sub hoste,
Quamvis haud fuerit res credita. Te quoque, Turne,
Dii poterant monuisse tuosque ostendere casus 230
Longe ante exitiumque tibi cum dira volucris
Per clypeum perque ora volans stridentibus alis
Omine turbavit mentem admonuitque futuri.
Nam tibi tempus erit magno cum optaveris emptum
Intactum Pallanta et cum spolia aurea balthei 235
Oderis; illa tibi stabit victoria magni.
Nam juvat haec ipsos inter praescisse legentes
Quamvis sint et adhuc confusa et nubila porro.
Haud aliter longinqua petit qui forte viator
Moenia si positas altis in collibus arces, 240
Nunc etiam dubias oculis et ad aethera turres
Surgentes procul aspiciat, tum protinus ille
Laetior ire viam et gressus glomerare valentes
Atque alacri levior menti labor ille videri
Quam cum nusquam ullae apparent quas petit arces. 245
Ergo adeo nisi mente prius, nisi pectore toto
Crebra agites quodcumque canis tecumque premendo
Totum opus aedifices iterumque iterumque retractes,
Laudatum alterius frustra mirabere carmen.
Nec te sors inopina regat casusque labantem. 250
Omnia consiliis animisque volentibus ultro
Certus age ac semper nutu rationis eant res.
Quandoquidem saepe incerti huc illucque vagamur
Inque alia ex aliis inviti illabimur orsa
Dum multa ac varians animis sententia surgit. 255
Nonne vides primis ut quidam saepius orsis

Disgrediuntur et obliti quasi cepta priora
Longe aliis haerent sermonibus artis egeni
Et longos peragrant tractus aliena canentes?
Ac velut in patriam longinqua si quis ab ora   260
Ire cupit post exitium durosque labores,
Ille tamen prono non qua via limite ducit
Carpit iter, sed nunc hic, nunc cunctatur et illic,
Dextra modo nunc laeva tenens, et ubique viarum
Plana terit recti oblitus compendia callis   265
Undique dum studio fontes collustrat inani
Fontesque fluviosque et habentes frigora lucos.
Nam quid opus gemmis armatos pingere currus,
Multa superque rotas, super axes sistere multa
Tunc cum bella manus poscunt atque arma fremit Mars?   270
Non ego Telmachus cum stratis se injicit altis
Sollicitus curem exutus cui tradat amictus
Detractos quantove emuniat obiice postes,
Nec cum Dulichio Tersitem dicis Ulissi
Invisum cupidi expectant audire legentes   275
Qua facie quibus aut humeris qualive capillo
Aut quo sit captus oculo an pes claudicet alter
An longo vertex ductu consurgat acutus.
Quam melior noster Drances, cui frigida bello
Dextera, consiliis sed enim non futilis autor,   280
Dives opum, pollens lingua et popularibus auris.
Multa sed Argivae fert indulgentia vocis
Quae nostros minus addeceant gravitasque Latini
Effugiat sermonis et inclementia linguae.
Non olim Aeneas patriae optet cernere fumum   285
Exul, inops, procul Idaeis a finibus errans,
Cujus amore tamen pulchre incendatur Ulisses
Ingenti desiderio patriaeque suorumque
Ardescens durosque optans finire labores.
Quid tibi nunc laevum ingenium moremque minorumque   290
Indignum referam? Saepe hi ut se plurima nosse
Ostentent pateatque suarum opulentia rerum
Quicquid opum est usquam sine more, sine ordine passim
Effundunt atque omnia versibus intercludunt,
Praecipue si quid summotum, si quid opacum   295
Atque parum vulgi notum auribus aut radiantis
De summa coeli ratione almave deorum
Natura aut animae arcano divinitus ortu.
Saepe etiam accumulant praeclara exempla virorum
(Carminis haud gratum genus) hinc atque inde petita,   300

Quamvis longe illis tempus locusque repugnet.
Ah ne te laudis capiat tam vana libido.
Nec sum animi dubius magnos quandoque poetas
Nostrosque Grajosque suis res addere opertas
Carminibus, solisque vias Lunaeque meatus   305
Syderaque alta poli, qua vi tumida aequora surgant,
Unde tremor terris, quamvis illi orsa sequantur
Longe alia, aut duri resonantes horrida Martis
Munera vel ruris dicentes commoda opimi.
At prius invenere locum et tempore capto   310
Talia subjiciunt parci, nec sponte videntur
Fari ea; rem credas ipsam tunc poscere, ita astum
Dissimulant, aditusque petunt super omnia molles.
Cur pater Anchises natum opportuna rogantem
Non doceat rursusne animae semel aetherae cassae   315
Ad coelum redeant inque altera corpora tranent?
Quandoquidem ut varium sit opus (namque inde voluptas
Semper grata venit) rebus non semper in iisdem
Versator, sed fas varios quasi sumere vultus.
Mutandae rerum facies: non omnia semper   320
Sunt eadem omnino; verum extra mille petantur
Longius argumenta, petantur mille colores.
Paulatim tamen (ut monui) huc allabere capto
Tempore, nec positis insit violentia rebus.
Omnia sponte sua veniant lateatque vagandi   325
Illa cupido potensque omnem labor occulat artem.
Sic pius Aeneas Lybicis ut redditus oris
Iliacas pugnas et picta ex ordine bella
Aspicit ac mediis mixtum se agnovit Achivis.
Nec temere quondam venturi haud inscius aevi   330
Res Italum in clypeo Romanorumque triumphos
Fecerat ignipotens pugnataque in ordine bella,
Stirpis ab Ascanio quondam, genus omne futurum.
Tum si quis Latio cretus de sanguine vates
Prosequitur varias oras moresque locorum   335
Maedosque Aethiopasque et dites arboris Indos,
Ah ferus ille nimis patriae tunc matus amore
Si non Italiae laudes aequaverit astris
Cui neque Medorum silvae neque Bactra neque Indi
Totaque thuriferis Panchaia certet arenis.   340
Salve magna parens frugum, Saturnia tellus
Clara olim sed nunc externis addita sceptris.
Atque ego qui potero gratis, siquando sinet res,
Quicquid agam quodcunque canam, non Herculis esse

Rangonis memor et laudum meminisse tuarum,   345
O praestans animi juvenis, spes maxima vatum!
Tu magnum mihi concilias ultro ipse Leonem.
Ocia tu mihi fecisti, me spernere vulgi
Insanas curas atque impia vota dedisti
Contentum parvo ob Musas modicoque beatum.   350
Quid tibi pro meritis tantis pro laudibus optem!
Dii coelum meriti vestris virtutibus olim
Sydereas sedes et lucida templa tenentes,
Hunc juvenem una omnes cunctis arcete periclis;
Atque illi in terris dantem orbi jura Leonem   355
Incolumem servate diu, fratremque Leonis,
Vatum praesidium angustis in rebus Iulum,
Quorum ope purpureo caput ille insigniit ostro
Romanos inter patres sacrumque senatum.
Hoc primum, tum magnanimos decora alta Latini   360
Nominis aspiciat fratres socia arma secutos
Laurenti Medicis post bella exhausta reverti
Quadrijugis omnes in equis, insignibus omnes
Velatos pariter lauri capita alta coronis,
Guidumque Annibalemque et spem virtutis avitae   365
Ludovicum, acres si sese Martis in artes
Tradiderit puer et duris assueverit armis.
Quare etiam egregii nec vos nec carmina vestra
Arguerim, vates, qui post quandoque legentum
Tedia longa animos renovatis carmine ficto   370
Dulce novumque aliquid referentes: seria ludo
Cedant interdum; neque ego post tribula dicta
Rastraque plaustraque et inflexo cum vomere aratra
Addubitem flere extincti miserabile funus
Romani ducis, aut ruris laudare quietem   375
Post vites Bacchi, post et sylvestria dona.
Hanc olim ob causam reges qui in proelia euntes
Dinumerant populosque moram traxere canentes
Aut Ligurum regi ob casum Phaetontis amati
Dum gemit et moestum musa solatur amorem   380
In silvis cano natas in corpore plumas,
Aut rursum Hyppolitum superas venisse sub auras
Paeoniis revocatum herbis et amore Dianae.
Nec vero interea quae cuique insignia, quae arma
Praetereunt, pingunt clypeos, atque Hercule pulchro   385
Pulcher Aventinus satus olim insigne paternum
Centum angues cinctamque gerit serpentibus hydram.
Saepe etiam loca amoena canunt et frondea Tempe.

Nunc variis pingunt cum floribus auricomum ver,
Nunc placidas liquidis inducunt fontibus umbras   390
Crebraque fluviorum in ripis spatiantur amoenis
Aut Veneti Eridani aut Aetholi Acheloi;
Tum Panes Faunosque canunt Dryadesque Napaeasque
Et centum aequoreas Nereo genitore sorores.
Vidi etiam qui jam perfecto munere longam   395
Subjecere moram extremo sub fine vagantes
Exactorum operum vacua dum carmina musa
In longum traherent, cujus dulcedine capti
Fessi animi cuperent iterumque iterumque redire,
Praecipue si non vacuus desit locus ipsis   400
Carminibus sed adhuc tercentum subdere versus
Suadet inexpletus numerus cursuque patescit
Area aperta et adhuc campispatia ampla supersunt.
Me nulla iccirco valeat vis vertere quin post
Naturas et apum dictas et liquida mella   405
Tristis Aristei questus monitusque parentis
Prosequerer vacuo sermone et Prothea vinctum;
Addam Threicij carmen miserabile vatis
Qualis populea queritur Philomela sub umbra,
Ut Rhodope, ut Pangaea fleant, Rhesi ut domus alta   410
Atque Getae atque Hebrus atque Actias Orithya,
Non secus Adriacis servati fluctibus olim
Centaurum ingentem nautae cum littora ad alta
Detorquent siccumque petunt qua lata profundi
Aequora constructis includit mollibus Anion.   415
Tum validas promunt vires alacresque lacertis
Incumbunt quando studio undique fusa juventus
Visendi; spumant late freta, nauticus astris
It clamor tonitruque arces testantur amico
Laetitiam portu donec conduntur in alto.   420
Saepe tamen memorandum inter ludicra memento
Immiscere aliquid per se mortalia corda
Quod moneat tangens humanae comoda vitae
Quodque olim jubeant natos meminisse parentes.
Hinc orbi sumus ut vitam moresque colamus   425
Quantum quisque valet, gravia in comune ferentes
Consilia atque graves monitus, non temnere divos,
Iustitiamque sequi, et non omnia fidere rebus
Humanis quia saepe vices sors lubrica mutat.
Nil tamen admoveas nisi dignum siqua magister   430
Praecipis in melius referens mortalia facta.
Nec tum cuncta tuis amplecti versibus optes.

Nempe piget tenues nimium cognoscere curas,
Si cum forte canis ruris praecepta colendi
Agricolam moneas ne sacris rite paratis   435
Ante aram in templis crescentes demetat ungues,
Utve sedens ignem propter nudare tegendas
Corporis abstineat partes cum plurima agrestis
Circumfusa focis avertit frigora pubes:
Talia non monitus per sese quique videbit.   440
At non exiguis etiam te insistere rebus.
Abnuerim si magna voles componere parvis,
Aut apibus Tyrios aut Trojugenas formicis
Solvere de Lybico properantes littore classem;
Haud tamen Argolici volitans foedissima quondam   445
Militis aequarit numerum cum plurima mulctram
Agglomerat sese circum; non magna sonantem
Arma ducesque decet tam viles decidere in res.
Nec dictis erit ullus honos si urgentibus Ajax
Trojanis post terga alta cum e caede cruentus   450
Vix pugna absistit similis dicetur asello
Quem pueri herboso pascentem pinguia in agro
Ordia stipitibus properant detrudere duris
Instantes quatiuntque sudes per terga, per harmos,
Ille autem campo vix cedere, et intereundum   455
Saepe hic atque illic avidis insistere malis.
Omnia conveniunt faciesque simillima rerum,
Credo equidem, sed turpe pecus, sed vilis asellus
Ah nimium, procerumque aures audire recusant
Quam multae circumvolitent mulctraria muscae;   460
Major honos apibus vitae et formica magistra est.
Hoc quoque non studiis nobis levioribus instat
Curandum ut quando non semper vera profamur
Possint illa tamen fieri atque simillima veris
Conveniant. Si forte igitur medio aequore belli   465
Congreditur Glauco Tydides, non roget alter
Tela tenens longis nimium sermonibus unde
Quave dono, quis sit, nec divi facta Lycurgi
Commemoret, neve ille dehinc quoque Bellerophontis
Contra fortia bella canat domitamque Chimeram   470
Et victos Solimos pulsas et Amazones armis.
Hac vice sermonum tanto in discrimine Martis
Haud opus est, cauti nec credent ista legentes.
Disce etiam, pulchri tibi si cura ordinis ulla est,
Cuncta semel fari tantum; repetita bis aures   475
Avertuntur et obtundunt fastidia fessos

Longa animos; namque ipse suo si forte poeta
Retulerit prius ore dolens quid fortis Achilles
Sponte Micenaeis sese subduxerit armis,
Nequicquam solo Aeacides in littore matri   480
Ipse eadem aequoreae lachrymans narrabit ad undas.
Nec deceat si audita prius referente poeta
Et verbis numerisque iisdem sua somnia Atrides
Ipse renarrarit ducibus populisque coactis.
Non sic Ausonius Venulus legatus ab Arpis   485
Cum redit Ethole Argiripa Diomedis ab urbe.
Ergo quaecunque alterius vis ore referri
Parce tuis verbis attingere, parce legentum
Auribus, et versu innumero ne quaere placere.
Altum aliis opus exurgat; tu nocte dieque   490
Exiguum meditator ubi mirentur et artem
Egregiam et vires fandi ingeniumque legentes.
Quod si longarum liber spatia ampla viarum
Ire velis seroque labore extendere longas
Iliadas, si res angustis finibus arcta est,   495
Protrahere atque moram passim licet addere gratam
Ingenio praesente. Viae sunt mille trahendi,
Mille modi. Tunc ficta juvat longeque petita
Inserere: aut ludos magnorum ad busta parentum
Concelebrant manesque vocant aut invia vivis   500
Heroas sub regna aliquo duce numine ducunt
Umbrarumque domos vacuas sontesque recensent
Damnatos Erebo, Titionque et Thesia Aloeique
Immanes natos et terrigenas Titanas
Terribilesque umbras referuntque horrentia Ditis   505
Monstra, canis triplices rictus, et Erinnydes atras,
Gorgones, Harpyias, Scyllasque Hydrasque Chimerasque
Et centum geminis dirum artubus Egeona.
Multum etiam hospitiis impendunt temporis olim
Regalesque epulas celebrant ubi multa repostis   510
Inter se vario dapibus sermone retractant.
Annua nunc patriis peragunt diis sacra periclo
Servati quondam laudesque ad sydera tollunt,
Nunc responsa canunt vatumque et somnia fingunt,
Nunc quoque ad arma deos ducunt mortalia iniquis   515
Certantes inter se odiis donec pater ipse
Concilium vocet atque indignas molliat iras.
Non etiam parvo studio rimantur ubique
Atque hinc atque illinc variarum semina rerum
Mille petunt operique addunt, Est saepius illic   520

Cernere naturas omneis moresque animantum
Et quae sub coelo nullo sunt praedita sensu,
Usque adeo, ut nuncque Trojani proelia belli
Inspiciam, quin ante oculos mihi si ferat usque
Clarius ipsa omnis rerum natura videnda   525
Mille trahens varios vultuque habituque colores.
An memorem quandoque omnes intendere vires
Cum libuit verbisque ipsam rem aequare canendo?
Seu dicenda atri tempestas horrida ponti
Ventorum et rabies fractaeque ad saxa carinae   530
Aut Siculo angusto aut implacido Euxino,
Sive cohorta repente lues cum multa ferarum
Corpora multa hominum leto data, sive Sicana
Dicendum quantis terra tonet Aetna ruinis
Prorumpens atram, horrendum, ad sydera nubem   535
Turbine fumantem piceo et candente favilla.
Audistin cum bella sonant horrentia et arma,
Arma fremunt miscentque equitum peditumque ruinas?
Ante oculos belli sese offert tristis imago
Non tantum ut dici videantur sed fieri res,   540
Unde sacris nomen Graii fecere poetis.
Armorum fragor audiri gemitusque cadentum
Et tormenta tonantia cum Vulcania dona
Aere cavo disclusa arcesque et tecta domorum
Saxa chalybsque petunt; circum gemit arduus aether   545
Saepe adeo horrescant ut corda legentibus ipsis.
Quis quoque cum captas evolvunt hostibus urbes
Temperet a lacrymis? Tectorum ad culmina crebras
Ire faces passimque domos involvere flammis
Cernere erit, trepidosque senes parvosque parentes   550
Amplexos, flentesque ipsas ad sydera matres
Tollentes clamorem hostes interque suosque,
Abstractasque nurus adytis arisque deorum
Et crinem laniare et tundere pectora palmis,
Hos fugere arreptas illos abducere praedas   555
Perque domos perque alta deum delubra furentes,
Atque hac atque illac tota discurrier urbe,
Tanta mole ruunt immissis artis habenis.
Quid cum animis sacer est furor additus atque potens vis?
Nam variant species animorum et pectora nostra   560
Nunc hos nunc illos multo discrimine motus
Concipiunt, seu quod nobis divinitus insit
Ingenium, seu quod coeli mutatur in horas
Tempestas hominumque simul quoque pectora vertit,

Seu quia non iidem respondent saepe labore   565
Sensus effoeti atque animus cum corpore languet,
Seu quia curarum interdum vacuique doloris
Interdum tristes caeco intus tundimur aestu.
Dii potius nostris ardorem hunc mentibus addunt
Credo equidem; felixque ideo qui tempora quivit   570
Adventumque dei et solitum expectare calorem
Paulisperque operi incepto subducere mentem
Mutati donec redeat elementia coeli;
Sponte sua veniet justum (ne accersite) tempus.
Interdum et sylvis frondes et fontibus humor   575
Desunt, nec strictis semper cava flumina ripis
Plena fluunt, nec semper agros ver vestit apricum.
Sors eadem incertis contingit saepe poetis;
Interdum exhausta languent ad carmina vires
Absumptusque vigor studiorumque immemor est mens   580
Torpescuntque animi et circa praecordia sanguis
Stat gelidus; credas penitus migrasse Camoenas.
Ah quoties aliquis frustra consueta retentat
Munera, nec cernit coelum se tendere contra
Adversosque Deos et non tollerabile numen!   585
Quidam etiam inventus qui saepe reduceret auras
Optatas veterum repetendo carmina vatum
Paulatimque animo blandum invitarit amorem
Donec collectae vires sensusque refecti
Et vigor ille redit veluti post nubila et imbres   590
Sol micat aerius. Unde haec tam clara repente
Tempestas? Deus, ecce Deus jam corda fatigat,
Altius insinuat venis penitusque per artus
Deditur atque faces acres sub pectore versat.
Nec se jam capit ille ardens calor asperaque intus   595
Vis agit attonitumque rapit mirabile vatem.
Huc atque huc furit ille animumque ad sydera tollit
Igneus exultantem animum atque exercet anhela
Oraque pectoraque et jactat jam non sua verba
Oblitusque hominem mirum sonat; haud potis ignem   600
Excutere invitum miratur se ire rapique
Praecipitem, te, Phoebe, vocans, te te evohe Bacche,
Evohe Bacche, fremens; cadit ars visque illa gerit rem
Omnipotens. Non ille dapum, non ille quietis
Aut somni memor absistit noctemque diemque   605
Indulget cantu moraque omnis iniqua videri.
Qualis ubi quondam pastorum lusus in arvis
Subjecit stipulas caudae tedamve flagrantem

Aut canis aut vulpis, rapidis fugit ocyor Euris
Atque huc atque illuc juga per deserta, per agros   610
Territa quacunque illa fugit trahit inscia secum
Pestem inimicam, eadem trepidi sibi causa furoris;
Talis Phoebeus vates rapiturque furitque
Incensus plenusque Deo stimulisque subactus.
Ergo diem noctemque alacres Phoebeja tractant   615
Munera: quod nocte insomni reperere, reponunt.
Mox, redeunte die, memoresque ex ordine jungunt
Carmina. Non unquam in stratis Aurora morantes
Attigit hos hiberna: umbris humentibus ultro
Surgunt ac dulci subducunt lumina somno: 620
Interea largo victum artus vulgus Iaccho
Egregiae nil laudis egens sopor opprimit altus.
Tum sensus vigiles, tum corda arrecta, laboris
Oblita hesterni, tum late cuncta silescunt.
Saepe etiam in somnis memores Phoebeja tractant   625
Munera, et inventi quondam qui saepe sopore
In medio versus Musis et Apolline dignos
Struxere in numerum quos dehinc mirantibus omneis
Surgentes socijs cecinerunt ordine laeti,
Tantus amor famae, tam praesens cura laborum.   630
Ne tamen o nimium, puer, o ne fide calori.
Non te fortuna semper permittimus uti
Praesentique aura dum caecum pectore numen
Insidet. At potius ratioque et cura resistat.
Freno siste furentem animum ac sub signa vocato   635
Et premere et laxas scito dare cautus habenas.
Atque ideo semper tunc expectare jubemus
Dum fuerint placati animi compressus et omnis
Impetus; hic recolens sedato corde revise
Omnia quae caecus menti subjecerat ardor.   640
Nam brevis ille calor cito desinit attonitumque
Atque hominem exanimi similem mutumque relinquit.
Non aliter Phrygiae matris post acta furentes
Sacra chori postque gelidi juga Dindymi et Idae
Frondosae lucos atque avia lustravere   645
Timpana tundentes tenta et cava cymbala palmis
Procumbunt lassosque artus in gramine ponunt.
Interea fessi permulcent pectora alumni
Pierides gremioque fovent placidumque soporem
Artubus infundunt lapsis sparguntque salubres   650
Largius ambrosiae succos atque oscula jungunt.
Naturam facilem juvenes optate deosque

Poscite, namque dabunt ipsi. Quaerenda labore
Ars erit humanisque opibus studioque perenni.
Fors aliquid nostri poterunt quoque munera versus 655
Hic prodesse; meo laeti gaudete labore:
Caetera longa dabit rerum experientia vobis.
Nec tamen hic fugiat vos nil conarier artem
Naturam nisi ut assimulet propiusque sequatur.
Nimirum divini agitant quodcumque poetae 660
Hanc unam ante oculos sibi constituere magistram.
Praesertim varios hominum moresque animorum
Et studia imparibus divisa aetatibus ingens
Est simulare labor sermonis imagine, tumque
Grandaevosque senes deceant juvenesque virentes 665
Foemineumque animum, quantum quoque rura colenti
Aut famulo distet quisquam alto e sanguine regum
Egregius. Neque enim placeat si sit gravis annos
Thelemacus supra, senior si Nestor inani
Gaudeat et ludo et canibus pictisve pharetris. 670
Et quoniam in nostro multi persaepe loquuntur
Carmine, verba illis pro majestate virumque
Ac rerum damus, et proprii tribuuntur honores
Cuique suus, sive ille deus seu foemina seu vir,
Mortalis cui conditio. Divum atque hominum rex 675
Ipse in concilio fatur si forte cohorta
Seditio paucis. At non Venus aurea contra
Pauca refert Troum indignos miserata labores.
Ingreditur furijs atque alta silentia rumpit
Acta furore gravique et Iuno foeta querelis. 680
Cumque etiam juveni gliscat violentia major
Ardens cui virtus animusque in pectore praesens,
Nulla mora in Turno nec dicta animosa retractat;
Stat conferre manum et certamine provocat hostem
Desertorem Asiae. Verum quantum ille feroci 685
Virtute exuperat tanto est impensius aequum
Et pietate gravem et sedato corde Latinum
Consulere atque omnes metuentem expendere casus.
Multum etiam intererit Dido ne irata loquatur
An pacato animo. Lybicas si linquere terras 690
Trojanus paret et desertum fallere amorem,
Saeviet ac tota passim baccabitur urbe
Mentis inops, immanis, atrox; verba aspera rumpet
Confusasque dabit voces incertaque et haerens
Quae quibus anteferat. Quantum ah distabit ab illa 695
Didone excepit Teucros quae nuper egenos

Solvere corde metum atque jubens secludere curas
Invitansque suis vellent considere regnis.
Nec te poeniteat fandique artisque magistros
Consulere interea ut Trojanos fallere possit   700
Arte Sinon structisque dolis impellare capta
Pectora quo libeat vel fati doctus Ulisses
Argivos longo fessos discedere bello
In patriam certos Trojaque redire relicta
Ore queat solo revocare fugamque paratam   705
Voce vetare. Tibi quid sanctum Nestora dicam
Qui toties inter primores Argivorum
Ingentes potuit verbis componere lites
Et mulcere animos et mollia fingere corda?
Tum nisi te orantes causas artisque magistri   710
Edocuere prius, Venerem quo carmine nato
Arma notho orantem sistes ante ora mariti
Cui toties notis illusit prodita furtis
Ut causas petat ex alto atque indagine captam
Ambiat occulta verborum callida mentem?   715
Hinc etiam ille labor sensusque animosque legentum
Fingere diversosque habitus dare ut imperet illis.
Egregius semper vates, seu tristia moerens
Evolvat, seu laeta canat, dulcedine mira
Inflectit sensus dulcem et labefacta dolorem   720
Insinuans per corda serit atque elicit imbrem
Ex oculis. Quem non Getici sors aspera vatis
Molliat amissam dum solo in littore secum
Te, dulcis conjux, solans testudine amorem
Te veniente die, te decedente sonaret?   725
Quid puer Euryalus cum pulchros volvitur artus,
Ah dolor, inque humeros lapsa cervice recumbens
Languescit moriens ceu flos succisus aratro,
Ardet adire animus mihi saepe et currere in ipsum
Volscentem puerique manum supponere mento   730
Labenti et largum frustra prohibere cruorem
Purpureo niveum signantem flumine pectus,
Nec parco lacrymis moesto permotus amore.
Postremo tibi siqua instant dicenda ruborem
Quae tenerum incuterent Musis adaperta chorisque   735
Virgineis, nullo vel praeter labere tactu
Dissimulans vel verte alio et rem subijce fictam.
Si pater omnipotens tonitru coelum omne ciebit,
Speluncam Dido dux et Trojanus eandem
Deveniant; nihil ulterius pudor addere curet.   740

Nam sat erit tellus quod prima et conscius aether
Connubij dent signum, ululentque in vertice Nimphae.
Neve aliis puer infelix heu Troilus armis
Ah nimium forti impar congrediatur Achilli
Quam quibus in Libyco conspexit littore pictum   745
Ipsum Anchisiades heros, dum victus anhelis
Fertur equis curruque haeret resupinus inani;
Ne tibi ne tanti fuerit reverentia veri.
Quid deceat, quid non vates sanctumque pudorem
Ostendent semper nostri patresque Latini;   750
Inventa ex aliis disce. Et te plurima Achivos
Consulere hortamur veteres Argivaque regna
Explorare oculis ditemque avertere gazam
In Latium atque humeris laetum spolia ampla referre
Aonio ex Helicone, ex Actaeo Aracyntho.   755
Haud longe minor inde tibi preclara reperta
Laus erit Argivum in patriam convertere vocem,
Si te fata sinunt prohibet nec dexter Apollo,
Quam si tute aliqua invenies minus obvia Graijs
Atque indicta prius cuiquam. Tantum absit ut ipse   760
Furta velim tegere et praedam celare relatam.
Aspice ut insignis peregrino incedat in auro
Fatidicae Mantus et Minci filius amnis,
Quam pulcher magni exuvias indutus Homeri
Fulgeat, utque viros victor supereminet omnes,   765
Utque suis parcens spoliorum semper amore
Ardescit Grajumque avidus populatur honores!
Ille quidem in patriam deducere vertice Musas
Nititur Aonio palmamque auferre Pelasgis
Gaudet et Ausoniae vires ostendere linguae,   770
Quis cultus, quantusque decor, quae copia fandi,
Quantus honos, Danaum invigilans contundere fastus;
Nec super ipse suo tantum molitur honore
Quantum comuni Italiae pro laude movetur,
Usque adeo laudis patriae juvat aemula cura.   775
Vatibus hinc etiam reges dominique potentes
Ingentis addunt animos qui laudis amore
Accensi ob patriam libertatemque tuendam
Magna audent propriisque hostes a finibus arcent.
Sed jam heu (tanta Italos inter discordia reges)   780
Cessit amor patriae et laudum generosa cupido
Inseditque animis heroum ignavia turpis
Nec pudet Italiam externis aperire tyrannis.
Tum simul immemores studiorum carmina vates

Dedidicere, simul Musas contemnere reges   785
Cepere et sanctis nihil indulgere poetis.
Spes tamen Ausoniae prostratae affulserat ingens
Nuper et egregiis animos erexerat ausis,
Heu, frustra; invidit laudi sors laeva Latinae
Necdum fata malis Italum exaturata quierunt.   790
Haec fuerat via sola decus laudemque priorem
Qua nostra poterant sperare amissaque sceptra.
Iamque urbes longe positae trepidare ducesque
Externi, jam dives Arabs, jam Nilus, et Indus
Egregij juvenis late decora inclyta Ethrusci   795
Magnum et ab antiquo devectum nomen Iulo
Audierant, Medicumque genus stirpemque deorum.
Iam tum ille insignes curas accinxerat ardens
Pro patriae decore, pro libertate sepulta
Antiquae Ausoniae, germani fretus amore,   800
Germani, qui nunc immenso praesidet orbi
Idem regnatorque hominum divumque sacerdos.
Iam tum illum Ausonidum juvenem manus omnis in unum
Conversique oculos conversique ora tenebant.
Iamque duces animis illum concordibus omnes   805
Velle sequi Martis pulchri in certamina euntem
Insignem pietate, insignem fortibus ausis.
Illum quadriiugo invectum per moenia curru
Roma triumphato vidisses protinus orbe.
Illum, Thybri pater, laetanti turbidus alveo   810
Tendentem spoliis alta ad Capitolia opimis
Exciperes Thuscus Thuscum sed sanguine mixtum
Romano patriumque gerentem pectore Martem.
Issent post currus capti longo ordine reges
Oblitusque minas minor iret barbarus hostis   815
Qui victis Solimis nunc atque Oriente subacto
Exultat fidens orbisque affectat habenas
Efferus, atque Italae jam jam (dolor) imminet orae.
Visendi studio passim Romana juventus
Per fora perque vias festa discurreret urbe.   820
Ipse sedens ingens frater solio aureus alto
Acciperet fratrem dulci lachrymatus amore
Barbaricumque aurum praedaeque juberet acervos
Sacratis adytis summaque reponier arce.
Una omnes huc tunc castae ex Helicone sorores   825
Migrassent Phoebusque pater, tunc laeta sonarent
Carmina, tum vates veterum decora alta virorum
Aequassent cantuque animos super astra tulissent.

Verum heu (Dij vestrum crimen) spes tanta repente
Italiae absunta ac penitus fiducia cessit; 830
Vatibus in miserum vertuntur carmina luctum:
Egregius juvenis moriens secum omnia vertit.
Da violas puer et mecum candentia plena
Lilia sparge manu ferrugineosque hiacynthos.
Condamus tumulum heroi sub Thusculo inanem 835
Et saltem hoc magnos manes cumulemus honorem
Dum patruus tanti turbatus funere amici
Ah nimio indulget luctu noctesque diesque
Et magnum nequit infelix explere dolorem.
Nos circum Dryades, nos circum et Oreades omnes 840
Montibus his passim sub desertis ululabunt
Et circumfusae reddent gemitum undique valles.

M. HIERONYMI VIDAE POETI

CORUM LIBER TERTIUS

AD ANGELUM DIVITIUM

Nunc autem linguae studium moremque loquendi
Quem vates Musaeque probent atque Autor Apollo
Expediam, curam extremam finemque laborum.
Discenda indicia et verborum lumina quae sint
Addita lustrandis rebus. Hic omne poetae   5
Durantes aevum impendunt, modo dicta virorum
Pendentes animis veterum qui versibus olim
Dicendi hanc nobis faciem peperere, modo ipsi
Perpetuo sese exercentes sponte labore
Dum mos ille animis longa assuetudine fandi   10
Haereat atque potens menteis sensim imbuat usus.
Ne tamen hinc ne te deterreat ultima meta,
Care puer, dulcis comes et mea magna voluptas.
Iam te Pierides summa en de rupe propinquum
Voce vocant viridique ostentant fronde coronam   15
Victori atque animis stimulos haerentibus addunt,
Iamque rosas calathis spargunt per nubila plenis
Desuper, et florum placido te plurima nimbo
Tempestas operit, gratumque effusus odorem
Ambrosiae spirat liquor et divina voluptas.   20
Ipse ingens autem patruus quem plurima semper
Turba canit circum vatum et dijs laudibus aequat
Te spectat praesensque animis praestantibus implet.
Audendum, puer, atque invicto pectore agendum.
Aspice ut ante alios juvenis Lipomanus in altum   25
Nititur et biiugi jamjam capita ardua montis
Contendit prensare manu quando omnia Musis
Posthabet atque unum colit almi Heliconis amorem
Nec curat sibi quod fortunae crimine iniquae
Abstulerit modo promissos sors invida honores.   30
Cui si purpureo debentia fata dedissent
Romanos inter patres fulgere galero,
Praesidium Musis magnum sacrisque poetis
Afforet atque suus doctis honor artibus esset.
Cura sit in primis tibi ea praediscere quantum   35
Intersit causas orantes atque poetas

Divinos, neque enim fandi mos unus utrisque
Haud eadem: omnino facies comunia quamvis
Plurima sint illis etiam conantur utrique
Affines pariter priscis audita Latinis   40
Verba loqui et paribus fandi splendescere formis,
Illi liberius campum arripuere palentem
Currentes, neque tanta fatigat fingere gressus
Compositos cura aut vinclis campacta per artem
Cogere sub numerum certo discrimine verba.   45
Hi vero duras leges ac temporis arcta
Praescripti spatia atque pedum cohibentia vincla
Solantur freti longe majore loquendi
Libertate palam facta atque infecta canentes.
Mille modis aperire datur mentisque latebras   50
Arcanosque animi sensus interprete lingua,
Longius et rerum indicia transferre petita
Quaesitique decent comptus magis atque colores
Externi, nec erit tanto ars deprensa pudori.
Hunc fandi morem (si dignum est credere) divi   55
Coelicolae exercent coeli in penetralibus aureis
Virgineus chorus ad terram quem detulit olim
Pieridum docuitque homines. Nempe hae Iovis aula
Syderei in media choreas agitare feruntur
Et canere immixtae superis Phoebique fruuntur   60
Colloquio vatumque inspirant pectora ab alto.
Nonne vides verbis ut veris saepe relictis
Accersant simulata aliundeque nomina porro
Transportent aptentque alijs ea rebus ut ipsae
Exuviasque novas res insolitosque colores   65
Indutae saepe externi mirentur amictus
Unde illi laetaeque aliena luce fruantur
Mutatoque habitu, nec jam sua nomina mallent?
Quamquam eadem norint queis cura est dicere causas
Orando, sontes legum compescere habenis   70
Dum cupiunt atris vel caros mortis amicos
Faucibus eripere et defletos reddere luci,
Parcius ista tamen delibant et minus audent.
Quin etiam agricolas ea fandi nota voluptas
Sollicitat genio cum festis saepe diebus   75
Indulgent, dum laetae seges, dum trudere gemmas
Incipiunt vites, sitientiaque aetheris imbrem
Prata bibunt, ridentque satis surgentibus agri.
Proinde olim hanc speciem propriae penuria vocis
Intulit indictisque urgens in rebus egestas.   80

Quippe ubi se vera ostendebant nomina nusquam
Fingere fas erat et veris simulata profari.
Paulatim accrevere artes hominumque libido;
Quodque olim usus inops reperit, nunc ipsa voluptas
Postulat ac laetos sermonibus addit honores.   85
Sic homines primum venti vis aspera adegit
Vitandique imbres stipulis horrentia tecta
Ponere et informi sedem arctam claudere limo;
Nunc amplae surgunt aedes ad sydera luxu
Regifico auratis trabibus Parijsque columnis   90
Dependentque altis lycni laquearibus aurei.
Haud secus ut mentes hominumque et pectora capta
Detineant ipsi vates mirantia, quamvis
Nomina sufficiat rebus natura canendis,
Laetantur tamen haud propriis lucem addere verbis.   95
Saepe ideo cum bella canunt incendia cernas
Maxima diluviumque ingens surgentibus undis
Aut tempestatem attollique fretique procellas.
Contra etiam saevos Mavors ferus adjuvat ignes
Cum furit accensis acies Vulcania campis,   100
Nec turbato oritur quondam minor aequore pugna:
Consurgunt animosi Austri certamine vasto
Inter se pugnantque adversis fluctibus undae.
Aspice ut inter se sua res insignia laetae
Permutentque juventque alternum, ut mutua sese   105
Altera in alterius faciem transformet et ora.
Tum specie capti gaudent spectare legentes
Cum simul hic illic ex re fas cernere eadem
Multa modis simulacra et mille figuras.
Ceu cum forte olim placidi liquidissima ponti   110
Aequora vicina spectat de rupe viator,
Tantum illic subjecta oculis immobilis unda est;
Ille tamen sylvas interque virentia prata
Inspiciens miratur aquae quae purior humor
Cuncta refert captosque eludit imagine visus.   115
Non aliter mentes nunc huc traducere vates
Nunc illuc variasque animis apponere rerum
Effigies curat venit unde immensa voluptas.
Sic quoque sordida humique jacentia tollit ad astra
Splendorem laetum adijciens et lumine vestit   120
Iucundo simul ut parcus dispendia vitat
Verborum notamque viam saltusque relinquit
Consuetas, alia invectus brevioris amore
Curriculi, et paucis spatium ingens passibus aequat.

Contemplator item si quando turpia dictu 125
Inconcessa pudor manifestius abnuit olim
Pandere quo nubis velamine circumfundant;
Tunc lux ipsa alias in rebus plurima votis
Exoptanda nocet tenebrisque obducere praestat.
Ceu ubi jam in venerem pecuaria solvere tempus 130
Pastores macie tenuant armenta volentes—
Quam semper vitare alias ante omnia tendunt—
Tunc autem nimio ne luxu obtusior usus
Sit genitali arvo et sulcos oblimet inertes
Sed rapiat sitiens venerem interiusque recondat. 135
Haud tamen obscura penitus caligine condunt;
Sublustri e nebula rerum tralucet imago
Et res interius dictis clarescit opacis.
Nec tutum fuerit rerum perstare sub umbra
Una eademque diu nisi forte assumpserit ora 140
Caesaris extinctus crudeli funere Daphnis;
Tum placeant sylvae potius pro moenibus urbis,
Pro patribus moestis pastores fontibus umbras
Inducant virides; tum cantet Lyctius Aegon
Carmina vel magnis pro vatibus Alphesiboeus. 145
Hic autem (vates audite ubicumque Latini)
Multi errant; namque in tenebris et saepe sub umbra
Luce palam tractanda agitant et nubibus abducunt
Intempestive rebus res assimulantes.
Exercent alij vim duram et rebus iniqui 150
Nativam eripiunt formam indignantibus ipsis
Inque aliam vertunt aegras nihil instar habentes.
Nunc ausi stabula alta lares hi dicere equinos,
Nunc hominum pastorem Agamemnona compellare.
Cumque etiam calor inter se frigusque repugnent 155
Quid siquis versu male prudens fingeret ambo
Castra locare manu ferventia frigidaque, olim
Opposita inter se, et paribus decernere signis!
Prestiterit vero faciem spolia et sua cuique
Linquere et interdum veris rem prodere verbis 160
Indiciisque suis quam dissimulare per umbram.
Saepe etenim alterutrum poteris conferre vicissim
Res rebus et utrasque suis exponere dictis;
Tum fuge verborum cautus dispendia paucisque
Includas numeris unde illa simillima imago 165
Ducitur atque eadem effigies, ne forte priorum
Oblitus sermonum alio traducere versum
Inque alia ex alijs videare allabier orsa

Atque incerta sequi nunc hac nunc protinus illac
Errando vagus et nullam tibi figere metam   170
Quam teneas, tantum correptus amore vagandi
Et referas nullum speratae laudis honorem:
Ceu ubi saepe nova captus dulcedine currum
Atque acres hortatus equos auriga pericli
Haud memor et passim manibus dimisit habenas,   175
Olli corripiunt spatium cursuque volucres
Nec mora nec requies ventos praevertere tendunt,
Hac illac donec fuso super axe solo acti
Procubuere; ruit simul ille irrisus et ausi
Paenitet; it coelo toto ingens aequore clamor.   180
Nunc age verborum qui sit delectus habendus,
Quae ratio, nam nec sunt omnia versibus apta,
Omnia nec pariter tibi sunt uno ordine habenda.
Versibus ipsa etiam divisa et carmina quantum
Carminibus distant tantum distare memento   185
Verba quoque inter se quamvis communia multa
Interdum invenies versus diffusa per omnes.
Multa decent scenam quae sunt fugienda canenti
Aut divum laudes aut heroum inclyta facta.
Ergo alte vestiga oculis aciemque voluta   190
Verborum sylva in magna. Tum commoda Musis
Selige et insignes verborum pascere honores
Ut pulcher puro versus tibi fulgeat auro.
Reijce degenerem turbam et nil lucis habentem
Indecoresque notas, nec sit non digna supellex.   195
Quo fieri id possit, veterum te semita vatum
Observata docebit. Adi monimenta priorum
Crebra oculis animoque legens et multa voluta.
Tum quamvis, longe siquis supereminet omnes,
Virtutem ex illo ac rationem discere fandi   200
Te jubeam cui contendas te reddere semper
Assimilem atque habitus gressusque effingere euntis
Quantum fata sinant et divum numina laeva.
Haud tamen interea reliquum explorare labores
Abstiteris vatum moneo suspectaque dicta   205
Sublegere et variam ex cunctis abducere gazam.
Nec dubitem versus hirsuti saepe poetae
Ipse ego lustrare et vestigare legendo
Sicubi sese inter quaedam illic comoda versu
Forte meo ostendant quae mox melioribus ipse   210
Auspiciis proprios possim mihi vertere in usus
Deterso prorsus prisca rubigine scabra.

Flumina saepe vides obducto turbida limo;
Haurit aquam tamen inde frequens concursus et altis
Important puteis ad pocula. Desuper illa   215
Occultis immissa canalibus influit omnemque
Illabens bibulas labem exuit inter arenas.
Nil adeo incultum quod non splendescere possit,
Praecipue si cura vigil non desit et usque
Mente premas multumque animo tecum ipse volutes.   220
Atque ideo ex priscis semper quo more loquamur
Discendum quorum depascimur aurea dicta
Assidui et raros semper populamur honores.
Aspice ut exuvias veterumque insignia nobis
Aptemus, nunc de Danais spolia ampla ferentes,   225
Nostrorum nunc furati decora inclyta vatum,
Atque hic atque illic nunc rerum clara reperta,
Nunc seriem atque animum, nec verbis parcimus ipsis.
Argolici res atque animum seriemque poetae
Sufficient, cultumque dabunt accomoda nostri   230
Verba satis nec non ostendent gentis Acheae
Inventa in melius qua possint arte referri.
Quaelibet Argivis fas demum vertere ab oris
In Latium: viden ut Trojanus origine ductor
Magnanimus Anchisiades accomodet arma   235
Saepe sibi Graium galeaeque insigne decorum
Ensemque clypeumque et levia tegmina crurum?
Tum victor potitur rapto; nunc fortis Atridae
Arma gerens, nunc exuvias indutus Achillis,
Nunc etiam errantis formam assimulatus Ulyssi   240
Verborum tenus; haec tantum de more parentum
Et patriae sonat haud mentitus caetera Grajus.
Cum priscis autem moliris furta Latinis
Cautius ingredere et raptus memor occule versis
Verborum indicijs atque ordine falle legentes   245
Mutato; nova sit facies, nova prorsus imago.
Munere (nec longum tempus) vix ipse peracto
Dicta recognosces veteris mutata poetae,
Nec venit in mentem quorum consederis agris
Purpureos flores atque inter lilia carpens.   250
Saepe palam tamen hi rapiunt cupiuntque videri
Omnibus intrepidi ac furto laetantur in ipso
Deprensi, seu cum dictis nihil ordine verso
Longe alios ijsdem sensus mira arte dedere
Exueruntque animos verborum impune priores,   255
Seu priscis cum certandi exorta libido est

Et possessa diu sed enim male condita victis
Extorquere manu et melioribus addere regnis
Instant vi multa, melius ceu saepe videmus
Atque sata atque solo mutato surgere plantas;   260
Pomaque se referunt succos oblita priores
In melius. Sic regna Asiae Phrygiosque penates
Trojus auspicijs posuit melioribus heros
In Latio quamvis (nam divum fata vocabant)
Invitus Phoenissa tuo de littore cessit,   265
Nec connubia laeta nec incepti Hymenaei
Flexerunt immitem animum. Tu victa dolore
Occidis, et curae vix ipsa in morte relinquunt,
Semianimesque micant oculi lucemque requirunt.
Numquam o Dardaniae tetigissent vestra carinae   270
Littora, fors nulli poteras succumbere culpae.
Quare agite et mecum securi accingite furtis
Una omnes, pueri, passimque avertite praedas,
It nigrum campis agmen ceu cum populantur
Certatim ingentem formicae farris acervum.   275
Infelix autem (quidam nam saepe reperti)
Viribus ipse suis temere qui fisus et arti;
Externae quasi opis nihil indigus aspernatur
Fida sequi veterum vestigia dum sibi praeda
Temperat, heu, nimium, atque alienis parcit, inanis   280
Iustitiae memor. Ignota regione viarum
Tum male per deserta vagus huc erret et illuc
Atque gubernaclo in tenebris sin sydere amico.
Nec longum tales unquam laetantur, at ipsi
Saepe suis superant monimentis illaudatique   285
Ante obitus proprios (vix dignum credere) famae
Saepe suae letum et foetus flevere caducos.
Quam cuperent casso potius cariusse labore
Seque olim indecores artis docuisse parentes!
Non tamen omnia te priscis fas fidere qui non   290
Omnia sufficient omnino; plura labore
Incumbent tentanda tuo. Sortitor honesta
Nomina cum primis; facilis labor. Aut ea rebus
Quondam ipsis sua principio imposuere Latini
Saturnusque senex Picus Faunusque Latinusque,   295
Aut ea nos alijs rebus traducimus ultro,
Ut docui, atque alijs porro servire jubemus
Non sua. Quaedam etiam nobis nova condere nulla
Religio vetat indictasque effundere voces.
Non tamen haec penitus fuerint ignota, sed usquam   300

Agnoscant genus et cognatam ostendere gentem
Possint et stirpis nitantur origine certae
Quam referant. Tum bina juvat conjungere in unum
Molliter inter se vinclo sociata jugali.
Verum plura nefas vulgo congesta coire   305
Ipsaque quadrifidis subniti carmina verbis,
Itala nec passim fert monstra tricorpora tellus.
Horresco diros sonitus et levia spargo
Invitus perterricrepas per carmina voces.
Argolici quibus haec usu concessa libido   310
Talia connubia et tales celebrent Hymenaeos,
Tergeminas immane struant ad sydera moles
Pelion addentes Ossaeque et Pelio Olympum.
Quin et si quando patriae penuria vocis
Obstabit, fas Grajugenum felicibus oris   315
Devehere informem massam quam incude Latina
Informant patriumque jubent dediscere morem.
Sic quondam Ausoniae succrevit copia linguae
Optima, et antiquis Latium nihil invidet Argis
Quod dites penitus carpendo exhausit Athenas,   320
Transtulit unde ingens aurum gemmasque nitentis
Craterasque scyphosque et comoda cymbia Iacco
Et carchesia Mulciberi informata caminis;
Multaque praeterea medijs erepta Mycenis
Graja genus nostris fulgent immixta, nec ullum   325
Apparet discrimen: eunt insignibus aequis
Undique per Latios et civis et advena fines.
Iam nostri cessit porro sermonis egestas;
Nusquam uber patriae, tibi nusquam opulentia deerit.
Vocis thesauris depromere cuncta licebit   330
Magne tuis Cicero, Latium cui plurima debet,
Aequalesque tui nati felicibus annis
Omnia sufficient large, nec audere deinde
Incumbet timidis adeo nova multa poetis.
Quod si forte tamen fatis urgebere iniquis   335
Indigus Argivorum opis, aude, ultroque fatere,
Nec Danaum te dissimula de more loquutum.
Quandoquidem incidimus scopulis aliquando malignis
Aut Maleae aut Scyllae puppes sorbentibus undis
Aut Strophadum (Grajo Strophades stant nomine dictae),   340
Praecipue furor ille animis cum injectus agitque
Praecipites (oestron Graij vertere vocantes).
Saepe etiam vidi veterum inter carmina vatum
Barbarico versus cultu gazaque superbos,

Belgicaque immisit trans Alpes esseda Gallus   345
In Latium Poenos contra Macedumque phalanges;
Nunc camuris onerosa vehunt ea cornibus uri.
Et dubitem ne deficiat me larga supellex
Verborum angustique premat sermonis egestas!
Quin et victa situ si te paenuria adaxit   350
Verba licet renovare; licet tua, sancta vetustas,
Vatibus indugredi sacraria; saepius olli
Aetatis gaudent insignibus antiquai,
Copia nec defit quorum nunc pervius usus.
Obsita sic aevo visuntur templaque et urbes,   355
Sicubi murorum apparent vix signa ruentum,
Tantus amor ritus artesque agnoscere avorum est.
Non tamen ille vetus squalor fuat undique et aspra
Verborum rubigo; juvant si rara vetusta.
Tum quoque si deerunt rebus sua nomina certa,   360
Fas illas apta verborum ambire corona
Et late circumfusis exponere dictis.
Quid memorem cum magna ducum referenda virumque
Nomina dura nimis dictu atque asperrima cultu?
Tum licet aut illos veterum signare parentum   365
Aut fluvij patrij aut urbis de nomine prisco.
Dura etiam nunc addentes nunc inde putantes
Pauca minutatim multa vi nomina laevant.
Titanas minor hinc labor Enceladique tumultus
Coeumque Iapetumque Othumque ferumque Ephialtem   370
Et socios canere ingentem rescindere Olympum
Atque Iovem astrifera conatos pellere ab arce
Quam Gallorum acies Itala virtute subactas
Cedentum nuper Latioque iterumque ruentum
Alpibus (Ausonidum sic vos voluistis inertes   375
Primores scelere immani) et turbantia regna
Insubrum, Eridani gentes, Venetosque togatos.
Quandoquidem minor est libertas nomina vana
Fingere, vera autem oderunt plerumque Camoenae;
Tunc vero si falsa tibi inducenda, Pelasgum   380
Aut aliquem referant aut non indicta profare;
Insolita oderunt aures nec nomina agrestum
Pastorumve indigna placent. Quid enim Ciceriscus
Faburnusque mihi cantet quae Mopsus et ipse
Tityrus aut Damon quondam cantare solebant?   385
At neque verborum causa vis nulla canentem
Consilium preter cogat res addere inanis,
Verba sed usque ipsis verbis servire jubeto.

Nec dubitem interdum vacuas et mente carentes
Incassum voces atque irrita fundere verba   390
Aut quae nullius fungantur munere sensus
Dives ut insigni tantum et conspectus amictu
Versus eat seseque superbo ostentet in auro.
Atque adeo quae sint ne vero quaere profecto
Illa: tibi occurrent ultro seque obvia passim   395
Sponte dabunt cum res ipsa exiget. Omnia sed tunc
Perpendes animo versus resonantia verba;
Saepe etenim quaedam ignarum te fallere possint
Ni vigiles mandatum et munus obire recusent
Furenturque operi clam sese et inertia cessent: 400
Caetera dum labor exercet concordia jussus
Quaeque suus, tantum illa dabunt umbramque sonumque.
Atque ideo quid ferre queant, quid quaeque recusent
Explorare prius labor esto, ac munera justa
Mandato et proprium cunctis partire laborem;   405
Obscuros aliter crepitus et murmura vana
Miscebis ludentque sonis fallacibus aures.
Saepe igitur ruptis vinclis exuta volutes
Verba et compactum quaesitor disijce versum;
Post iterum refice et partes in pristina redde   410
Partibus avulsis. Numquam te libera fallent
Nexibus incautum resoluto carmine verba;
Tum dolus ammotisque apparet nubibus error.
Nec vero facile est etiam concludere versus
Postquam parta animo jamdudum clara reperta.   415
Tum vates sibi centum aures, tum lumina centum
Exoptat dubius curae dulcisque laboris.
Dividit huc illuc animum cunctamque pererrat
Naturam rerum versatque per omnia mentem
Quis rebus dexter modus aut quae mollia fandi   420
Tempora; fixae haerent species in pectore rerum.
Nec mora nec requies dubio sententia surgit
Multa animo variansque; omnes sed dividit ille
In facies metuitque etiam tutissima et haeret
Ambiguus. Nunc multa animum, nunc consulit aures,   425
Nunc vinclis partes aptare et stringere verba
In numerum et versu assiduo decus addere torno,
Nunc agitare animo siqua olim audita recursent
Sponte sua et memorem mentem excitat atque repostis
Thesauris depromit opes, laetusque laboris   430
Ipse sui parto fruitur. Tum multa repente
Fors inopina aperit cunctanti aliudque putanti

Dum coelum aspectat suspensus opemque moratur.
Iamque haec jamque illa attentat, texitque retexitque
Incertus; nunc aedificat, nunc structa labore   435
Multo sponte ruit melioraque sufficit usque
Et varijs indefessus conatibus instat.
Quid non assiduus vincat labor! Omnia tandem
Dura domat patiens vatis mora. Quippe canenti
Saepius occurrunt haud dictu mollia ubi haeret   440
Cura diu multoque exercita corda labore.
Nunc hos nunc illos aditus facilemque requirit
Fortunam et scopulo longum luctatur iniquo;
Vertitur huc atque huc et vestigantia in omnes
Corda rapit partes atque omnia mente pererrat   445
Durus et insistens animis haud cedere certus
Dum se qua ostendat facilis via. Denique, multa
Aut vi aut coeli ac Fortunae munere victor,
Exultat domitoque animis it ad aethera monstro.
Ast ubi nulla viam nec vis nec dextra aperit sors   450
Nec prodest fessas aut crebra resumere vires
Aut Musis aptum captare ad carmina tempus,
Invitus cura absistit tristisque relinquit
Cepta infecta pedem referens, velut urbe viator
Siquis tendat iter campis cui se amnis abundans   455
Ecce viae medio obijciat spumisque fragosos
Post imbrem volvens late in freta concita fluctus
Horrescit, ripasque moratus obambulat anceps
Audeat attentare vadum pedibusne vel undis
Inijiciat sese saltu superetque natando.   460
Tum vitae metuens retro redit aeger iterque
Aut alia tenet aut alio sub tempore differt.
Hoc tamen eveniet paucis, vis daedala fandi
Tot se adeo in facies, tot sese vertit in ora,
Mille trahens varios verborum ambage colores.   465
Ne quid inexpertum ne quid dimittat inausum,
Omnia fit. Nempe illa parum prodesse sub vera
Sensit ubi forma se protinus induit ultro
Atque alium atque alium in vultum mutabile monstrum:
Quin etiam egregij hoc procurant usque poetae   470
Sponte sua quamvis etiam succedere possent
Una eademque via facili sibi multa labore.
Nec nisi versicolor sit fandi copia credunt
Posse placere diuque animos novitate tenere:
Aspice ubi variat crebro tenor ille figuris   475
Mutatis aures illectas quanta voluptas

Detineat, quali pertentet pectora motu.
Ergo omnem curam impendunt ut cernere nusquam
Sit formas similes, naturae exempla secuti
Naturae omniparentis; habent namque omnia porro 480
Dissimilem inter se formam quaecumque sub astris
Vitales carpunt auras, genus omne ferarum
Atque hominum pictae et volucres mutaeque natantes.
Saepe videbis eos solitis rem pandere verbis,
Nunc nebula arcanos verborum adducere sensus, 485
Perpetui nunc sermonis longo ordine ferri,
Nunc haerere, interque rogantes quaerere multa.
Ecce improvisi compellant vocibus ultro
Saepe aliquem longe absentem, desertaque et antra
Et solos montis affantur; saepe salutant 490
Sylvasque fluviosque et agros sensuque carentes
Speluncas velut haec sint responsura vocata,
Et vos o vacui compellant nomine saltus.
Praeterea verbis inimicos addere sensus
Oppositis dum dissimulant aliudque videbis 495
Saepe loqui atque aliud simulata obducere mente
Et proferre animo penitus contraria dicta.
Sic verusque piusque Sinon, sic fida Lacaena
Deiphobo, Drancesque dedit tot stragis acervos
Egregius passimque insignijt arva tropheis. 500
Scilicet haec liceant causas orantibus; ipsi
Non autem vates ausint eadem omnia fando
Liberius. Quin ecce juvat super aethera quondam
Tollere res nec sit fas tantum credere dictis;
It caelo clamor, tremit omnis murmure Olympus. 505
Nec mora bis vocem ingeminant urbisque ruinas
Fataque proeliaque et sortem execrantur iniquam,
O patria, o rapti necquicquam ex hoste penates
Clamantes, cecidit, pro Iuppiter, Ilion ingens.
Quid cum Neptunum dicunt mare, vina Lyaeum, 510
Et Cererem frumenta, patrumque et nomine natos
Significant? urbesque juvat pro civibus ipsis
Effari. Timor iccirco cum invaserit Afros
Africa terribili tremet horrida terra tumultu.
Unum pro cunctis etiam fas prodere, et omnes 515
Fontes atque amnes Acheloja pocula signant.
Nec verborum animos tantum variare figuris
Diversis quantum juvat ipsa coloribus usque
Pingere verba. Viden quam dispar saepius ijsdem
Ordine connexis aut hoc aut partibus illo 520

Fortuna eveniat! Male quaedam saepe videbis
Incipere in primo sermonem limine jacta
Quae si verborum retroverso ordine in finem
Conijcias medijs aut partibus intercludas
Responsent longe melius mage grata legentum 525
Auribus, usque adeo refert regioque locusque.
Fas fuit et partes interdum ingentia in ambas
Verba interpositis proscindere seque parare
Obijcibus, tum deterere atque abstraxi secando
Exiguam partem et strinxisse fluentia membra. 530
Vidistin? cum saepe aliquid cepere profari
Nulla mora est, tum proinde silent medijsque morantur
Vocibus (oblitos dictorum saepe putares
Atque sui) subitoque aliud discrimine multo
Diversum primis sermonibus interruptis 535
Subijciunt; redeunt mox deinde et capta priora
Perficiunt memores atque intervalla relinquunt
In medio clauduntque suis hinc finibus inde.
Quid sequar ulterius? Quanta dulcedine captas
Detineant aures vocem cum rursus eandem 540
Ingeminant ultro alterius nil vocis egentes!
Tum neque Parnasi vobis juga, tum neque Pindi
Ulla moram faciunt tam dulci carmine tactis,
Pierides, sed enim decurritis ocyus ac vos
Iungitis et socias voces et carmina vestra; 545
Pan etiam Arcadia neget hoc si judice praesens,
Pan etiam Arcadia dicet se judice vanum.
Quae vobis, quae non, vates, jam copia nota!
Quae facies! quae forma! suum nec Graecia morem
Deficit atque suas nobis dat habere figuras. 550
Sed meme interea longe tempusque vigorque
Effugit amplecti conantem versibus omnes
Dicendi formas. Citius comprendere possem
Quam varij in pratis spectentur vere colores,
Quot folia in sylvis hyemis sub frigore primo 555
Lapsa cadant. Adeo tot se in miracula sermo
Transformat vatum, tot sese vertit in ora.
Quorum nulla tamen major prudentia quam se
Aut premere aut rerum pro majestate canendo
Tollere. Nunc igitur videas summittere mentem 560
Verborum parcos humilique obrepere gressu
Textaque vix gracili deducere carmina filo;
Nec mora nunc verbis opulentos divite gaza
Cernere erit fluere ac laxis decurrere habenis

Fluxosque undantesque; redundat copia laeta 565
Ubere felici, verborumque ingruit horror
Perpetuus densoque citus fluit agmine sermo
Hibernarum instar nivium cum Iuppiter Alpes
Frigidus aerias petit et juga cana revestit.
Ergo illi per aperta volant strepituque feruntur 570
Saltibus in vacuis ingenti viribus usi
Omnibus atque animis freti ventisque secundis
Percurrunt alacres pleno lata aequora velo.
Interdum vero cohibent undantia lora
Non humiles, non sublimes, media inter utrumque 575
Littus arant veluti spacia et confinia radunt
Utraque, nec quicquam effusi nec copiae egeni.
Hactenus haec. Mihi nunc faciles da protinus aures,
Care puer; majora vocant. Procul ecce per auras
Auditur dulcis late concentus, ab aethra 580
Dulcia Castalides modulantur carmina divae.
Sit mihi fas, divae, vestros nunc prodere cantus
Tam varios quales suspensis auribus haurio
Admirans vestraeque loqui discrimina vocis
Arcanos numeros tacitasque in carmine leges. 585
Illa quidem divina animis illapsa voluptas
Oblectat varie sensus, sed pandere verbis
Difficile; intactus labor hactenus. Hic mihi, divae,
Este bonae. Favet ipsa altro dea mater amorum,
Alma Venus, perquam (nisi vana est fama) repertum est 590
Quodcumque humanas aures dulcedine tangit.
Illa olim tereti spumosa per aequora concha
Vecta ibat, bijugi mordebant aurea frena
Delphines curvisque secabant marmora caudis,
Lora regebat amor. Pulchram maria humida alumnam 595
Excipere plausu laeto, subsidere fluctus
Undaeque iratique Euri tumidaeque procellae,
Littora laetari. Liquidi gens squammea ponti
Undique visendi studio fluit omnibus antris
Et turpes phocae et dorso horrentia cete. 600
Ecce autem dictu horrendum mirabile monstrum
Prima hominis facies cui, desinit alvus in anguem,
Terribilis visu ponti fera deserit antra
Capta deae forma, subitoque fit obvia et illi
Vim parat. Exclamat dea turpi exterrita monstro 605
Luctaturque deosque implorat voce marinos.
Desuper aligerum frustra trepidum agmen amorum
Tendere curvatos arcus pavidaeque parenti

Auxilium levibus nequicquam ferre sagittis.
Instabat fera et hirsutis nivea ora lacertis   610
Oraque collaque vexabat, scelus, oscula captans.
Et vim passa foret monstro supposta Dione
Aurea deformi, socio ni ex agmine Triton
Ter spumante cava insonuisset ab aequore concha.
Audiit excitus fundo Neptunus ab imo;   615
Exciti affluxere dei Inousque Palaemon
Nereusque Glaucusque et Phorci exercitus omnis
Una omnes Veneri auxilio. Pater ipse tridentem
Neptunus dextra quatit exitiumque minatur
Absterretque feram et pontum deturbat in imum.   620
Excepere deam vitreis Nereides antris
Exanimem multoque metu fovere trementem.
At rex undarum domitor pro munere tali
Tritonem affecit pretio et dedit ipse profundi
Custodem sociosque pari subjunxit honore   625
Qui spumosa cava streperent per caerula concha
Taliave posthac ausint maris horrida monstra.
Iamque illi inter se servantes humida regna
Responsare procul diverso ex aequore cantu
Ceperunt vario alterni, quo carmine captae   630
Nereides stupuere, chori stupuere marini.
Exin summa leves celeri per marmora motu
Ad diversa pedes vocum discrimina morunt.
Una omnes junxere chorum Oceanitides, una
Plauserunt pedibus choreas, Clothoque levisque   635
Cymodoce Drymoque et candida Dejopeja
Et Nereja Xantho et Neptunine Arethusa
Atque Atte atque Ephyre et fusis Galathea capillis
Una omnes canere atque salo insultare liquenti
Una omnes, ipsaeque sonant pugnantibus undae   640
Fluctibus, alta sonant ingenti murmure Nerei
Stagna, procul vasto responsant littora pulsu.
Nec mora quae stagnis, quae fluminibusque vagantur
Nymphae etiam simili cecinerunt carmina ritu
Et coetu cinxere lacus. Gens ilice nata   645
Indocile atque hominum durum genus admirati
Murmura captabant gelida cum nocte quiescunt
Omnia, cum tacet omnis ager sylvaeque silescunt;
Tum procul audiri stringenti flumine ripas
Clarius arguti saxis obstantibus amnes   650
Naiadumque chori mulcentes aethera cantu.
Atque ita mortales duri monstrantibus undis

Paulatim sese cantu assuevere rudesque
Ore sonos primum tentarunt, inde cavae orbi
Miranti ostensus subito testudinis usus   655
Tibiaque et septem imparibus compacta cicutis
Fistula. Tum gelidi calamo pineta Lycaei
Pan capripes tenuit mirantia, condidit arces
Amphion cythara Dyrcaeus, movit Arion
Delphinos curvos, tum saxa sequentia traxit   660
Saxaque et intonsas sylvas Oeagrius Orpheus,
Usque adeo varia illa animis discrimina vocum
Grata auresque tenent mira dulcedine captas.
Quod genus Aonij simulac sensere poetae
Qui primum paribus jungebant omnia vinclis   665
Carmina contextuque pari et compagibus ijsdem,
Ipsi etiam variare modos cepere canendo
Et numeris tandem gratus labor additus ipsis.
Principio fas per senos consurgere versum
Semper ad alta gradus perque omnes tendere cursum.   670
Verum non eadem vis omnibus aut vigor idem,
Nam quamvis cunctis pariter spatia aequa viarum
Incumbant superanda, tamen velocius hic se
Saepe rapit celerique fugam secat ocyor Euro;
Ille autem tardis sese fert passibus aegre   675
Ignavus fessosque incedens vix trahit artus.
Immo age, quando juvat quae vis quae robora cuique
Discere vel quae quamque viae fortuna sequatur,
Huc geminas nunc flecte acies turbamque sonantem
Agminis alipedis toto sursum aspice clivo,   680
Dum senos per quisque gradus se tollere certat.
Aspice ut hic volucri properet pede tangere metam
Perpetuumque rapit supera ad fastigia cursum,
Nec requiescet enim donec superaverit omnis
Enitens ad summa gradus. Contra ille quietem   685
Segnis amat creberque moram trahit et piger haeret
Atque hic atque illic interrumpitque laborem.
Cernis ut hic primo jam nunc in limine cessat
Fessus anhelanti similis similisque cadenti,
Rursum iter inceptum collectis viribus urget.   690
Hic animo frustra primis congressibus ardet,
Iamque gradus primos superavit, jamque secundos
Successu laetus, sed dum fastigia prensat
Tertia, genua labant medijsque procumbit in ausis.
Ulterius fert ille pedem: sed nec tamen ipse   695
Fortuna longum laetatur; deficit aeger

Nec potis est quartam cursu contingere metam.
Ecce omnes alius pernix pede transit et acri
Corde impune putans volat ac spes arrigit et jam
Extremo aspirat post quinta pericla labori;   700
Invidit fortuna, cadit meta ecce sub alta
Pronus humi frustra exultans certamine. Paucis
Perpetuo tranare datum spatia ultima cursu.
Quid! qui post primos casus redit acrior ira
Ad pugnam, incendit vires et conscia virtus   705
Et pudor, evadit subito spatia ultima campi
Exuperansque animis haud ille in fine quiescit
Sed rapit ulterius cursus atque altera victor
Metitur spatia atque addit rursum altera, donec
Deficiat vires extremas spiritus aeger.   ,   710
Perpetuosque ideo verborum ducere tractus
In longum versus consertos saepe videbis
Enodesque artus ut respirare legentes
Haud valeant fessi et vocem renovare quiete.
Tu creber, tu necte moras, tibi saepe quiescant   715
Carmina quae velut imparibus sint aspera nodis
Qualis longa seges, qualis fluvialis harundo.
Quod si perpetuo perstabunt ducta tenore
Omnia, nullus erit concentus, nulla voluptas
Vocis, nempe lupos ululatu imitabere longo   720
Flabraque ventorum per densos sibila lucos.
Contemplator ubi guttae de montibus altis
Humida praecipitant lacrimanti fornice in antra
Pulsantes interrupto sola saxea lapsu
In numerum quantum juvet haud aequalibus aures   725
Distinctus intervallis sonor. At magis udis
Liquidis in venis si forte exuberat humor
Stiriaque incipiat lentum manare tenore
Perpetuo, prior illa voluptas deseret aures
Actutum querulae mutato murmure aquai.   730
Haud aliter vatum continget versibus ipsis
Ni varios secti in numeros persaepe quiescant
Nunc hic nunc illic; neque enim considere semper
Uno eodemque gradu liceat, nec fine quies est
Cunctis parta ipso quamvis obiere laborem   735
Quisque sum jussi confecto munere cursus;
Quidam etenim socios adeuntque juvantque sequentes
Consertique simul vadunt concordibus ausis.
Quod si quisque sui tantum memor ultima postquam
Attigerit spatia et proprii confine laboris   740

Considat socium oblitus decorisque salutisque
Hic illic disjectam aciem incompactaque versum
Agmina et invalidam passim ac sine robore turbam
Cernere erit nulloque labantes foedere partes.
Adjuvat et numeros sonus ipse ac dissonus ordo   745
Verborum, et diversa juvat dare versibus ora
Diversosque habitus, ne qualis primus et alter,
Inde alter rursus talem se ostenderit ultro.
Ille pedum melior motu et pernicibus alis,
Hic membris ac mole valens. Ille acer et ardens   750
Ingreditur, subit hic incessu ignavius aegra
Membra trahens tardo molimine subsidendo.
Ille viam tacito lapsu per levia radit,
Hic strepitu ingenti inter se allidentibus usque
Scrupea per pedibus loca calcem calce retrudit.   755
Inde alius subit egregio pulcherrimus ore
Cui pulchrum membris Venus omnibus afflat honorem;
Contra alius rudis informes ostentat et artus
Hirsutumque supercilium ac caudam sinuosam,
Ingratus visu ac sonitu illaetabilis ipso.   760
Non adeo hic possum vos o nec vestra silere
Corpora, terribiles frates, immania, partus
Monstrosi, quos non senis insistere plantis
Contentos quasi pes deformat septimus, ultraque
Ingentem trahitis caudam et producitis alvum,   765
Haud impune tamen. Nam qui subito inde sequuntur
Infensi opponunt subito se extremaque caudarum
Incidunt immane volumina vertice acuto.
Dissimiles habitus igitur diversaque versum
Ora vides multo et varios discrimine vultus.   770
Nec vero hae sine lege datae, sine mente figurae,
Sed facies sua pro meritis habitusque sonusque.
Omnibus invigilant vates et tempora captant
Apta, et suspensos sonus auribus excitat omnis.
Nec tantum verbis, ipso sed carmine signant   775
Res etiam vocumque sono et concordibus aptant
Verborum numeris. Hinc sibila saepe sonare
Carmina saepe vides ultro aspras stridere voces
Ut rerum strepitum strepituque et murmure versus
Assimiles imitentur. Ubi spumare reductis   780
Convulsum remis rostris stridentibus aequor
Ostendunt, cani spumas maris aere ruentes,
Tunc longe sale saxa sonant, tunc et freta ventis
Incipiunt agitata tumescere, littore fluctus

Illidunt rauco, atque refracta remurmurant unda   785
Ad scopulos, cumulo insequitur praeruptus aquae mons;
Nec mora, Trinacriam videas procul intremere omnem
Funditus et montes concurrere montibus altos.
Cum vero nautas miseratus cerula Nereus
Lenijt in morem stagni placidaeque paludis,   790
Labitur uncta vadis abies et levia radit.
Hoc etiam solers mirabere saepe legendo,
Sicubi Vulcanus sylvis incendia misit
Aut agro stipulae flamma crepitante cremantur;
Carmine nec levi dicenda est scabra crepido.   795
Tum si laeta canunt, hilari quoque carmina fronte
Incedunt laetumque sonant haud segnia verba,
Seu si vere novo rident prata humida, seu si
Panditur interea domus omnipotentis Olympi.
Mane novo varioque sonant aviaria cantu;   800
Contra autem sese tristes inamabile carmen
Induit in vultus, si forte invisa volucris
Nocte sedens serum canit importuna per umbras,
Ut quondam in bustis aut culminibus desertis.
Verba etiam res exiguas angusta sequuntur   805
Ingentesque juvant ingentia. Cuncta gigantem
Magna decent: vultus immanes, pectora lata
Et magni membrorum artus, magna ossa lacertique.
Hinc etiam geritur siquid molimine tardo,
Haud cita verba volant, pariter sed tarda laborant   810
Carmina vi multa, seu quando gleba coactis
Aeternum frangenda bidentibus, aequore seu cum
Cornua velatarum obvertenda antennarum.
At mora si fuerit damno, properare jubebo,
Si se forte cava extulerit mala vipera terra   815
Sole novo, cape saxa manu, cape robora pastor,
Ferte citi flammas, date tela, avertite pestem.
Ipse etiam versus ruat in praecepsque feratur
Praecipitans ruit in gremium cum Oceani nox
Aut cum perculsus graviter procumbit humi bos.   820
Cumque etiam requies rebus datur, ipsa quoque ultro
Carmina paulisper cursu cessare videbis
In medio interrupta; quierunt cum freta ponti
Postquam aurae posuere, quiescere protinus ipsum
Cernere erit versum et medijs subsistere ceptis.   825
Quid dicam? senior cum telum imbelle sine ictu
Invalidus jecit defectis viribus aeger,
Ipse etiam tardo nam tunc versus pede languet;

Nec tu illum aspicies telo discludere turres,
Disturbare domos, praefractaque quadrupedantum 830
Pectora pectoribus perrumpere, sternere turres
Ingentes totoque ferum dare funera campo.
Ille autem Musis carus cui contigit aure
Talia non surda sentire accommoda rebus
Carminaque et numeros studio concludere curat 835
Concordes dictis. Sed enim laudandus et ille
Pura fluunt nitido cui semper carmina amictu
Lumine clara suo, externae nihil indiga lucis.
Nam neque (si tantum fas credere) defuit olim
Qui lumen iocundum ultro lucemque perosus 840
Obscuris tenebris nebulaeque immiscuit atrae
Et multo noctis se circumfudit amictu
Indicijs nunc ignotis, nunc vocibus usus
Ambiguis, nunc perturbatis ordine verbis
Inverso, longos gaudens nunc ducere tractus, 845
Tantus amor noctis miseris, ea cura latendi.
Quod superest, quae dehinc etiam peragenda poetae
Expediam, postquam casus evaserit omnes
Signaque perpetuum perduxit ad ultima carmen
Exultans animo victor laetusque laborum. 850
Non Italas jam tum passim secura per urbes
Carmina vulgabit; ah ne sit gloria tanti
Et dulcis famae semper male suada cupido.
At patiens operum potius metuensque pericli
Addet sponte moram atque diu congesta tenebit 855
Clausa domi, donec ferventem mente calorem
Paulatim exuerit foetusque abolerit amorem
Ipse sui annorum labentium munere magno
Oblitusque alio curam traduxerit omnem.
Interea fidos adit haud securus amicos 860
Utque velint inimicum animum frontisque verendae
Dura supercilia induere et non parcere culpae,
Atque iterum atque iterum rogat, admonitusque latentis
Grates laetus agit vitis, et peccata fatetur
Sponte sua, quamvis etiam damnetur iniquo 865
Iudicio et falsum queat ore refellere crimen.
Tum demum redit et post longa oblivia passim
Incipit hic illic veterem explorare laborem.
Ecce autem nova se ante oculos fert undique imago,
Rerum longe alia species, mutataque ab illis 870
Carmina quae tantum ante recens compacta placebant;
Miratur tacitus nec se cognoscit in illis

Immemor, atque operum piget ac sese increpat ultro.
Tum retractat opus culpatum et cuncta novare
Carmina prosequitur, commissa piacula doctae   875
Palladis arte luens. Nunc haec nunc reijcit illa
Omnia tuta timens, et inania multa recidit
Submittens meliora. Premit tumida, aspera levit
Atque inculta domat subigens calamoque retractat
Vulnera juncturasque madendo nectit hiantes   880
Attondetque comas stringens sylvamque fluentem
Luxuriemque minutatim depascit inanem
Exercens durum imperium, dum funditus omnem
Nocturnis instans operis operisque diurnis
Versibus eluerit labem et commissa piarit.   885
Tum siqua est etiam pars imperfecta relicta,
Olim dum properat furor ingenijque morari
Tempestas vetat, absolvit, ac versibus affert
Invalidis miseratus opem claudisque medetur.
Arduus ille labor; verum hic durate, poetae,   890
Gloria quos movet aeternae pulcherrima famae.
Nec semel attrectare satis: verum omne quotannis
Terque quaterque opus evolvendum verbaque versis
Saepius immutanda coloribus, omne frequenti
Saepe retexendum carmen per singula cultu.   895
Quod non una dies fors afferet altera, et ultro,
Nullo olim studio, nulla olim in carmine cura,
Deprensae per se clarescent tempore culpae
Quaeque latent variae densa inter nubila pestes.
Quin etiam doctum multum juvet ille laborem   900
Qui varias caeli creber mutaverit oras
Nunc huc nunc illuc, gelidi vel Tyburis arces
Vel sylvas et prata petens sub Thusculo amoena.
Namque etiam mutant animi, genioque locorum
Diversas species, diversos pectora motus   905
Concipiunt, nostrisque novae se mentibus addit
Ultro aliquid semper lucis tenebraeque dehiscunt,
Atque novos operi semper fas addere cultus.
Verum esto hic etiam modus. Huic imponere curae
Nescivere aliqui finem medicasque secandis   910
Morbis abstinuisse manus ac parcere tandem
Immites, donec macie confectus et aeger
Aruit exhausto velut omnis sanguine foetus
Nativumque decus posuit, dum plurima ubique
Deformat sectos artus inhonesta cicatrix.   915
Tuque adeo vitae usque memor brevioris, ubi annos

Post aliquot (neque enim numerum neque tempora pono
Certa tibi) addideris decoris satis atque nitoris,
Rumpe moras; opus Italiae dimitte per oras
Depositisque novum exuvijs nitidamque juventam   920
Perque manus perque ora hominum permitte vagari.
Continuo laeto te dulces undique amici
Gratantes plausu excipient ac praemia solvent
Laudis, et ad caelum tua terris cognita virtus
Succedet, nomenque tuum sinus ultimus orbis   925
Trans Indum Gangemque procul, trans ultima Bactra
Audiet, ac seri post saecula longa nepotes
Accipient, nullo ingens abolebitur aevo.
Et dubitamus opes humiles contemnere avari
Nec potius sequimur dulces ante omnia Musas?   930
O fortunati quibus olim haec numina laeva
Annuerint praecepta sequi quaeve ipse canebam
Iussa modo plenus Phoebo attonitusque furore.
Nec satis hic artes aut ullae hominumve labores,
Et mea dicta parum prosint ne desuper adsit   935
Auxilium ac praesens favor omnipotentis Olympi.
Ipse viam tantum potui docuisse repertam
Aonas ad montis longeque ostendere Musas
Plaudentes summi choreas in vertice clivi,
Quo me haud ire sinunt trepidum fata invida et usque   940
Absterrentque arcentque procul, nec summa jugi unquam
Fas prensare manu fastigia. Sat mihi si te,
Si te olim longe aspiciam mea fida secutum
Indicia exuperasse viam summoque receptum
Vertice et haerentes socios juga ad alta vocantem,   945
Angele, si tecum vadentem passibus aequis
Accoltum juvenem aspiciam quem saepe maligno
Sudantem clivo dulci miserantur amore
Pierides fessumque sinu super ardua tollunt
Parnasi juga. Saepe antro sylvisque recondunt
Secretis puerum egregium placitoque fruuntur
Amplexu et dulci pia libant oscula cura,
Dum legit intactae lauri de fronde coronam
Insignem patruique audet se tollere supra
Divinas laudes famaeque aspirat avorum.   955
Sed non nulla tamen nostri quoque gratia facti
Forsan erit; me fida olim praecepta canentem
Stipabunt juvenes denso circum agmine fusi
Et vocem excipient intenti atque ora tenebunt
Una omnes. Tum fata meae si tempora vitae   960

Aequa dabunt nec me viridi succiderit aevo
Impia mors, olli gelida tardante senecta
Languentem et sera defessum aetate magistrum
Certatim prensa super alta cacumina dextra
Saepe trahent ultro. Fors et quandoque juvabit   965
Subvectare humeris (nostrorum grata laborum
Praemia) subnixumque ferent per aprica locorum
Et vitrei invalidum sistent ad flumina Serij
In patriam cantantem, ubi magno sacra Maroni
Solemnesque dapes solvemus et annua dona   970
Et tumulum viridi in ripa statuemus inanem,
Felices vatis manes animamque vocantes.
Tum simul illius laudes ac facta canemus
Certatim alternisque choris tollemus ad astra
Primus ut Aonijs Musas deduxerit oris   975
In patriam et Grajum Romana per oppida carmen
Sparserit, ut juvenis Siculas inflarit avenas,
Utque idem Ausonios animi miseratus agrestes
Extulerit sacros ruris super aethera honores,
Triptolemi invectus volucri per sydera curru.   980
Res demum ingressus Romanae laudis ad arma
Excierit Latium omne Phrygumque instruxerit alas,
Verba Deo similis. Decus a te principe nostrum
Omne, pater, tibi Grajugenum de gente trophaea
Suspendunt Itali vates tua signa secuti.   985
Te propter Graij (quae plurima turba) poetae
Cedunt Italiae. Elysijs te Graecia campis
Miraturque auditque ultro assurgitque canenti.
Te sine nil nobis cultum; tibi maxima rerum
Verborumque fides uni. Omnes ora Latini   990
In te oculosque ferunt versi; tua maxima virtus
Omnibus auxilio est. Tua libant carmina passim
Assidui primis et te mirantur ab annis.
Nemo tibi frustra certaverit: omnia cedant
Secla nec invideant primos tibi laudis honores,   995
Fortunate operum; tua praestans gloria fama,
Quo quemquam sperare nefas, sese extulit alis.
Nil adeo mortale sonas; tibi captus amore
Ipse suos animos, sua munera laetus Apollo
Addidit ac multa praestantem insignijt arte.   1000
Quodcumque hoc opis atque artis nostrique reperti,
Uni grata tibi debet generosa juventus
Quam docui et rupis sacrae super ardua duxi,
Dum tua fida lego vestigia, te sequor unum,

O decus Italiae, lux o clarissima rerum.   1005
Te colimus, tibi perpetuas sacravimus aras
Et tibi rite tuum semper dicemus honorem
Carminibus. Salve vates sanctissime! quando
Laudibus augeri tua gloria nil potis ultra
Et nostrae nil vocis eget. Nos aspice ab alto,   1010
Pectoribusque tuos castis immitte calores,
Insinuans, pater, atque animis tete insere nostris.

BIBLIOGRAPHY

ABBREVIATIONS

LCL   Loeb Classical Library
LLA   Library of the Liberal Arts
OCT   Oxford Classical Texts
TCT   Teubner Classical Texts

CHIEF EDITIONS AND TRANSLATIONS OF THE *DE ARTE POETICA*

For a detailed list of all known editions and translations of the De arte poetica the reader is referred to Mario Di Cesare's *Bibliotheca Vidiana: A Bibliography of Marco Girolamo Vida* (Florence, 1974), pp. 167–98. The following list contains a selection of important editions with significant circulation; all of these I have examined personally.

Marci Hieronymi Vidae Cremonensis De Arte Poetica Libri III. . . . Rome, 1527.

M. Hieronymi Vidae Cremonensis De Arte Poetica Libri Tres. Paris, 1527.

This probably unauthorized edition, which presents a text significantly different from either the 1517 manuscript or the 1527 *editio princeps*, is discussed briefly above, pp. 199–200.

Marci Hieronymi Vidae Cremonensis . . . Poemata Omnia. . . . Cremona, 1550.

Marci Hieronymi Vidae, Cremonensis. . . . De arte poetica Libri Tres. Ed. Tho. Tristram. Oxford, 1723.

Vida's *Art of Poetry* Translated into English Verse, by the Reverend Mr. Christopher Pitt, A.M. London, 1725.

This is the first edition of what became the standard English translation of Vida's *De arte poetica*.

Marci Hieronymi Vidae . . . Poemata omnia. . . . Ed. J. Antonio and Cajetano Volpi. Padua, 1731.

This great collected edition is the source of the text photographically reproduced above.

Marci Hieronymi Vidae . . . Poemata quae extant omnia. . . . Ed. Richard Russel. London, 1732.

Les quatres poëtiques: d'Aristote, d'Horace, de Vida, de Déspreaux. Trans. and comm. M. L'Abbé Batteux. Paris, 1771.

The Art of Poetry. The Poetical Treatises of Horace, Vida, and Boileau, with the Translations by Howe, Pitt, and Soame. Ed. A. S. Cook. Boston, 1892.

This book was reprinted in 1926, in New York.

OTHER WORKS

AESCHYLUS. *Septem quae supersunt tragoediae*. Ed. Gilbert Murray.2d ed. OCT. Oxford, 1966.

AIGNER, JOSEPH. *Die Christliche-lateinische Muse*. Vol. II. Munich, 1825–28.

ALBERSON, HAZEL S. "Marcus Hieronymus Vida." Unpublished Ph.D. Dissertation. University of Wisconsin, 1935.

APOLLODORUS. *The Library*. Trans. James George Frazer. 2 vols. LCL. London, 1921.

ARIOSTO, LODOVICO. *Orlando furioso*. Ed. Dino Provenzal. 4 vols. Biblioteca Universale. Milan, 1935.

ARISTOTLE. *Aristotele-Poetica*. Ed. Augusto Rostagni. 2d ed. Turin, 1945.

——. *Aristotelis categoriae et liber de interpretatione*. Ed. L. Minio Paluello. OCT. Oxford, 1961.

——. *Aristotelis De arte poetica liber*. Ed. Rudolf Kassel. OCT. Oxford, 1965.

——. *The "Art" of Rhetoric*. Trans. John Freese. LCL. London, 1959.

——. *Nicomachean Ethics*. Trans. H. Rackham. LCL. London, 1962.

——. *Politics*. Trans. H. Rackham. LCL. London, 1959.

——. *Rhetorica ad Alexandrum*. Trans. H. Rackham. LCL. London, 1957.

ATKINS, J. W. H. *Literary Criticism in Antiquity*. 2 vols. New York, 1952.

AUGUSTINE, SAINT (AURELIUS AUGUSTINUS). *Confessions*. Trans. William Watts. 2 vols. LCL. London, 1942–46.

BALDWIN C. S. *Medieval Rhetoric and Poetic*. New York, 1928.

——. *Renaissance Literary Theory and Practice*. New York, 1939.

BASIL, SAINT. *De legendis antiquorum libris*. Trans. Leonardo Bruni. Venice, 1478.

BATTEUX, CHARLES. *Les quatres poëtiques*. Trans. M. L'Abbé Batteux. 2 vols. Paris, 1771.

BEMBO, PIETRO. *Prose della volgar lingua*. Ed. Mario Marti. Padua, 1967.

BEMBO, PIETRO, and PICO DELLA MIRANDOLA. *Le Epistole "De Imitatione" di Giovanfrancesco Pico della Mirandola e di Pietro Bembo.* Ed. G. Santangelo. Florence, 1954.

BOCCACCIO, GIOVANNI. *Boccaccio on Poetry.* Trans. Charles Osgood. LLA. New York, 1962.

BOILEAU-DESPREAUX, NICHOLAS. *Oeuvres.* Ed. Georges Mongredien. Classiques Garnier. Paris, 1961.

BOLGAR, R. R. *The Classical Heritage.* New York, 1964.

BOWRA, C. M. *Pindar.* Oxford, 1964.

BUTCHER, S. H. *Aristotle's Theory of Poetry and Fine Art.* New York, 1957.

CAMPANA, A. "The Origin of the Word 'Humanist,' " *Journal of the Warburg and Cortauld Institute,* IX (1942), 60–73.

CASSIRER, ERNST, and PAUL O. KRISTELLER, eds. *The Renaissance Philosophy of Man.* Chicago, 1948.

CASTELVETRO, LODOVICO. *Poetica d'Aristotele vulgarizzata e sposta.* Basel, 1576.

CASTIGLIONE, BALDASSARE. *Il Libro del cortegiano.* Ed. V. Cian. Florence, 1947.

CASTOR, GRAHAME. *Pléiade Poetics.* Cambridge, 1964.

CICERO, MARCUS TULLIUS. *Brutus and Orator.* Trans. G. L. Hendrickson and H. M. Hubbell. LCL. London, 1962.

——. *De natura deorum.* Trans. H. Rackham. LCL. London, 1961.

——. *De oratore.* Trans. E. W. Sutton and H. Rackham. 2 vols. LCL. London, 1959.

——. *Somnium Scipionis.* Ed. Carl Meissner. TCT. Leipzig, 1897.

[Pseudo-] CICERO, MARCUS TULLIUS. *Rhetorica ad Herennium.* Trans. Harry Caplan. LCL. London, 1964.

CICCHITELLI, VINCENZO. *Sulle opere poetiche di Marco Girolamo Vida.* Naples, 1904.

COOK, A. S. *The Art of Poetry.* Boston, 1892.

COOPER, LANE. *A Bibliography of the Poetics of Aristotle.* Cornell Studies in English XI. New Haven, 1928.

CURTIUS, ERNST R. *European Literature and the Latin Middle Ages.* Trans. Willard Trask. New York, 1953.

DANTE ALIGHIERI. *Il convivio.* Ed. and comm. by G. Busnelli and G. Vandelli, with an introduction by M. Barbi. 2d ed. Florence, 1968.

——. *De vulgari eloquentia.* Ed. Aristide Marigo. 3d ed. Florence, 1968.

——. *The Divine Comedy.* Trans. and comm. by Charles S. Singleton. 6 vols. Princeton, 1970–75.

DI CESARE, MARIO A. "The *Ars poetica* of Marco Girolamo Vida and the Manuscript Evidence," in *Acta Conventus Neo-Latini Lovaniensis, Proceedings of the First International Congress of Neo-Latin Studies, Louvain 23–28 August 1971,* pp. 207–18. Ed. J. IJsewijn and E. Kessler. Louvain and Munich, 1973.

——. *Bibliotheca Vidiana: A Bibliography of Marco Girolamo Vida.* Florence, 1974.

——. *Vida's Christiad and Vergilian Epic.* New York, 1964.

ELSE, GERALD F. *Aristotle's Poetics: The Argument.* Cambridge, Mass., 1963.

——. "Homer and the Homeric Problem," in *Lectures in Memory of Louise Taft Semple*, pp. 315–65. Ed. D. W. Bradeen et al. Princeton, 1967.

——. *The Origin and Early Form of Greek Tragedy.* Cambridge, Mass., 1967.

ENNIUS, QUINTUS. *The Annals of Quintus Ennius.* Ed. Ethel Steuart. Cambridge, 1925.

ERASMUS, DESIDERIUS. *The Adages of Erasmus.* Trans. and comm. by Margaret Phillips. Cambridge, 1964.

——. "Ciceronianus," in Izora Scott, *The Imitation of Cicero*, pt. 2, pp. 19–130. New York, 1910.

——. *De duplici copia commentaria duo.* Paris, 1535.

FARAL, EDMOND. *Les Arts poétiques du XIIe et du XIIIe Siècle.* Paris, 1924.

FERGUSON, WALLACE K. *Europe in Transition.* Boston, 1962.

——. *The Renaissance in Historical Thought.* Boston, 1948.

FICINO, MARSILIO. *Opera omnia.* 2 vols. Facsimile edition. Turin, 1959.

FLETCHER, JEFFERSON B. *Literature of the Italian Renaissance.* New York, 1934.

GABOTTO, FERDINANDO. *Cinque lettere di M. G. Vida.* Pinerolo, 1890.

GILMORE, MYRON P. *The World of Humanism.* New York, 1962.

GIRALDUS, LILIUS GREGORIUS. *De poetis nostrorum temporum.* Ed. Karl Wotke. Berlin, 1894.

GRAY, HANNA H. "Renaissance Humanism: The Pursuit of Eloquence," in *Renaissance Essays*, pp. 199–216. Ed. Paul O. Kristeller and Philip P. Wiener. New York, 1968.

GRUBE, G. M. A. *The Greek and Roman Critics.* Toronto, 1965.

HATHAWAY, BAXTER. *The Age of Criticism: The Late Renaissance in Italy.* Ithaca, 1962.

HESIOD. *Hesiodi Carmina.* Ed. A. Rzach. TCT. Leipzig, 1902.

HOMER. *Iliad.* Ed. D. B. Monro. 2 vols. 5th ed. OCT. Oxford, 1963.

——. *Odyssey.* Ed. and comm. by W. B. Stanford. 2 vols. London, 1965–67.

HORACE, QUINTUS FLACCUS. *Opera.* Ed. E. Wickham and H. Garrod. OCT. Oxford, 1959.

JAEGER, WERNER. *Aristotle*, 2d ed. Oxford, 1948.

——. *Paideia: The Ideals of Greek Culture.* Trans. Gilbert Highet. 3 vols. Oxford, 1944.

KRISTELLER, PAUL O. *The Classics and Renaissance Thought.* Martin Classical Lectures XV. Cambridge, Mass., 1955.

KRISTELLER, PAUL O. and PHILIP P. WIENER, eds. *Renaissance Essays.* New York, 1968.

LANCETTI, VINCENZO. *Della vita e degli scritti di Girolamo Vida*, 2d ed. Milan, 1840.

LEFÈVRE-DEUMIER, JULES. *Etudes biographiques et littéraires*. Paris, 1854.

LESKY, ALBIN. *Greek Tragedy*. London, 1965.

——. *A History of Greek Literature*. 2d ed. New York, 1963.

LONGINUS. *On the Sublime*. Ed. and comm. by D. A. Russell. Oxford, 1964.

LUCAN, MARCUS. *The Civil War*. Trans. J. Duff. LCL. London, 1928.

MACROBIUS. *Macrobius*. Ed. Francis Eyssenhardt. TCT. Leipzig, 1868.

MAGGI, LORENZO, and BARTHOLOMEW LOMBARDI. *In Aristotelis librum de poetica communes explicationes*. Venice, 1550.

MAZZACURATI, GIANCARLO. *Misure del classicismo rinascimentale*. Naples, 1967.

MIRIAM JOSEPH, SISTER. *Rhetoric in Shakespeare's Time*. New York, 1962.

NOVATI, FRANCESCO. "Sedici lettere inedite di M. G. Vida, Vescovo d'Alba," *Archivio storico lombardo*, XXV (1898), 195–281; *ibid.*, XXVI (1899), 1–59.

OTIS, BROOKS. *Virgil: A Study in Civilized Poetry*. Oxford, 1963.

OVID, PUBLIUS. *P. Ovidius Naso*. Ed. Rudolph Merkel. TCT. 3 vols. Leipzig, 1867–68.

PADELFORD, F. M. *Select Translations from Scaliger's Poetics*. Yale Studies in English XXVI. New York, 1905.

PAUSANIAS. *Description of Greece*. Trans. W. H. S. Jones. LCL. 5 vols. London, 1918–35.

PETRARCA, FRANCESCO. *Francisci Petrarci opera*. 2 vols. Basel, 1554.

PICO DELLA MIRANDOLA, GIOVANNI. *De hominis dignitate, Heptaplus, De ente et uno, e scritti vari*. Ed. Eugenio Garin. Florence, 1942.

PINDAR. *The Works of Pindar*. Ed. C. M. Bowra. OCT. Oxford, 1935.

PIRCHER, ALOIS. *Horaz und Vida*. Merano, 1895.

PLATO. *Platonis opera*. Ed. J. Burnet. 5 vols. OCT. Oxford, 1899–1906.

PLUTARCH. *Moralia*. Trans. Frank Babbitt. 14 vols. LCL. London, 1927.

POLIZIANO, ANGELO. *Prose volgari e poesie latine e greche*. Ed. I. del Lungo. Florence, 1867.

POPE, ALEXANDER. *The Poems of Alexander Pope*. Ed. John Butt et al. 6 vols. London, 1961–69.

QUINTILIAN. *Institutio oratoria*. Trans. H. E. Butler. 4 vols. LCL. London, 1963.

——. *On the Early Education of the Citizen-Orator*. Ed. James Murphy. LLA. New York, 1965.

RABELAIS, FRANCOIS. *Oeuvres complètes*. Ed. Jacques Boulenger. Paris, 1955.

SABBADINI, REMIGIO. *Storia del ciceronianismo e di altre questioni letteraria nell' età della rinascenza*. Turin, 1885.

SAINTSBURY, G. E. B. *A History of Criticism and Literary Taste in Europe*. 3 vols. Edinburgh and London, 1902.

——. *Loci Critici*. New York, 1903.

SALUTATI, COLUCCIO. *Epistolario di Coluccio Salutati*. Ed. Francesco Novati. 4 vols. Rome, 1893–1911.

SALVATORE, NICOLA. *L'arte poetica di Marco Girolamo Vida*. Foligno, 1912.

SANDYS, J. E.   *Harvard Lectures on the Revival of Learning.* Cambridge, Mass., 1905.

SANTANGELO, GIORGIO.   *Pietro Bembo e il principio d'imitazione.* Florence, 1950.

SCALIGER, JULIUS CAESAR.   *Poetices libri septem.* Lyons, 1561.

SCHEVILL, FERDINAND.   *The Medici.* New York, 1949.

SCOTT, IZORA.   *The Imitation of Cicero.* New York, 1910.

SEIGEL, JERROLD E.   *Rhetoric and Philosophy in Renaissance Humanism: The Union of Eloquence and Wisdom, Petrarch to Valla.* Princeton, 1968.

SENECA, LUCIUS ANNAEUS.   *Opera quae supersunt.* Ed. Fredericus Haase. 3 vols. Leipzig, 1881.

SERVIUS.   *In Vergilii carmina commentarii.* Ed. George Thilo and Herman Hagen. TCT. Leipzig, 1881.

SIDNEY, SIR PHILIP.   *An Apology for Poetry.* Ed. Geoffrey Shepherd. Edinburgh, 1965.

SIKES, E. F.   *The Greek View of Poetry.* London, 1931.

SISMONDI, J. C. L. DE.   *History of the Italian Republics.* London, 1906.

SMITH, GREGORY, ed.   *Elizabethan Critical Essays.* 2 vols. Reprint. Oxford, 1964.

SPERONI, SPERONE.   *Dialogi di M. S. Speroni.* Venice, 1543.

SPINGARN, JOEL E., ed.   *Critical Essays of the Seventeenth Century.* 3 vols. Reprint. Bloomington, 1963.

——.   *A History of Literary Criticism in the Renaissance.* New York, 1899.

STANFORD, W. B.   *The Ulysses Theme.* Oxford, 1954.

STATIUS, PUBLIUS.   *Statius.* Trans. J. H. Mozley. 2 vols. LCL. London, 1928.

SUETONIUS.   *Suetonius.* Trans. J. C. Rolfe. 2 vols. LCL. London, 1928–30.

SYMONDS, J. A.   *The Renaissance in Italy.* 2d ed. 2 vols. New York, 1935.

TACITUS, CORNELIUS.   *Dialogus of Tacitus.* Ed. Alfred Gudeman. Boston, 1898.

TILLYARD, E. M. W.   *The English Epic and Its Background.* London, 1954.

TIRABOSCHI, GIROLAMO.   "Notizia e descrizione di un Codice MS. della Poetica del Vida," in *Nuovo Giornale dei Letterati d'Italia* (Modena), XIV (1778), 158–77.

——.   *Storia della letteratura italiana.* 16 vols. Milan, 1824.

TOFFANIN, GIUSEPPE.   *L'umanesimo al concilio di Trento. In appendice: M. Gerolamo Vida, Elogio dello stato (De rei publicae dignitate).* Bologna, 1955.

TRABALZA, CIRO.   *La critica litteraria del rinascimento: Storia dei generi litterari Italiana.* Milan, 1915.

TRINKAUS, CHARLES.   *In Our Image and Likeness: Humanity and Divinity in Italian Humanist Thought.* 2 vols. Chicago, 1970.

VERGIL, PUBLIUS.   *P. Vergili Maronis opera.* Ed. R. A. B. Mynors. OCT. Oxford, 1969.

VIDA, MARCUS HIERONYMUS.   *The Christiad.* Trans. J. Cranwell. Cambridge, 1768.

——. *Marci Hieronymi Vidae Cremonensis Albae Episcopi Christiados libri sex.* Cremona, 1535.

——. *M. Hier. Vidae Cremonen. Albae Episc. Dialogi de rei publicae dignitate.* Cremona, 1556.

——. *Marci Hieronymi Vidae Cremonensis Albae Episcopi Poemata Omnia.* . . . Cremona, 1550.

——. *Marci Hieronymi Vidae Cremonensis Albae Episcopi Poemata Omnia.* . . . , Ed. J. Antonio and Cajetano Volpi. 2 vols. Padua, 1731. Published by Cominus, referred to as "Cominiana" edition in Notes and Commentary.

VOEGELIN, ERIC. *Plato and Aristotle.* Order and History, Vol. III. Baton Rouge, La., 1957.

WEINBERG, BERNARD. *A History of Literary Criticism in the Italian Renaissance.* 2 vols. Chicago, 1961.

——. *Trattati di poetica e retorica del cinquecento.* 4 vols. Bari, 1970–74.

WETMORE, M. N. *Index verborum Vergilianus.* New Haven, 1911.

WOODWARD, WILLIAM H. *Studies in Education during the Age of the Renaissance.* Cambridge, 1906.

INDEXES

INDEX OF PARALLEL PASSAGES, TEXT OF 1527 AND OF C. 1517

This listing of parallel passages is constructed to aid comparison of the two texts; the format adopted will, it is hoped, allow the reader to proceed with reasonable ease from one text to the relevant material in the other. The blocking of the material is almost purely mechanical: that is, I generally included in a single series all lines possible until I was confronted with five or more continuous lines of text peculiar to either version. I have, however, made a very few exceptions to this rule, particularly in the massively revised Book 3 where clarity seemed likely to be served thereby. Material peculiar to the text of c. 1517 (abbreviated *Cr.* for "Cremona") is marked with an asterisk; material peculiar to the Rome version of 1527 (*A.V.* for "authorized version"), with a dagger. I generally assimilated lines where possible: that is, if three or more words in a line were identical in the two texts, and the sense largely the same, I gave them as parallel. In the case of more complete rewording but parallel sense I made an ad hoc decision based on identity of function and syntactic similarity of the lines. The dubious cases were few enough, however.

Text of 1527 (Rome)	*Text of c. 1517*
BOOK 1	BOOK 1
1-8	1-12 (*ll. 6-9)
9-26†	
	13-20*
	21-50 (= *A.V.* 1.515-41; *ll. 48-50)
27-30	51-54
	55-109* (Save that *Cr.* 1.98 = *A.V.* 1.33; *Cr.* 1.103 = *A.V.* 1.37; *Cr.* 1.107, 108 = *A.V.* 1.39, 40)
31-40† (Save that *A.V.* 1.33 = *Cr.* 1.98; *A.V.* 1.37 = *Cr.* 1.103; *A.V.* 1.39, 40 = *Cr.* 1.107, 108)	
41-49	110-17
50-191 (†ll. 88, 99, 119-20, 191)	118-261ᵃ (*ll. 125, 151, 152, 172, 173, 186, 187, 195, 199, 200, 252, 256)
192-201†	
202-15 (†ll. 214-15)	261ᵇ-78 (*ll. 270-73, 277, 278)
216-305 (†ll. 260-62)	279-380 (*ll. 282, 292, 311, 316-17, 328-33, 336, 349, 363, 376)

306-11 (†ll. 308, 309)
312-63 (†ll. 314, 352, 353)

364-78

379-97 (†ll. 389, 390)

398-423 (†ll. 398, 399)

424-58 (= *Cr.* 3.416-62; *Cr.* 426, 427, 433, 435, 436, 438, 445, 446, 459, 460)
459-73 (†ll. 459, 460)
474-80†

481-91 (†l. 483)

492-514 (†ll. 495, 500-502)

515-44 (= *Cr.* 1.21-47; †ll. 542-44)
545-63 (†ll. 554-56)

BOOK 2

1-16 (†ll. 13-16; cf. *A.V.* 2.16 to *Cr.* 2.70)

17-63

64-73*
74-97 (†ll. 96, 97)

98-99

100-108

109-23 (†ll. 117, 118)

124-90 (†ll. 179, 180)

191-238 (†ll. 203, 218, 219, 222, 223)

381-85*
386-97 (*ll. 387, 389, 390, 393-97)
398-450 (*ll. 404, 406, 412, 419, 441)
451-68*
469-84 (*l. 479)
485-92*
493-511 (*ll. 499, 500)
512-29*
530-57 (*ll. 532, 536, 537; note: *A.V.* 1.412-14 = *Cr.* 1.533-35)

558-72 (*ll. 558, 563)

573-82*
583-94 (*ll. 586, 588)
595-600*
601-21 (*ll. 611-12)
622-37*

638-53

BOOK 2

1-12

13-20*
21-79 (*ll. 26-29, 34-35, 41-42, 45, 53)

80-105 (*ll. 84-87)
106-26*
127-28
129-34*
135-44 (*l. 139)
145-55*
156-69 (*l. 164)
170-211*
212-83 (*ll. 242, 264, 265, 271-74)
284-89*
290-340 (*ll. 305, 319-22)

341-67*

239-46 (†l. 241)
247-59 (= *Cr.* 2.395-411: **Cr.* 400-
404)

260-77 (= *Cr.* 2.377-94)

278-81

282-314 (†ll. 300-303)
315-24†
325-45^a (†ll. 328, 334-36, 341; much
reworking throughout)

345^{b}†
346 (= *Cr.* 2.519)
347 (= *Cr.* 2.515)
348†
349-50 (= *Cr.* 2.516-17)
351-55†
356-61 (= *Cr.* 2.509-13; l. 359 = *Cr.*
2.499)
362-66†

367-440 (†ll. 418, 419)

441-54

455-551 (†ll. 458, 505-7, 512)

552-63†
564 (= *Cr.* 2.780)

368-76 (*ll. 370, 371-72)

377-94 (= *A.V.* 2.260-77)
395-411 (= *A.V.* 2.247-59; **Cr.*
400-404)

412-20*
421-24
425-40*
441-73 (*ll. 459-61, 472, 473)

474-98 (*ll. 477, 487-89, 491, 493,
496)
499 (= *A.V.* 2.359)
500-508*

509-13 (= *A.V.* 2.356-61)
514*
515 (= *A.V.* 2.347)
516-17 (= *A.V.* 2.349-50)
518*
519 (= *A.V.* 2.346)
520-26*
527-605 (*ll. 543-46, 562, 597, 598,
603)
606-24*
625-40 (*ll. 628, 629)
641-57*
658-764 (*ll. 660, 703, 705, 710,
712, 713, 720, 721, 734, 749-50,
755; ll. 760-61 = *A.V.* 3.262-63)
765-86* (l. 780 = *A.V.* 2.564; l. 783
= *A.V.* 2.566)

565†
566 (= Cr. 2.783)
567-603 (†ll. 573, 579)

787-832 (*ll. 791, 792, 795, 796, 801, 806, 807, 812-13, 825-28)
833-42*

BOOK 3

BOOK 3

1-5

1-5
6-11*

6

12

7†

13*

8-14

14-20
21-45* (Cr. 3.42 = A.V. 3.111)

15†
16-19 (= Cr. 3.841-42, 843, 847)
20†
21 (= Cr. 3.838)
22†
23-25 (= Cr. 3.463-65)

46-47 (= A.V. 3.110, 109)
48*
49 (= A.V. 3.112)

26-27
28-38†
39-43 (= Cr. 3.478-83; *Cr. 480)

50-51

52* (cf. A.V. 3.45, 151)
53-54 (= A.V. 3.114-15)
55-61 (= A.V. 3.76-83)

44-50

62-68
69-72 (= A.V. 3.86-89)
73 (= A.V. 3.106)
74-90 (= A.V. 3.90-105; *Cr. 3.75; Cr. 3.89, 90 = A.V. 3.105, 104)
91-95*

51-75
76-83 (= Cr. 3.55-61)
84-85†
86-89 (= Cr. 3.69-72)
90-105 (= Cr. 3.74-90; *Cr. 3.75; Cr. 3.89-90 = A.V. 3.105, 104
106 (= Cr. 3.73)
107-8†

96-121 (*ll. 98, 119, 120)

109-10 (= *Cr.* 3.47, 46)
111-13 (cf. with *Cr.* 3.502-3ᵃ)
114-15 (= *Cr.* 3.53-54)
116-29 (= *Cr.* 3.503ᵇ-16)
130-42 (= *Cr.* 3.488-500; *Cr.*
  3.498-99 retouched to coincide
  with Vergilian original)
143-47 (= *Cr.* 3.539-47; *Cr.* 3.542-45)
148-52† (cf. l. 150 with *Cr.* 3.52)
153-59 (= *Cr.* 3.150-53; †ll. 155,
  156, 157, 159; *Cr.* 3.152)

122-49* (with l. 136 cf. *A.V.* 2.125; l.
  137 = *A.V.* 2.44)
150-53 (= *A.V.* 3.153-55, 158)
154-58*
160-69   159-68
                                     169-80*
170-215   181-228 (*ll. 225-26)
                                     229-42* (cf. *A.V.* 1.41-49)
216†
217-56   243-89 (*ll. 249, 250, 274, 275,
                                       281-83; *Cr.* 3.286-87 = *A.V.*
                                       3.254, 253)
257-63† (ll. 262-63= *Cr.* 2.760-61)
264-66   290-92
                                     293-97*
267-71   298-303ᵃ
                                     303b-13 (= *A.V.* 3.305-15)
272-87   314-34 (*ll. 321-23, 331, 333)
                                     335-42*
288-304   343-62 (*ll. 347, 355, 356; *Cr.* 354 =
                                       A.V. 3.301)
305-15 (= *Cr.* 3.303ᵇ-13)
316-19 (= *Cr.* 3.527-30)
320-26 (*ll. 324, 325)
327 (cf. *Cr.* 3.373; note, with the   363-69 (*ll. 365, 366)
  French dedication, the change in
  this line)
328†

                                     370-72*
                                     373 (cf. *A.V.* 3.327 and note)
                                     374-85*
329-31   386-88
332-42 (= *Cr.* 3.397-407)

343-49 (= *Cr.* 3.389-95)

389-95 (= *A.V.* 3.343-49)
396*
397-407 (= *A.V.* 3.332-42)
408-12

350-54
355-69†
370-81 (= *Cr.* 3.746-60; *ll. 751,
754, 755; *A.V.* 374 = *Cr.* 3.753;
A.V. 375 = *Cr.* 3.750)
382-83 (= *Cr.* 3.771-72)
384-85†
386-439 (= *Cr.* 3.780-832; **Cr.*
3.782, 800, 829; †*A.V.* 3.400-401,
435, 436)
440-54 (= *Cr.* 3.558-76; **Cr.* 567,
570-73)
455-541 (= *Cr.* 3.847-945; **Cr.*
3.855, 858, 870-80, 902, 903, 920,
924, 926, 927; *A.V.* 3.487 = *Cr.*
3.885; *A.V.* 3.488 = *Cr.* 3.890;
A.V. 3.489 = *Cr.* 3.891; *A.V.*
3.490-93 = *Cr.* 3.886-89)

413-15*
416-62 (*A.V.* 1.424-58; *ll. 426,
427, 433, 435, 436, 438, 445, 446,
459, 460)
463-65 (= *A.V.* 3.23-25)
466-77*
478-83 (= *A.V.* 3.39-43; *l. 480)
484-87*
488-500 (= *A.V.* 3.130-42; *Cr.*
3.498-99 retouched to coincide
with Vergilian original)
501*
502-3ᵃ (cf. *A.V.* 3.111-12)
503ᵇ-16 (= *A.V.* 3.116-29)
517-30 (*Cr.* 527-30 = *A.V.* 3.316-19)
531-38* (cf. *A.V.* 2.166-69)
539-47 (= *A.V.* 3.143-47; *ll.
3.542-45)
548-57*
558-76 (= *A.V.* 3.440-54; *ll. 567,
570-73)
577-745*

746-60 (= *A.V.* 3.370-81; *ll. 751,
754, 755; *Cr.* 3.750 = *A.V.* 3.375;
Cr. 3.753 = *A.V.* 3.374)
761-70*
771-72 (= *A.V.* 3.382-83)
773-79*
780-832 (= *A.V.* 3.386-439; *Cr.*
782, 800, 829; †*A.V.* 400-401, 435,
436)
833-37*
838 (= *A.V.* 3.21)
839-46 (= *A.V.* 3.16-19; *ll. 841,
843-45)
847-945 (= *A.V.* 3.455-541; *ll. 855,
858, 870-80, 902, 903, 920, 924,
926, 927; *Cr.* 3.885 = *A.V.* 3.487;
Cr. 3.890 = *A.V.* 3.488; *Cr.* 3.891
= *A.V.* 3.489; *Cr.* 3.886-89 = *A.V.*
3.490-93)

542-92 (†il. 553, 555, 556)   956-1012 (*ll. 965, 966, 969-72, 974,
986, 989^b-990^a, 1008)

INDEX OF NAMES,
TEXT OF 1527, ROME

The reader who wishes to follow Vida's references in the 1517 version to a particular figure or place should begin by using the Index of Parallel Passages (pp. 283 ff.) in conjunction with the citations below. I have given references in the General Index to those of his contemporaries whom Vida mentions in the 1517 text only.

GENERAL INDEX

There is a separate index for proper names occurring in the 1527 (Rome) text of the *De arte poetica*, and another listing the line numbers of parallel passages in the texts of c. 1517 and of 1527 (Rome). These two should allow the reader to move about in the two major versions of the poem with considerable ease. I have included in this index the names of contemporaries whom Vida mentions in the 1517 version of the poem. The internal reference system of the edition will be of further help to the reader: that is, any reference to the text of the *De arte poetica* (Rome, 1527) may lead the reader to further material in the commentary pertinent to his interest, and any reference to the commentary will lead the reader back to the text.